Globalisation and Development

Globalisation and Development: Perspectives and Policies

Achiransu Acharyya
Soumyadip Chattopadhyay
Apurba Kumar Chattopadhyay

GYAN

Published, 2019

Published by

Gyan Publishing House
5, Ansari Road
Daryaganj, New Delhi-110002
Phone: 011-47034999, 9811692060
www.gyanbooks.com
E-mail: books@gyanbooks.com

Printed at: G. Print Process, Delhi.

Cataloging in Publication Data—DK
Courtesy: D.K. Agencies (P) Ltd. <docinfo@dkagencies.com>

International Conference on Globalisation and Development (2018 : Santiniketan, India)
Globalisation and development : perspectives and policies / [editors], Achiransu Acharyya, Soumyadip Chattopadhyay, Apurba Kumar Chattopadhyay.
pages cm
"Most of the chapters were presented as papers at the International Conference on Globalisation and Development organised by the Department of Economics and Politics, Visva-Bharati under the UGC-SAP (DRS-II) Programme"—Preface.
Includes bibliographical references.
ISBN 9788121215633

1. Globalization—Economic aspects—India—Congresses. 2. Globalization—Economic aspects—Developing countries—Congresses. 3. Economic development—India—Congresses. 4. Agriculture—Economic aspects—India—Congresses. 5. Sustainable agriculture—India—Congresses. 6. Globalization—Social aspects—India—Congresses. I. Acharyya, Achiransu, editor. II. Chattopadhyay, Soumyadip, editor. III. Chattopadhyay, Apurba Kumar, 1963- editor. IV. Visva-Bharati. Department of Economics & Politics. UGC-Special Assistance Programme. DRS – II, organizer. V. Title.

LCC HC435.3.I58 2018 | DDC 338.954 23

Contents

Preface

This book examines the impact of globalisation on the developing economies of the world in general and Indian economy in particular. Divided into three parts, it evaluates the impact of globalisation on the Indian macro-economy, especially on trade in goods and services, movement of capital, financial flows and their impact on the Indian economy. It tries to address the advantages of globalisation as also the fears and concerns from globalisation. The book contains seventeen chapters in total. Most of the chapters were presented as papers at the *International Conference on Globalisation and Development* organised by the Department of Economics and Politics, VISVA-BHARATI under the UGC-SAP (DRS-II) programme. The chapters have been divided into three sections. The first part containing seven chapters talks about the impact of globalisation in developing economies, especially with reference to India. It discusses various macroeconomic issues with respect to globalisation such as innovation, capital movement and capital adequacy as also growth and employment under globalisation. The second section, containing seven chapters, is based on issues related to impact of globalisation on agriculture and environment in India. The third section, containing three chapters, is based on studies in various other aspects of Indian society, such as education, gender and demography that are affected from globalisation. We are thankful to our colleagues for their assistance in organizing the seminar.

VISVA-BHARATI
Santiniketan
September, 2018

Achiransu Acharyya
Soumyadip Chattopadhyay
Apurba Kumar Chattopadhyay

Introduction

The process that has come to be known as globalisation generally meaning the progressively greater influence being exerted by worldwide economic, social and cultural processes over national or regional ones— is clearly leaving its mark on the world of today. This is not a new process. Its historical roots run deep. Yet the dramatic changes in terms of space and time being brought about by the communications and information revolution represent a qualitative break with the past. In the light of these changes, it is important for a country like India, with its huge population and a large number of poor people, to understand how globalisation can help in development of the economy. Globalisation clearly opens up opportunities for development. We are all aware -and rightfully so- that national strategies should be designed to take advantage of the potential and meet the requirements associated with greater integration into the world economy. This process also, however, entails risks: risk generated by new sources of instability in trade flows and, especially, finance; the risk that countries unprepared for the formidable demands of competitiveness in today's world may be excluded from the process; and the risk of an exacerbation of the structural heterogeneity existing among social sectors and regions within countries whose linkages with the world economy are segmented and marginal in nature. Many of these risks are associated with two disturbing aspects of the globalisation process. The first is the bias in the current form of market globalisation created by the fact that the mobility of capital and the mobility of goods and services exist alongside severe restrictions on the mobility of labor. This is reflected in the asymmetric, incomplete nature of the international agenda that accompanies the globalisation process. This agenda does not, for example, include mobility. Nor does it include mechanisms for ensuring the global coherence of the central economies' macroeconomic policies, international standards for the appropriate taxation of capital, or agreements regarding the mobilisation of resources to relieve the distributional tensions generated by globalisation between and within countries. These shortcomings are the reflection of an even more disturbing problem: the absence of a suitable form of governance in the contemporary world, not only in economic terms (as has become particularly evident in the financial sector) but in many other areas as well. This lack of governance can be attributed, in its turn, to the sharp divergence between global problems and political processes that continue to be pursued within national and, increasingly, local frameworks. An important dimension of the globalisation process -but certainly not one of the main focuses of attention in discussions on the subject- is the gradual spread of ideas and values with regard to civil and political rights, on the one hand, and economic, social and cultural rights, on the other. These ideas and values are gradually laying the foundations for the concept of global citizenship.

A series of economic reforms, implemented in the early 1990s, effectively opened India's hitherto closed economy to international trade and capital flows. This opening came at a time when rapid growth of cross-border trade and capital flows was forging national economies into an expanding global economy—a process that has come to be known as globalisation. The economic reforms were intended to promote integration of India's economy into this expanding global economy. Openness to international trade and capital flows, it was believed, would substantially increase both the pace and the employment intensity of economic growth. Many economists had for long argued that the policy of import substitution under protection, pursued till the end of the 1980s, had stunted economic growth in India by pre-empting specialisation in accordance with comparative advantage, benefits of scale economies and steady technological progress. Increased openness to international trade, on this view, could be expected to bring about growth acceleration by promoting specialisation in accordance with comparative advantage (thus bringing the benefits of economies of scale) and by facilitating technological change. These growth-enhancing effects of openness to international trade, it was also thought, would be further reinforced by openness to inflow of foreign capital, as this would allow the investment rate to rise above the domestic saving rate. These anticipated developments on the growth front were also expected to bring about faster improvement in employment conditions. In the first place, growth acceleration itself could be expected to increase the pace of improvement in employment conditions. Moreover, openness to trade was expected to increase the employment intensity of growth by altering the composition of output. Since India's comparative advantage was believed to lie in unskilled-labor-intensive industries, openness to trade was expected to encourage growth of such industries It was widely held at the time that the earlier policy of import substitution under protection had stunted employment growth because it encouraged growth of capital-intensive industries.

These arguments and expectations obviously derive from the current mainstream economic theory. Since India has abundant supply of unskilled labour together with scarcity of capital and skilled labour, standard trade theory suggests that India has comparative advantage in the production and export of goods that require intensive use of unskilled labour. So, openness to trade should allow this comparative advantage to come into play, thereby bringing the benefits of specialisation and economies of scale. As for capital flows, the standard view is that capital should naturally flow from developed economies, where it is plentiful and hence earns poor return, to developing economies such as India, where it is scarce and hence earns high return. So, openness to capital flows can be expected to raise India's investment rate above the domestic saving rate. In addition, foreign capital should bring with it new technologies and management methods, which would contribute to productivity growth.

This book seeks to provide an empirical assessment of the extent to which the expectations have been borne out by the actual experience. This volume has put together seventeen articles, which examine some of the important issues on globalisation and development in India. The articles are organised into three parts; each part includes a set of articles addressing a particular issue. The following sections provide a summary of the major findings of the articles.

I

The first part of the volume includes seven articles studying various aspects of Globalisation and Development. The first article titled *Globalisation and its Impact on India* is written by former Governor of the Reserve Bank of India, Dr. C. R. Rangarajan. In his article, Dr. Rangarajan tries to first give a historical perspective on globalisation and its meaning for India. He mentions that globalisation has been a historical process with ebbs and flows. During the Pre-World War I period of 1870 to 1914, there was rapid integration of the economies in terms of trade flows, movement of capital and migration of people. The 19th century had witnessed some revolutionary breakthroughs in communication and transport with the emergence of railroad, steamship and telegraph. However, after the 20th century globalisation mainly moved to movement of international trade and capital and financial flows that have been witnessed by India over the past decade. However, Dr. Rangarajan has expressed his concerns about globalisation for India. The first major concern that he expresses is that globalisation leads to a more unequal distribution of income among countries and within countries and the second fear he expresses is that globalisation leads to loss of national sovereignty and that countries are finding it increasingly difficult to follow independent domestic policies. However, he mentions that there are two changes with respect to international trade which may work to the advantage of the developing countries. First being the vacating of certain areas of production by industrially advanced countries which can be filled in by developing countries. Second, a globalised economy with increased specialisation can lead to improved productivity and faster growth. His conclusion is that what will be required is a balancing mechanism to ensure that the handicaps of the developing countries are overcome.

One of the most important aspects of globalisation is technological innovation. The chapter by Saurav Roy Choudhury titled *Innovation and Regulation: An Inverted U-Relationship'* investigates the relationship between Government regulation and innovation taking the case of the American economy. He tries to create a simple model of innovation as a function of government regulation where regulation effects innovation through added regulatory and compliance costs as well as indirectly through its effect on product market competition. Using a panel dataset compiled from patent data of firms of USA he finds a strong evidence of an inverted-U relationship.

Pranab Kanti Basu in his article *Globalisation and Development: Perspectives* interprets globalisation as an epoch of time, a particular period of history and aims is to construct a perspective on globalisation and development that contests the mainstream analytic from a 'class' perspective. By using a Marxian frame of analysis he tries to show that the form of extraction of surplus from labouring people is significant for determining nature of any economy. He interprets globalisation as a feudo-capitalist order since the controller of production is not a profit earner but a rentier.

Among the countries that have benefitted the most from globalisation, one must include the South East Asian countries. In his paper *Dreaming the Asian Economic Community and Beyond: Current Status, Reform Options and Possible Lessons*, Soumyadip Chattopadhyay focuses on key measures taken by ASEAN Economic Community towards making Southeast Asia a fully integrated production base for international capital by eliminating regional barriers to trade and investment and creating infrastructure to connect the national market. In his paper he identifies the challenges therein and proposes measures to streamline the process of integration and their implications for regional growth and prosperity. The paper argues for putting due emphasis on domestic policy reforms, regional and international cooperation and institution building to ensure competitiveness and inclusivity of this growing region.

The problem of Non-Performing Assets in banks has always been a concern, mainly because of the far reaching impact that banks have on the economy as a whole. Akash Barua in his article titled *Dynamic Capital Adequacy Ratio for Bringing Equilibrium in Lending in the Banking Industry: A Study of the Five Largest Banks in India*does a study of the five largest Indian banks and comes to the conclusion that the capital adequacy ratio is incapable of reducing risks in banks in terms of growing Non Performing Assets. His study shows that non-performing assets continued to rise regardless of the banks maintaining high capital adequacy ratios. He develops a ratio which he terms as the Marginal Cost of Lending and comparing it across banks shows that not all banks are similarly efficient based on their capital requirement. Under the circumstances, he forms a dynamic capital adequacy ratio which will reflect the inherent risks of banks that would lead them to create a self-correcting mechanism which prevents low quality lending and help reduce the problem of NPAs.

With the clear indication of growing financial integration of money market and monetary policies post financial reforms, and globalisation in India,

Deepanjali Das in her article *An evaluation and multiple-step ahead forecast of the post-reform LAF period in a globalised environment through autoregressive model* aims at firstly screening the different facets of liquidity conditions. With the phase wise segregation of the time period 2008-2016 under study, her goal is to work out correlation coefficients of monetary policy instrument and the money market instruments. Her aim behind the choice of such time scenario is to note the outcome from any volatile effect seeping in though globalisation.The study provides insights to the behavior of the selected financial instruments for effective operation of call market and money market.

The last chapter in the category of Globalisation and Development is a study of the impact of globalisation on the Indian state of Kerala. Written by Ruchi Bhalla, Naresh Mallik and Surendra Meher, the paper titled *Impact of Globalisation on Economic Growth and Employment in India with special reference to Kerala* focuses on the linkage between globalisation and its impact on employment and development in Kerala. Their data analysis reveals that globalisation had a positive impact on economic growth but the effect on employment is a mixed one. Reason being lack in skills due to low enrollment in higher education of people in the State, as also low participation of females in workforce and lack of skill-based education among them. The study concludes that in order to reap the benefits of globalisation, it is necessary to have expansion of higher education, reduction in gender disparities in education and promotion of skill development programmes.

II

The articles in Part II are on the impact of Globalisation on Trade and Environment. While on the one hand globalisation can enhance trade in agriculture for developing countries through technology and innovation as also integration of markets, it has also the potential to wipe out small and poor farmers from the market. Moreover, agriculture under globalisation could have long term negative effects on the environment due to higher use of fertilizers and pesticides. Under the circumstances, the seven articles in Part II discuss the various impact of globalisation on agriculture and the environment.

An often unrecognised consequence of globalisation is change in lifestyle including diets, particularly among the urban middle class, as a result of increased global inter-connectedness through travel and communications. Consumers in large, urban centres are more exposed to non-traditional foods as a result of their access to food retail outlets and marketing campaigns. Large urban markets create the scope for the establishment of large supermarket chains, and they attract foreign investments and advertising from global corporations. Non-traditional foods are more accessible as a result of trade liberalisation and declining costs of transportation and communication. In the first of the articles under this segment, Achiransu Acharyya in his article titled *Globalisation and Sustainable Agriculture in India* shows that it is important to understand, especially for a country like India having the largest population in the world to adapt itself to a sustainable form of agricultural development for the future without harming the environment as also the future generation. The negative impact of the Green Revolution, especially due to high use of fertilizers and pesticides as also overuse of groundwater has led to loss of soil fertility and drastic lowering of the groundwater table. Along with this, due to climate change, India's hydro-climatic regime is expected to alter significantly over the course of the 21st century. Under this crisis, the paper argues for a path of agricultural development that is sustainable and adaptive to climate change. The paper argues that taking help of globalisation, India can use technology, such as Internet of Things (IoT) and Climate Smart Agriculture (CSA) as well as human capital to mitigate the above mentioned problems.

Mohd. Adil and Pragya Sharma in their article titled *Trends and Dimensions of India's Agricultural Trade under WTO Regime* argue that rapid globalisation has created a need for liberalisation in all sectors of India including agriculture.An assessment of trade performance of Indian agriculture during pre and post WTO period has been made in the study proving a picture of linkage between trade liberalisation in India and Agriculture under WTO regime and shows that there has been insignificant benefit to Indian agriculture in the post WTO regime as the trade balances in agriculture have been unfavorable. Exploring the reasons for such losses in Indian agriculture after WTO formation, the study suggests that lack of infrastructure, education, skills among farmers, lack of efficiency increasing technologies, inadequate credit facilities in this sector have decelerated the growth. They suggest for formulation and implementation of structural reforms within agriculture sector so as to reap the benefits of global participation and competition.

Rama Ghosh in her article *Globalisation and Water: The Dynamics of Privatisation and Water Markets* suggests that the natural resource water is becoming more and more a private property rather than a public or common property. She suggests that the alarming imposition of provision of drinking water is now not solely a State responsibility anymore, inviting newer players in the supply side of the drinking water sector.

In his article titled *Collective Action for Common Property Resource Conservation as an Antidote to the Destruction of Adivasi Livelihoods being wrought by Globalisation* author Rahul Banerjee suggests that need for collective action for the management of common property resources and the importance of this for both livelihood promotion and climate change mitigation as an antidote to the ravages wrought by the commercial and extractive processes unleashed by globalisation. Taking the example of a watershed which is part of the Jhabua Hills agro-climatic zone in Madhya Pradesh, he shows that local institutions through cooperation have used the favourable legal provisions to ensure that the Bhils of Alirajpur are able to secure their rights and entitlements and gain justice from the modern economic and political systems that govern this country.

Maniparna Syam Roy in her article titled *Need for developing System of Integrated Environmental and Economic Accounts to address Sustainable Development Goals* has argued for green accounting for all countries to address the issue of sustainability and can be used by policymakers for monitoring development pathway on sustainable development direction.

Technical change is a major driving force for economic growth and development. Post globalisation, there has been an acceleration of technical change that has favoured skill bias of labour force. Although individual skills are captured through educational level, in the long-run what matters is the un-observable ability inherent in an individual argues Saheli Das and Mita Keswari Mehra in their paper titled *An Empirical Analysis of Ability-Biased Technical Change with Environmental Constraints.* They attempt to empirically capture the simultaneous effects of skill-biased technical change and environmental quality change on different economic variables like, within-group and between-group wage inequalities, income distribution, economic welfare and other variables through the channel of individual ability-differentiation.Their empirical analysis shows that environment-friendly ability-biased technical change improves economic welfare for all the countries of the world. However, ability-differentiation affects economic welfare differentially for developed and developing countries with respect to income distribution.

Pragya Sharma and Sanatan Nayak in their paper titled *Globalisation and Groundwater Management: Challenges in Indian Agriculture* by using data from various secondary sources have tried to analyze the export pattern of India and its impact on groundwater resources in India. They show that since globalisation period, country's share in total export of water intensive crops such rice, sugarcane, cotton, soybean, wheat has been substantially high and so has been the increase in groundwater abstraction. Their data analysis show that groundwater use splurged in connotes that states like Punjab, Rajasthan, Madhya Pradesh, Maharashtra, Karnataka, Tamil Nadu and Uttar Pradesh which produce higher quantity of water-guzzling crops have groundwater development of more than fifty per cent which is definitely not a positive sign. Therefore, increased production of such crops for meeting trade demands poses to be a challenge in groundwater management. Thus, the study suggests that trade liberalisation should not be done at the cost of water resource base depletion. They suggest adoption of water-efficient technologies in agriculture, farmer awareness and community management of groundwater to prevent such over-exploitation of water resources.

III

The last section contains three articles looking at the impact of globalisation on various social sectors. L. Clement Baskar in his article titled *An Empirical study on Higher Education under Globalisation in India* examines the present status of higher education under globalisation in India, especially in the State of Tamil Nadu. He discusses the major challenges that globalisation has brought to higher education. He suggests that in the higher education segment of India, substantial improvement is possible in both quantitative and qualitative terms post globalisation. The major objective of the paper is to make an attempt to identify any significant impact on higher education due to globalisation. He argues that globalisation is expected to have a positive influence on the volume, quality and spread of knowledge through increased interaction among the various States.

Globalisation has impacted upon gender relations in complex and contradictory ways.The opening-up of new spaces by the apparent weakening of the nation-State holds open the possibility of undermining the traditional gender hierarchies and devising new bases for gender relations. In her article titled *Gender Inequality in India after a quarter century of Globalisation* author Shobana Karthikeyan in her study investigates the payoffs to Indian women from 25 years of globalisation. The study looks at education-related changes, employment-related changes and few social issues. Results show that globalisation has delivered a mixed bag of results for Indian women. While on the one hand, the literacy levels of women has gone up, it can be noticed that women only pursue selective courses. The proportion of the working age women has gone down significantly.

Modernisation process in every single country has been nourished by demographic evolution. Sk. Md. Azharuddin and Meeta Keswani Mehra in their article *Revisiting the Demographic Transition: A Unified Growth Approach*, utilizes a unified growth theory model to describe the long-run economic growth and demographic evolution of an economy. Using a two period overlapping generations model with two sectors: agriculture and manufacturing, the paper characterizes the transition of the economy from a subsistence pre-industrial Malthusian epoch to a period of sustained modern economic growth. Using average years of schooling as a measure of child quality and total fertility rate as an indicator of the number of children born, the empirical analysis finds a long-run negative and a significant relationship between total fertility and average years of schooling for post-independent India, implying a child quality-quantity trade-off.

Achiransu Acharyya
Soumyadip Chattopadhyay
Apurba Kumar Chattopadhyay

List of Contributors

1. **C.R. Rangarajan,** *Former Governor,* Reserve Bank of India and *Chairman,* Madras School of Economics
2. **Saurav Roy Choudhury,** *Professor of Finance & Economics,* Department of Business, Capital University, Columbus, Ohio, USA. **Email:**-sroychou@capital.edu
3. **Pranab Kanti Basu**, *Professor*, Department of Economics and Politics, Vidya Bhavana, Visva-Bharati, Santiniketan, West Bengal. **Email:**pranabkbasu@gmail.com
4. **Soumyadip Chattopadhyay,** Assistant Professor, Department of Economics and Politics, Vidya Bhavana, Visva-Bharati, Santiniketan, West Bengal. **Email:** soumyadip.chattopadhyay@gmail.com
5. **Akash Barua**, *Assistant Professor of Finance,* Indian School of Business & Finance **Email:**akash.baruah@pibm.in
6. **Deepanjali Das**, *Research Scholar*, Dept. of Economics, Babasaheb Bhimrao Ambedkar University, Lucknow. **Email:**deepanjali505@gmail.com
7. **Ruchi Bhalla**, *Research Scholar*, Dept.of Economics, Babasaheb Bhimrao Ambedkar University, Uttar Pradesh. **Email:**bhallaruchi27@gmail.com
8. **Naresh Mallik**, *Research Scholar*, Dept.of Economics, Jawahar Lal Nehru University, New Delhi. **Email:** nareshmallik@gmail.com
9. **Surendra Meher,** *Assistant Professor*, Dept.of Economics, Babasaheb Bhimrao Ambedkar University, Uttar Pradesh.
10. **Achiransu Acharyya**, *Assistant Professor*, Department of Economics and Politics, Vidya Bhavana, Visva-Bharati, Santiniketan, West Bengal. **Email**: achiransu@gmail.com
11. **Mohd.Adil**, *Research Scholar*, Department of Economics, Aligarh Muslim University, Uttar Pradesh. **Email**:adileco88@gmail.com
12. **Pragya Sharma,** *Research Scholar*, Department of Economics, Babasaheb Bhimrao Ambedkar University, Lucknow, Uttar Pradesh. **Email:**pragya.kabir@outlook.com

13. **Raina Ghosh**, *Research Scholar*, Centre for the Study of Regional Development School of Social Sciences, Jawaharlal Nehru University, New Delhi. **Email:**rainaghosh@hotmail.com

14. **Rahul Banerjee**, *Director*, Khedut Mazdoor Chetna Sangath (KMCS), Jhabua, Madhya Pradesh.**Email:**rahul.indauri@gmail.com

15. **Maniparna Syam Roy,** Assistant Professor of Economics, Asutosh College, Kolkata. **Email:**maniparnasr@gmail.com

16. **Saheli Das**, Ph.D Scholar, Centre for International Trade and Development, Jawaharlal Nehru University, New Delhi. **Email:**sahelidas.2008@gmail.com.

17. **Meeta Keswari Mehra**, Professor, Centre for International Trade and Development, Jawaharlal Nehru University, New Delhi. **Email:**meetakm@gmail.com

18. **Pragya Sharma**, Research Scholar, Department of Economics, Babasaheb Bhimrao Ambedkar University, Lucknow, Uttar Pradesh. **Email:**pragya.kabir@outlook.com

19. **Sanatan Nayak**, Professor, Department of Economics, Babasaheb Bhimrao Ambedkar University, Lucknow, Uttar Pradesh. **Email**: sanatan5@yahoo.com

20. **L. Clement Baskar**, Assistant Professor and Head, Department of Economics, Government Arts & Science College, R. K. Nagar, Chennai. **Email:**clementbaskar@gmail.com

21. **Shobana Karthikeyan**, Assistant Professor, Department of Economics, Madras Christian College, Chennai. **Email**:shobykarthik@gmail.com

22. **Sk. Md. Azharuddin,**Ph.D. Scholar, Center for International Trade and Development, School of International Studies, Jawaharlal Nehru University, New Delhi. **Email:**azharlowa@gmail.com

23. **Meeta Keswani Mehra**, Professor of Economics, Center for International Trade and Development, School of International Studies, Jawaharlal Nehru University, New Delhi. **Email:**meetakm@gmail.com

Part - I

Globalisation and Economic Development

Chapter - 1

Globalisation and its Impact

C.R. Rangarajan

1. Introduction

Globalisation has become an expression of common usage. Unfortunately, it connotes different things to different people. To some, it represents a brave new world with no barriers. For some others, it spells doom and destruction. We need to have a clear understanding of what globalisation stands for, if we have to deal with a phenomenon that is willy-nilly gathering momentum, even though there is some deceleration, of late.

2. Globalisation and its Meaning

As we begin analyzing the implications of globalisation, several questions arise. What is globalisation? Is it purely an economic concept? Is this a new phenomenon? What are the benefits of globalisation? Who gets hurt in the process of globalisation? Does globalisation lead to inequity? What are the complementary institutions and policies that countries can build to protect themselves or to gain maximum benefits? Where does India stand in this race for globalisation? Is she a potential gainer or loser?

Broadly speaking, the term 'globalisation' means integration of economies and societies through cross country flows of information, ideas, technologies, goods, services, capital, finance and people. The essence of globalisation is connectivity. Cross border integration can have several dimensions – cultural, social, political and economic. In fact, some people fear cultural and social integration even more than economic integration. The fear of "cultural hegemony" haunts many. However, we use the term globalisation in this lecture in the more limited sense of economic integration which can happen through the three channels of (a) trade in goods and services, (b) movement of capital and (c) flow of finance. Besides, there can also be a channel through movement of people.

2.1 Historical Development

Globalisation has been a historical process with ebbs and flows. During the Pre-World War I period of 1870 to 1914, there was rapid integration of the economies in terms of trade flows, movement of capital and migration of people. The 19th century had witnessed some revolutionary break throughs in communication and transport with the emergence of railroad, steamship and telegraph. Keynes wrote in 1920 "What an extraordinary episode in the progress of man that age was which came to an end in August 1914!......The inhabitant of London could order by telephone, sipping his morning tea in bed, the various products of the whole earth... he could at the same time and by the same means adventure his wealth in the natural resources and new enterprise of any quarter of the world...". The Pre-World War I period witnessed the growth of globalisation mainly led by the technological forces in the fields of transport and communication. There were fewer barriers to flow of trade and people across the geographical boundaries. Indeed there were no passports and visa requirements, no non-tariff barriers and no restrictions on fund flows.

The pace of globalisation, however, decelerated between the First and the Second World War. The inter-war period witnessed the erection of various barriers to restrict free movement of goods and services. Most economies thought that they could thrive better under high protective walls. After World War II, all the leading countries resolved not to repeat the mistakes they had committed previously by opting for isolation.

Although after 1945, there was a drive to increased integration; it took a long time to reach the Pre-World War I level. In terms of percentage of merchandise exports and imports to total output, the US could reach the pre-World War level only around 1970.Most of the developing countries which gained independence from the colonial rule in the immediate Post-World War II period followed an import substitution industrialisation regime. The Soviet bloc countries were also shielded from the process of global economic integration. However, times have changed. In the last three decades, the process of globalisation has proceeded with greater vigor. The former Soviet bloc countries are getting integrated with the global economy. More and more developing countries are turning towards outward oriented policy of growth. Yet, studies point out that trade and capital markets are no more globalised today than they were at the end of the 19th century. However, there are more concerns about globalisation now than before because of the nature and speed of transformation. What is striking in the current episode is not only the rapid pace but also the enormous impact of new information technologies on market integration, efficiency and industrial organisation.

The first two decades of the 21st century have seen an extremely surprising turn in attitude. Until 2008, the concerns about globalisation were voiced by the developing countries. Post 2008, it is the developed countries which are turning their heads against globalisation and voicing dissatisfaction with the current status.

3. Gains from Globalisation

The gains and losses from globalisation can be analyzed in the context of the three types of channels of economic globalisation identified earlier.

3.1 Trade in Goods and Services

According to the standard theory, international trade leads to allocation of resources that is consistent with comparative advantage. This results in specialisation which enhances productivity. While the classical theory of comparative advantage was based on assumptions of perfect competition, constant returns to scale and fixed technology, the "new trade theory" which takes into account imperfect competition, increasing returns to scale and changing technology also comes to the conclusion that openness leads to improved rates of growth. The new trade theory talks of dynamic gains from international trade. It is accepted that international trade, in general, is beneficial and that restrictive trade practices impede growth. That is the reason why many of the emerging economies which originally depended on a growth model of import substitution have moved over to a policy of outward orientation. Obviously, even in relation to trade in goods and services, there is one concern. Emerging economies will reap the benefits of international trade only if they reach the full potential of their resource availability. This will probably require time. That is why international trade agreements make exceptions by allowing longer time to developing economies in terms of reduction in tariff and non-tariff barriers. Special and differentiated treatment has become an accepted principle. It is a strange turn of events that as the developing countries are moving forward, the developed countries are complaining of discrimination and turning towards protectionism.

3.2 Movement of Capital

Capital flows across countries have played an important role in enhancing the production base. This was very much true in 19th and 20th centuries. Capital mobility enables the total savings of the world to be distributed among countries which have the highest investment potential. Under these circumstances, one country's growth is not constrained by its own domestic savings. The inflow of foreign capital has played a significant role in the development of the East Asian countries. The current account deficit of some of these countries had exceeded 5 per cent of the GDP in most of the period when growth was rapid. In fact, at the peak, the foreign capital inflow into Malaysia in 1993 was 17.4 per cent of its GDP, while in Thailand in 1995 it was 12.7 per cent of the GDP.

Capital flows can take either the form of foreign direct investment or portfolio investment. For developing countries the preferred alternative is foreign direct investment. Portfolio investment does not directly lead to expansion of productive capacity. It may do so, however, at one step removed. Portfolio investment can however be volatile particularly in times of loss of confidence. That is why countries want to put restrictions on portfolio investment. But, in an open system such restrictions cannot work easily. Even in relation to foreign direct investment, two aspects have raised concerns. First, there is always the fear that some part of the domestic economy will be controlled by external factors. In India, it is very often referred to as the "East India Company Syndrome".

However, there is an increasing realisation on the part of transnational companies also not to act in a manner inconsistent with the policies of countries in which investment is made. For example, in East Asian crisis it was found that foreign direct investment was a stable element. While to some extent fresh capital inflow was moderated, there was no outflow of foreign direct investment. The second aspect of concern in relation to foreign direct investment has been the fact that a significant part of foreign direct investment has been in the form of cross border mergers and acquisitions. It is felt that FDI entry through the takeover of domestic firms is less beneficial because such foreign acquisitions do not add to the productive capacity but simply transfer ownership and control from domestic to foreign hands. While this is correct, it overlooks the fact that the funds released to the domestic entrepreneurs because of the acquisition can be utilised for expanding capacity by the domestic entrepreneurs. Whether or not mergers and acquisitions lead to technological up gradation in the short-term is not clear. However, it is reported that over the longer term, effects could be different. Cross border mergers and acquisitions can be followed by transfer of new or better technology, when acquired firms are restructured to increase the efficiency of their operations. While foreign direct investment is beneficial, public policy will have to set the conditions under which private capital is invited.

3.3 Financial Flows

The rapid development of the capital market has been one of the important features of the current process of globalisation. While the growth in capital and foreign exchange markets have facilitated the transfer of resources across borders, the gross turnover in foreign exchange markets has been extremely large. It is estimated that the gross turnover is around $ 1.5 trillion per day worldwide. This is of the order of the hundred times greater than the volume of trade in goods and services. Currency trade has become an end in itself. The expansion in foreign exchange markets and capital markets is a necessary pre-requisite for international transfer of capital.

However, the volatility in the foreign exchange market and the ease with which funds can be withdrawn from countries have created often times panic situations. When one country faces a crisis, it affects others. It is not as if financial crises are solely caused by foreign exchange traders. What the financial markets tend to do is to exaggerate weaknesses. Herd instinct is not uncommon in financial markets. When an economy becomes more open to capital and financial flows, there is even greater compulsion to ensure that factors relating to macro-economic stability are not ignored. Opening of the capital account need not preclude moderate controls, either price based or regulatory on capital flows. Controls should be selective, designed to achieve the specific objective of containing speculative capital. While there is, no doubt, that countries benefit by capital flows, the need to keep a watchful eye on foreign exchange markets becomes essential. What applies to trade may not necessarily apply to finance in full measure. However, while stringent capital controls may be adopted as a temporary shield as part of crisis management, they cannot be a permanent feature. Capital account convertibility must proceed in stages.

4. Concerns and Fears

On the impact of globalisation, there are two major concerns. These may be described as even fears. Under each major concern there are many related anxieties. The first major concern is that globalisation leads to a more unequal distribution of income among countries and within countries. The second fear is that globalisation leads to loss of national sovereignty and that countries are finding it increasingly difficult to follow independent domestic policies. These two issues have to be addressed both the oretically and empirically.

The argument that globalisation leads to inequality is based on the premise that since globalisation emphasizes efficiency, gains will accrue to countries which are favorably endowed with natural and human resources. Advanced countries have had a head start over the other countries by at least three centuries. The technological base of these countries is not only wide but highly sophisticated. While trade benefits all countries, greater gains accrue to the industrially advanced countries. This is the reason why even in the present trade agreements, a case has been built up for special and differential treatment in relation to developing countries. By and large, this treatment provides for longer transition periods in relation to adjustment.

However, there are two changes with respect to international trade which may work to the advantage of the developing countries. First, for a variety of reasons, the industrially advanced countries are vacating certain areas of production. These can be filled in by developing countries. A good example of this is what the East Asian countries did in the 1970s and 1980s. Second, international trade is no longer determined by the distribution of natural resources. With the advent of information technology, the role of human resources has emerged as more important. Specialised human skills will become the determining factor in the coming decades. Productive activities are becoming "knowledge intensive" rather than "resource intensive". While there is a divide between developing and the advanced countries even in this area – some people call it the digital divide - it is a gap which can be bridged. A globalised economy with increased specialisation can lead to improved productivity and faster growth. What will be required is a balancing mechanism to ensure that the handicaps of the developing countries are overcome.

Apart from the possible unequal distribution of income among countries, it has also been argued that globalisation leads to widening income gaps within the countries as well. This can happen both in the developed and developing economies. The argument is the same as was advanced in relation to unequal distribution among countries. Globalisation may benefit even within a country those who have the skills and the technology. The higher growth rate achieved by an economy can be at the expense of declining incomes of people who may be rendered redundant. In this context, it has to be noted that while globalisation may accelerate the process of technology substitution in developing economies, these countries even without globalisation will face the problem associated with moving from lower to higher technology. If the growth rate of the economy accelerates sufficiently, then part of the resources can be diverted by the state to modernize and reequip people who may be affected by the process of technology up gradation.

The second concern relates to the loss of autonomy in the pursuit of economic policies. In a highly integrated world economy, it is true that one country cannot pursue policies which are not in consonance with the world wide trends. Capital and technology are fluid and they will move where the benefits are greater. However, this is not a new phenomenon. For example, in the days of gold standard, maintenance of the external value of the currency in terms of gold content became paramount. Domestic monetary policy actions were subordinated to this overriding consideration. In fact, the fixed exchange rate system under the Bretton Woods arrangement also imposed similar constraints. In a more or less fixed exchange rate regime, no country can allow its inflation rate to be out of alignment with the inflation rate in the rest of the world. Of course, the flexible exchange rate regime which is now prevalent, gives little more autonomy in the pursuit of domestic monetary policy. It is, however, impossible for any country to have domestic autonomy, fixed exchange rate and free capital flows. This is the famous impossibility theorem. As nations come together whether it is in the political, social or economic arena, some sacrifice of sovereignty is inevitable. The constraints of a globalised economic system on the pursuit of domestic policies have to be recognised. However, it need not result in the abdication of domestic objectives.

Another fear associated with globalisation is insecurity and volatility. When countries are inter-related strongly, a small spark can start a large conflagration. Panic and fear spread fast. The only hope here is that despite integration, different parts of the world economy can be at different phases of the business cycle. The downside to globalisation essentially emphasizes the need to create countervailing forces in the form of institutions and policies at the international level. Global governance cannot be pushed to the periphery, as integration gathers speed.

Empirical evidence on the impact of globalisation on inequality is not very clear. The share in aggregate world exports and in world output of the developing countries has been increasing. In aggregate world exports, the share of developing countries increased from 20.6 per cent in 1988-90 to 29.9 per cent to 2000. It stands at 34.3 per cent in 2015 (Table 1.1).

Table 1.1: Share in Aggregate World Exports

Year	*Major Industrial Countries*	*Developing Countries*	*Asia*	*Africa*
1988-90	55.5	20.6	10.8	2
1995	50	26.9	17.5	1.8
2000	47.7	29.9	19.1	2.1
2015	34.3	36.6	22.1	1.7

Source: Various Issues of World Economic Outlook, IMF.

Similarly the share in aggregate world output of developing countries has increased from 17.9 per cent in 1988-90 to 40.4 per cent in 2000. It has touched in 2015 57.6 per cent (Table 1.2).

Table 1.2: Share in Aggregate World Output

Year	*Major Industrial Countries*	*Developing Countries*	*Asia*	*Africa*
1988-90	62.7	17.9	7.2	1.7
1995	46.2	41.2	24.4	3.3
2000	45.4	40.4	25	3.2
2015	31.5	57.6	35	3.1

Source: Various Issues of World Economic Outlook, IMF.

The growth rates of the developing countries in terms of GDP have been higher than those of the industrial countries. These growth rates have been in fact higher in the 1990s than in the 1980s. There is a significant difference in growth rates during 2001-15 (Table 1.3).

Table 1.3: Key Average Growth rates

	Major Industrial Countries			*Developing Countries*			*Asia*			*Africa*	
	1982-91	*1991-2001*	*2001-15*	*1982-91*	*1991-2001*	*2001-15*	*1982-91*	*1991-2001*	*2001-15*	*1991-2001*	*2001-15*
GDP	3.3	2.7	1.7	3.6	3.8	5.9	6.8	7.2	8.0	2.5	5.6
Exports (Volume)	5.5	6.4	4.0	3.3	7.2	6.9	8.1	10.3	10.1	4.5	3.8
Imports (Volume)	6.1	6.5	3.6	1.8	7.4	7.9	6.5	9.2	9.9	4.9	8.1

Source: World Economic Outlook 2017, IMF.

All these data do not indicate that the developing countries as a group have suffered in the process of globalisation. In fact, there have been substantial gains. But within developing countries, some of the South Asian countries have done better. As far as income distribution within the countries, it is difficult to judge whether globalisation is the primary factor responsible for any deterioration in the distribution of income. Capital flows into developing countries as a percentage of their GDP have also shown a rise (Table 1.4).

Table 1.4: Capital Inflows as a % of GDP

Developing Economies	
Year	*FDI inflow*
1975	0.63
1985	0.54
1995	1.87
2005	3.12
2015	2.41

Source: World Development Indicators, World Bank, 2018.

5. India and the External Sector

India's economic policy towards foreign trade and foreign investment in the first four decades after India's Independence was restrictive. Import substitution constituted a major element of country's foreign trade and industrial policies. The approach to foreign investment was equally constrained. The deficit on the current account was met mainly by borrowing and particularly from official sources. India's share in world exports which stood at 1.91 per cent in 1950 fell to 0.58 per cent in 1992. In the wake of the economic crisis that overtook the country in 1991, the approach to and content of economic policy underwent a far reaching change. This change was reflected in trade and investment policies. An outward orientation began to emerge. Tariff rates have been steadily brought down while quantitative controls have been dismantled. Foreign investment policy has become proactive. Majority ownership by foreign investors is allowed over a wide spectrum of industries.

Authorised foreign institutions are allowed to invest in Indian stock markets. The exchange rate of the rupee is by and large determined by the forces of supply and demand, although the central bank does intervene to avoid instability and volatility.

How has the Indian economy fared as a result of the steady opening up? India's growth rate has definitely been higher in the period following 1992-93, even though there are concerns about falling growth rate in the last few years. In relation to the external sector, the situation has been comfortable. The current account deficit has remained around 1.2 per cent of GDP in the last few years, even though in the current year it may be higher. This however is not a source of concern as the capital flows have been more than adequate. In fact, in recent years the only year in which there was a hiccup was in 2013. The increasing integration has not resulted in a jolt to the economy. On the contrary, the broad macro-economic indicators have shown an improvement. The share of merchandise trade and services to Gross Domestic Product has touched 56.5 percent. FDI inflows have touched $36 billion in 2016-17.

What should be India's attitude in this environment of growing globalisation? At the outset it must be mentioned that opting out of globalisation is not a viable choice. Our aim must be to wrest maximum benefits out of international trade and investment.

India must work towards making the international trading arrangements not being loaded against developing countries. The objective must be to create an environment for 'free and fair trade'. Some of the developed countries particularly the United States has grievances against the developing countries and more particularly against China of manipulating the exchange rate and of dumping goods. This is only partially true. There are genuine concerns which developing countries have and they must be taken care of.

As far as trade is concerned, India must focus on improving its competitiveness so that its share in world exports increases. India's share in world exports now stands at 1.65 percent. India is heavily dependent on the import of crude oil and crude oil prices have shown wide fluctuations. In fact, we do have a high trade deficit. The Current Account Deficit is low because of the surplus on account of services. Perhaps, maintaining the current account deficit at around 1.2 per cent on GDP would be desirable as far as India is concerned.

On the capital account, many changes have been made with respect to the flow of foreign direct investment. Except in a limited set of areas, we should allow foreign direct investment to come in. As far as portfolio investment is concerned, with these inflows coming into the Indian market in a big way, the Indian stock market is very much subject to external shocks.

India's economic policy will be determined by domestic factors. We are not an open economy like Singapore or Malaysia. We should create appropriate conditions within the economy in such a way that capital will flow into areas where we need the most. We also need to be careful in maintaining stability as we grow faster.

6. Conclusion

To conclude, globalisation, in a fundamental sense, is not a new phenomenon. Its roots extend farther and deeper than the visible part of the plant. It is as old as history, starting with the great migrations of people across the great land masses. Only recent developments in computer and communication technologies have accelerated the process of integration, with geographic distances becoming less of a factor. Is this 'end of geography' a boon or a bane? Borders have become porous and the sky is open. With modern technologies which do not recognize geography, it is not possible to hold back ideas either in the political, economic or cultural spheres. Each country must prepare itself to meet the new challenges so that it is not being bypassed by this huge wave of technological and institutional changes.

Nothing is an unmixed blessing. Globalisation in its present form though spurred by far reaching technological changes is not a pure technological phenomenon. It has many dimensions including ideological. To deal with this phenomenon, we must understand the gains and losses, the benefits as well as dangers. To be forewarned, as the saying goes, is to be forearmed. But we should not throw the baby with bath water. We should also resist the temptation to blame globalisation for our failures. Most often, as the poet said, the fault lies in us.

Risks of an open economy are well known. We must not, nevertheless, miss the opportunities that the global system can offer. More than many other developing countries, India is in a position to wrest significant gains from globalisation. However, we must voice our concerns and in cooperation with other developing countries modify the international trading arrangements to take care of the special needs of such countries. At the same time, we must identify and strengthen our comparative advantages. It is this two fold approach which will enable us to meet the challenges of globalisation which is willy-nilly becoming defining characteristic of the new millennium.

Chapter - 2

Innovation and Regulation: An Inverted-u Relationship?

Saurav Roy Choudhury*

Abstract

This paper investigates the relationship between Government regulation and innovation. It creates a simple model of innovation as a function of government regulation. In this model, regulation effects innovation through added regulatory and compliance costs as well as indirectly through its effect on product market competition. The rate of innovation is initially fostered through increasing but low levels of innovation; however, as the direct and indirect costs of regulation increases exponentially, this reduces the rate of innovation. Using a panel dataset compiled from US patent data of US firms in USPTO and NBER and the regulation data from the Regdata 3.0 project over a long time-series from 1976-2014, I find strong evidence of an inverted-U relationship.

1. Introduction

Innovation has long been considered as an engine of economic growth. So, one of the objectives of public policy should be to create a conducive environment that will foster innovation. Government regulation can promote innovation by addressing market failure and increasing competition but can also prove to be an impediment to innovation by increasing barriers to entry, slow the reallocation of capital, and reduce competition. Our paper using a novel dataset of patents and regulations in the US markets from 1976 to 2014, find an inverted "U" relationship between innovation and regulation.

Researchers have been analyzing government regulation for decades due to its importance as a means of addressing market failure (Pigou, 1938).

---

* The author is thankful for useful comments and suggestions by the participants at the International Conference on Globalization and Development in Visva Bharati University in Santiniketan, India and the Mid-West Economics Association conference in Cincinnati, USA.

However, regulations may not always be for best interests (Stigler, 1971), and they may have unintended adverse consequences (see Peltzman [1975]. Bailey and Thomas (2015) finds support for the hypothesis that regulation inhibits business growth and job creation while protecting larger, existing businesses.

But as a healthy competitive environment is imperative for innovations to foster, it may be necessary for the Government to devise policies that would result in increased competition and reduce monopoly and oligopoly pressures. In the US, federal regulations have accumulated over many decades, piling up over time. When regulators add more rules to the pile, analysts often consider the likely benefits and compliance costs of the additional rules. Build-up of regulations over time has a greater effect on innovations than analyzing of a single rule in isolation. Regulations can have a cumulative and detrimental effect on innovation and, over time, have a real impact on American economic growth and development. Ashford et al. (1985) finds regulatory stringency to be the most important factor influencing technological innovation.

2. Model

Regulation can also indirectly affect innovation through its effect on product market competition. I create a simple model of innovation where government regulation and competition[1] are the only factors that will affect innovation. Other factors like talent, the state of nature, the condition of the economy remain unchanged.

Let the government regulation be denoted by a variable r, which can take any value from $[0, \infty)$. The competition c is a function of regulations, which means the value of the competition is a real number $c(r)$] when the level of government regulation is r. I denote the innovation activities as a function of product market competition. According to Aghion et. al. (2005), the degree of competition and innovation level in an industry has an inverted-U shaped relationship. Again, when regulation increases, entry barriers are removed, anti-trust laws are present, predatory behavior by large firms become subject to heavy penalty and all these measures actually contribute to higher competition. But with higher regulation, the rate at which competition increases, tends to decline and in the limit can decrease competition.

I assume that $c' > 0$ with $c'' > 0$ and $\lim_{r \to \infty} c(r) \to \infty$. When the level of competition prevailing in an industry itself depends on regulation, then the level of innovative activities becomes an indirect function of regulation. Initially, with higher competition, firms have more incentive to innovate in order to protect their positions in the market. However, with the entry of more firms, every firm loses out on its market share. Hence firms feel discouraged when ther are many similar "neck-to-neck" firms. This acts as an indirect disincentive for innovation.

The cost of regulation is denoted by *g(r)*. This cost includes direct costs like compliance costs and indirect costs that complicates and distorts the decision-making processes of firms, the dead-weight costs that arise from compliance burden on businesses, that causes them to divert valuable time and resources from innovation activities to compliance efforts of increasing regulations. Taken in isolation, a single regulation should cross the cost benefit test, but the accumulation of regulations over time will gradually lead to duplicative, obsolete, conflicting, and even contradictory rules, and the multiplicity of regulatory constraints. At higher levels of regulations, the required rules, procedures themselves become barriers to entry for small firms. Without loss of generality, I can assume that this cost increases at an increasing rate, i.e. $g' > o$ with $g'' > o$and $\lim_{r \to \infty} g(r) \to \infty$. Thus we can write the innovation function in a simple additive separable form as

$$I(r) = c(r) - g(r)$$

This function can be illustrated in figure 1.1. As we can see the *c(r)* is increasing and concave, while the *g(r)* function is increasing and convex. They intersect at 0 and at *r*. The distance between these two curves initially increases, reaches a maximum at *r** and then declines. Thus, if we plot innovation *I* as a function of regulation *r*, we get the inverted-U shaped curve as shown in figure 1.1.

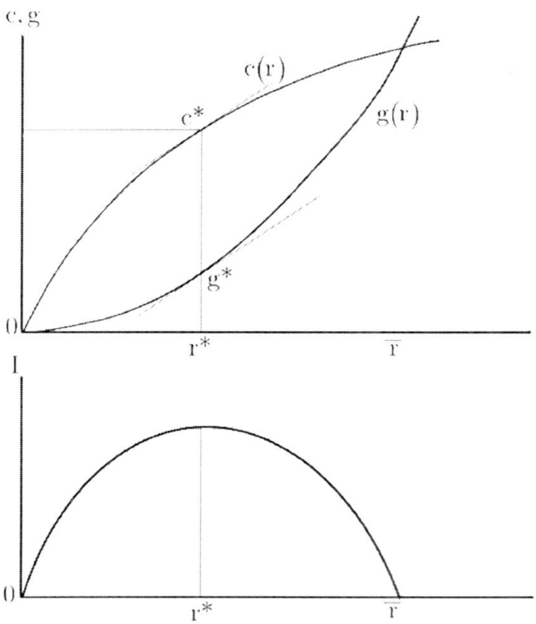

Figure 1.1: Inverted "U" Innovation as a function of Regulation.

3. Data

Our measure of innovation activity in industries is looking at patent counts and patent citations. There are more than 8 million patent data available just for the US since 1976. In order to match the time period of the patent data to the regulation data, I confine my database from 1976 to 2014, which reduces my sample to 2.5 million patents granted. I could then match about 40% of the patents to the name of specific publicly traded firms in the Compustat database. Of these patents, about 35% were not included in the NBER data and hence excluded. Then, I include only the firms that have unique firm identifiers in Compustat with the 3 digit NAICS codes. Table 2.1 lists the industry description and the corresponding NAICS codes for industries that could match with the Regulation dataset (Regdata 3.0), discussed later in this section.

Table 2.1: Industry Descriptions of the 40 NAICS Codes.

NAICS	*Industry Description*	*NAICS*	*Industry Description*
111	Crop Production	454	Non-store Retailers
211	Oil and Gas Extraction	481	Air Transportation
212	Mining (except Oil and Gas)	482	Rail Transportation
213	Support Activities for Mining	483	Water Transportation
221	Utilities	493	Warehousing and Storage
311	Food Manufacturing	512	Motion Picture and Sound Recording Industries
312	Beverage and Tobacco Product Manufacturing	515	Broadcasting (except Internet)
321	Wood Product Manufacturing	517	Telecommunications
322	Paper Manufacturing	518	Data Processing, Hosting and Related Services
324	Petroleum and Coal Products Manufacturing	519	Other Information Services
325	Chemical Manufacturing	522	Credit Intermediation and Related Activities
326	Plastics and Rubber Products Manufacturing	523	Securities and Commodity Contracts
327	Nonmetallic Mineral Product Manufacturing	524	Insurance Carriers and Related Activities
331	Primary Metal Manufacturing	525	Funds, Trusts, and Other Financial Vehicles
333	Machinery Manufacturing	541	Professional, Scientific, and Technical Services
334	Computer and Electronic Product Manufacturing	551	Management of Companies and Enterprises
335	Electrical Equipment and Component Manufacturing	561	Administrative and Support Services
336	Transportation Equipment Manufacturing	562	Waste Management and Remediation Services
423	Merchant Wholesalers, Durable Goods	621	Ambulatory Health Care Services
424	Merchant Wholesalers, Nondurable Goods	713	Amusement, Gambling, and Recreation Industries

For each year, I sum the patents generated by all firms under a specific NAICS code to come up with the total patent counts for each of the 40 industries. Figure 1.2 shows the average yearly patent counts across the 40 industries which show an increasing trend since 1976. As a robustness check, I also use cite-weighted patents as another proxy for innovation. more As the value of individual patents can differ greatly, Hall et al. (2005) find that cite-weighted patents carry more information about the quality of the patents than raw patent counts.

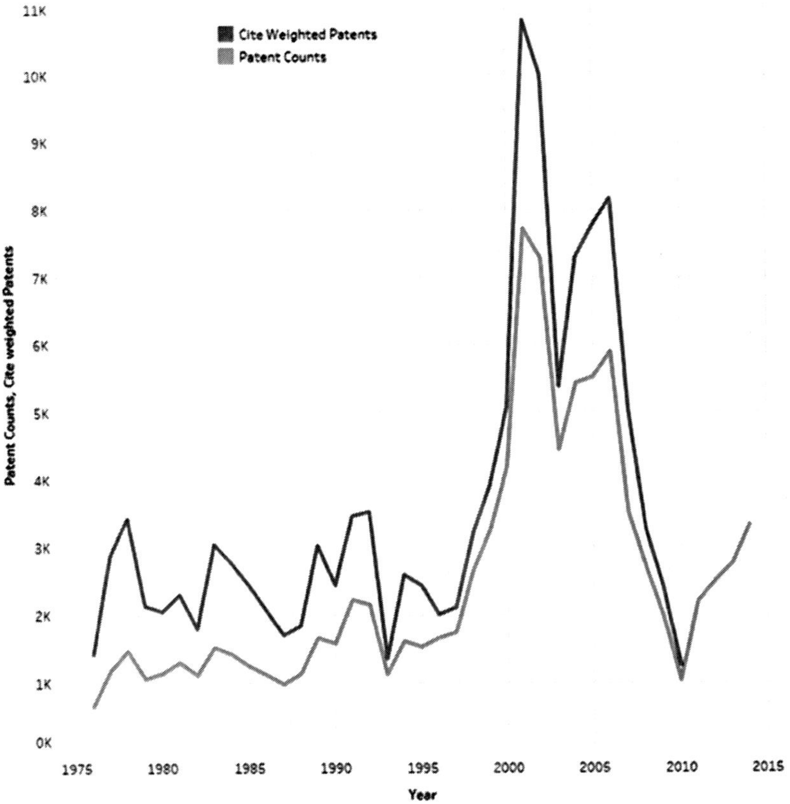

Figure 1.2: Trends of Patent Counts and Cite-Weighted Patents for the 40 representative Industries over 1976-2014

They find an extra citation per patent increases the market value of the patenting firm by 3%. I follow the methodology by Hall et al. (2005) to weight each patent by the number of future citations, which is the number of subsequent citations received by a firm's patents. Following standard procedures, I use patents that are ultimately granted, dated by year of application, and weight these by future citations through 2014. To deal with censoring I estimate only until 2010, allowing for a four-year window of future citations for the last cohort of patents in the data. Figure 1.2 shows the trends in the patent counts and cite-weighted patents for the 40 representative industries. I also include a full set of time dummies, which control the fact that patents taken out later in the panel have less time to be cited than patents taken out earlier in the panel I find a high correlation between these two proxies of innovation and if we do not measure innovation success across firms, but across industries, the patent counts are a good proxy for innovation. The innovation seems to pick up sharply during the mid-1990's and fall sharply around the time of the great recession in the US.

The source of Government regulations is a project initiated by the Mercatus Center at the George Mason University. The project, called Reg Data, annually quantifies federal regulations by industry and regulatory agency for all federal regulations. The data measures regulation for industries at the two, three, and four-digit levels of the North American Industry Classification System (NAICS). The RegData 3.0 database (McLaughlin et. Al, 2017) uses text analysis to count binding constraints in the wording of regulations, as codified in the Code of Federal Regulations (CFR[3]) and to measure the applicability of regulatory text to different industries.

There are two broad types of regulation data available, one based on restrictions (*IRR*) and the other on word counts (*IRW*)—at four CFR levels of granularity: title, chapter, part, and paragraph. I can use this database to study the determinants of industry regulations and to study regulations' effects both across industries and time[4]. Figure 1.3 shows the accumulation of regulatory restrictions and regulatory Word counts over our sample period from 1976-2014 across the 40 industries in the dataset. There has been a steady growth in both those measures over three long periods, with two quick intermissions when the growth rate slowed dramatically and the number of restrictions even declined 1983-84 and 1995-1996). Since the great recession of 2008-09, the regulation has grown sharply. According to Regdata project, "these periods do not match up neatly with any president or party; rather, regulatory accumulation seems to be a bipartisan trend—or perhaps a bureaucratic trend independent of elected officials' ideologies"[5]. Both these measures of regulatory stringency are closely correlated.

There are papers using Regdata which has looked at the relationship between regulation and various measures of productivity, entrepreneurship, and growth. The evidence has been mixed. Davies (2014) using a Regdata dataset from 1997 through 2010 found that least regulated industries experienced higher per cent growth in output per person, in output per hour,

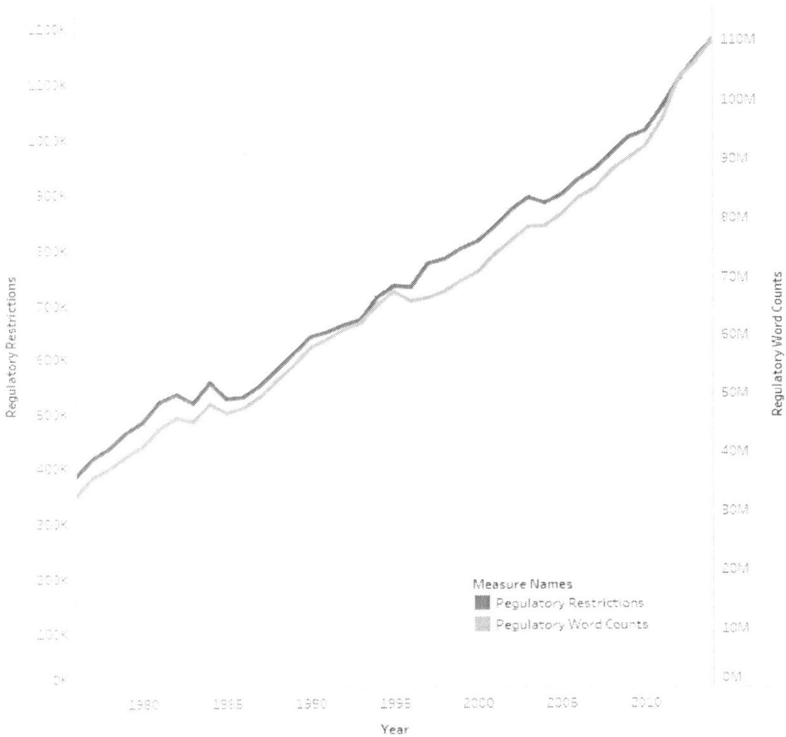

Figure 1.3: Accumulation of Federal Regulatory Restrictions and Regulatory Word Counts.

and a decline in unit labor costs. Over the same period, the most regulated industries experienced a lower 33 per cent growth in output per person, a 34 per cent lower growth in output per hour, and an increase in unit labor costs. But, Goldschlag and Tabarrok (2014) using Regdata found no evidence that higher regulation causes declining entrepreneurship levels in the US. Coffey et al. (2017) Regdata 3.0 document that the economic growth in the United States has, on average, been slowed by 0.8 per cent per year since 1980 owing to the cumulative effects of regulation. They concluded that if regulation had been held constant at levels observed in 1980, the US economy would have been about 25 per cent larger than it actually was as of 2014.

To compare the regulations and innovations in an industry, I create relative measures of innovation (regulation), I divide the total number of patents (regulation) granted in an industry by the total patents(regulation) of all the 40 industries in our sample. This gives the relative innovation (regulation) strength of each industry. Figure 1.4 shows the patents and regulations by industry. Patent % for each industry is calculated by the total number of patents in that Industry divided by the sum of the patents of the 40 industries in the data set. Similarly, the Regulatory Restrictions % gives the regulatory

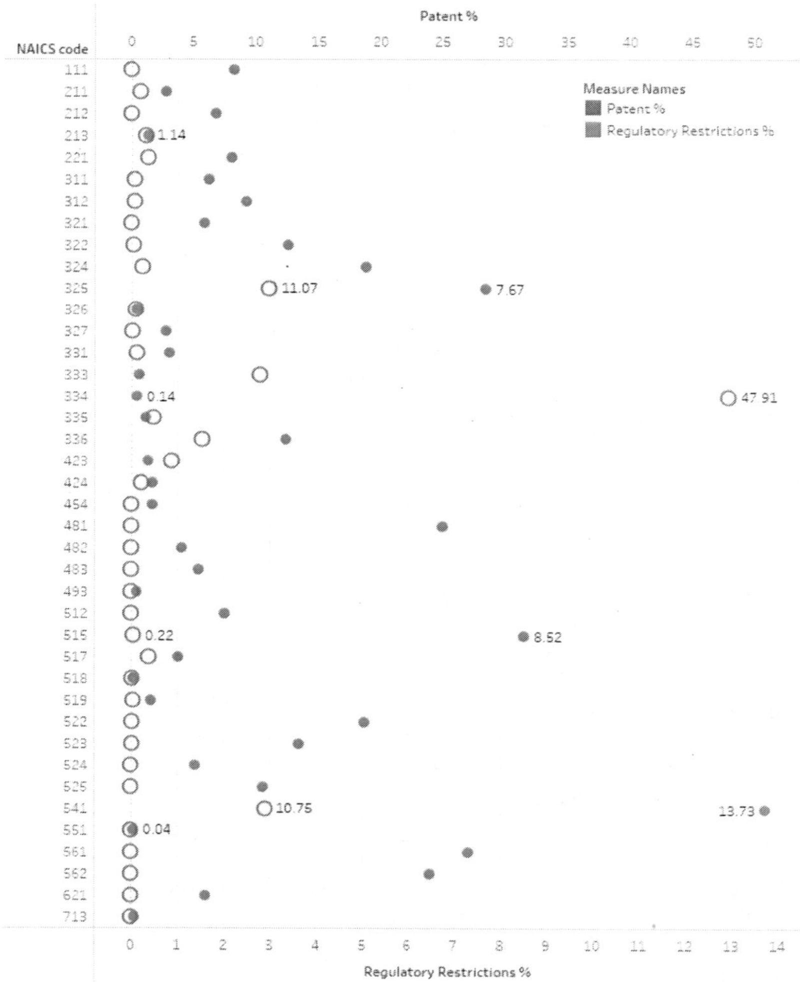

Note: Patent % for each industry is calculated by the total number of patents in that Industry divided by the sum of the patents of the 40 industries in the data set. Similarly, the Regulatory Restrictions % gives the regulatory restrictions for a specific industry as a percentage of the Sum of the total Regulatory Restrictions of all the 40 industries in the data set. The industry descriptions corresponding to the specific NAICS codes are in Table 1. The period for the data is from 1976 to 2014.

Figure 1.4: Relative Patent Counts and Regulations by Industry.

restrictions for a specific industry as a percentage of the Sum of the total Regulatory Restrictions of all the 40 industries in the data set. The industry descriptions corresponding to the specific NAICS codes are in Table 2.1. The period for the data is from 1976 to 2014. There are some interesting findings, the industry with the highest percentage of patents of 47.91%, Computers and Electronic Product Manufacturing (NAICS 334) has only 0.14% of the regulation attributed to them. Conversely, the Broadcasting industry (NAICS 515) which excludes the internet account for 0.22% of the patents but 8.52% of the regulations. Again, most industries do not show any clear pattern, the percentage contribution to patents and the percentage attributed by regulation are somewhat similar (NAICS 213, 326, 326, 335, 424, 493, 518, 551, and 713).

Following the standard literature, I employ the inverse Lerner (i.e., 1- Lerner index) as a measure of the intensity of competition[6]. Consistent with our theoretical model, a value close to 1 implies perfect competition. Lerner is estimated as the median gross margin from the three-digit industry. There is some evidence of an inverted-U relationship between innovation and competition in Aghion et al. (2005), but when I run a regression of patent counts on the inverse Lerner and the square of the inverse Lerner, the linear term is positive whereas the squared term is negative but insignificant.

Table 2.2 reports the descriptive statistics of the key variables. The data on regulation and patents are quite skewed across industries.

Table 2.2: Descriptive Statistics

Variable	*Mean*	*Std. Dev.*	*Min*	*Max*
Regulatory Restrictions (IRR)	19,634	28,162.6	190.87	97,502.4
Regulatory Word Counts (IRW)	1,695,317	2,387,531	18,397	7,375,309
Raw Patent counts	8,075	10,497	1	37,175
Cite Weighted Patent counts	16,961	23,188	1	79,640
1- Lerner Index (Competition)	0.865	0.413	0.632	0.973

Notes: IRR is Industry Regulatory Restrictions index, and IRW is the industry Regulatory Word, Count index, obtained from Regdata 3.0 project. *'Competition'* is the *(1- Lerner Index)* whereLerner is estimated as the median gross margin from entire Compustat database in the three-digit NAICS industry code. Raw patent counts are obtained from National Bureau of Economic Research match with the US Patent and Trademark Office data. Each patent count is weighted by the number of future citations to create Cite Weighted Patents. Estimation period is 1976-2014, except for Cite Weighted patents (1976-2010), where I allow a four-year window of future citations for the last cohort of patents in the data.

4. Methodology

Consider the first moment of the relationship between a count based measures of innovation (raw patent counts and cite-weighted patents), $INNOV_{it}$, of industry *i* in period *t* and our measures of regulation (*REG= IRR and IRW*) and competition as measured by inverse Lerner index, ($COMP_{it}$). The ordinary least squares (OLS) model specification is

$$(1)\ ln(INNOV_{it}) = \beta_o + \beta_1 \ln(REG_{it}) + \beta_2 (\ln(REG)_{it})^2 + \beta_3 COM_{it} + \eta_i + \tau_t$$

where η_i is a industry fixed effect, and τ_t are time dum-mies.

Because of the count based and highly skewed nature of the patent and citations data (see Table 2.2), I use the standard Poisson regression model. The Poisson specification is given by

$$(2)\ E(INNOV_{it}|REG_{it}, \eta_i, \tau_t) = e^{(\beta_1 REG_{it} + \beta_2 (REG_{it})^2 + \beta_3 COM_{it} + \eta_i + \tau_t)},$$

where η_i is a industry fixed effect, and τ_t are time dum-mies.

5. Results

Table 2.3 contains the results. Columns (1) and (3) report the ordinary least squares (OLS) estimates, where *In (Patent Counts)* is the dependent variable. Columns (2) and (4) correspond to Poisson regressions on *Patent Counts*. Columns (1) and (2) has Industry Regulatory Restrictions (IRR) index as the Regulation variable and Columns (3) and (4) has regulation measured

Table 2.3: Innovation and Regulation

Estimation Method	*OLS*	*Poisson*	*OLS*	*Poisson*
Regulation measure	*Regulatory Restrictions*		*Regulatory Word Counts*	
Dependent Variable	*Ln(Patents)*	*Patents*	*Ln(Patents)*	*Patents*
	(1)	(2)	(3)	(4)
Regulation	0.032*	0.036**	0.056**	0.039**
	(0.015)	(0.013)	(0.029)	(0.019)
Regulation squared	-0.013*	-0.004**	-0.025**	-0.005***
	(0.006)	(0.001)	(0.011)	(0.001)
Competition	1.319**	7.430***	1.245**	7.289***
	(0.592)	(2.120)	(0.621)	(2.145)
No. of Observations	1560	1560	1560	1560

Notes: Notes:Columns (1) and (3) are OLS regressions on *ln(Patent counts)*. Columns (2) and (4) correspond to Poisson regressions on *Patent Counts*. IRR is Industry Regulatory Restrictions index and IRW is the industry Regulatory Word Count index. 'Competition' is the *(1- Lerner Index)* whereLerner is estimated as the median gross margin from entire Compustat database in the firm's three-digit industry. Estimation period is 1976-2014. For OLS regressions I use *ln(IRR)* and *(ln(IRR))*^{2} for column (1) and *ln(IRW)* and *(ln(IRW))*^{2} for column 2, respectively. For the Poisson regressions, I scale the IRR and IRW by 10,000 and 100,000, repectively. All regressions have control for a full set of the year and industry dummies. The standard errors are in parenthesis are clustered in the three-digit industry. ***, **,* denote significance at 1%, 5% and 10% levels, respectively.

by Industry Regulatory Word Counts (IRW). For the Poisson regressions, I scale the IRR and IRW by 10, 000 and 100, 000, repectively. Across all columns in Table 2.3, the coefficient on Regulation is positive and significant. For OLS regressions I use *ln(IRR)* and $ln(IRR)^2$ for column (1) and *ln(IRW)* and $ln(IRW))^2$ for column 2, respectively. This result seems to be due to economic as well as statistical significance. The coefficient on the squared term is negative and significant across all columns. This implies an inverse "U" shape as predicted by the model. This result seems to be due to economic as well as statistical significance.

In table 2.4, I repeat the economteric models replacing raw patent counts by cite-weighted patents. The columns (1) and (3) report the ordinary least squares (OLS) estimates, where *ln(Cites)* is the dependent variable. Columns (2) and (4) correspond to Poisson regressions on cite-weighted patents or *Cites*. Our results are qualitatively similar to table 2.3. This is due to the fact that there is a high correlation between patent counts and cite-weighted patents in an industry.

Table 2.4: Innovation and Regulation

Estimation Method	*OLS*	*Poisson*	*OLS*	*Poisson*
Regulation measure	*Regulatory Restrictions*		*Regulatory Word Counts*	
Dependent Variable	*Ln(Cites)*	*Cites*	*Ln(Cites)*	*Cites*
	(1)	(2)	(3)	(4)
Regulation	0.035*	0.048*	0.055**	0.049**
	(0.015)	(0.025)	(0.032)	(0.024)
Regulation squared	-0.014**	-0.004**	-0.023*	-0.004***
	(0.006)	(0.001)	(0.011)	(0.001)
Competition	1.323***	7.386***	1.244**	7.270***
	(0.358)	(2.182)	(0.627)	(2.145)
No. of Observations	1400	1400	1400	1400

Notes: Columns (1) and (3) are OLS regressions on *ln(Cites)* where Cites are patents weighted by the number of future citations. Columns (2) and (4) are *Poisson* regressions on *Cite Weighted Patent countsor Cites*. IRR is Industry Regulatory Restrictions index and IRW is the industry Regulatory Word, Count index. *'Competition'* is the *(1- Lerner Index)* whereLerner is estimated as the median gross margin from entire Compustat database in the firm's three-digit industry. Estimation period is 1976-2010. For OLS regressions I use *ln(IRR)* and $(ln(IRR))^2$ for column (1) and *ln(IRW)* and $(ln(IRW))^2$ for column 2, respectively. For the Poisson regressions, I scale the IRR and IRW by 10,000 and 100,000, repectively. All regressions have control for a full set of the year and industry dummies. The standard errors are in parenthesis. ***, **,* denote significance at 1%, 5% and 10% levels, respectively.

6. Conclusion

There is some agreement among economists that some level of government regulation is needed to prevent market failure and anti-trust issues such as larger firms buying-up of promising competitors, and potential monopsony power over suppliers and vendors. But there is a trade-off between innovation and regulation. The positive effects of regulation promote innovation. However, the accumulation of regulations over time leads to duplicative, obsolete, conflicting, and even contradictory rules, and the multiplicity of regulatory constraints that stymies innovation. Based on a dataset on patent counts and regulation index grouped by 40 industries from 1976-2014, I find robust evidence of an inverse "U" shape relationship between innovation and regulation, even after controlling for competition and industry effects.

References

Aghion, Philippe, Nick Bloom, Richard Blundell, Rachel Griffith, and Peter Howitt, (2005), "Competition and Innovation: An Inverted-U Relationship," Quarterly Journal of Economics, 120(2), pp. 701–728.

Ashford, A. A., C. Ayers, and R. E. Stone. 1985. Using Regulation to Change the Market for Innovation. Harvard Environmental Law Review 9(2): 419-466.

Bailey, M.N., C. Hulten and D. Campbell, (1992), "Productivity dynamics in manufacturing plants," Brookings Papers: Microeconomics (Brookings Institute, Washington, DC), pp. 187-249

Coffey, Bentley and McLaughlin, Patrick A. and Peretto, Pietro F.,(2016) "The Cumulative Cost of Regulations." MERCATUS WORKING PAPER; Duke I&E Research Paper No. 2016-45. Available at http://dx.doi.org/10.2139/ssrn.2869145

Davies, Antony.(2014) "Regulation and Productivity." Mercatus Research. Arlington, VA: Mercatus Center at George Mason University

Goldschlag, Nathan and Tabarrok, Alexander T., (2014) "Is Regulation to Blame for the Decline in American Entrepreneurship?" (2014). GMU Working Paper in Economics No. **15-11**. Available at SSRN: http://dx.doi.org/10.2139/ssrn.2559803

McLaughlin, Patrick A. and Sherouse, Oliver and Francis, Daniel and Gasvoda, Michael and Nelson, Jonathan and Strosko, Stephen and Richards, Tyler, Regdata 3.0 User's Guide (August 31, 2017). Available at SSRN: https://ssrn.com/abstract=3044802 or http://dx.doi.org/10.2139/ssrn.3044802

Hall, Bronwyn H., Adam Jaffe, and Manuel Trajtenberg, (2005), "Market Value and Patent Citations," RAND Journal of Economics, **36(1)**, pp. 16-38.

Notes

1. Intuitively, when product market is competitive, firms are compelled to get involved in innovative activities in order to preserve its position in the industry vis-a-vis their contenders. However, as the industry nears the perfectly competitive state, the rate of diffusion tends to be very high and firms are very often discouraged to conduct any innovative R&D. In such cases either the firms do not innovate at all or they conduct mostly imitative types of R&D activities.

2. The CFR is published annually and contains all regulations issued at the federal level in the US. The CFR is divided into 50 titles, each of which corresponds to a broad subject area. Each title is nominally divided into parts that cover specific regulatory areas within the broad subject area given by the title. Each title is also physically divided into volumes to permit publication in conveniently sized bindings.
3. For a list of papers that have used or references Regdata, go to https://quantgov.org/research/
4. Source: Patrick A. Mclaughlin and Oliver Sherouse- Regdata 3.0, Available at http://www.quantgov.org
5. See Aghion et al. (2005) for a discussion on why the inverse Lerner is appropriate in these kinds of models.

Chapter - 3

Globalisation and Development: Perspectives

Pranab Kanti Basu

1. Globalisation

Every social phenomenon, including an epoch of world history that is marked out by certain traits that other epochs do not display, is open to be constructed from various perspectives. This is true of our current concern – globalisation, a term which is used to denote a definite period of history. However, there are views that contest this position claiming that this trend was quite pronounced in much earlier periods, too. We will not enter this terrain.

Our aim is to construct a perspective on globalisation and development that contests the mainstream analytic from a 'class' perspective. We will start from the accepted attributes of globalisation to theoretically critique it from our perspective and build an alternative analytic.

So, what is globalisation? OECD (2013) defines globalisation as 'a process of deeper integration between countries and regions of the world'. It goes on to elaborate its characteristics: 'Globalisation is a process in which economies have become increasingly integrated and inter-dependent. *Globalisation is dynamic*rather than an end state...Globalisation is not inevitable – it can reverse, indeed the growth of world trade in goods and services slowed in recent years following the global financial crisis' (emphasis added).

Let us try to break this down. 'Dynamic' implies that its characteristics are historically and geographically contingent.In other words there is a certain fluidity of character within the era.Cross border integration of supply chains and production processes has become an important feature of globalisation in the recent phase of globalisation. This is what is referred to as 'Global Value Chain' (GVC). OECD says as much: "The geographic dispersion of industrial and service activities, for example research and development, sourcing of factor inputs, production and distribution, and the cross-border networking of companies, for example through joint ventures and the sharing of assets." This will be our focus: GVCs in the post-Fordist era.

As we have stated at the outset, like every economic phenomenon, globalisation can be viewed from various perspectives. Perspectives depend on what you are curious or passionate about. Schematically speaking there are two kinds of perspectives. First, the policy perspectives concerned with ways of conserving the system by making it 'better' or more bearable. In contrast there are the critical perspectives that try to understand the structural faults that make the system incapable of delivering its promise.

I take the latter perspective. Within this broad perspective I use a Marxian frame of analysis. The basic proposition of this analytic is that the form of extraction of surplus from labouring people is significant for determining nature of economy. The labouring people constitute a set of classes, say, workers, tenant farmers, etc. Literally in opposition to them stand the class/classes that appropriate the surplus (i.e. what the labouring people produce in excess of their needs). These could be the owners of the factories – the industrial capitalist – or, say the landlord. There are other classes that are necessary to the surplus appropriating classes for furnishing the conditions for appropriation of surplus – the merchants, the money lenders, the public servants who defend the right to extract surplus, etc. Thus when I say that I will be using a Marxian perspective I imply that this is a class focussed analysis as distinct from the individual focussed analysis of mainstream analysis. I shall be using information and tools that are already in the public domain to first present a picture of contemporary global world. I will then briefly introduce Marx's method and go on to view the painted picture from that perspective. Two contributors whose works have particularly influenced this piece are Selwyn (2016) and Roy (2018).

2. Fordism

To put this period in perspective we have to contrast it with the preceding phase of world capitalism. This is, of course, a contentious issue: how should one periodise? I am using a standard scheme that Marxists and some non-Marxists adhere too. The current period is referred to as post-Fordist and the preceding as Fordist. 'Fordism' was coined to denote the capitalist order from the first to the sixth decade of the twentieth century. Capitalism of this phase displayed certain common traits. The most significant was the inauguration and spread of large-scale assembly line production of standardized commodities. This began with the production of the Model T-Ford automobile in 1908. Previously, automobiles were custom built. This was the first time that a large number of standardized cars were produced in anticipation of a market. The process of standardisation was itself significant: conveyor belt technology was used in production for the first time. A fascinating narration of this turn can be read by the interested reader in Harry Braverman's *Labour and Monopoly Capital.* It is also vividly told in Charlie Chaplin's *Modern Times.* This technology soon spread to mass consumption goods production and on to capital goods production. Obviously, this implied that a very buoyant mood prevailed where there was anticipation of sustained and increasing demand. The large consumer goods market was sustained partly by rising real wages that resulted from a vigorous Trade Union movement itself aided by the coming together of large number of workers in huge integrated factories.

The driving force behind increasing profits and capital accumulation in the period preceding this was fragmentation and analysis of work in the factory through 'Time and Motion Studies' (this period is usually referred to as the period of Taylorism after Francis Taylor who was the inventor of 'scientific management'). In the Fordist period emphasis shifted to coordinating the fragments of the production process (that had been created by the industrial division of labour) within the integrated factory, more efficiently through the use of technology, most importantly the conveyor belt.

3. Post-Fordism and Global Value Chains

From the seventies of the twentieth century began the new age of capital that has been named 'post-Fordism'. Fragmentation and outsourcing as opposed to production within integrated factory marked the period. This trend was necessitated by the decreasing advantage in material manufactures of leading industrial nations.

Capital located in the industrialised nations wanted to take advantage of lower wages and less state regulation of environment and workplace norms in the underdeveloped world. This was facilitated by the neoliberal policies of increased trade and investment flows forced on nations through IMF, WB, WTO. Fragmentation and geographical/international relocation of fragments of production processes also decreased the power of TUs, which had become a concern for capital. Outsourcing over the globe has been seen in the literature as the production of value addition through a global chain. Hence the popular nomenclature: Global Value Chain (GVC). The growth of GVCs has been facilitated also by the development of IT that allows strong governance of the chain through instant flow of information back and forth. The developed nations shifted from material manufacture to reaping benefits through governance of GVCs.

Kaplinsky (2000) presents the structure of GVCs schematically:-

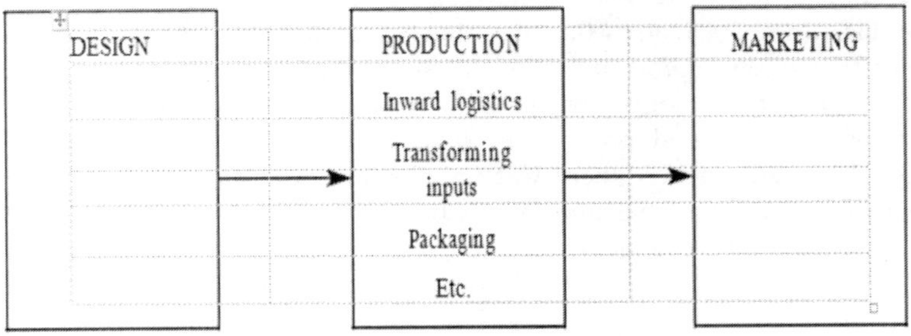

The location of the segments of the GVCs is, broadly, geographically specific. The middle segment is located in the less developed spaces while the extremities are located in the developed areas.

Source: Kaplinsky (2000)

Figure 2.1: A Simple Value Chain

The middle rectangle is located in the poor countries. This is highly competitive and the returns are poor. What Kaplinsky illustrates is the cause for the developed countries gaining unequally from GVCs. This is because, typically, the production units located in the poor countries are numerous and also numerous such locations compete with one another. Because of the large number of job seekers it is also possible to produce in sweatshops and manage to earn profit at the low prices at which the products are sold to the segment on the right. As Kaplinsky (2000) remarks "As more and more countries have developed their capabilities in industrial activities, so barriers to entry in production have fallen and the competitive pressures have heightened". This leads to situations that cannot be called contractual worker–capitalist relations but are rather 'sweat shops'. '[t]he prime motivation behind offshoring is the desire to reduce labour costs…a U.S.-based factory worker hired for $21 an hour can be replaced by a Chinese factory worker who is paid 64 cents an hour' Charles Whalen (2005). **Lions share** of the marketed value of the product of GVC accrues to the developed nations in the form of **rent** for knowledge and power based activities: **governance, marketing and design. Deployed to maintain and extend monopoly control** Quite grotesquely this situation is summarised in a diagram called the smile curve.

'Usually, the value created in a GVC is unevenly distributed among its participants. The allocation of value depends on the ability of participants to supply sophisticated, hard-to-imitate products or services.Increasingly, the supply of such products or services stems from forms of KBC [knowledge-based capital] such as brands, basic R&D and design, and the complex integration of software with organisational structures' (OECD (2013).

To anticipate, 'value addition' here is used to indicate solely the appropriation of market values by agencies in various locations. This has nothing in common with the sense in which value is used by classical political economy and Marx to denote, stated rather heuristically, the labour contribution. The bottom of the trough is of course the most miserable – the sweat shops of Bangladesh, India, Malaysia, etc. the further up you move towards any extreme of the smile the geographical location approaches the rich countries.Below we present the disaggregation of 'value addition' in a few GVCs to illustrate our contention.

3.1 Importance of GVCs

Though the significance of the GVCs, today, is widely recognised, let us substantiate the point for those who may not be conversant with the literature. The 2013 World Investment Report estimates that now over 80 per cent of global trade flows through global production networks led by transnational corporations. The ILO on the other hand estimates that one in five jobs in the world are somehow linked to GVCs. Using the OECD WTO database on Trade in Value Added, a prominent research paper, Banga (2014), shows that 67% of total global value created under global value chains, accrue to OECD countries while share of NICs and BRICs countries is 25%. Only 8% of total value added is shared among all other developing countries and Least Developed Countries (LDC).

The rise of global value chains (GVCs) in the past two decades has dramatically altered the world economy. But with the increasing complexity and sophistication of cross-border production-sharing activities, the use of only official trade data (such as gross exports and imports) and GDP statistics has not revealed the significance and nature of changes in the global business cycle. An important reason is that indicators based on official trade and production data cannot identify and distinguish which types of trade are GVC activities and which are not, thus making it difficult to evaluate the relation between changes in global trade and changes in GDP growth.

4. Conceptualising GVCs from a Marxist perspective

I would propose that the term feudo-capitalist fits the description of GVCs. The reasons for this will be elaborated as we proceed.WTO and other defenders of GVCs claim that poor countries at the point of entry into the GVC may be in bad position on the 'smile curve' but there is always the possibility of nations moving up the ladder through policy effort. Assuming some can manage a positional shift, there must some who occupy the trough of the curve, otherwise GVC would not have any comparative advantage. Governors of GVCs, developed nation states and international economic organisations will do all in their power to ensure that such does not happen – patents, copyrights, immobility of labour and all the rest of the instruments of economic warfare are deployed to prevent such possibility.

In the rest of the chapter we elaborate the proposition that the current order can be described as feudo-capitalist (and the consequences analysed) using the Marxian understanding of rent modified to suit the era of globalisation marked by predominance of GVCs.

To elaborate our proposal we have to schematically look into Marx's theory of surplus appropriation by capital to see how the analytic needs to be modified because of the entry of GVCs

4.1 Marx's Scheme

4.1.1Production of *Surplus Value*

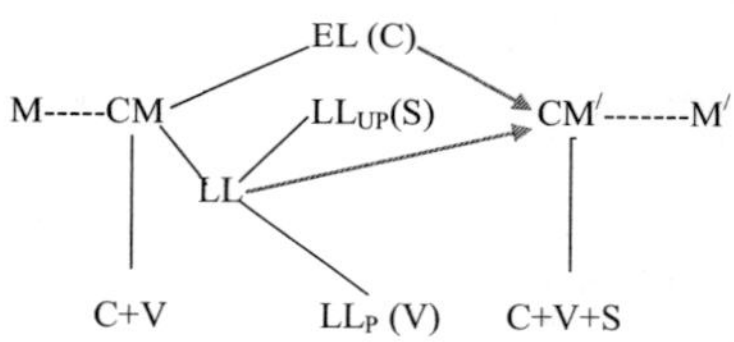

EL (C)	: Embodied Labour(Constant Capital)
LL	: Live Labour
LL_{UP}(S)	: Live Labour which unpaid (Surplus Value)
LL_P (V)	: Live Labour which is paid back to the labourer as wage (Variable Capital)
——	: Free exchange.
→	: Production Process/labour process.

The productive capitalist invests M to buy inputs or commodities, CM. Note that we are using CM instead of the familiar 'C' used in *Capital*. This is to differentiate this from constant capital for which also Marx uses the symbol 'C'. CM contains two components: *embodied labour* or *constant capital* and *live labour*. The former contains the non-labour inputs like fuel, raw materials, wear and tear of machinery, etc. Labour has already been spent in their production and therefore the value (grossly the labour hours spent) that this component adds to the products is constant (since it is already fixed) and equal to its own value (C). Live labour, i.e. the labour power actively engaged in this factory in transforming the raw materials into finished products with the aid of machinery, fuel, etc. is purchased at its value (V). This investment is called investment in *variable capital*, because its contribution to the value of the finished product CM' is not given beforehand, unlike in the case of EL, which has already been rendered and is therefore given. The capitalist has contracted with the labourer that against a wage payment whose value is V the labourer will work for a day. Now the length of the working day is liable to variation for various political and economic reasons.

For example when the economy is in the downturn of the cycle, work opportunities are low and the worker can be cajoled to work for longer hours. Besides, the workers render *alienated labour*, and therefore are averse to work diligently in the factory. This means that unlike the independent artisans who take pleasure in their work, the workers have sold their labour power to the capitalist and the labour time only goes to add to the wealth of the capitalist. Besides, given the fragmentation of work, the labourer has no idea of his own contribution to the final product, in these senses he/she is alienated. Thus, they have to be coerced. So how successfully they can be made to work for the agreed time is variable. Hence, the term 'variable capital'.In any case they have to contribute some value to 'S' in addition to the value of their work time (i.e. is in excess of the time that is necessary to make the wherewithal for the worker's sustenance for a day). Else the capitalist has no reason to hire them. This additional value is LL_{UP} and is the source of surplus value – the value addition by which CM' exceeds CM. So we have the circuit M-CM-CM′-M′, $CM' > CM \rightarrow M' > M$. In the notations of Vol. I of Capital we have: M-C-C′-M′, $C' > C$! $M' > M$

4.1.2 Redistribution of surplus among enterprises

The surplus value is distributed between the various capitalist enterprises so as to ensure equal rates of profit in these enterprises. Here Marx like the classical economists Smith and Ricardo was assuming an equilibrium state. Such distribution of surplus value Requires transformation of (labour) values of commodities to prices of production in a non-proportionate manner. Let us elaborate this.

Investment in V generates S, not investment in C. The greater the proportion of V to C in any line of production (Marx calls the inverse, C/V, 'organic composition of capital'), the greater will be the proportion of S to capital invested (or the rate of profit in value terms) in a line of production. So equalisation of rates of profits in price terms requires divergence of prices of production from (labour) values: the greater the excess of organic composition (C/V) from average (C/V) greater will be the excess of prices of production over values. The converse will hold for lines of production where (C/V) is less than average. This can be shown by simple algebra:

The rate of $\prod$ (in value terms) $= S \div (C+V) = (S/V) \div (C/V + 1)$

S/V (rate of exploitation) is assumed to be the same across lines of production. So the rate of $\prod$ in terms of value is lower than average where C/V (organic composition of capital) is higher than average; higher where C/V is lower than average C/V. But equilibrium under capitalism requires equalisation of rt. of $\prod$ in terms of prices (i.e. in terms of money) in all lines of production.

This is achieved through *transformation of value into Production Price (P) or value form.* $P >$ Value, where $C/V >$ average C/V so rate of $\prod$ in terms of value is lower, $P =$ Value, where $C/V=$ average C/V, $P <$ Value where $C/V<$ average C/V, So rate of $\prod$ in terms of value is higher than average. *There is a redistribution of value from lines of production with lower C/V to those with higher C/V.*

4.1.3 Subsumed Payments

But productive capital (i.e. capital engaging hired labour to produce commodities and so extracting S) cannot appropriate entire S. It has to make *subsumed* class payments to obtain the necessary conditions of extraction of surplus value. It has to pay rent to the landlord; trade margin to merchant; taxes to state to ensure its law and its order; interest to the money lender.

The problem with Marx's formulation as I see it is that the subsumed class payments are not integrated into the price system. A fuller discussion of this problem is outside the scope of this discussion. I have discussed this elsewhere, Basu (2008). There are some insights in volume III of *Capital,* where he discusses ***absolute ground rent***, i.e. rent solely paid by capitalist farmer to gain access to land whose ownership has been monopolised by landlords. Integrating rent into the price-value system gives some critical insights into the nature of globalisation in the post-fordist age marked essentially by the domination of GVCs. For that we have to understand the idea of rent as used by Marx.

4.1.4 Rent

In the Marxian sense a part of rent is what you get from monopoly ownership of non-produced – goods or services not having value but commanding a market price. Karl Polyani calls these 'fictitious commodities'. We are concerned with this rent. Though borrowed from the Ricardian idea Marx extended the concept of rent by introducing the idea of *absolute ground rent* (AGR). AGR is solely a claim on surplus by dint of monopoly ownership of a non-produced good (not attributable to some additional productivity of a plot, which is Ricardo's 'differential rent'). Hence the concept of AGR can be extended to explain claims generated by monopoly over resources other than land (tangible or intangible) that give access to conditions of production and marketing. Monopoly over resources requires exercise of power, something that mainstream economics suppresses. A lot of work has been done showing how the international economic organisations, particularly WTO work to create differential regimes of mobility of services and access to resources. (e.g. immobility of labour; mobility of other services) The National Working Group on Patent Laws has done much work. I have detailed some of the discriminatory regulations of WTO that help maintain monopoly (Basu, 2008).

4.2 Analytical characteristics GVC

We will tweak Marx's notion of rent to understand the current situation. Marx argued that rent is a species of subsumed class payment made by the productive capitalist from appropriated surplus value to ensure some condition of production like access to factory land. We argue that given the *central role played by the governor of the GVC, who is also the rent appropriator*, it is not a subsequent payment but the first claim. Also the middle rectangle or the *bottom of the trough of Smile Curve may contain non-capitalist productive units*, like cottage producers (though whether the sweatshops of Shanghai, Bangalore and Dhaka can be called capitalist enterprise is moot point). Largest share or revenue generated by GVCs appropriated as rent akin to absolute ground but disguised as profit in the accounts. We propose that rent is not subsumed payment out of surplus value appropriated by capitalist but is a prior claim of the governor of the GVC. Hence rent is price determining not price determined. Greater the 'efficiency' in governance or management of the chain, greater is the rent. *If rent is price determining and rent depends on monopoly maintained by efficient governance of GVC then there must be redistribution of (labour) value from outside the GVCs to the GVCs. This process similar to the process of redistribution of value from enterprises with low C/V to those with high C/V.*

Within Marxian value-price theory there is redistribution of value from lines of production with lower 'organic composition of capital' to lines of production with higher 'organic composition'. With the rise of GVCs the concept of equalisation of rates of profit on which Marxian price theory rests needs to be tweaked to the analytic of the capitalist order compliant with current reality. Greater the efficiency of governance, less the competition and greater the redistribution of values to GVC governors.

My tentative proposal is that this process works through the displacement of goods produced outside these chains to poor buyer market segments. These markets, typically earn lower rates of profit. This redistribution causes increase in exploitation rate of labour outside the GVCs. This is achieved through lowering of wages; lengthening of working day; reduction or abrogation of social security expenditures by employers. All for maintaining a minimum rate of profit on capital invested outside the chain. The wages in the materially productive sector within the GVCs (located in the poor countries) is lowered because increasing competition at the bottom of the trough, as already seen. But this is insufficient to ensure the high 'value addition' in the mainstream sense (as shown in the tables and charts) without a redistribution of labour values from outside the GVCs to the Governors of the chains.

5. Conclusion

I call the emerging order feudo-capitalist for two reasons. The controller of production is not a profit earner but a rentier. The source of surplus is often not contractual labour employment – extraction of SV through sale and use of labour power at its value, but coercive exploitation – the sweatshops which, in Marxian terms amounts to depression of wages below the value of labour power. Marx mentions this in passing in Vol III of *Capital* but with the rider: "This is mentioned here only empirically". Non-capitalist exploitation is interwoven with capitalist exploitation in GVCs. What insights does such analyses give beyond the mainstream analysis?

(i) The 'value added' analysis embodied in literature such as the 'smile curve' literature cannot conceive the source of surplus.
(ii) Expansion of GVC does not mean expanded reproduction of productive capital but expanded reproduction of elements of governance and control within GVCs.
(iii) Exclusionist character of globalisation in the PF era: worldwide jobless expansion of supply chains.
(iv) This causes decline in profitability of investment for production of articles of mass consumption. This ties up with financialisation that complements post-fordist production processes: there is a wall of finance seeking investment opportunities and failing to find them in productive avenues gets diverted to financial markets that recurrently breakdown from overburden.

This phase of globalisation is more invasive in many senses. Marketing has always been strategically important for capitalist enterprises. But the marketing divisions were tasked with marketing the output of the materially productive divisions. True there were/are market surveys, but these are very tentative and given a permanent employee strength, the assignment is to market what is produced. Now marketing and designing combine as principle elements of global chain to determine the nature of product. The workplace being mobile – you can shift the productive unit out of Bangalore to Dhaka – the product quality and mix can be easily changed.

The fulcrum of the order is Consumerism, generation of esoteric desires of niche consumers. You have mobiles with increasing megapixel cameras by the day; dual cameras with Amir Khan clicking a dog and a cat (not that I understand the messages of most advertisements). As Marx had argued in *Capital (Vol. I),* use value that was divorced from exchange values in the course of commodity production.

In this era exchange values become the simulacra of use values. Honestly is an INR 16, 000 walking shoe anywhere near that useful for walking. I have suggested elsewhere that the reality (in the sense of use values) has ceased to exist for the niche consumers of the GVCs (Basu, forthcoming). The target segments are persuaded to need what is produced. It is a kind of mind control captured aptly by Baudrillard's concept of the 'simulacra'. The consumers are as much the products of the GVCs.

Importance

The 2013 World Investment Report estimates that now over 80 per cent of global trade flows through global production networks led by transnational corporations. The ILO on the other hand estimates that one in five jobs in the world are somehow linked to global value chains.

Using the OECD WTO database on Trade in Value Added, this paper shows that 67% of total global value created under global value chains, accrue to OECD countries while share of NICs and BRICs countries is 25%. Only 8% of total value added is shared among all other developing countries and Least Developed Countries (LDC) Banga (2014)

The rise of global value chains (GVCs) in the past two decades has dramatically altered the world economy. But with the increasing complexity and sophistication of cross border production-sharing activities, the use of only official trade data (such as gross exports and imports) and GDP statistics has not revealed the significance and nature of changes in the global business cycle. An important reason is that indicators based on official trade and production data cannot identify and distinguish which types of trade are GVC activities and which are not, thus making it difficult to evaluate the relation between changes in global trade and changes in GDP growth.

References

Banga, Rashmi. *Linking into Global Value Chains Is Not Sufficient: Do You Export Domestic Value Added Contents?* Journal of Economic Integration, Vol. 29, No. 2, June 2014. 267. http://dx.doi.org/10.11130/jei.2014.2

Baudrillard,Jean.'Simulations and Simulacra'in *Jean Baudrillard, Selected Writings*, ed. Mark Poster (Stanford; Stanford University Press, 1988), pp.166-184 accessed from www.stanford.edu/.../**Baudrillard/Baudrillard_Simulacra**.html

Basu, P K (2008) *Globlisation: Anti-text,* Aakar Books, Delhi.

Basu, P K (forthcoming) 'Financialisation and the Business of the Soul' in Partha Chattopadhyay (ed.) *A century of Revolutions.* Orient Blackswan.

Conroy, M, D, Murray and P, Rosset. (1996). *A Cautionary Tale: Failed US Development Policy in Central America*. Boulder: Lynne Rienner.

Gereffi, Gary (2014) Global value chains in a post-Washington Consensus world, *Review of International Political Economy*, 21:1, 9-37, DOI: 10.1080/09692290.2012.756414

Global Value Chain Development Report 2017. International Bank for Reconstruction and Development/The World Bank

Kaplinsky, R. (2000) 'Globalisation and Unequalisation: What Can Be Learned from Value Chain Analysis?', Journal *of Development Studies, 37:2, 117-146*, DOI: 10.1080/713600071

Kraemer, K, G, Linden, and J, Dedrick. (2011). "Capturing value in Global Networks: Apple's iPad and iPhone." University of California, Irvine, University of California, Berkeley, y Syracuse University, NY.http://pcic. merage. uci. edu/papers/2011/ value_iPad_iPhone. Pdf

Marx, K *Capital Vol. I and III,* Progress Publishers, Moscow.Available at Marxist.org.

Norfield, T. (2012). 'T-Shirt Economics: Labour in the Imperialist World Economy.' http://column.global-labour-university.org/2012/08/t-shirteconomics-labour-in-imperialist.html

OECD. 2013.*New Sources of Growth: Knowledge-Based Capital: Key Analyses and Policy Conclusions – SynthesisReport*. Available athttp://www.oecd.org/sti/inno/knowledge-based-capital-synthesis.pdf

Roy, Satyaki. 2018. Global Production Network: The New Template of Power and Profit in the Regime of Empire. Lecture delivered at International Conference "Capital in the East". Kolkata.

Selwyn, Benjamin. 2016. *Global Value Chains or Global Poverty Chains? A new research agenda* Working Paper No. 10. Centre for Global Political Economy,University of Sussex

Whalen, C. (2005). 'Sending Jobs Offshore from the United States,' *Intervention: A Journal of Economics* 2 (2): 33-40.

Chapter - 4

Dreaming the Asian Economic Community and Beyond: Current Status, Reform Options and Possible Lessons

Soumyadip Chattopadhyay

Abstract

In conformity with the serious efforts at economic integration among the ASEAN member states since 1990s, the ASEAN Economic Community (AEC) aims to make Southeast Asia a fully integrated production base for international capital by eliminating regional barriers to trade and investment and creating infrastructure to connect the national market. This paper focuses on key measures towards this aim, identifies the challenges therein and proposes measures to streamline the process of integration and their implications for regional growth and prosperity. Although, the ASEAN member states have experienced significant progress on tariff elimination, non-tariff measures (NTMs) to trade and investment have remained significant in the ASEAN region. Lack of transparency and coherence has unnecessarily compounded the trade facilitation costs in the region. The 'ASEAN minus x' principle has been utilised to provide protection to key domestic sectors and their interests. Socio-political contestations over the distribution of economic power and resources in the ASEAN member states make the formation of the AEC complex and problematic. Therefore, the paper argues for putting due emphasis on domestic policy reforms, regional and international cooperation and institution building to ensure competitiveness and inclusivity of this fastly growing region.

1. The Perspective

In 1967, Indonesia, Malaysia, Philippines, Singapore, and Thailand together formed the Association of Southeast Asian Nations (ASEAN) mainly to foster regional peace and security. Brunei Darussalam joined in 1984, and Cambodia, Lao People's Democratic Republic (Lao PDR), Myanmar, and Viet Nam (CLMV) joined between 1995 and 1999. Economic cooperation and integration among the member states began in the late 70s through a preferential trade agreement followed by the establishment of the ASEAN Free Trade Area (AFTA) and further complemented by the ASEAN Framework Agreement on Services (AFAS) and the ASEAN Investment Area (AIA) agreement in the 1990s. In 2007, the ASEAN launched the ASEAN Economic Community (AEC) Blueprint with the aims of making southeast Asia a fully integrated production base for international capital by eliminating regional barriers to trade and investment and creating infrastructure to connect the national market. Economic potentials of this Blueprint are enormous as the formation of AEC coupled with regional trade pacts is expected to increase the regional GDP by 5.3 per cent (Petri *et al.*, 2012) and, if ASEAN can maintain it's solid growth momentum, the member states will collectively be the world's fourth largest economy by 2050 (Lamy, 2017).

In fact, over the past 50 years ASEAN has experienced extraordinary economic progress with deepened intra-ASEAN cooperation. In 2016, ASEAN ranked the 6th worldwide in terms of its combined GDP and the 3rd in Asia. ASEAN has also emerged as the world's fourth largest traders after China, the U.S. and Germany. Despite few fluctuations across various sectors and sub-sectors arising out of global economic uncertainties, ASEAN has been recognised to be among the few regions in the world with remarkable growth in the inflows of FDIs. All these attest the emergence of ASEAN as the new growth pole at present.

At the same time, global socio-economic-political environment have witnessed some significant developments having wider and deeper implications for the realisation of the AEC (Lamy, 2017; Maria *et al.*, 2017). First, following the Brexit decision in UK and the outcome of the U.S. Presidential election, anti-globalisation and anti-trade sentiments have started to find footholds in many political discourses. Popular dissatisfaction with globalisation has increased the demand for adoption of protectionist policies. The phenomenon Great Trade Slowdown also indicates the structural slow down of world trade growth (Contantinescu *et al.*, 2015). Second, in recent times, the centre of economic gravity has shifted towards Asia with China, India and ASEAN, owing to their huge mass of people in middle income and consuming class, emerging as the dominant drivers of the global market and economic growth. Third, technological change in the garb of digital revolution is altering the economics of globalisation by significantly cutting down the communication and transaction costs. Digitisation is, in particular, assumed to increase productivity and expand market access of the small and medium size enterprises (SME) which are the principal driver of regional integration in the region. In other words, the changing global environment provides the ASEAN member states opportunities to achieve higher levels of economic growth and development through regional economic integration. At the same time, such integration would negatively affect some segments of production network (e.g., inability of some SMEs in adapting to new technologies) and society (e.g., digitisation engendering a 'hollowing out' of the labour market). So, the AEC faces the challenges of providing economic growth an inclusive character by minimizing the costs inflicted upon the vulnerable groups by the forces of regional integration.

The blueprints of the AEC have acknowledged both the opportunities and challenges inherent in the process of regional economic integration. In particular, the AEC aims to integrate ASEAN into the global economy and create a single market and production base where goods, services, capital and labour flow freely, so that equitable development can be realised within the region (ASEAN, 2008). The four major components of the AEC Blueprint are:

(A) *A Single Market and Production Base*: By bringing down the barriers to trade and thereby creating a single market and production, the ASEAN member states would get benefit from economies of scale and efficiency in production network processes. This, in turn, would boost intra-regional trade and investment flows to the region.

(B) *Competitive Economic Region*: By invoking a regional standard in trade policy and for the business operating environment, an attempt has been made to promote ASEAN as a competitive economic bloc.

(C) *Equitable Economic Development*: By focussing on development of the SMEs and Initiative for ASEAN integration (IAI), an attempt has been made to narrow the development gap between members and to accelerate economic integration of the CLMV (Cambodia, Lao PDR, Myanmar and Vietnam) members.

(D) *Integration into the Global Economy*: By undertaking coherent approach regarding external economic relations and enhanced participation in global supply networks, the ASEAN member states strive to integrate themselves better as a bloc into the global supply chain.

Importantly, the ASEAN Secretariat's 'AE Scorecard' reported that only 66, 68, 68 and 86 per cent of the above mentioned four components of integration measures were completed respectively (ASEAN Secretariat, 2012). As these scores were based on member states' self reporting, the scholars have expressed their scepticisms regarding the actual state of progress. Acknowledging the vision of the AEC in achieving inclusive and dynamic regional integration, the present paper focuses on key measures towards this aim, identifies the challenges therein and proposes measures to streamline the process of integration. In particular, the paper takes an analytical perspective of key strategies including non-tariff measures (NTMs), trade facilitation, services development, connectivity and production networks which provide the framework for free trade amongst members of the ASEAN and formation of the ASEAN Economic Community (AEC). It also discusses their implications for regional growth and prosperity.

2. ASEAN's Economy - A Macroeconomic Overview

Before discussing the economic relations among the ASEAN member states in merchandise trade and trade in services, it is useful to begin the analysis with observations based on key macroeconomic indicators of ASEAN.Of late, ASEAN has made extraordinary economic progress to reach a total GDP of US$ 2.55 trillion in 2016 from US$ 0.58 trillion in 1999 when it first achieved the full membership of ASEAN-10 (Table 4.1). In terms of growth rate,

Table 4.1: ASEAN's Macro economy: Selected Indicators

Indicators	*1967*	*1999*	*2010*	*2016*
GDP at Current Prices (US$Tn)	0.02	0.58	1.93	2.55
GDP Growth Rate (%)	4.3	3.4	7.5	4.8
% Share of ASEAN in World GDP (% based on US$ PPP)	3.3	4.8	5.6	6.2
Per Capita GDP (US$ at Current Prices)	122	1135	3268	4021

Source: ASEAN Secretariat

ASEAN is projected to achieve 4.8 per cent in 2017. This performance is quite praiseworthy at the backdrop projected global growth rate of 3.5 per cent in 2017 (Figure 4.1). ASEAN member states account for 6.2 per cent of

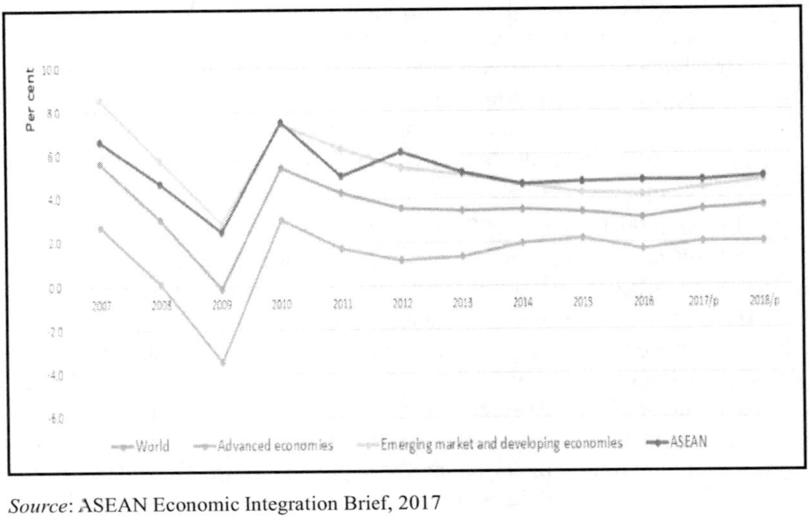

Source: ASEAN Economic Integration Brief, 2017

Note: p-projected

Figure 4.1: Trend in GDP Growth

world GDP in 2017 (Table 4.1). The standard of living has also improved considerably as reflected through almost 3.5 times increase in average nominal GDP per capita in 2016 as compared to 1999 (Table 4.1).

Strong domestic demand for both consumption and investment and improved external demand following recovery in major economies have continued to support the growth potential of the region (AIB, 2017). On the other hand, economic uncertainties related to changes in trade policy and monetary policy of the advanced economies has disrupted the regional economic activities in the region. This is evident from a decline of 2.28 per cent in total trade and a decline of 2 per cent in global FDI flows in the region between 2015 and 2016 (AIB, 2017). Intra-ASEAN trade with it's share of 23.48 per cent of total trade remained as the largest market for ASEAN (Figure 4.2). China, with 16.01 per cent share of total trade, emerged as the ASEAN's largest external trade partner; followed by EU-28 at 10.35 per cent and Japan at 9.99 percent. In terms of the FDI, intra-ASEAN FDI flows remained solid at USD 23.95 billion, an increase of 12.22 per cent year on year. EU-28 accounted for 31.50 per cent of total FDI inflows in the region followed by intra-ASEAN inflow with 24.76 per cent share. Given the expected recovery in global trade in near future, the ASEAN trade scenario and ASEAN's FDI is also expected to experience some improvements and this necessitates stronger economic integration.

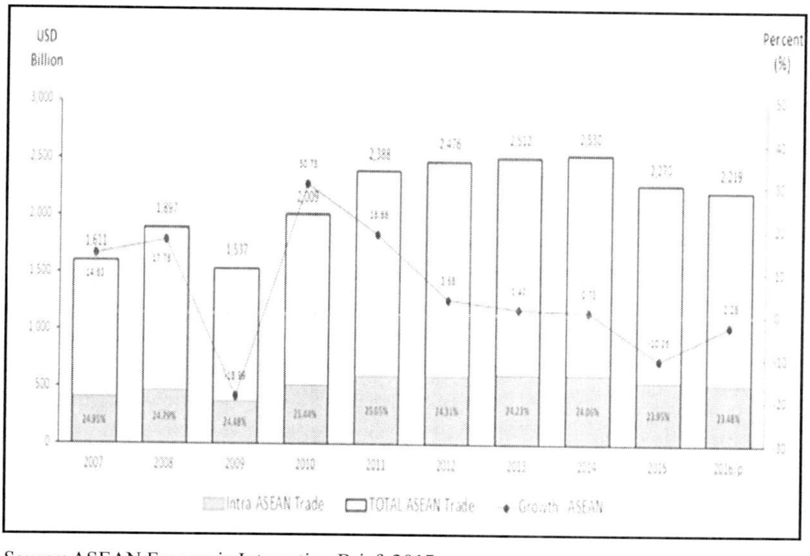

Source: ASEAN Economic Integration Brief, 2017.

Figure 4.2: Trend of Total Trade in ASEAN and Share of Intra ASEAN Trade

In the global production networks and supply chain, services are becoming increasingly important. In conformity with the global trend, services sector is generally the most significant and continuously increasing sector in ASEAN economies. Correspondingly, ASEAN's export and import of services have increased significantly over the recent years (Figure 4.3). The prevailing level of export of services is slightly more than 1.5 times the value of exports in 2010 whereas the imports increased 1.4 times during the same period. It needs mention here that, the region has now transformed itself into a net exporter of services.

Another crucial feature of the region is that, despite being one of the most developed parts of the Global South, Southeast Asia experience overwhelming presence of small and medium sized enterprises (SMEs) along with the presence of large informal sectors that operate alongside small number of large enterprises. CARI (2013) reported that upto 98 per cent of the businesses are SMEs. Moreover, the manufactured products have dominated the ASEAN exports (Ing *et al.*, 2017). These products accounted for over half of ASEAN

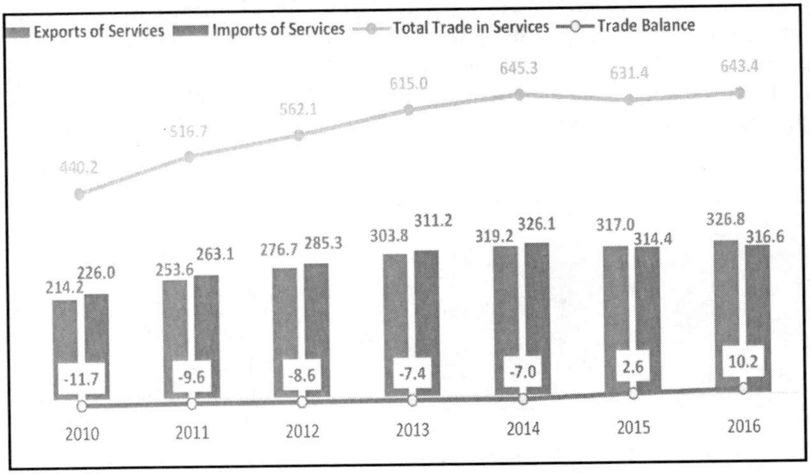

Source: EXIM Bank, 2018

Figure 4.3: Trend in ASEAN's International Trade in Services (US $ Billion)

member countries' exports except those with large hydrocarbon exports (Indonesia, Myanmar, and Brunei Darussalam). As the trade in manufactured products is largely driven by the global value chain, each country attempts to specialize in production according to it's comparative advantage. Resulting economic interconnectedness is expected to contribute to the overall reduction in poverty in the region.

3. Facilitating Trade in Goods in ASEAN

ASEAN Trade in Goods Agreement (ATiGA)– the Path Taken So Far

As per the latest Report of the ASEAN Secretariat total trade in the region stood at USD 2.22 trillion in 2016 (AEIB, 2017). As mentioned in the previous section, the intra-ASEAN trade remained as the largest market for ASEAN and largely dominated by the exports of manufactured products. Producers of these products are part of the cross border value chains where the multinational companies distribute productive tasks across countries according to their comparative advantage. Consequently, the member countries have experienced increasing incidence of industrial specialisation and high level of economic dependence on their regional partners.

Clearly, trade in goods turns out to be crucial to the Asian Economic Community (AEC) project as further progress towards achieving the goals of this block, in its entirety, begins with trade in goods. ATiGA, which took effect on May 17 2010, is meant to be a concrete step toward establishing a full-fledged AEC and provides the governing framework for Intra-ASEAN trade. Earlier in the 1990s, the ASEAN Free Trade Area (AFTA) aimed to raise the bloc's competitive edge as a production base through (a) the reduction of tariffs, (b) elimination of non-tariff barriers on intra-ASEAN trade and (c) attracting FDI. In particular, a scheme of Common Effective Preferential Tariff (CEPT) among ASEAN members was adopted for tariff reduction to between zero and 5 per cent by 2010. However, in the absence of any common external tariff on goods imported from outside the trade bloc, each ASEAN member states used to apply import tariffs based on its national schedules.

Removal of tariffs within the ASEAN has been one of the key elements for ensuring free flow of goods and establishing a single market and production base as envisaged by the AEC. The ASEAN member states have experienced significant progress on tariff elimination. The ATiGA rates for all ASEAN member states declined from 2.58 per cent in 2007 to 0.54 per cent in 2014 whereas the corresponding MFN rate stood at 6.90 per cent in 2014 (Figure 4.4). In the case of ASEAN-6 (Brunei Darussalam, Indonesia, Malaysia, the Philippines, Thailand and Singapore), the average ATiGA rate is negligible and for CLMV (Cambodia, Lao PDR, Myanmar and Viet Nam), the same has exhibited a declining trend over the period under consideration. Similarly, the share of tariff lines at the ATIGA rate of zero per cent has increased across the ASEAN member states over the same period (Figure 4.5). The shares of ATIGA tariff lines at ATIGA zero per cent stand at 99.2 per cent for the ASEAN-6. For, the CLMV the corresponding shares increased to 72.6 per cent in 2014 from 46.5 per cent in 2007 and this is expected to increase even further to 90.8 per cent in 2015.

Non-tariff Measures and their Implications for Regional Integration

Importantly, trade facilitation is not just about reduction in trade tariff and attendant reduction in cross border transaction cost. Removing non-tariff barriers to trade and investment is also of crucial importance especially in the context of ASEAN's unique manufactured products based network production structure. In practice, complex network distribution of productive task in

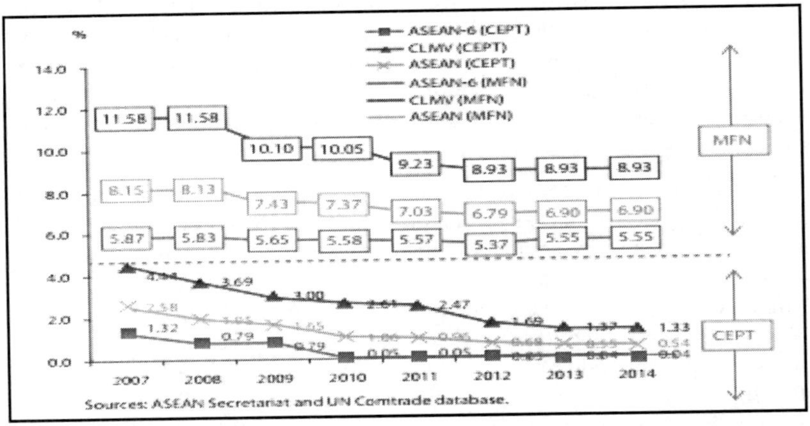

Sources: ASEAN Secretariat and UN Comtrade database.

Figure 4.4: ASEAN's CEPT/ATIGA Rates and Applied MFN Rates

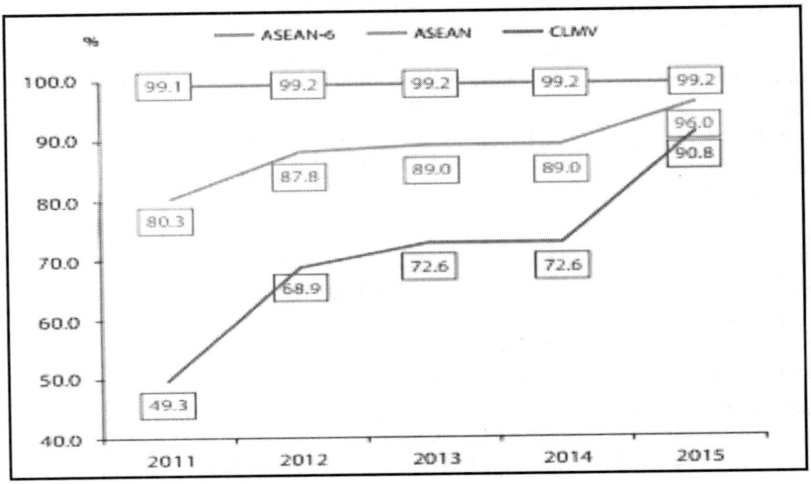

Sources: ASEAN Secretariat.

Figure 4.5: Share of Tariff Lines at 0% in the ATIGA Tariff Schedule.

manufacturing in the ASEAN member states has made each of the state increasingly economically dependent on the regional partners. Given such high interdependence, the real practical challenge is to devise a diverse array of policy interventions to reduce the vulnerability of the region to any external economic shocks and to strengthen the regional integration.

In practice, non-tariff barriers to trade and investment have remained significant in the ASEAN region (Jones, 2015). Ing and Cadot (2017) have noted that increase in the incidence of non-tariff measures (NTMs) was even faster amongst the ASEAN+6 partnersthan amongst member states themselves during 2000–2015.The foreign business sector engaged in trade with ASEAN member states often complain about the difficulties they face in exporting and importing in the region (Maria *et al.*, 2017).Apart fromsanitary and phytosanitary (SPS) regulations and technical barriers to trade (TBT) regulations, the NTMs include policies related to licensing, price-control measures, and distribution restrictions. Rising number of NTMs in the ASEAN region is explained in terms of the member states' imperative to fulfil certain non-trade objectives, for example food safety or environmental protection. At the same time, NTMs can also be used as instruments of trade policy in a distortionary manner because NTMs are more opaque and complex than tariffs. All these make the regional trading environment vulnerable specifically to a complex web of institutional arrangements that lacks coherence and a large stock of non-tariff measures (NTMs) subject to weak disciplines.

Decoding the Rules of Origin

In this subsection, we discuss some of the trade facilitation measures and their implications for ASEAN's economic integration.Rules of Origin (RoO) is one of the key components of the cross-border ASEAN Trade Facilitation Work Program. As per the RoO under ATiGA, a product can be said to originate from the ASEAN country where "working or processing of the goods" takes place, so long as the goods have an "ASEAN regional value content" (RVC) of at least 40 per cent. From purely quantitative angle, Ing and Cadet (2016) estimated the ad-valorem equivalent (AVE) of RoO as about 3.40 percent. Moreover, the authors find that the ad valorem equivalent for the lower-skilled and more labour-intensive goods (e.g., textiles and leather product) are at least two to nearly three times the average for all products and, therefore, hurts their export potentials. Also the RoO varies substantially across sectors with different implications across the member states. Further, the problems of fragmentation and lack of consistency make the RoO quite arbitrary in nature and therefore distort the production and investment decisions.

It needs mention here that trade pattern of the region is based on the principles of comparative advantage framework under which medium- or high-income countries tend to specialise in the upstream (manufacturing) part of value chains while the low-income ones tend to specialise in the downstream (assembly) part. Ing and Cadet (2017) considered the generic value chain of a cotton shirt. For this product, the upstream operations (spinning, weaving, dying and cutting), being capital and energy intensive, are best located in middle income countries or in China. On the other hand, the labour intensive downstream operations of assembly are best located in low income countries with lower labour costs. In such set up, the low income countries are expected to accrue benefits in terms of higher jobs and reductions in the poverty level.

However, Ing and Cadet (2017) argued that attractiveness of the low income countries as location for downstream operations in the value chain depends not only on lower labour costs but also on those countries' (i) preferential access to developed markets and (ii) unrestricted access to the semi-finished products to be assembled. Here the combination of complex regional arrangement and RoO can distort the investment and production decision. For example, in case the investors have option to invest in Vietnam *vis-a-vis* in CLM countries, he would prefer to locate the entire textile-garment production (all the way down from the yarn to the garments) in Viet Nam, provided the investor enjoys preferential access to the United States market for eligible garments. Even if we assume the CLM countries enjoy preferential access to U.S. markets, their attractiveness as investment location is less as their garments fail to meet the eligibility criteria. Therefore, the nature of current market access and the RoO could result in concentration of garment industries in Vietnam at the expense of CLM countries.

Clearly, the policy makers face an uphill task of promoting balanced trade led development in the region. It is, indeed, a challenge to coordinate both the forward linkage (ensuring CLM countries' preferential access to U.S. market) and backward linkage (ensuring RoO to allow for the export of garments assembled from fabric produced in countries at competitive costs). The SMEs, producing lower skilled and more labour intensive goods, may be allowed to use 'self-certification scheme' in which the integrator-exporter self-certify subject to appropriate control along the supply chain. Adoption of 'Advance Ruling Mechanism' as a trade facilitation tool can be beneficial for the SMEs as that would allow the importer/ exporter, prior to importation or exportation, to utilise a competent customs authority to determine whether or not the concerned product qualifies as an originating product.

Dealing Effectively with the NTMs

The non-tariff measures impose three types of costs on the businesses and thereby affect the investment decision. Enforcement costs are related to the companies' compliance efforts to the NTMs. Costs related to changes in the sources of input (e.g., from low grade to high grade) are known as sourcing costs. Process adaptation costs relate to the adjustment in the production process (e.g., through changes in capital equipments) for meeting NTM standards.

Except the sourcing costs, the other two costs are fixed costs and can have different effects depending on the nature of the product, nature of the firm (local vs foreign, small vs large) and nature of the users.

One of the most difficult challenges faced by the ASEAN regarding the NTMs is related to the lack of transparency and coherence which unnecessarily compound the trade facilitation costs. Further, fixed and lumpy nature of two components of NTMs affects SMEs more than the large enterprises. Establishment of national NTM inventories with details of NTMs and regulatory information can bridge the information gap. In ASEAN, the ERIA has come with such inventories of all NTMs and all products covered by each NTM, at the most detailed level. Timely data updation and availability of the same at each country's trade portal are also of crucial importance. Ensuring coherence in NTMs among the member states can be very challenging as, firstly, the NTMs often serve legitimate non-trade objectives and secondly social optimality of such objectives vary with respect to the country's level of development. In other words, difficulty in streamlining the NTMs at regional level calls for approaching the same through the angle of national regulatory-improvement agendas and promoting regulatory supervision bodies in all ASEAN member countries, each with a mandate to review and improve key business-relevant regulations.

Maintaining standards and ensuring conformance is the other major problems faced by the SMEs of the ASEAN member states. SMEs often fail to meet the conformity assessment requirements due to lack or inadequacy of internationally recognised quality infrastructure (ADB and UNESCAP, 2009). In other words, their inability in getting foreign accreditation from established internationally recognised accreditation bodies reduces their competitiveness in the global value chain. Thus, it has become imperative for the ASEAN member states to invest in better-quality national infrastructure, including internationally recognised testing and certification institutions, such as Malaysia's Standards and Industrial Research Institute, and to streamline certification procedures.

An analysis of 'Logistic Performance' of ASEAN member nations provides more insights into challenges and opportunities that members face in their performance of trade logistics. Logistics connectivity would critically influence the overall process of AEC development.Logistics is conceived as the process of planning, implementing and controlling the effective and efficient flow of goods and services from the point of origin to the point of consumption in order to meet some requirements of users/consumers. The Word Bank constructs the *Logistic Performance Index (LPI)* based on six dimensions: (a) efficiency of the customs clearance process, (b) quality of trade and transport related infrastructure, (c) ease of arranging competitively priced shipments (f) competence and quality of logistics services, (g) ability to track and trace consignments and (h) frequency with which shipments reach the consignee within the scheduled or expected time. Consequently, LPI provides indirect estimates of costs of poor logistics along with the sources of those costs.

In terms of LPI, there exists disparity among the ASEAN member states and the same become significant compared to top performers like Germany (Table 4.2) (ASSOCHAM, 2016). Involvement of the ASEAN member states in regional production network or value chains has significantly contributed to their high economic growth. Being a part of that value chain, any firm has

Table 4.2: LPI Scores (2014) of ASEAN Member States and Selected Other Non-ASEAN Member states

Country	*Overall*	*Customs*	*Infrastructure*	*International Shipments*	*Logistic Quality and Competence*	*Tracking and Tracing*	*Timeliness*
Brunei	NA	NA	NA	NA	NA	NA	NA
Cambodia	2.74	2.67	2.58	2.83	2.67	2.92	2.75
	(83)	(71)	(79)	(78)	(89)	(71)	(181)
Indonesia	3.08	2.87	2.92	2.87	3.21	3.11	3.53
	(53)	(55)	(56)	(74)	(41)	(58)	(50)
Laos	2.39	2.45	2.21	2.5	2.31	2.2	2.65
	(131)	(100)	(128)	(120)	(129)	(146)	(137)
Malaysia	3.59	3.37	3.56	3.64	3.47	3.58	3.92
	(25)	(27)	(26)	(10)	(32)	(23)	(31)
Myanmar	2.25	1.97	2.14	2.14	2.07	2.36	2.83
	(145)	(150)	(137)	(151)	(156)	(130)	(117)
Philippines	3	3	2.6	3.33	2.93	3	3.07
	(57)	(47)	(75)	(35)	(61)	(64)	(90)
Singapore	4	4.01	4.28	3.7	3.97	3.9	4.25
	(5)	(3)	(2)	(6)	(8)	(11)	(9)
Thailand	3.43	3.21	3.4	3.3	3.29	3.45	3.96
	(35)	(36)	(30)	(39)	(38)	(33)	(29)
Vietnam	3.15	2.86	3.34	2.93	3.11	3.15	3.55
	(48)	(56)	(34)	(70)	(48)	(54)	(47)
India	3.08	2.72	2.88	3.2	3.03	3.11	3.51
	(54)	(65)	(58)	(44)	(52)	(57)	(51)
China	3.53	3.21	3.67	3.5	3.46	3.5	3.87
	(28)	(38)	(23)	(22)	(35)	(29)	(34)
Germany	4.12	4.1	4.32	3.74	4.12	4.17	4.36
	(1)	(2)	(1)	(4)	(3)	(1)	(4)

Source: http://www.worldbanl.com/content/dam/worldbank/document.trade/LPI2014.pdf

Note: Figures in the parentheses indicate country rank out of 160 countries.

to bear some direct costs associated with moving goods (such as freight costs, port and handling charges, agent fees and miscellaneous payments) and also some indirect costs related to lack of predictability and reliability of the supply chain. The later part of the cost form a significant part of logistics costs and, in turn, undermines the competitive strength of ASEAN firms trying to diversify into higher value production via international supply chain. Quite obviously, the logistic costs happen to be much lower for the firms in countries with good logistic performance and, so, these firms can leverage logistics as a strategic source of competitive advantage. Moreover, in global production chains, predictability and reliability of supply chains for imported inputs and components are as important as they are for exports. In essence, predictability and timeliness in the production chains improves the quality of the logistics environment in which a firm operates and, thus, enhances it's competitiveness in the global market.

Bureaucratic delays and paperwork involved in the customs and clearance procedures increase delays and costs of transit (ASSOCHAM, 2016). For example, in Myanmar, it takes *at least* 12 days to put an export consignment (standard 20 feet container) from factory gate to ship whereas in Korea it takes only 16 hours to complete the same task (Table 4.3). Border

Table 4.3: Liner Shipping Connectivity Index (LSCI) of ASEAN Member States and Selected Other Non-ASEAN Member states, 2004-2016

Country	*2006*	*2011*	*2016*
Brunei	3.26		3.86
Cambodia	2.93	5.36	5.61
Indonesia	25.24	25.91	27.19
Laos	NA	NA	NA
Malaysia	69.20	90.96	106.79
Myanmanr	2.54	3.22	6.37
Philipines	16.48	18.56	17.81
Singapore	86.11	105.02	122.70
Thailand	31.89	36.70	44.32
Vietnam	15.14	49.71	62.84
India	42.90	41.52	46.24
Sri Lanka	37.31	41.13	63.21
China	113.10	152.06	167.48
Korea	71.92	92.02	115.61

Source: http://unctadstat.unctad.org

compliance (customs formalities) cost U.S. $ 772 for a standard 20 feet container in Myanmar compared with just U.S. $ 185 in Korea. This clearly demonstrates that trade competitiveness of many of the ASEAN member countries can be improved by streamlining trade procedures and thereby, cutting down the transaction costs. Overall, enhanced logistics can reduce the cost of economic operations and fuel economic growth with the potential of narrowing the development gaps by sharing the benefits of growth with poorer locations and communities in the region.

'ASEAN minus x' Stymieing the Process of Regional Integration

Member states in ASEAN are heterogeneous economies with varying levels of income, economic development, structural characteristics and institutional readiness to trade facilitation. The more financially developed 'IMPST' group of countries (Indonesia, Malaysia, the Philippines, Singapore, and Thailand) are generally considered as developed whereas 'BCLMV' countries (Brunei, Cambodia, the Lao PDR, Myanmar, and Viet Nam) are categorised as less developed. To narrow the development gap, emphasis has been placed on the 'ASEAN minus x' principle that allows regional integration projects to advance without full participation of each member states. In practice, this principle has been utilised to provide protection to key domestic sectors and their interests (Jones, 2015). A study by ERIA (2012) noted that the integration of aviation markets was permitted to follow the 'ASEAN minus x' principle. Indonesia, ASEAN's biggest aviation market, categorically protected the Garuda and other domestic airlines that struggled to compete with the low cost carriers in the region. Conversely, Malaysia has strongly supported regional aviation integration as the Air-Asia has competitive advantage in the region. The aviation industries in other newer member countries have not been successful in acquiring politico-economic weight necessary for securing protection. Similarly, in case of automotive component, Malaysia has adopted protectionist stance and the same component has been put into the AEC's 'sensitive' list which is equivalent to NTBs. In other words, such domestic interest driven adherences to the AEC Blueprint could stymie the process of regional integration.

Strengthening Connectivity – Opportunities and Challenges

Improved connectivity is central to realizing the ambitious goals of the AEC. As mentioned earlier, competitiveness of the dominant manufacturing sectors depends in part on the quick and predictable flow of parts and components from both domestic and cross-border sources. Therefore, improved ASEAN connectivity can enhance the competitiveness of ASEAN firms, make them investment-attractive and connects them within the region and with rest of the world and thus leads to formation of dynamic economic community in the ASEAN region. ASEAN nations have put up considerable efforts into growing their connectivity by roads, rail, ship, and air in order to connect more than 600 million people who live and work in the region. The Singapore-Kunming Rail Link (SKRL: Connecting Singapore, Malaysia, Thailand, Cambodia and Vietnam to Kunming, China), Kaladan Multimodal Transit

Transport Project (connect Kolkata with Sittwe port in Myanmar), maritime transport system (designating 47 ports for upgrades to their ship and cargo capacity) etc. are some of the initiatives taken in the region to achieve greater transport integration and inter-modal interconnectivity by 2025. The ASEAN Power Grid (APG) and the Trans-ASEAN Gas Pipeline (TAGP) aims to facilitate energy integration at a regional level. Moreover, several agreements like the ASEAN Framework Agreement on the Facilitation of Goods in Transit, the ASEAN Framework on the Facilitation of Inter-State Transport and the ASEAN Framework Agreement on Multimodal Transport have been taken. For air transport, ASEAN has three important agreements in force and they are: the Multilateral Agreement on Air Services, the Multilateral Agreement on the Full Liberalisation of Passenger Air Services, and the Multilateral Agreement on the Full Liberalisation of Air Freight Services. Implementation of all the agreements is expected to allow for greater responsiveness to the demands of the changing flow of goods and people in the region.

However, ERIA (2012) expressed it's concern regarding unsatisfactory state or progress of many of the schemes. A major problem to intra-ASEAN trade is poor quality of road connectivity. There are many missing highway links besides poor condition of roads in some countries which do not facilitate movement of large trucks for trade. For example, only about 15 per cent of total road length in Myanmar is paved. Railway links are almost nonexistent and even when exists, the railway gauge mismatch hinders the cross border movement of goods. For example, Thailand and Myanmar have metre gauge railway tracks whereas India has broad gauge (1, 676 mm) railway tracks. The ports are not well equipped with multimodal transport facilities. Clearly, poor transport linkages nullify much of the benefits of geographical contiguity and, thereby, hamper effective regional cooperation.

It is also important to note that socio-political power relations have also constrained the effective implementation of some of the infrastructure projects. For example, APG's attempt to build cross-border energy infrastructure required the reduction of domestic subsidies to energy consumers. Chattopadhyay and Jha (2014) reported that the ASEAN-5 governments spent US$34 billion alone on energy subsidies in 2010 and 44 per cent of the same went to electricity. Business sectors close to the state power (e.g., petrochemicals and cement in Indonesia) and individual consumers were the principal beneficiaries of these subsidies. Consequently, this is quite challenging for many ruling coalitions in the ASEAN member states to take the decision of subsidy reduction and even adoption of such decision produced social unrest (Jones, 2015).

Similarly, the TAGP's aim to connect the ASEAN region's gas exporters (Indonesia, Malaysia and Myanmar) to its gas consumers through a planned network of 16 bilateral pipelines has been constrained by the governments' tendencies to tightly control the resource sectors via imposition of higher tax on exports or explicit reservation of resources for domestic use. In some other cases, for example the Thiland-Myanmar pipeline, Myanmar military junta's desperate need for gas export revenue acted as a catalyst for project completion. Pipelines for linking Indonesia's Natuna gas fields to peninsular Southeast Asia have suffered due to their lack of commercial viability (Wilson, 2015). Overall, country level socio-political factors have influenced the progress of implementation of different infrastructural projects in particular and the larger goal of regional integration in general.

4. Understanding Trade in Services – Stories of Unmet Challenges

Growing share of trade in services has been one of the prominent trends in recent years in the world economy and international economic relation. ASEAN is also not an exception to this trend. By 2015, eight ASEAN member states had a service share in GDP exceeding 40%, in three countries the share was over 50%, and in Singapore it was above 70%. Increasing per capita income, forces of globalisation and digital revolution facilitate the dramatic growth of tradable services (Findlay, 2017). Actually, household demand (e.g., income elasticity of demand for tourism services), export demand, and demand from other sectors (firms' demand for intermediate inputs) largely influence the demand for services (Eichengreen and Gupta, 2011). Being a part of the global value chain firms are increasingly contracting out the provision of modern service activities. Also, it has been found that the shares of service components in manufacturing in the ASEAN member states are increasing (Maria *et al.*, 2017). Thus, ASEAN is well positioned to benefit from a service development and liberalisation having significant implications for the economies of the region.

Services can significantly contribute to productivity growth and therefore can become an important driver of overall economic growth. Findlay (2017) discusses several channels through which services induce productivity and they include: increase in productivity by contracting out services to specialists, by application of ICT to services, increasing tradability of services resulting in gains from international specialisation and increasing tradability leading to greater scope of competition and technology transfer. In other words, the possibility of productivity growth is higher both within the service sector as well as the other interconnected sectors within the global system. Therefore, it has become imperative to embed the facilitation and integration the service sector development within the AEC framework to better capture the benefits of the services revolution.

Availability of good quality ICT and a commitment to free trade in technology related products are important prerequisites for capturing the benefits of service revolution. Institutional quality determining the nature of contracting between services and the interconnected sectors is also crucial. Beverelli et al. (2017) found that countries with high institutional capacity (and therefore the ability to contract out) benefit the most from services trade policy reforms in terms of increased productivity in downstream industries. Extent of competitiveness in the services sector significantly influences the prices of the services as well as scope of innovation. Apart from these, removing barriers to trade and investment in services is also important. He et al. (2012) and Van der Marel (2017) reported that higher degrees of restrictiveness are associated with poorer performance in services. Hoekman and Shepherd (2017) also reported that decreasing services trade restrictiveness has a positive indirect impact on the manufacturing sectors that use services as intermediate inputs in production. Quality of infrastructure (such as power shortages, chaotic urban transportation etc.) has negative impacts on growth of the service sectors (Nasir *et al.*, 2016). Emergence of specialist service providers also depends on access to skilled labour. Such access improves the ability of the firms to respond to competition in the open market and this, in turn, make those firms less hostile to the policies related to opening up of service markets. Nasir *et al.*, (2016) found positive relationship between availability of graduates and productivity of the modern service sectors.

There are, however, considerable risks in the development of services sector as the outcome can turn out to be unequal in nature. Firms with access to good quality of infrastructure would have higher productivity and outperforms the other firms in the sector. Skilled labourers would be able to accrue substantial benefits of increased wages whereas the semi-skilled and unskilled workers would remain outside these services sector networks. This clearly engenders greater income inequality unless the large numbers of low–skilled labourers are being incorporated in the manufacturing sectors. Further, there are risks of market failures in the service sectors as services production and consumption occur simultaneously. Such nature of transactions makes the services sector quite vulnerable to the lack of information. It is really difficult for the consumers to prejudge both the quality of the service providers and the services received. Given the large infrastructural investment requirement for these sectors, firms that are first investing initially enjoy the advantage of being first movers, leading to barriers to entry by new competitors (Findlay, 2017).

Till date, many attempts have been made to facilitate the trade in services in the ASEAN region. The ASEAN Framework Agreement on Services (AFAS) has made improvements in the number of sectors included (called the extensive margin) and within sectors (called the intensive margin). Mutual recognition agreements (MRAs) for professional services have been framed to ease the movement of professional employees within the ASEAN region through mutual recognition of professional qualification. By late 2012, ASEAN negotiated eight MRAs covering various professions including in engineering, nursing, architectural services, medical and dental services, accountancy, and hospitality. Air transport is the other area that has experienced noticeable services integration in ASEAN (Ahsan *et al.*, 2015).

In spite of all these provisions, the actual implementations have demonstrated remarkable variations among the ASEAN member states. For example, in case of medical practitioners, Thailand has taken protectionist stance in MRA negotiations whereas the creation of a region wide professional certification scheme for 'ASEAN Architects' has been strikingly liberal in nature. Such variations can be explained in terms of observed socio-political contestations over the distribution of economic power and resources in the ASEAN member states (Jones, 2015). In Thailand, the Medical Council is dominated by the well paid local doctors who feared greater competition from immigrants in case of liberal MRAs. Private hospitals could afford to employ doctors with higher salaries. The other probable beneficiaries of liberal MRAs were the public hospitals. But they were so geographically dispersed that they failed to lobby coherently in favour of liberal MRA. The medical universities hold their reservation against the liberal MRA in fear of losing state subsidy in training medical practitioners. As a result, the Thai Medical Council took a protectionist stance in ASEAN negotiation in the form of insistence on maintaining qualifying examinations in Thai. Conversely, for architectural services, the APEC engineer project enabled architects from participatory member states (Malaysia, Thailand, Philippines and Singapore) to practice freely in their jurisdiction. The motivation of architects to further enhance their business prospect acted as one of the facilitators. Unlike medical education, the universities did not get any subsidy for educating the domestic architects. Also, the universities were less hostile to the MRA due to the possibilities of recruiting foreign students. Thus, given the contested nature of MRA negotiation, the trade in services is likely to be contentious and this, in turn, makes the formation of AEC complex and problematic.

Moreover, policy decisions have sometimes been taken deliberately to discriminate the foreign providers, e.g, through limits on availability of licenses. It has to be noted, for instance, that some of the member states like Brunei, Myanmar, Cambodia and Laos do not have competition policy and laws to date (Nambiar, 2015) and such absence acts as barriers to trade and investment. Therefore, coordination of regulation among different ASEAN member states is extremely crucial and the process involves sharing of experiences and systematic efforts to build capacity (Findlay, 2017).

5. Summing Up and the Way Forward

The analysis in the previous sections indicates that there is significant potential for expanding mutually beneficial economic relations among the ASEAN member states. ASEAN can be a more formidable economic force provided it strengthens itself within the region. Envisioning AEC is an important step to utilize that potential as the idea is based on convergence of interests of ASEAN member states to deepen and broaden economic integration through specific rules and regulation with clear timelines. Importantly, effective trade and investment facilitation are more important than merely having liberalised market. The growth of anti-globalisation attitudes in the world in general and in ASEAN in particular could seriously undermine the ASEAN moves towards the creation of the AEC. Therefore, any issues related to domestic policy reform, regional and international cooperation and institution building should be tactfully addressed to ensure competitiveness and inclusivity of this fastly growing region. In particular, on the basis of learning from the successes and failures of the current experiences of AEC formation, we point out below the areas that require immediate attention for realizing the dream of AEC by accommodating differences among the ASEAN member states.

Firstly, we need to accept that the journey towards equitable economic development in the ASEAN region will take time. Even the early starters of regulatory reforms in Asia-Pacific region, e.g., Australia and New Zealand have not been able to complete transition. Obviously, the CLMV countries would face tougher challenges to modify regulatory practices to suit their socio-economic environment.

Secondly, governance is the key to AEC formation. Rules and regulation aiming at facilitation of trade and investment would be effective only when these are transparent and well coordinated among the different ASEAN member states. For example, the creation of an institutional mechanism at the ASEAN Secretariat for continuous NTM data collection and dissemination would bring in the much needed to NTM transparency in the region. This would be particularly beneficial for the SMEs that lack capacity and political clout to navigate the opaque and complex set of rules and regulations.

Thirdly, the region requires regular investments in human capital both to ensure to supply of skilled labourers as well as skill enhancement of the unskilled labourers. This would enhance the environment for accelerated technology transfer, adaptation, and even innovation. Further, there is an urgent need to streamline the MRAs because without the free flow of skilled labour and free trade in services, it will not be possible to establish ASEAN as a region that can attract FDI.

Fourthly, the concerns of the small and medium enterprises (SMEs) have to be given specific attention. Mechanisms to connect the SMEs to the industrial and service clusters andproduction networks locally, regionally, and globally should be backed up by the proactive efforts by the ASEAN member states to inform and train SMEs on how to internalise the opening opportunities available to them. Arguably, the growth of the SMEs perfectly fits into the inclusive approach to economic cooperation that would enable the less-developed members to take advantage of the benefits of integration.

Fifthly, it is extremely important to pay due attention to the coherence of the regional measures with other domestic measures and policies. Equally important are the institutions and capacity building strategies in each member state as the regional measures are ultimately implemented at the national level.

Lastly, the major regulatory reform is a political decision. The framing and implementation of reform measures crucially depends on the socio-political contestation over the distribution of economic resources. So, the vital elements in realisation of AEC dream are the willingness of the dominant economic interests and efforts to develop trust and confidence in each other. It is equally important to address the information and perception gaps and mindsets that hinder the pace of economic cooperation among the ASEAN member states. On a positive note, the recent ERIA survey demonstrates peoples' strong aspirations in favour of an integrated and equitable ASEAN (Maria *et al.*, 2017). This, in turn, calls for neutralizing every ideological and informational blinders to operationalize the vision of establishing a larger Asian Economic Community.

References

Ahsan A, A Mattoo, B Gootiiz, J S Saez, M Molineuvo, and P Walkenhorst (2015): ASEAN Services Integration Report: A Joint Report by the ASEAN Secretariat and the *World Bank*, Washington, DC: The World Bank.

ASEAN Secretariat (2017):*ASEAN Economic Integration Brief*, No 01, June, Jakarta: ASEAN Secretariat.

ASEAN Secretariat (2012): *ASEAN Economic Community Scorecard: charting progress towards regional economic integration*, Jakarta: ASEAN Secretariat.

Asian Development Bank (ADB) and United Nations Economic and Social Commission for Asia and the Pacific (UNESCAP) (2009), *Designing and implementing trade facilitation in Asia and the Pacific*, Manila: ADB.

Beverelli C, M Fiorini, and B Hoekman (2017): "Services trade restrictiveness and manufacturing productivity: the role of institutions', *Journal of International Economics*, 104(C), 166–82.

CARI [CIMB ASEAN Research Institute] (2013): "The ASEAN Economic Community: the status of implementation, challenges and bottlenecks', Kuala Lumpur, June.

Chattopadhyay D and S Jha (2014): "The impact of energy subsidies on the power sector in Southeast Asia", *Electricity Journal*, 27 (4): 70-83.

Constantinescu, C., A. Mattoo, and M. Ruta (2015), 'The Great Trade Slowdown: Cyclical or Structural?,*IMF Staff Working Paper*, WP/15/6, Washington, DC: International Monetary Fund.

Eichengreen B and P Gupta (2013): "The two waves of service-sector growth", *Oxford Economic Papers*, 65(1), 96–123.

ERIA [Economic Research Institute for ASEAN and East Asia] (2012): "Mid-term review of the implementation of AEC blueprint: executive summery", Jakarta.

EXIM Bank (2018): *Strengthening ASEAN India partnership: trends and future prospects*, January, Mumbai: India.

Findlay C (2017): "Bringing ASEAN into the global services network revolution" in R S Maria, S Urata and P S Intal (Jr) (eds) *The ASEAN Economic Community into 2025 and beyond*, Vol 5, Economic Research Institute for ASEAN and East Asia (ERIA), Jakarta.

He X and C Findlay (2014): "Policy restrictions and services performance: evidence from 32 countries", *Journal of International Commerce, Economics and Policy*, 5(1), 1–19.

Hoekman B and B Shepherd (2017): "Services productivity, trade policy and manufacturing exports", *World Economy*, 40, 499–516.

Ing L Y and O Cadot (2017): "A More integrated ASEAN: facilitating trade in goods" in R S Maria, S Urata and P S Intal (Jr) (eds) *The ASEAN Economic Community into 2025and beyond*, Vol 5, Economic Research Institute for ASEAN and East Asia (ERIA), Jakarta.

Jones L (2015): "Explaining the failure of the ASEAN economic community: the primacy of domestic political economy", *The Pacific Review* (http://dx.doi.org/10.1080/09512748.2015.1022593)

Lamy P (2017): "The ASEAN Economic Community: preparing for tomorrow in today's world", ASEAN Economic Integration Brief, No 01, June, Jakarta: ASEAN Secretariat.

Maria R S, S Urata and P S Intal (Jr) (2017): "The ASEAN Economic Community into 2025and beyond", in R S Maria, S Urata and P S Intal (Jr) (eds) *The ASEAN Economic Community into 2025 and beyond*, Vol 5, Economic Research Institute for ASEAN and East Asia (ERIA), Jakarta.

Nambiar S (2015): "India's relationship with ASEAN: Seizing trade and investment opportunities" in *ASEAN India economic relations opportunities and challenges* – Proceedings of the Third Roundtable on ASEAN India Network of Think Tanks (AINTT) (25-26 August 2014, Hanoi, Vietnam), RIS, New Delhi: India.

Nasir S and K Kalirajan (2016): "Information and communication technology-enabled modern services export performances of Asian economies", *Asian Development Review*, 33(1), 1–27.

Petri P A, M G Plummer and F Zhai (2012): "The ASEAN Economic Community: a general equilibrium analysis", SSRN, 21 November.

The Associated Chambers of Commerce and Industry of India (2016): *India ASEAN trade and investment relations: opportunities and challenges*, July, New Delhi.

Van der Marel (2017): "Reforming services: what policies warrant attention?', Policy Brief, 1/2017, European Centre for International Political Economy *(ECIPE)*, http://ecipe.org//app/uploads/2017/06/5F_17_PB_Reforming-Services_V5.pdf.

Wilson J D (2015): "Regionalising resource security in the Asia-Pacific: the challenge of economic nationalism", *Australian Journal of International Affairs*, 69 (2): 224-245.

Chapter - 5

Dynamic Capital Adequacy Ratio for Bringing Equilibrium in Lending in the Banking Industry: A Study of the five largest Banks in India

Akash Baruah

Abstract

The problem of Non-Performing Assets in banks has always been a concern, mainly because of the far reaching impact that banks have on the economy as a whole. There has always been a trade off in banks in terms of tighter regulation and higher risk taking. Arguments have been made in the past that banks tend to make riskier loans with tighter regulations. But it can be noticed that not all banks are efficient of the same degree and thus not all banks should be regulated on the same scale. This paper does a study of the five largest Indian banks and comes to the conclusion that the capital adequacy ratio is incapable of reducing risks in banks in terms of growing NPAs. Data suggests that non-performing assets continued to rise regardless of the banks maintaining high capital adequacy ratios. In the paper, we develop a ratio termed as the Marginal Cost of Lending and compare it across banks to find out that not all banks are similarly efficient. Thus having the same capital requirement does not incentivize banks to perform better neither does it penalize them. This led to the formulation of a dynamic capital adequacy ratio, by taking into account the Marginal Cost of Lending, which will reflect the inherent risks of banks. The purpose of the study is to create a self-correcting mechanism which prevents low quality lending and help reduce the problem of NPAs. Traditionally a higher capital ratio reflected the safety of the banks in terms of its loss absorbing capacity, but a higher dynamic capital ratio will reflect its inherent risks.

1. Introduction

1.1 General Overview

The Indian banking sector has been recently grappling with the problem of mounting bad assets. The Reserve Bank of India (RBI) has issued many guidelines in order to help the banks solve this problem but the progress has been very slow. The severity of the problem can be gauged from the fact that the balance sheet of the five largest lenders of India, which are State Bank of India, Punjab National Bank, ICICI Bank, Canara Bank and Bank of Baroda, accounted for 32.27% of India's Gross Domestic Product (GDP), as of 2017. The basic issue which the regulators face is that all the measures to resolve bad assets are *ex-post* and therefore their actions are generally behind the curve. We found that the banks enjoyed a very high CRAR all throughout the study period and yet was not able to resolve the issue of rising bad assets. The reason for this is that the banks were adjusting to the capital requirements mostly through the numerator which is made up of Tier I and Tier II capital. According to (Estrella et al. 2000) the banks were able to set aside large amounts of profits as reserves and also raise capital from the market, mostly on favorable terms. Thus, even though the GNPAs were rising, lending kept on increasing with the fallacy of higher CRARs (Acharya 2003). The basic feature of a capital requirement is to make banks safer, but in spite of the high capital ratios GNPAs were added at an unsustainable pace. This increased the inherent risks in banks and posed threats towards a systemic slowdown of the economy.

This fundamental problem of the CRAR not being reflective of the inherent risks in banks in terms of mounting bad assets led to the formulation of the dynamic CRAR. *Firstly,* a particular bank fails if it is not being able to honor its liabilities. It defaults on its liabilities when the assets financed through those it goes bad. Hence, creation of bad assets is positively correlated with bank failure. Therefore, there should be more responsible creation of assets for greater financial stability.

Secondly, there should be some mechanism to encourage efficiency in banks by incentivizing them for undertaking better lending practices (Cohen & Scatigna 2014). Banks should be incentivized for aiming at higher profits through lower risks and not for higher profits through higher risks. Profitability of a bank should not be a criterion for allowing it to lend more, instead the underlying quality of its assets should be. We have seen to the run up of the Financial Crisis of 2007, that how profitability can be a driver of irresponsible lending and what its consequences can be. Thus, the dynamic CRAR would allow banks to have different CRARs based on their efficiency, which is a reflection of their asset quality and NPA levels. This will incentivize banks to earn profits through responsible lending and factor in the efficiency of the banks (Dio 2003).

Thirdly, we need to bring equilibrium in lending in the banking industry through a dynamic CRAR. With a constant CRAR not all the banks are lending at their optimum level, some are over lending and others are under lending (Allen et al. 2000). This is because both efficient and inefficient banks are subject to the same set of regulations and are lending with the same amount of freedom. Thus good banks are not incentivized by giving them the capacity to lend more and bad banks are not penalised by allowing them to lend at the same rate. Thereby the banking sector is not in equilibrium. We try argue for a situation in which each bank can lend at its optimum level by a discriminatory dynamic CAD and thereby leading to an equilibrium in the whole banking system. The same can be seen in a financial market where different coupon rates are paid on different bonds, which is also a reflection of the underlying efficiency of the companies issuing them. It can be further stated that as the company improves its efficiency, it can borrow at better market rates and thereby increase its leverage. The dynamic coupon rates keep a check on the standard of the company and provides it with an incentive to keep improving.

1.2 Model Overview

We first develop a ratio by taking Addition of GNPA/"Advances and establish the *Marginal Costof Lending.* The MCL gives us a very good insight on the amount of assets going bad as apercentage of amount of assets being created and gives us an understanding of the efficiency of the bank. This ratio would appraise us about the bank's deteriorating lending quality and call for preventive measures.

We then define a *bankruptcy model;* in which we prove that the CRAR is incapable of reducing lending in situations of mounting bad assets. It is only because that the MCL has a steeper slope than the MRL (Revenue/"Advances), banks reduce lending in response to growing NPAs.

Further the MCL ratio is added to the base capital requirement to come up with the dynamic CRAR. It is argued that a rising dynamic CRAR is a reflection of higher risks in banks and therefore they try to converge towards the base rate by becoming more efficient.

In this paper we do an empirical analysis of the top five largest banks of India through their financials. All the data used in the study has been taken from their Annual Reports and RBI database, starting from 2007 till 2017. The rest of the paper is structured as follows, in section 2 we do an asset quality review of the five banks and state certain specific reasons for the growing NPAs. In section 3 we define the *Marginal Cost of Lending Ratio* and explain how important it is for identifying potential risks in banks. In section 4 we develop the bankruptcy model to validate that the CRAR was unable to reduce the mounting bad assets problem and in section 5 we explain the dynamic CRAR, its derivation and provide a simulation to explain how the banks CRAR would have looked like if they were dynamic. In Section 6 we provide a final conclusion and sum up the results of our findings.

2. Asset Quality Review

2.1 Impact Analysis

Generally, the Reserve Bank of India (RBI) inspects the books of accounts of banks annually because of its yearly financial survey. In accordance with this, an exceptional inspection was organised during the month of August in FY 2015-16 and was termed as Asset Quality Review (AQR). During a normal routine financial inspection, RBI scrutinizes a small sample to examine if the classification of assets were done in accordance with the repayment schedule.

This time however, the AQR was done on a much larger sample size, which included most of the large borrower accounts, to assess if the classification was done keeping the prudential norms in mind. Through this almost 200 accounts were recognised and were directed to be classified as non-performing.

As a result of this exercise the GNPAs of the five banks in 2015 amounted to 126, 816 Crores (Cr) and net NPAs to 66, 052 Cr. The addition of new GNPAs was also an astonishing high number of 73, 485 Cr. These figures had a very strong momentum and witnessed high growth rates in the following year of 2016, with GNPAs, net NPAs and addition of new GNPAs amounting to 252, 371 Cr, 144, 432 Cr and 175, 714 Cr. The Net NPAs had a growth of 118.66 % in 2016, which was a reflection of the deteriorating asset quality situation of the Indian banks. This was because most of the banks were reluctant to classify their loans as non - performing and were resorting to ever - greening of accounts. However, in 2017 the growth in the Net NPAs were low at 7.96% due to the efforts from the RBI through Various Schemes such as the Strategic Debt Restructuring Scheme (SDR), Joint Lenders Forum (JLF), 5/25 Scheme etc.

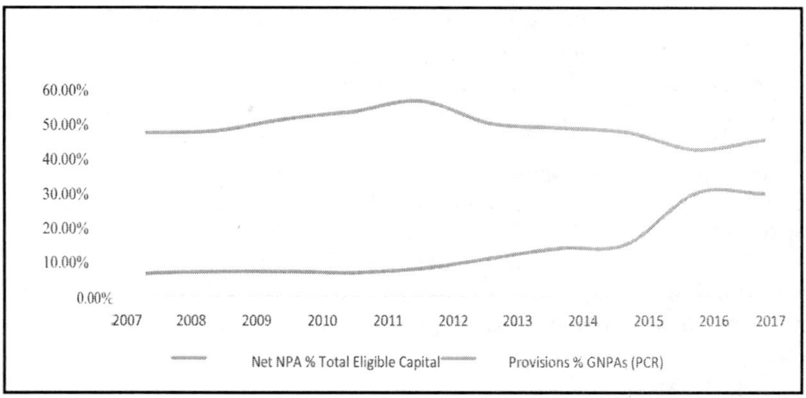

Figure 5.1 - Alarming Ratios.

The ever – greening of accounts, which amounted to the banks not taking any steps to resolve the issue, allowed the NPAs to keep on growing. This resulted in the addition of new GNPAs growing from 11, 232 Cr in 2007 to 175, 713 Cr in 2016. Therefore, the banks were required to undertake some tough measures for providing permanent solution to the problems at hand, which resulted in the write offs increasing from 38, 483 Cr in 2015 to 62, 169 Cr in 2017. Even though the banks profit margins were hit by this step, it was necessary to send a strong signal to the markets and the world community.

The severity of the problem can be understood from the figure above, which shows the trend of two important ratios of the five banks calculated on a consolidated basis. We can see that the Provisions/GNPAs ratio, also known as the Provision Coverage Ratio, started to decline from 2012 and continued to fall until 2016. It was only in 2017 that it had risen, after the dual impact of higher provisioning requirements and declining GNPAs. Another ratio is the Net NPA/Total Eligible Capital, in which the denominator is the aggregate of Tier 1 and Tier 2 capital. This ratio gives an idea about the loss in eligible capital if the whole of Net NPA would have to be written off. A rise in the ratio is an indication of the deteriorating asset quality of the bank and is a reflection of the underlying inherent risks (Cao and Chollete 2014). We can see that the ratio started to increase from 2012 and kept on increasing until 2016 and peaked at 29.91 %. One thing which can be interpreted from figure 5.1 is that both the lines in the graph should diverge from each other in order to indicate financial stability and the convergence of the same would indicate deteriorating financial health of the banks.

2.2 Reasons for Deteriorating Asset Quality

A thorough analysis of the data, collected from the sample of five banks, revealed certain patterns which explained why the banks were unable to recognize the severe mounting bad assets problem. We have classified our findings into three broad categories in accordance with what the data had to reveal.

Kicking the can down the lane is exactly what the bankers propagated and the problem remained unaddressed for so long. At each and every point of time an attempt could have been made to resolve the issue, but nobody was willing to take the difficult steps. It can be seen from figure 5.2 that the increase in addition of GNPAs started from 2008 whereas the write offs remained constant. This led to the start of the widening of the gap between the GNPAs and the write offs. In fact, in 2012 there was a dip in the write offs, whereas the addition in GNPAs continued its exponential rise.

Moral Hazard

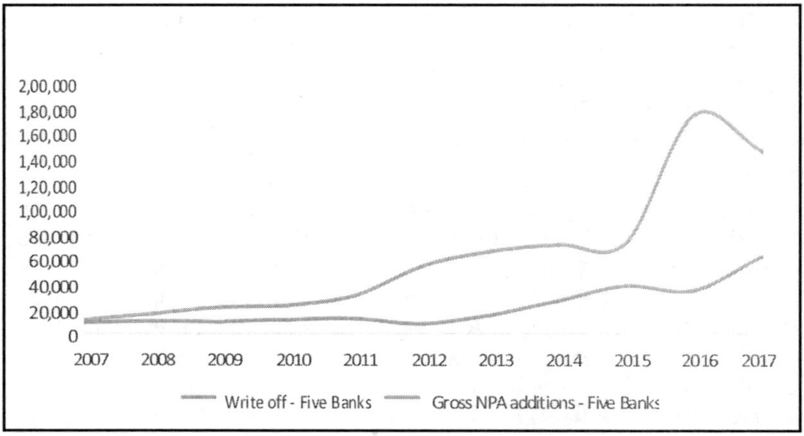

The increase in write offs from 2013 was not enough to compensate the growing bad assets problem and the gap was at its peak in 2016. The diverging trend was a matter of serious concern for the bankers and the regulators, to which they reacted considerably very late. But 2017 brought in some hope as both the figures started to converge, with addition of bad assets declining and write offs picking up. The reason why writing off is so difficult because it brings about a reduction in the bank's balance sheet along with huge negative publicity.

Solvency Problem

The risk in a bank increases as the bad assets or GNPAs expand. The banks need to provision for these bad assets. But we know that a bank's profits

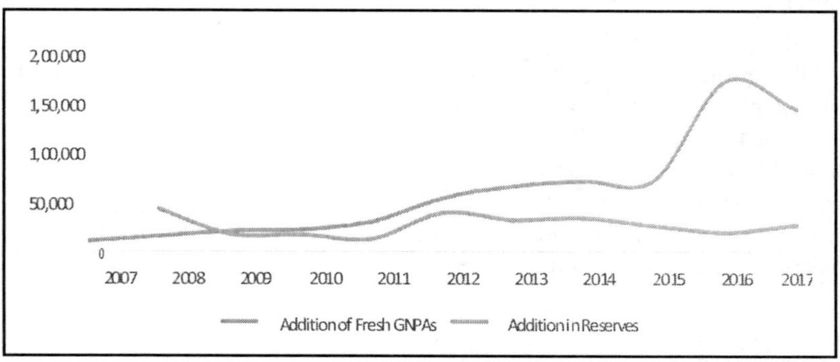

Figure 5.3 - Solvency Problem.

are limited and thus if the level of bad assets increases beyond a certain point, it would not be able to provide for them. This leads to a situation where a bank's reserves are used up and poses a threat to its solvency. Later on when we develop the Bankruptcy Model, this issue will be dealt with in detail. It can be seen from figure 5.3 that initially in 2009, the gap between the Addition of GNPAs and Addition in Reserves was very low and hence any rise in bad assets could have been provided for without much difficulty. But the situation started to change after 2011 and the gap between the two extended. As the GNPAs diverge from the PAT, bank's ability to provide for bad assets through profits diminishes.

Therefore, probability of provisions entering into the reserves of banks increases and thereby makes them riskier (Andrle et al. 2017). The risk is in terms of losses eroding away all the eligible capital (Tier1 and Tier 2) and forcing the bank into liquidation. The situation worsened from 2015 and reached its peak in 2016. Though we have seen some trends of reversal in 2017, there is still a long way to go before we can think to relax.

Recognition Problem

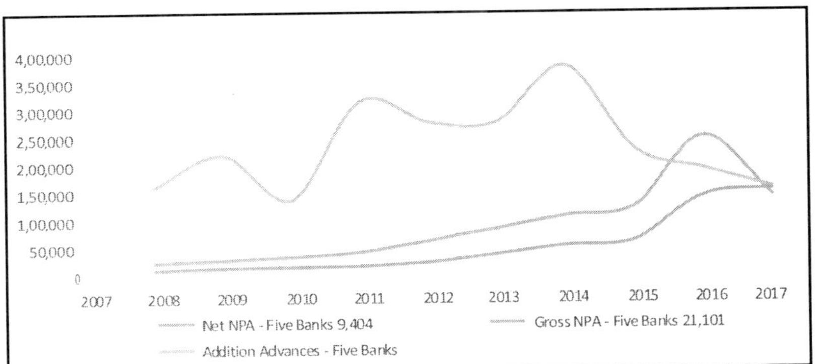

Figure 5.4 - Recognition Problem.

It's a normal practice to recognize growing bad assets in the system and take appropriate measures to tackle it. One of the ways of resolving a bad assets problem is reducing the amount of lending and becoming more cautious in one's approach. We can see from figure 5.4 that the GNPAs started to increase from 2011 and had a steady growth until 2014. Then it had a very steep rise and reached its peak in 2016. But the addition in advances kept on happening despite the evident rise in bad assets. It was only after 2014, that the banks slowed down its lending and also started to take other remedial measures such as write offs. The constant increase in advances is a clear sign of lack of acceptance and complacency on the part of the bankers in terms of assessing the bad assets situation. The Net NPA was also diverging from the Gross NPA, which shows that write off as a measure was not adequately adopted. Serious steps regarding recognizing the situation was taken only after 2015 when the addition in advances started to decline and the Net NPAs started to rise.

Thus these three reasons give us an understanding as to why the five banks resulted in the situation in which they are now and sheds light on the probable reasons of their mismanagement. The threats to bank failure are very evident and needs to be dealt upon with sincerity for a proper resolution.

3. Marginal Cost of Lending

3.1 Derivation of the Ratio

Every firm needs to be efficient by making maximum utilisation of their resources. The Banks need to make the best possible use of their capital and see to it that they generate the least amount of NPAs. What we have seen from our analysis is that the CRAR is not an adequate reflection of the inherent risks in banks and neither does it enlighten us on the degree of efficiency in bank lending. This led to the derivation of a ratio by taking Addition of GNPA/" Advances, which would appraise us on the amount of assets going bad per rupee of advances.

We do not take the negative values of the ratio into consideration while doing our analysis, as a negative number implies that the bank has actually contracted its lending. The ratio should have a downward trend with positive values. An efficient bank will have the ratio decreasing, with the denominator increasing and the numerator decreasing, but never approaching zero. The numerator can be zero only if a bank does not have any of its loans turning bad and is highly efficient.

Marginal Cost of Lending (MCL)

$$= \frac{\text{Addition of GNPA}t_n}{\Delta \text{Advances}n}$$

$$= \frac{\Delta\ \text{GNPA}n + \text{Write Off}t_n}{\Delta \text{Advances}n}$$

$$= \frac{(\text{GNPA}t_n - \text{GNPA}t_{n-1}) + \text{Write Off}t_n}{\Delta \text{Advances}t_n}$$

$$= \frac{(GNPAt_{n-1} + \text{Addition of } GNPAt_n - \text{Write Offt}_n) - (GNPAt_{n-2} + \text{Addition of } GNPAt_{n-1} - \text{Write Offt}_n) + \text{Write Offt}_n}{\Delta Advancest_n}$$

$$= \frac{(GNPAt_{n-1} - GNPAt_{n-2}) + (\text{Addition of } GNPAt_{n-1} - \text{Addition of } GNPAt_n) + \text{Write Offt}_n}{\Delta Advancest_n}$$

$$= \frac{\Delta GNPAt_{n-1} + \Delta \text{Addition of } GNPAt_n + \text{Write Offt}_{n-1}}{\Delta Advancest_n}$$

* The calculation of the above equation can be checked from annexure 1

(a) Addition of GNPAs - Amount of bad assets added each year during time period tn

(b) "Advancest$_n$ – Amount of advances added each year during time period tn

(c) "GNPAt$_n$ – Amount of GNPAs added each year during time period tn

(d) Write Offt$_n$ - Amount of bad assets written off each year during time period tn

This ratio tells us about the amount of assets going bad each year as a percentage of the amount of assets created. If we find the ratio increasing, it can be implied that there are issues with the productivity and efficiency of that particular bank in terms of its lending. An analysis and breakdown of the ratio reveals that the previous period's "GNPA and Write off also affects the current periods MCL. Thus this allows us to identify trends that might be accumulating from several previous years and thereby help us to prevent further building up of risks in the system.

3.2 Inefficiency of the CRAR

We can see from the figure above that the consolidated MCL (MCL of the five banks) started to increase from 2011 and had a steep rise from 2014 when the AQR was called in by the RBI. But the inefficiency of the banks in terms of rising bad assets was not fully reflected through the CRAR as it remained well above the Basel III requirements. A high CRAR implied that the bank was well capitalised and inherently less risky, but it did not reflect its lending productivity. Thus a rising MCL appraises us of the loss in productivity and the rise in bad assets, which is lacking through the CRAR.

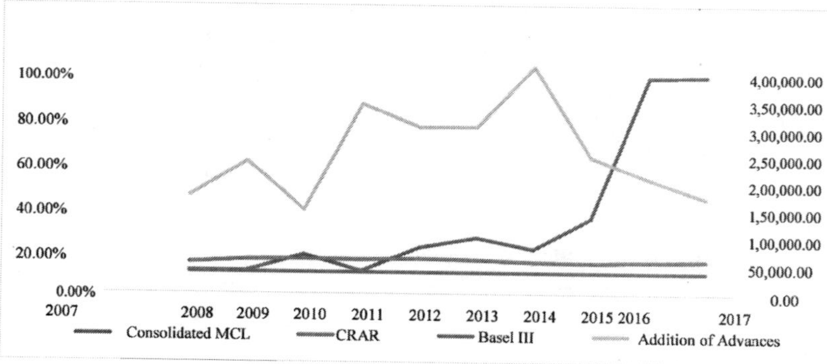

Fig 5.5 - Inefficincy of CRAR.

The Formula for the CRAR is:

$$\frac{\text{Total Eligible Capital}}{\text{Credit Risk Weighted Assets + Market Risk Weighted Assets + Operational Risk Weighted Assets}}$$

The rising MCL of the five banks from 2014 meant that the GNPAs per rupee of advances were increasing and the adjustment of the CRAR should have happened through the denominator, which is by reducing lending. We can analyze from figure 5.5 that the adjustment of the CRAR happened through the numerator, as the advances kept on increasing. This phenomenon continued from 2011 till 2014, but from 2014 the adjustment finally started to happen through the denominator, as the reduction in advances can be seen. If the MCL was made public, investors would have factored this in their valuations and asked for higher returns. Subsequently, higher dividends and interest payments would have required the banks to adjust through the denominator as raising capital would become costly. A rising MCL indicates that something is not correct with the lending function of the bank and hence calls for a check on the credit expansion. This is one of the main reasons why the CRAR has not been able to reduce risks in terms of growing NPAs, as the market does not factor in the efficiency and the CRAR is adjusted through easy raising of capital.

4. The Bankruptcy Model

4.1 Derivation of the model

We first define another ratio called the Marginal Revenue of Lending (MRL) which tells us the revenue earned per unit of lending. The ratio is as follows:

Marginal Revenue of Lending (MRL)

$$= \frac{\Delta \text{ Reservestn}}{\Delta \text{ Advancestn}}$$

MRL tells us how productive a bank is in terms of its lending. This ratio increasing signifies that the assets created by the banks are generating revenues and resonate efficiency of the bank.

The Bankruptcy Model:

Let X be the amount of GNPAs

Let Y be the amount of provisions required

Let Z be the amount of profits earned in a particular period tn

Let time = $t_1, t_2 \ldots\ldots t_n$

$\{0, 1\} \rightarrow$

$\rightarrow \beta_{1*} \text{ GNPA}_{tn} \leq Z_{tn} \rightarrow$ ❶

The above equation ❶ can only hold true when $Z_{tn} > Y_{tn}$,

Let Q be the reserves at the time t_{n-1}

Now, if $Y_{tn} > Zt_n$, the following condition will hold true at any time t_n for *avoiding bankruptcy*

$\rightarrow \beta_{1*} \text{ GNPA}_{tn} \leq (Ztn + Q) \rightarrow$ ❷

Profit is appropriated to various reserve accounts, Reserve_{tn} (R) = Profit_{tn} + $\text{Reserves}_{tn}\text{-}_1$

1* $\quad tn \leq R_{tn} \rightarrow$ ❸ $\rightarrow$

Now we divide both sides by equation by Δ Advancest_n

$$\frac{\beta_{1*} \text{ GNPAtn}}{\Delta \text{ Advancest}_n} \leq \frac{R_{tn} \rightarrow ❹ \rightarrow}{\Delta\text{Advancest}_n}$$

We know that, $\text{GNPA}^t{}_{n} = \text{GNPA}_{tn-1} + \text{Addition in GNPA}_{tn} - \text{Write Offt}_n$ and $R_{tn} = R_{tn-1} +$

Δ R Now equation ❹ can be written as,

$$\rightarrow \beta_{1*}\left(\frac{\text{GNPAtn-1}+}{\Delta\text{Advancestn}} \frac{\text{Addition in GNPAtn}}{\Delta\text{Advancestn}} - \frac{\text{Write Offtn}}{\Delta\text{Advancestn}}\right) \leq \frac{R_{tn-1}}{\Delta\text{Advancestn}} + \frac{\Delta R}{\Delta\text{Advancestn}}$$

$$\rightarrow \beta_{1*}\left(\frac{\text{GNPAtn-1 - Write Offtn}}{\Delta\text{Advancestn}} + \frac{\text{Addition in GNPAtn}}{\Delta\text{Advancestn}}\right) \leq \frac{R_{tn-1}}{\Delta\text{Advancestn}} + \text{MRL}$$

$$\rightarrow \frac{\text{GNPAtn-1 - Write Offtn}}{\Delta\text{Advancestn}} + \text{MCL} \leq \frac{R_{tn-1}}{\Delta\text{Advancestn}} + \text{MRL} \longrightarrow ⑤$$

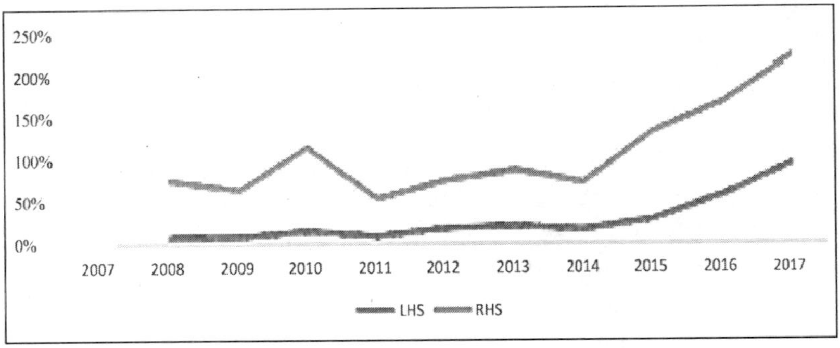

** The bankruptcy ratio is calculated with the model developed above. The calculations can be checked from annexure 2*

Equation ❺ should hold true at all points in time for the bank to remain solvent. IF the Left hand side (LHS) of the equation becomes greater than the Right Hand Side (RHS), the provisioning requirement will be greater than the profit for the current period and previous period's reserves combined. This would imply that the going concern capital of the bank has eroded away and would call for liquidation. Thus if the GNPA in the previous period increases, the write off in the next period should also increase. Now when the GNPA on the LHS increases, the reserves on the RHS should decrease. This assumption comes from the fact that when the GNPAs are on the rise, the banks would reduce their lending to curtail future accumulation of bad assets. Therefore, the RHS cannot be adjusted at will and the adjustment has to be done on the LHS through the increase of write offs.

But the banks can take another decision, which is to increase lending. When the advances increase, the revenues also increase. Therefore, an increase on the LHS can be adjusted through increased revenues on the RHS, revenues being part of reserves, which is contrary to solving the main problem of rising GNPAs. In theory, advances can keep on growing and so also revenues, even when GNPAs are on the rise. But the only phenomenon which keeps a check on the banks in terms of lending when the GNPAs are on the rise, is the slope of the MRL and the MCL. As the MCL has s steeper slope than the MRL, an increase in lending might lead to a situation in which the LHS increases at a much faster rate than the RHS. Therefore, this is the natural process through which a bank is made to put a check on its lending. But the banks can always delay the process by raising easy capital, as equity forms a part of the reserves. Hence the RHS is adjusted by other ways which allows the banks to keep on lending. We can look at figure 5.6 for understanding the steepness of the MRL and MCL and Figure 5.7 for understanding the delaying process.

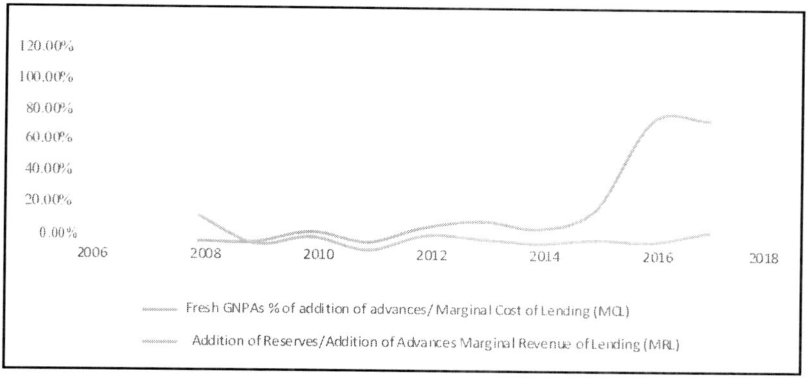

Figure 5.6 MCL and MRL.

In figure 5.6, we can see that from 2015 there is a steep rise in the MCL in comparison with the MRL. This reflects the fact that whenever recognition of bad assets happens and there is a steep rise in the GNPAs, the slope of the MCL will rise at a much faster rate than the slope of the MRL. Hence the convexity of MCL is much higher than the MRL.

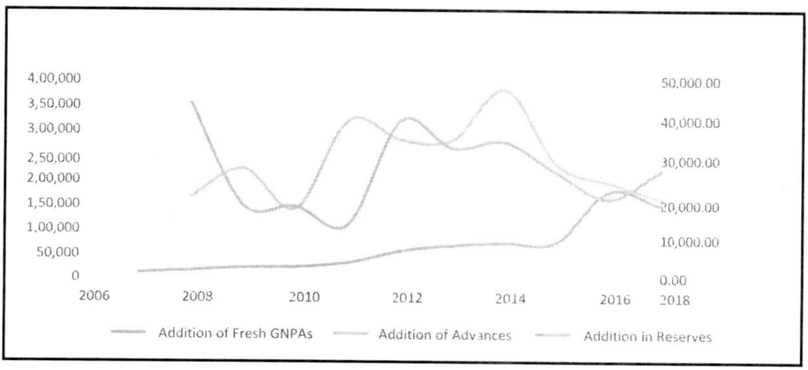

Fig 5.7 - Delay Process.

Figure 5.7 helps us to understand the delaying process to some extent. As we can see that there was an increase in addition of reserves and addition of advances from 2011 till 2014, even if the GNPAs were on the rise. It was only after 2014, when the AQR was called in by the RBI that the reserves and advances started to decline. The GNPAs also had a steep rise from 2014, mostly on account of the intervention of the RBI and its push to make the banks recognize the bad assets problem. This tells us the delaying mechanism of the banks, who delayed the recognition of bad assets from 2011 till 2014 and perhaps allowed the problem to grow bigger (Acharya 2001). During this time, it kept on its lending drive and hence adjusted to the RHS with higher reserves.

5. The Dynamic CRAR Model

5.1 Derivation of the model

The CRAR has been unable to reduce risks in banks in terms of lower GNPAs and also to reflect its efficiency and productivity, as established earlier from 3.2 – Inefficiency of CRAR. We make the CRAR reflective of the efficiency and productivity of the bank and address the fundamental problem of adjustment of the CRAR through the numerator. We have to make certain assumptions for developing the model.

1. All the banks start of from the same CRAR as set by the regulator
2. No bank has the tendency to pile up reserves. Hence profits earned are lent out and not transferred to reserves
3. The dynamic CRAR cannot go below the standard base CRAR, unless altered by the regulatory authority
4. 50 % of (MCLtn*Base CRARtn) will be added to Base CRARtn, to make it dynamic
5. The adjustment from dynamic $CRARtn_{-1}$ to dynamic CRARtn will be done in the ratio 90:10, where 90 % will be adjusted through the numerator and 10 % through the denominator

The General CRAR as per BASEL III recommendations is:

$$\text{CRAR} = \frac{\text{Total Eligible Capital}}{\text{Credit Risk Weighted Assets} + \text{Market Risk Weighted Assets} + \text{Operational Risk Weighted Assets}}$$

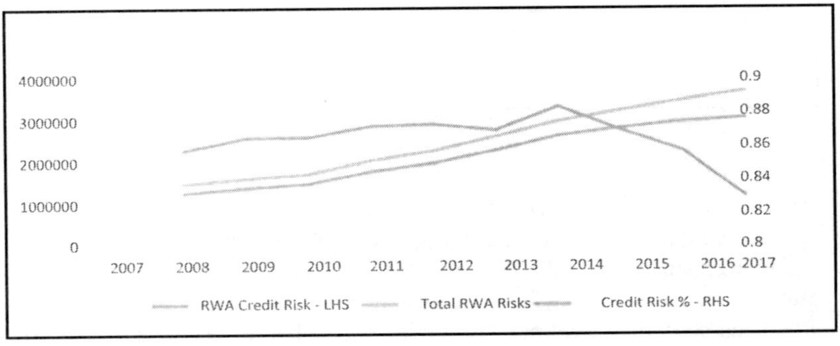

Fig. 5.8.

We have concentrated more on the credit risk part of the Risk Weighted Assets (RWA), because it accounts for the largest portion of the RWAs. On average it accounted for 86.5 % of the total RWAs of all the five banks combined from 2008 till 2017 (Fig 5.8).

The Model

→ Dynamic $CRAR_{tn+1}$ = dynamic CRARtn + 50 % (dynamic $CRAR_{tn*}MCL_{tn+1}$)

= **dynamic CRARtn+ (dynamic CRARtn*$MCLtn_{+1}$) → ❶**
2

Now the adjustment requirement will be,

= (dynamic $CRARtn_{+1}$- dynamic CRARtn)

This adjustment will be done in the ratio 90:10, where in the 90% of the adjustment will be done through the numerator and 10% through the denominator. Thus from equation 1 we can say that the MCL in Yeartn is going to decide how much the CRAR changes from Yeartn-1 to Yeartn and therefore makes the *CRAR dynamic*. As the MCL increases the CRAR also increases, similarly when the MCL decreases your CRAR reduces. But the CRAR cannot go below the *threshold*, which is set by the regulator. This implies that when the firm will be operating at optimum efficiency, it will have the threshold limit as its CRAR. Thus an increase in the dynamic CRAR would not only amount to locking up of funds but will also result in direct reduction of lending, through the mandatory 10% reduction in the denominator. This structure will bring in competition among the banks to operate at the optimum level and have the maximum amount of funds at disposal for lending. A self-correcting dynamic CRAR will help better monitor, manage and control risk in terms of growing NPAs. Another feature is that, a rising dynamic CRAR signifies problems within the firm and calls for thorough internal investigation. Whereas a normal rising CRAR will reflect a stable and robust firm and fails to reflect the inherent inefficiency.

5.2 Interpreting results from the model

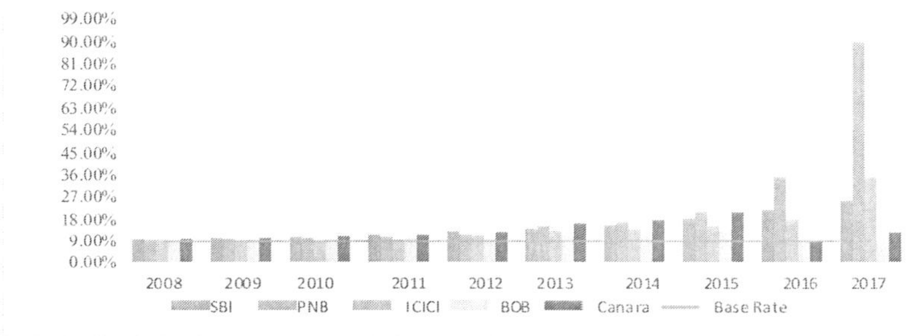

Fig 5.9 - Dynamic CRAR.

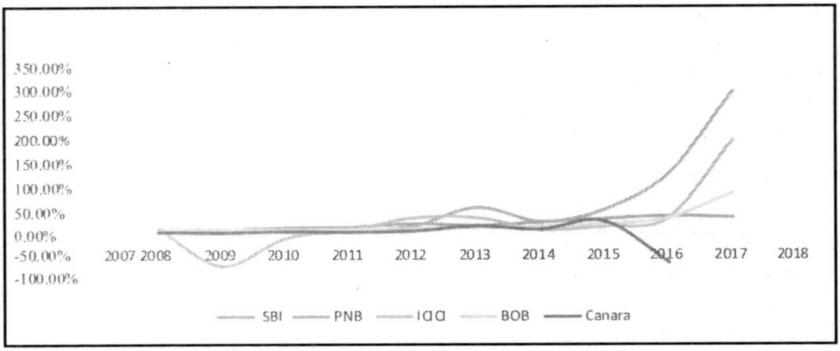

Fig 5.10 - MCL Trend

We have done a simulation on the five banks of our study, in which we calculated the dynamic CRAR of each bank from 2008 till 2017, using the model described in *section 5.1*. In figure 5.8 we can observe how the dynamic CRAR changes from 2008 and starts to rise from 2013, pushing the banks away from their optimal level of functioning. The only bank which moves back towards the optimum level of 9% is Bank of Baroda in 2016, mainly because of its steep cut in lending. These changes in the dynamic CRAR can be justified by looking at the MCL trends in figure 5.9. The MCL of the five banks started to rise from 2013 and took a very steep upward turn from 2014 onwards. This rising MCL resulted in the change of the dynamic CRARs across all the banks, signifying inherent problems. Only Bank of Baroda was able to reverse back towards the base rate because of the steep reduction in its MCL in 2016.

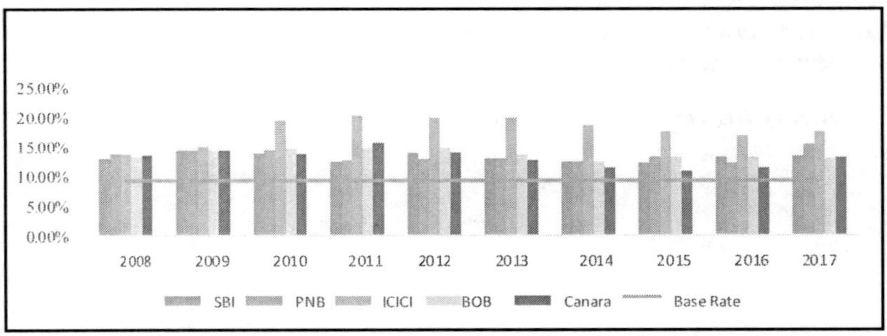

Fig 5.11 - Static CRAR

The static CRAR was well above the BASEL III base rate of 9% for all the banks. Figure 5.10 depicts a very optimistic scenario in which everything looks in order. The banks seem to be capitalised well above the required amount and thus poses no threat to the banks in terms of their solvency. What it completely fails to capture is their productivity and efficiency in terms of lending. The main reason for this is that the banks were able to adjust the CRAR through its numerator, as argued before in section *3.2*. Hence the latent problem of growing NPAs remain unattended.

6. Conclusion

The dynamic CRAR brings in equilibrium in the banking industry through the following ways:

1. It will reflect the inherent risk of the banks and differentiate them on the basis of efficiency
2. Due to the classification on the basis of risk and performance, there would be better allocation of resources as savings will shift from relatively bad to relatively good banks. Thus the good banks would have more funds at disposal for lending.
3. Dynamic CRAR will initiate competition among the banks in terms of bringing the CRAR as close as possible towards the base rate and hence operate at the optimal level. Banks will try to free up as much reserves as possible and increase their lending.
4. This competition among the banks to operate at the optimum level will bring in ***equilibrium in lending in the banking industry***.

References

Estrella, A., & Park, S. (2000), *Capital Ratios as Predictors of Bank Failure*, FRBNY Economic Policy Review.

Cohen, H. B., & Scatigna, M. (2014), *Banks and capital requirements: channels of adjustment*, Bank for International Settlements working papers No. 443.

Dio, G. (2003), *The Foundations of Banks' Risk Regulation: A Review of the Literature*, HEC Montréal, CIRPÉE and CREF working paper 03-08.

Cao, J., Chollete, L. (2014), *Capital Adequacy and Liquidity in Banking Dynamics*, UiS Working Papers in Economics and Finance.

Andrle, M., Tomšík, V., & Vlèek, J. (2017), *Banks' Adjustment to Basel III Reform: A Bank-LevelPerspective for Emerging Europe*, International Monetary Fund WP/17/ 24.

Acharya, V., (2001), *A Theory of Systemic Risk and Design of Prudential Bank Regulation*, Working Paper, Stern School of Business, New York University.

Acharya, V., (2003), *Is the international convergence of capital adequacy regulation desirable?*, Journal of Finance 58 (6).

Allen, F., & Gale, D. (2000), *Bubbles and crises*, The Economic Journal 110, pp. 236–255.

Bénétrix, A., Lane, P., & Shambaugh, J. (2015), *International currency exposures, valuation effectsand the global financial crisis,* Journal of International Economics, vol. 96 (January), pp. 98-109.

Annexure - 1

CANARA BANK											
Asset Quality Check	**Mar '07**	**Mar '08**	**Mar '09**	**Mar '10**	**Mar '11**	**Mar '12**	**Mar '13**	**Mar '14**	**Mar '15**	**Mar '16**	**Mar '17**
Provisions	446	373	658	787	739	599	933	1,561	4,254	10,745	12,419
Net NPAs	927	899	1,507	1,800	2,347	3,386	5,278	5,965	8,740	20,833	21,649
Gross NPA	1,493	1,416	2,168	2,590	3,089	4,032	6,260	7,570	13,040	31,638	34,202
Addition of Fresh GNPAs	1,272	1,426	2,378	3,266	3,508	4,590	5,819	8,444	10,908	24,724	11,652
GNPAs Write offs during the year	1,571	1,504	1,482	2,844	3,009	3,695	3,591	7,134	5,434	6,126	9,088
Addition of Advances		8,732	30,981	24,138	48,912	21,222	9,687	58,891	28,968	-5,321	17,294
PAT	1420.81	1,565	2,072	3,021	4,026	3,283	2,872	2,438	2,703	-2,813	1121.9222

Annexure - 2

	2007	2008	2009	2010	2011	2012	2013	2014	2015	2016	2017
B1	49.96%	47.31%	47.85%	51.20%	53.52%	56.61%	50.08%	48.77%	47.49%	42.53%	45.37%
GNPA	21,101	27,133	32,142	37,221	45,982	66,368	88,452	110,437	126,816	252,371	286,794
Write off	9,303	9,937	9,795	11,499	12,065	7,881	15,154	26,489	38,483	34,898	62,169
Addition in Advances	0	163,900	221,162	140,125	318,024	279,812	280,005	380,920	230,310	193,592	160,296
MCL		9.74%	9.64%	16.32%	9.67%	19.47%	23.70%	18.86%	31.91%	90.77%	91.22%

LHS		**7.83193%**	**8.362%**	**15.900%**	**9.409%**	**18.730%**	**21.029%**	**17.129%**	**29.988%**	**58.798%**	**95.213%**
		7.83171%	6.95341%	13.60113%	7.73861%	13.42613%	15.81925%	14.13847%	26.14797%	55.44564%	81.16783%
Provisions	10,541	12,836	15,378	19,059	24,611	37,568	44,295	53,856	60,221	107,338	130,109
Reserves	82,534.73	126,530.66	144,827.81	162,836.26	176,160.04	215,804.91	248,590.54	282,928.06	309,644.94	329,671.48	356,867.75
MRL		26.84%	8.27%	12.85%	4.19%	14.17%	11.71%	9.01%	11.60%	10.34%	16.97%
RHS		**77.20%**	**65.48%**	**116.21%**	**55.39%**	**77.13%**	**88.78%**	**74.27%**	**134.45%**	**170.29%**	**222.63%**

Chapter - 6

An Evaluation and Multiple-step Ahead Forecast of the Post-reform Liquidity Adjustment Facility (Laf) Period in A Globalized Environment through Autoregressive Model

Deepanjali Das

Abstract

"The progressive globalisation of financial institutions and services over the last two decades has led to a complex web of interconnected markets, institutions, services and products. Institutions transcended borders; markets became accessible in real time and financial services were available from everywhere. In short, financial markets and institutions declared 'death of distance' and 'conquest of location."

An effective monetary policy transmission onwards to the real sector depends on the extent of integration of the financial market. Therefore the greater the financial markets are integrated the quick is the trickle down speed to real economy along with the desired effect. With the clear indication of growing financial integration of money market and monetary policies post financial reforms, my study aims at firstly screening the different facets of liquidity conditions. With the phase wise segregation of the time period 2008-2016 under study, the goal is to work out correlation coefficients of monetary policy instrument and the money market instruments. This way there is an attempt to show the extent of association between the rates of the various segments of the financial market. The aim behind the choice of such time scenario is to bring in note the outcome from any volatile effect seeping in though globalisation. To take in consideration the brevity of the study the contagious upshot of Global Financial crisis on the following duration is looked over here. It spread to India through financial and real channel and primarily via the confidence channel. Such out-of-country stance creeps in and marked a setback to the ongoing policy choices of the RBI from monetary tightening in response to heightened inflationary tensions to monetary easing in opposition to a facile inflationary environment. In the eve of the financial crisis observers suggested a gradual move towards a framework keener to the inflation targeting adopted in other emerging economies (Rajan, 2008).

The study in question is a drive to examine the behavior of weighted average call money rate ranging from 2008Q1 to 2016Q4.The weighted average call money market being second biggest financial variable in the financial market, the study aims to observe call money rates time series data and test via forecasting it through an integrated AR (Autoregressive) model. Based on the already given data, a one-step ahead (static) forecast on the 2008-2016 time series is conducted, keeping in mind the AR's assumptions. The data is tested for stationarity with Augmented Dickey – Fuller test, serial correlation through Breusch Godfrey LM Test. Then through ACF and PACF, the best AR model is chosen. The analysis is inclined towards the extent of volatility in the instrument over the years since the after effects of global financial crisis. The above is to test whether such uncertainty throws ruins in the way RBI assumes to work their way in the road to a stable economy.

As the empirical analysis rolls down through a uni-variate time series, the analysis deduces a much stabilised and secured monetary policy transmission mechanism since the adoption of the new monetary policy regime with the taking up of liquidity adjustment facility. Even after being hovered under the influence of Global Financial crisis, the economy performed much well comparatively in terms of price stability and financial capacities. The study will give insights to the behavior of the selected instruments and also provoked the reason behind calling of such a response. An attempt is also made to predict a static one-step ahead ex-ante forecast after the thorough rummage of the best ARMA (p, q) model.

1. Introduction

An efficient monetary policy transmission mechanism is a runway for the central bank to reach out to the ultimate real economy. It is the mechanism, where financial market being the primary nodule, that brings the assumed extent of effect. Money market which market brings about equilibrium between demand and supply of short term funds, bring about influences in the liquidity conditions in the economy's financial environment. It is the mechanism which brings short term demand and supply of funds equilibrium, provides a thruway to the central bank to influence the liquidity position in the financial system. But the degree of achievement of the RBI's observations outreach depends chiefly on the country's financial market development and the confines of market integration along the various lines of domestic financial market instruments. The added the integration, in all likelihood, further will be the potency of MPTMs.

The issues that are dealt are the following:

(1) The nature of market. (2) The direction and the speed of achievement of RBIs pre-determined observations (3) Responses to it in the following time upturns. Thus for a well-trodded response, central bank aims for a better liquidity conditions via appropriate money market functioning. Money market instruments (unsecured) promote market discipline when addressing to information asymmetry, due to continuous peer monitoring under exposure to non-payment. Such is the variable under study i.e. call money markets, currently being used by RBI as operating target in a monetary policy framework.

2. Review of Literature

2.1 Why money market instrument?

It's been more than a decade of substantial development in the Indian Money Market in various facets changing its course of monetary operations from direct quantity based instrument to indirect price based instrument; enhancing its transmission efficacy in consonance to international practice. Financial tools of short maturities up to 1 year are viewed as a good money stand-in. So is the money market short term instruments i.e. weighted average call money rate (WACMR). Setting an equilibrating mechanism of demand and supply of short term funds, it provides an interceding hand in influencing the country's financial system and consequently the real economy. Money market is the foremost and significant node in the chain of monetary policy transmission mechanism under sustaining disadvantage of limited control over long term interest rates. As the central bank directly sets the rates of this instrument, the changes signals financial market, whereby multifarious members of the financial system adjusts their rate of return, riding on the extent and effectualness of the sensitivity of the transmission mechanism which in turn depends on the development confines of a country's financial system.

Recording the consequential nature of the instruments, money markets progression is carefully monitored and catechized by central banks. Moreover, my observing the WACMR, dealing with un-collateralised loans, it promotes market discipline in sustenance against information asymmetry. After the global crisis, greater attention was given to assets liquidity stance which even led to operating call money rates as inter-bank rates. The instrument became more employable in the quest to reach improved monetary signaling, thus, a commanding role in the MPTMs along the lines of growing money markets and inter-linkages among them across the country. This has called for fine-tuning the existing monetary policy regime.

2.2 New operating procedure

With the recommendations of Narsimham Committee (1988) monetary policy operating procedure undergo some changes like introduction of Interim Liquidity Adjustment Facility (ILAF) which transformed into full LAF by 2000 beginning with periodical modifications and financial market developments[2]. It operated through fixed repo and reverse repo rate. It helped to evolve interest rate as an instrument of monetary transmission while operating policy rate dwindle between repo and reverse repo rate according to the liquidity conditions. This was a great drawback in the procedure where often call rate remain unbounded in times of financial stress.

The new operating procedure which began since 2011 kept intact the essence of the LAF framework but imbibed some new improvements negating the confusion arising from the altering policy rate and improving the signaling accuracy. The weighted average call money rate was explicitly apprehended as the operating target of monetary policy while repo rate being the only independently varying policy rate. The revised corridor was defined with a fixed width of 200 basis points. The repo rate was placed in the middle of the corridor, with the reverse repo rate 100 basis points below it and the MSF rate 100 basis points above it.

RBI's Internal Group examined the money market and brought in focus the highly skewed nature of the market where though with a high turnover in Indian money market, call money market lacked depth and brought volatility and financial scarcity in the market. This instrument is accepted as an inter-bank rate which suffices for the short term liquidity emergencies of banks arising from day to day operations.

The plotting of the call rate is as below

	CALLRATE
Mean	6.911759
Median	7.240000
Maximum	10.70000
Minimum	3.180000
Std. Dev.	1.787640
Skewness	-0.716876
Kurtosis	3.002236
Jarque-Bera	9.250421
Probability	0.009802
Sum	746.4700
Sum Sq. Dev.	341.9352
Observations	108

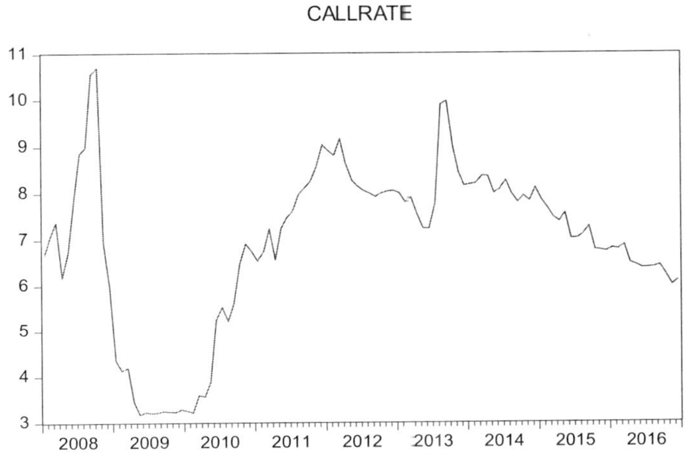

3. Methodology

The study in question is a drive to examine the behavior of weighted average call money rate ranging from 2008Q1 to 2016Q4 which also involves the monetary regime shift in respect of monetary policy operating procedure. The readings of various literatures divulge mostly that there is an increasing yet partial integration between monetary and financial market instruments but my study concentrates concisely over the period of aftermath of Global Financial crisis. As I am conducting an AR (Autoregressive) model on the uni-variate time series data for the forecasting, the various CLRM assumptions need to be fulfilled. The data is tested for stationarity with Augmented Dickey – Fuller test, serial correlation through Breusch Godfrey LM Test. Then through ACF and PACF, the best AR model is chosen. A one step-ahead static forecast is used for the time period 2008Q1-2016Q4.

4. Limitations

If we look over the period of study relevant to the aim of observations, the analysis confines to 2008-2016 tends to be small enough to decipher. Moreover, our cynosure is to test monetary policy decisions and its impact, via behavior of weighted average call money rate. This contracts the analysis to a partial equilibrium model where we a concerned with only the second largest money market instrument i.e. WACMR keeping other factors aside and constant. This makes it a short-run analysis exemplary of the financial market instruments behavior in a month-to-month basis.

4.1 Empirical Analysis

In a uni-variate time series modeling we will try to capture the dynamics of ACFs. We require Data Generating Process as we want to capture and determine the dynamic properties of Y_t. Moreover, real life time series data displays a larger variety of ACFs and any such DGPs will allow a restrictive pattern of ACFs so that we can fit ACF of real TS.

Therefore we find a combination of DGPs type and parameters that best matches the sample autocorrelation function and data stationarity properties with smallest residual variances to be judged by use of information criteria. The estimation and forecasting of uni-variate time series models is carried out through Box-Jenkins (B-J) methodology(1976)[3] which has following three steps:

- Identification
- Estimation
- Diagnostic

4.2 Stationarity

Thus, to get along with the properties we first check the stationarity of the series under consideration.

Null Hypothesis: CALLRATE has a unit root

Exogenous: Constant

Lag Length: 1 (Automatic - based on SIC, maxlag=12)

		t-Statistic	*Prob.**
Augmented Dickey-Fuller test statistic		-2.259977	0.1869
Test critical values:	1% level	-3.493129	
	5% level	-2.888932	
	10% level	-2.581453	

MacKinnon (1996) one-sided p-values.

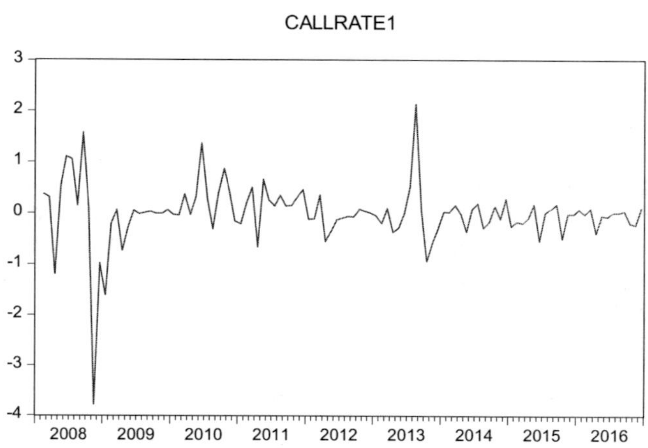

Null Hypothesis: D(CALLRATE) has a unit root
Exogenous: Constant
Lag Length: 0 (Automatic - based on SIC, maxlag=12)

		t-Statistic	*Prob.**
Augmented Dickey-Fuller test statistic		-7.968448	0.0000
Test critical values:	1% level	-3.493129	
	5% level	-2.888932	
	10% level	-2.581453	

*MacKinnon (1996) one-sided p-values.

Now that the data is stationary and we have, say, 15 years of data, we can use 1-10 years to learn about the rest 10-15 years. This will further lead us to forecasting.

4.3 Autocorrelation Function

Now, after testing for stationarity, we will observe the ACFs and its dynamics. With 36 lags, below is the result of a correlogram results.

lags	*AC*	*PAC*	*Q-stats*	*Prob.*
1	0.243	0.243	6.5211	0.011
2	-0.035	-0.100	6.6566	0.036
3	0.003	0.039	6.6573	0.084
4	-0.096	-0.118	7.6992	0.103
5	-0.078	-0.022	8.4027	0.135
6	-0.076	-0.071	9.0708	0.170
7	0.058	0.102	9.4681	0.221
8	-0.018	-0.086	9.5056	0.301
9	0.000	0.041	9.5056	0.392
10	-0.031	-0.081	9.6216	0.474
11	-0.032	0.018	9.7435	0.554
12	0.036	0.022	9.9012	0.625
13	-0.011	-0.013	9.9158	0.701
14	-0.034	-0.050	10.064	0.757
15	-0.010	0.013	10.078	0.815
16	-0.046	-0.067	10.352	0.848
17	-0.029	0.014	10.458	0.883
18	-0.077	-0.099	11.229	0.884
19	-0.161	-0.139	14.663	0.744
20	0.020	0.084	14.715	0.792
21	0.090	0.044	15.823	0.779
22	-0.105	-0.173	17.340	0.744
23	-0.100	-0.054	18.723	0.717
24	0.086	0.094	19.769	0.710

(Contd...)

25	0.059	0.015	20.268	0.733
26	-0.041	-0.049	20.510	0.767
27	0.022	-0.000	20.579	0.806
28	-0.041	-0.091	20.826	0.833
29	0.064	0.149	21.431	0.843
30	-0.076	-0.174	22.296	0.843
31	-0.105	-0.029	23.977	0.811
32	-0.019	-0.059	24.031	0.843
33	0.010	0.045	24.045	0.872
34	0.015	-0.040	24.083	0.896
35	-0.027	-0.011	24.205	0.915
36	-0.001	-0.116	24.205	0.933

After 1st lag, ACFs dies of quickly and so is the state of PACFs. Experiencing such behavior we can conclude that an ARMA (p, q) model will be a better choice. But our second task is to decide the value of p and q i.e. the number of lags. For that I have conducted a various model with different values of p and q, this will give us various AIC and SIC for variety of p and q lags. We will then go with the smallest AIC and SIC values for the best model. Below are the different AIC and SIC values:

Model (p,q)	*AIC*	*SIC*
ARMA(0,0)	1.8440	1.8689
ARMA(1,0)	1.8074	1.8576
ARMA(0,1)	1.7897	1.8397
ARMA(1,1)	1.7796	1.8550
ARMA(2,0)	1.8560	1.8813
ARMA(0,2)	1.8426	1.8676
ARMA(2,1)	1.7893	1.8398
ARMA(1,2)	1.7966	1.8469
ARMA(2,2)	1.8608	1.9113

On observing the above table, we get the smallest values of AIC and SIC for the ARMA (1, 1). We will run ARMA (1, 1) model and get the following results.

The generic linear function is in the form of $Y_t = f(Y_{t-1}, Y_{t-2}, \varepsilon_{t-1}, \varepsilon_{t-1}) + \varepsilon$. As the above series models both Y_{t-1} and ε_{t-1}, this is an ARMA type Data Generating Process.

Dependent Variable: CALLRATE1

Method: Least Squares

Date: 01/22/18 Time: 09:27

Sample (adjusted): 2008M03 2016M12

Included observations: 106 after adjustments

Convergence achieved after 15 iterations

MA Backcast: 2008M02

Variable	*Coefficient*	*Std. Error*	*t-Statistic*	*Prob.*
C	-0.009632	0.066488	-0.144870	0.8851
AR(1)	-0.518545	0.180540	-2.872190	0.0050
MA(1)	0.791411	0.130718	6.054326	0.0000
R-squared	0.102347	Mean dependent var		-0.009057
Adjusted R-squared	0.084916	S.D. dependent var		0.607332
S.E. of regression	0.580974	Akaike info criterion		1.779672
Sum squared resid	34.76568	Schwarz criterion		1.855053
Log likelihood	-91.32263	Hannan-Quinn criter.		1.810224
F-statistic	5.871805	Durbin-Watson stat		1.920076
Prob(F-statistic)	0.003847			
Inverted AR Roots	-.52			
Inverted MA Roots	-.79			

4.4 Stability

Through characteristics equation we will determine the hidden stability to check whether the ARMA process is stable or explosive via values of (λ) lambda.

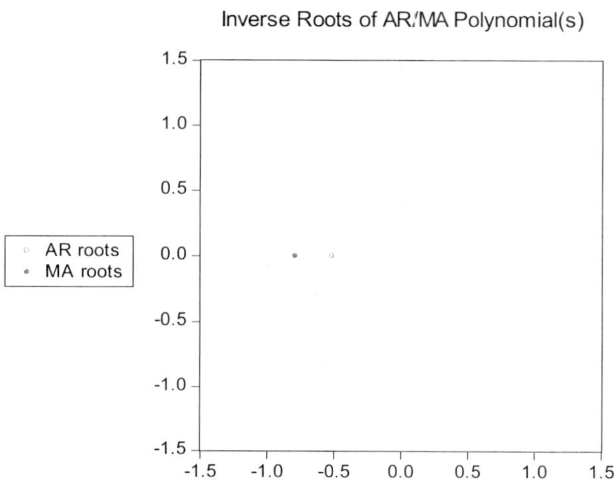

The ARMA process is stable if the absolute values of our solution (ë) are less than 1 or inside the unit circle. This is actually the case with our case and thus, we can state that out series has a stable process.

4.5 Residual Autocorrelation

Below is the graphical representation of residual ACFs.

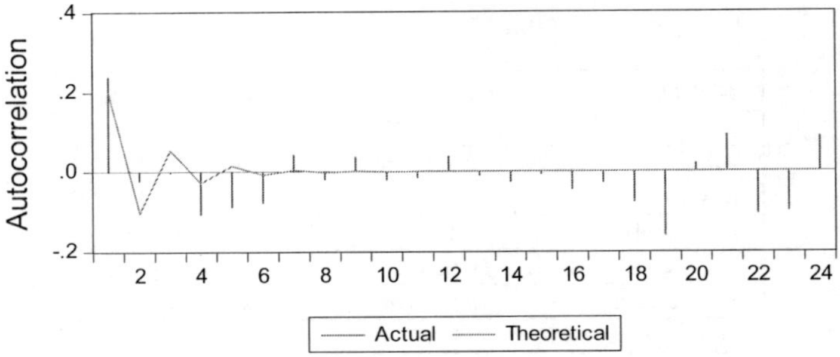

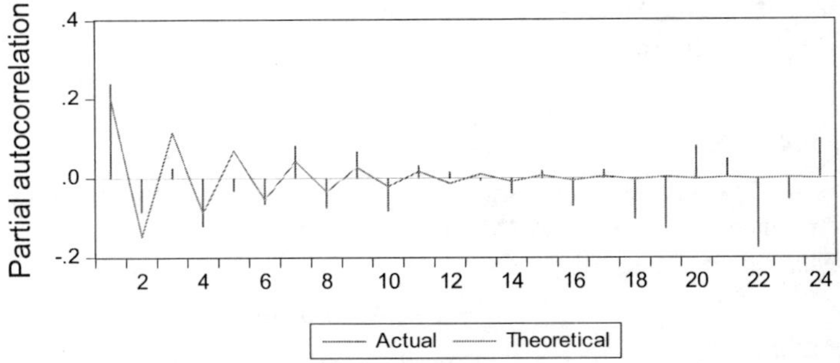

To test it, I have conducted an autocorrelation LM test.

Breusch-Godfrey Serial Correlation LM Test:

F-statistic	0.439173	Prob. F(2,101)	0.6458
Obs*R-squared	0.913255	Prob. Chi-Square(2)	0.6334

As the probability value greater than 0.05, our series is not auto correlated.

4.6Modelling

CALLRATE1 = - 0.00963215340584 + [AR (1) = - 0.518545275778, MA (1) = 0.79141140857]

ESTSMPL = "2008M03 2016M12"

@coef(1) = -0.0096322

@coef(2) = -0.5185453

@coef(3) = 0.7914114

Estimated S.E. = 0.5809740

4.7 Forecasting

While forecasting, I used static forecast method because through static method of forecasting, with each step ahead prediction, the previous forecasted value result is taken into account. Such facility is unavailable if we go with dynamic forecast method.

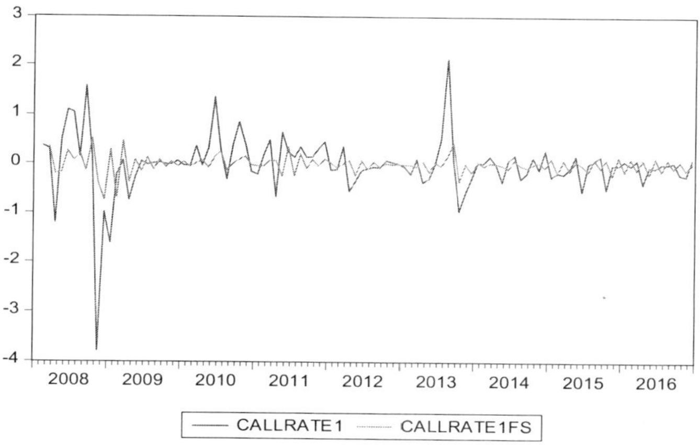

Looking at the forecasted data against the actual differenced data, we can see clearly that at the end quarter of 2008, there are disparate figures and same is the variation alongside 2013 Q4. Except these two highlighted time periods, all the other time period shows pretty good prediction by this ARMA (1, 1) model.

5. Conclusion

Such was the consequence of not going by the rules exemplified in the financial crisis which is ever more spreading outward. And the country diseased by such crisis is obviously trammeled with interruptions in the growth rates. Followed by the failing of the leading institutions, the entire financial market faced acute crisis. Albeit, the upheaval originated in the developed countries, it stretched its wings widely through various mechanisms[1]. The global financial crisis has not only affected the US but engulfed the whole world in total, depending upon the magnitude with which it was opened to the world economy globally.

India being integrated increasingly into the global economy, it was stroked by the spill-over impact of the financial crisis. The all told GDP growth rate almost downgraded from the high of 10.6 per cent of 2006Q4 to the low

5.8 per cent of 2008Q4, summed as an upshot both through the trade flows and financial channel. It has been recognised by the Prime Minister of India that *"...it is a time of exceptional difficulty for the world economy. The financial crisis, which a year ago, seemed to be localised in one part of the financial system in the US, has exploded into a systemic crisis, spreading through the highly interconnected financial markets of industrialised countries, and has had its effects on other markets also. It has choked normal credit channels, triggered a worldwide collapse in stock markets around the world. The real economy is clearly affected. ...Many have called it the most serious crisis since the Great Depression."* India feared downside risk primarily out of dreadful reversal of the capital flow. Banks stopped lending to one another suffused by ominous fear as trust vanished. In its dealing the lack of availability of dollars due to difficulty in raising funds abroad, it handicapped domestic financial system for additional credit, adding tension to domestic credit market. The universal de-leveraging process undertaken as a measure leading to cash flow reversal and simultaneous depreciation of rupee brought all-round fluctuations in the overnight money markets like WACMR (Patnaik and Shah (2010)).

The earliest indirect outreach of the global financial crisis was experienced by the money market, which tightened expeditiously, bringing about a sharp upshot of call money rates contributed by the US. This cannot be deciphered clearly through the model described earlier due to the untimely and unannounced financial turmoil.

But even after this, the banks of India had a far-less impact, given their strong capital-to-risk (weighted) assets ratio (CRAR), keeping in conscience the fact that it does not have any direct exposure to toxic assets outside and limited off-balance sheet activities. RBI maintained bounteous liquidity conditions in the form of variety of financial instruments though giving rise to inflationary conditions. RBI announced a slew of measures between 2008Q1 and 2009Q1 like slashing off the CRR from 9 % to 5% to foster credit expansion bridging way for increased money multiplier. As can be seen from the result graph, the adjustment of market interest rate in response to policy rates is not aligned but surely adjusts with a period of lag. The credit lending channel of monetary policy transmission mechanism, without doubt, is much faster than the transmission in other segments. This highlights the point that India's MPTMs has a differential impact along the different sections of financial market.

References

Reddy, Y. V., "Parameters of Monetary Policy in India", February 2002, RBI, at the 88th Annual Conference of The Indian Econometric Society at Madras School of Economics, Chennai.

Tobin, J., "A General Equilibrium Approach to Monetary Theory", February 1969, Journal of Money, Credit and Banking, Vol. No. 1, pp. 15-29.

Swamy, V. and Sreejesh, S., "Financial Instability, Uncertainty and Bank Lending Behavior." 2012, MPRA Paper No. 47518.

Kuttner, K. N. and Mosser, P. C., "The Monetary Transmission Mechanism: Some Answers and Further Questions", May 2002, FRBNY Economy Policy Review.

Bhattacharya, R., Patnaik, I. and Shah, A., "Monetary Policy Transmission in and Emerging Market Setting", January 2011, IMF Working Paper 11/5.

Bernanke, Ben S. and Blinder, Alan S., "Credit, Money and Aggregate Demand", May 1988, The American Economic Review, Volume 78, No. 2, PP. 435-439. Nath, G. and Ghose, P., "The Indian Call Money Market."

Deepak, M., "How does the Reserve Bank of India Conduct its Monetary Policy?", August 2011, Reserve Bank of India, delivered at the Indian Institute of Management (IIM), Lucknow.

Swamy, V. and Sreejesh, S.,"Financial Instability, Uncertainty and Bank Lending Behavior." 2012, MPRA Paper No. 47518.

Patimaporn, U. and Phumchusri, N., "A comparison study between time series model and ARIMA model for sales forecasting of distributor in plastic industry." February 2014, IOSR Journal of Engineering (IOSRJE), 2250-3021, ISSN (p): 2278-8719 Vol. 04, Issue 02 (February. 2014), pp 32-38.

Jarett., E. J. and Kyper E., "ARIMA modeling with intervention to forecast and Analyze Chinese stock prices." April 2011.

Mohanty, D.,"Global financial crisis and monetary policy response in India", Speech delivered at the 3rd ICRIER- Annual Conference in New Delhi, 12 November, (2009).

Gupta, A. S., "Sustaining Growth in Period of Global Downturn: A Case of India", United Nation Conference on Trade and Development, UNCTAD, (2010).

Rajya Sabha Secretariat, "Global Economic Crisis and its impact on India", Research Unit, June 2009.

Dullien, S., Kotte, D., Marquez, A. and Priewe, J., "The Financial and Economic Crisis of 2008-2009 and Developing Countries", UNCTAD Publication, December 2010.

Chapter - 7

Impact of Globalization on Economic Growth and Employment in India with Special reference to Kerala

Ruchi Bhalla, Naresh Mallik, Surendra Meher

Abstract

Focusing on the linkage between globalisation and its impact on employment and development Bhalla (2008) mentioned that advent of globalisation may result in increased displacement of unskilled or low skilled labour as demand would be more high-skilled centric. Considering it, in this paper, using secondary level data, we have tried to assess the impact of globalisation on economic growth and employment in India with special reference to Kerala. Our data analysis revealed that globalisation had a positive impact on economic growth but the effect on employment is a mixed one. From 1993 to 2000, 24.18 million jobs were added. According to Bhalla (2008) the number of unemployed in India rose from 3.98 million in 1973-74 to 9.15 by 1999-00 and further to 11.21 million by 2004-05. Against this backdrop, we have made an assessment of employment in most literate state of the country viz. Kerala. Data depicted that unemployment levels are highest in Kerala and its prime reason being lack in skills. Kerala has shown a very dismissal picture in terms of higher education enrolment which can be treated as a proxy for skill-based education. As per NSSO 68th around Kerala has only 21% persons enrolled in higher education in 2011. Another reason for high unemployment rates is low participation of females and lack of skill-based education among them. Thus, the study concludes that skill and employability of Indian labour force is quite low and therefore globalisation has proved not been very rewarding. Globalisation and free trade enables countries especially developing ones to utilise their abundant labour and increase flow of trade but this can be done only when labour force is well equipped to compete with world. In order to reap the benefits of globalisation, the study suggests expansion of higher education, reduction in gender disparities in education and promotion of skill development programmes.

1.1 Introduction

Globalisation is a process of gradual integration of countries or economies through unrestricted movement of goods, services and capital which also involves movement of knowledge, ideas, technology and culture. The economic reforms in India since 1991 are a major contributor to the process of globalisation so far as these reforms enabled the economy to progress in varied ways. Economic policy changes since globalisation have been done with the belief that globalisation would help in achieving accelerated economic growth in India and aid in creating employment opportunities by favouring labour-intensive growth. But, did the expected effects took place? The answer is partly 'yes'. The favourable effect of globalisation on economic growth probably did occur with a lag and was confined to certain sectors of the economy, while, in terms of inducing a labour-intensive growth path in India and creating immense employment opportunities, globalisation could not provide much. In this paper, we have worked on this aspect and tried to address two objectives. Primarily, we have assessed the impact of globalisation on growth and employment by analysing their respective trends from liberalisation period. Further, we explore the varied reasons behind adverse impact of globalisation on employment with special reference to Kerala.

1.2 Globalisation and its Impact on Economic Growth, Employment in India

Indian economy experienced a sharp rise in growth after globalisation. Meher & Bhalla (2017) in their study analysed the growth of Gross Domestic Product in various sectors of the country. It has been seen during early fifties, growth rate of GDP was merely 2 to 3 per cent. The GDP growth did not pick up even during sixties and seventies in their early years. However, during the period of 1990s growth rate as well as GDP in all the sectors has seen a sharp increase due to the implementation of globalisation. Growth rate of the economy reached a peak of 8 per cent during 1999-00 and 8.9 per cent in 2010-11. But, the benefits of globalisation are reaped more by service sectors such as Financing, Insurance, real estate and business services. Focusing on employment data, it is revealed that (as estimated by Behera 2012) from 1993-94 to 1999-00 24.18 million jobs were added and highest recorded from 1999-00 to 2004-05 where 59.22 million jobs were added.

However, in the subsequent NSS periods, net job addition is only 0.55 million. Consequently, employment growth was highest during the period 1999-00 to 2004-05 i.e. it grew at the rate of 2.81 per cent and only 0.02 per cent from the period 2004-05 to 2009-10 at the all India level. This period experienced a negative growth in employment for both rural female and urban female category. Economic survey 2014-15 noted that annual compound growth of employment during 1999-00 to 2004-05 was 2.8 per cent which declined to

0.5 per cent during the period 2004-05 to 2011-12. It is further noted that during period 2009-10 to 2011-12 13.9 million workforce were added which did not keep pace with the increase in labour force i.e. 14.9 million during same phase. Our study further manifested that the quality of employment in post globalisation era changed rapidly. It could be seen that as on 2009-10 more than 90 per cent workers constituted self -employed and causal workers in rural areas. Out of them more than 50 per cent workers were self -employed. During 68th round i.e. in 2011-12, there appears to be some rise in the proportion of regular workers. The scenario is almost same for rural female as well, but proportion of regular female workers is somewhat less than male workers. In urban area, however, more than 40 per cent workers happened to be regular workers and the proportion of causal labour is less than rural areas.

During the latest NSS round, the percentage of self -employed has increased in both rural as well as urban areas. It may be asserted that percentage of self -employed workers have increased due to the scope arises out of the integration of the economies. As the generation of open trade and increased in exports were facilitated the casual labours saw the remunerative effect of it. Nevertheless, skill and employability of Indian labour force is quite low and it may not be expected that self-employment so created in the advent of globalisation would be so remunerative. A study by Jha (2009) reveals that only 5.06 per cent are vocationally trained in total labour force in India compared to 98.8 per cent in Korea Republic, 75.33 in Germany 78.11 per cent in Canada.

The impact of globalisation was also seen in the front of employment and poverty. The period from 1999-00 to 2004-05 seen as aboom for employment growth, but thereafter it declined significantly. Some scholars found reduction in employment elasticity with respect to output (Papola 2012, Behera 2012, Sharma 2007). It has been established that the process of globalisation replaced millions of workers with new technology. Globalisation has compelled employers to become efficient in order to sustain competition. As a result, cost reduction techniques were being followed by the employers leading to use of more capital and labour-saving technology. People with adequate skills and training found themselves absorbed in lucrative service sector. Globalisation has further made a clear-cut divide between organised and unorganised sector. Most of the workers took shelter in the informal sector due to structural adjustment programmes initiated and employers found it suitable to use technology to make them competitive resulted in displacement of workers. Poverty ratio also appears to decline during post globalisation. But in absolute terms millions of populations are still in the clutches of poverty. Workers in informal sector and other causal workers are found to be more vulnerable than workers in formal sector. Therefore, it is high time to include the poor and informal workers in the process of globalisation. An integrated policy is required to create adequate employment opportunities to take the advantage of globalisation. Employment generation schemes specially 'gainful self-employment' and wage employment programme with due emphasis on rural asset building must be continued. Skill development training for the unemployed is essential to find gainful employment. Further, a host of social security schemes need to be initiated for the poor and informal workers.

1.3 Globalisation and its impact on Kerala

For the purpose of further scrutinizing the impact of globalisation on Indian economy we focussed our study on the most developed state in terms of social development. The famed Kerala model is all about social sector development. Till 2001, Kerala focused only upon the first-generation development i.e. attaining a decent standard of living and ignored the employment and growth aspect. Due to this it has largely suffered from unemployment and low per capita income (Human Development Report, 2005).

According to the reports of CDS, 1975, Kerala model has always given a higher priority to the development of people in terms of education and health while growth perspective of development has been considered secondary. It can be seen through Table 7.1 that NSDP has increased during 2001 and 2011 at all India level as well as in Kerala. But, in Kerala this rise is majorly due to rise in service sector share. The era of globalisation is said to be beneficial for the Indian economy specially in terms of employment. The question whether the era has been beneficial for the most prosperous state or not is answered in this paper. Kerala is one state in the country, which had to suffer a lot as a result of the process of integration of economy with the international market place much before the advent of globalisation. In fact, for Kerala, globalisation started the moment the colonial raiders set foot on its soil, inaugurating the western conquest of India.

Table 7.1: Per capita Net State Domestic Product at constant prices (in Rupees)

	(1993-94)	*(2004-05)*	*(2011-12)*
Kerala	7838	32351	52808
India	7690	24143	38048

Source- RBI, Handbook of Business Statistics, 2017.

Subhramanya et.al (1995) mentioned that even though domestic product has increased material base has declined to a large extent. This pattern of growth has posed several employment challenges in the state. Overall, Kerala has tried to accelerate its per capita income but the approach towards expansion is bit questionable. Deeper analysis of the economic profile of Kerala reveals that the state is "human development lopsided". Thus, considering literacy levels in this context table 7.2 shows that Kerala has exceeded the national average level in case of literacy rates.

Table 7.2: Literacy rates

	1991			*2001*			*2011*		
	Female	*Male*	*Persons*	*Female*	*Male*	*Persons*	*Female*	*Male*	*Persons*
Kerala	86.1	93.6	89.8	87.9	94.2	90.9	92.1	96.1	94
India	39.3	64.1	52.2	53.7	75.3	64.8	65.5	82.1	74.0

Source- Census,1991, 2001 and 2011.

Focusing on the education aspect, we assess the enrolment ratios in higher education (table 7.3) and data reveals that overall enrolment in Kerala (23.1) is higher than the national share of 20.4 per cent as per 2011-12. Still, enrolment ratio's in higher education in Kerala is low, which is a serious matter of concern and a cause for high unemployment rates in the state.

Table 7.3: Enrolment ratio in Higher Education

STATES	*2011-12*			*2004-05*		
	Male	*Female*	*Total*	*Male*	*Female*	*Total*
Kerala	19.3	26.9	23.1	8.15	9.96	9.08
All India	21.6	18.9	20.4	11.58	8.17	9.97

Source: All India Survey on Higher Education 2011-12, 2004-05.

With higher opportunities in terms of certain basic capabilities, access to school's education the state has made phenomenal progress in human capital formation (CDS-UN, undated). Though human development is one way through which an economy can attain development but this would reap benefits only when implemented in an effective way. In Kerala, these high levels of education have not been matched by employment opportunities and have thus resulted in educated unemployment. Table 7.4 reveals that unemployment rates are the highest in Kerala for both rural and urban labour force.

Table 7.4: Unemployment rates (per1000) according to current weekly status

	68th round		*61st round*		*50th round*	
	Rural (persons)	***Urban (persons)***	***Rural (persons)***	***Urban (persons)***	***Rural (persons)***	***Urban (persons)***
Kerala	107	85	156	180	89	129
India	20	24	82	83	29	56

Source: NSSO: 68th, 61, 50th round.

Table 7.5: Technical Education and Unemployment Rates in India

State	% enrolment in Diploma Courses 2011			Unemployment rate as per 68th round		
	Male	Female	Total	Male	Female	Total
Kerala	15.48	26.79	21.16	41	232	98
India	19.57	9.33	14.68	26	39	29

*Source** All Indian Survey on Higher Education 2011-12

NSSO 68th round on Employment and Unemployment Rates

Technical education includes diploma courses viz certificate courses, polytechnics, ITI's, integrated courses. Imparting technical and vocational education has been the key focus of Eleventh and Twelfth Five Year Plan. The shifting focus of the government from general education to skill education is due to the low level of quality education among Indian students. The above table depicts the position of technical education in Indian states. It specifies the enrolment rate of persons in the age group of 15-29 years. The All India level specifies a very dismissal picture.

As per AISHE only 14% of people got enrolled in diplomas. Figures of female are very depressing only 9% got enrolled in 2011. Kerala which is always appreciated for its general education level has not been able to enrol its population in skill level courses. Only 20% of total population got enrolled in diplomas courses with females again heading with 26% than males. Technical education is a form of higher education and ensuring quality education requires good enrolment in vocational education. Investment in technical education also helps to cure many social evils like that of unemployment, poverty etc. The major drawback in the development of Indian economy is the present of unemployment. One cause of unemployment is the demand and supply gap in the present labour force. At present India is suffering from educated unemployed. One cause of unemployment is the demand and supply gap in the present labour force. At present India is suffering from educated unemployed. As per the Census report 2011 Ten million Indians with graduate, post-graduate and technical degrees were looking for work, meaning that 15% of all Indians with the highest levels of education were seeking job as of 2011(Economic Survey 2015). According to NSSO 68th unemployment rate is around 30% with Kerala having the highest unemployment rate.

Overall, India's unemployment rate grew from 6.8 per cent in 2001 to 9.6 per cent in 2011, based on official Census data. The problem India is facing is the lack of skill education that imparts the demand of white collared jobs. Placing cherry on the top of India's unemployment is the state which is appreciated for its human development model. According to the Census 2011, Kerala is on the top of unemployment rates. More than 30% of the total population is educated unemployed. Imparting education is not the only way of development. Imparting quality education and skilling the masses is one of the remedy to get rid of this serious social evil. The problem with Kerala is of educated unemployment suffering from lack of skill education. Kerala has the highest rate of graduate unemployed at over 30% persons unable to fetch jobs. Considering, gender statistics, literature and data suggests that in Kerala females who are highly qualified are mostly unemployed. The unemployment rates for females according to NSSO 68th round was 232 which is highest among all the states. Now, the question arises if females are highly qualified then why they are not able to fetch jobs, one of its reasons being lack of technical and vocational education.

As per the recent Labour Survey on Labour Force Participation Rate, Kerala women have one of the lowest participation rates in India. Only 23% of women are employed and is economically active. The reason of the low participation is the faulty education system that prevails in the state of Kerala, predominance of arts and science colleges with conventional courses, huge fees charged in the self- financing colleges, lack of professional colleges in the government sector, gender discrimination etc (Anandan and Anchayil, 2015). According to the Hindu Report on unemployment female's unemployment rate is high due to the lack of skills which is required in private companies.

Another reason of high rate of unemployment can be Kerala's low per capita NSDP. Though per capita in Kerala on an average is 7.4 which is quite low as compared to other states. Kerala cannot be placed in the 'virtuous cycle' of development as its Human Development indicators have not translated into good economic growth numbers

1.4: District wise Literacy and Unemployment in Kerala

In this section, literacy and unemployment rates of the districts are studied. As per the data the most literate state of the state has the highest unemployment rate.

Micro analysing the unemployment trends, we have considered district wise data on literacy rates and unemployment rates. From the table 7.6, we may conclude that globalisation has not impacted employment favourably as unemployment rates are significantly higher even in the most literate state of the country. This is primarily due to lack of skills in our population which is nowadays the need of the hour. All districts have high unemployment rates (depicted in Table 7.5) Kannur having the highest (16.1 percent) followed by Alappazuha (15.6 percent), Kottayam (14.2 percent) and Kasaragod (12.6 percent) as of 2011.

Table 7.6: District wise Literacy rate, Growth rate and Unemployment rate in Kerala

Districts	*Literacy rate 2001-02*	*Growth rate 2001-02*	*Unemploy-ment rate 2001*	*Literacy rate 2011-12*	*Growth rate 2011-12*	*Unemploy-ment rate 2011*
Alappuzha	93.4	6.38	21.7	95.7	8.43	15.6
Ernakulam	93.2	6.74	24.5	95.9	6.98	9.3
Idukki	88.7	9.18	9.6	92	2.95	8.3
Kannur	92.6	6.7	25.5	95.1	8.76	16.1
Kasaragod	84.6	9.28	27.7	90.1	10.37	12.6
Kollam	91.2	9.35	15	94.1	7.5	10.9
Kottayam	95.8	6.85	16.5	97.2	7.39	14.2
Kozhikode	92.2	8.78	13.1	95.1	8.02	6.9
Malappuram	89.4	6.61	12.3	93.6	7.3	6.3
Palakkad	84.3	7.46	11.2	89.3	8.42	7.9
Pathanamthitta	94.8	9.49	22.9	96.5	8.37	12.2
Thiruvananthapuram	89.3	8.69	34.3	93	9.63	11.4
Thrissur	92.3	7.98	10.4	95.1	8.55	9.9
Wayanad	85.2	-15.11	13.2	89	6.93	5.7

Source: Kerala economic review (various issues)

A simple correlation technique was performed for the two periods i.e. 2001 and 2011 depicted in Table 7.7 and 7.8. The analysis depicts that there is positive relationship between literacy rate and unemployment rate. According to the analysis the more the people are literate the more the unemployment rate. This relationship shows that globalisation has not been able to increase the employment opportunities for the people of Kerala. The literate person is not able to find the appropriate job for himself. Various scholars have specified that globalisation has not been able to increase the base for formal employment.

Table 7.7: Correlation Matrix of Literacy rates and unemployment rates in Kerala (2001)

	Literacy rate2001	*Unemployment rate 2001*
Literacy rate 2001	1.000	
Unemployment rate 2011	0.122	1.000

Table 7.8: Correlation Matrix of Literacy rates and Unemployment rates in Kerala (2011)

	Literacy rate2001	*Unemployment rate 2001*
Literacy rate2011	1.000	
Unemployment rate 2011	0.492	1.000

Overall, the share of total workers in Kerala has not increased to a greater extent and the growth rate at national level is higher (shown in table 7.9). The era of pre-globalisation period (1987-88) to the beginning of the globalisation has witnessed a growth rate of just 3.39 and 1.82 in India and Kerala respectively. The period after the reforms witnessed a negative growth till 2004-05 in Kerala economy while just 2% growth rate was witnessed in the overall economy. The reason behind the low participation rate specially among the females in Kerala economy is due to the more importance given to human development indicators and low focus on the skill-based knowledge and also the lack of industries setting up in the economy (T.P Srinivasan 2001). The overall growth rate for the period 1987-88-2011-12 shows a negative participation of people in Kerala as well as India.

Table 7.9: Growth rate of Total Workers in Kerala and India

	1987-94	*1994-2000*	*2000-2005*	*2005-2011*	*1987-2011*
Male (Kerala)	2.76	12.45	0.38	0.93	4.53
India	3.54	2.28	1.69	9.66	5.09
Female (Kerala)	-0.14	0.62	-1.63	1.41	0.19
India	3.10	1.43	2.80	-1.43	1.46
Persons	1.82	-7.75	-2.57	2.64	-1.53
India	3.39	2.00	2.10	-8.71	-0.95

*Source**NSSO (Various rounds).

For further analysing the employment trends, we have studied the occupational structure of Kerala. Table 7.10 divulge that in Kerala the share of other workers is highest with 73.6 per cent in 2001 and 80.50 per cent in 2011.Other workers are followed by Agricultural labourers (11.39 percent), Cultivators (5.77 percent) and 2.35 per cent Household industry workers in 2011.

Table 7.10: Occupational Structure

	2001				**2011**			
	Culti-vators	**Agri-cultural labours**	**Household industry worker**	**Other workers**	**Culti-vators**	**Agri-cultural labours**	**Household industry workers**	**Other workers**
Kerala	7.0	15.8	3.6	73.6	5.77	11.39	2.35	80.50
India	31.7	26.5	4.2	37.6	24.6	30.0	3.8	41.6

Source- Census 2001 and 2011.

1.5: Concluding Remarks

The study concludes that skill and employability of Indian labour force is quite low and therefore globalisation has proved not to be very rewarding.

Globalisation and free trade enables countries especially developing ones to utilise their abundant labour and increase flow of trade but this can be done only when labour force is well equipped to compete with the world. From the case of Kerala state, we may also state that not mere increasing literacy levels would help in people to get employment as new-age jobs demand high skills. Thus, in order to reap the benefits of globalisation, the study suggests expansion of higher education, reduction in gender disparities in education and promotion of skill development programmes.

References

Bhalla G.S (2008). 'Globalisation and Employment Trends in India'. *The Indian Journal of Labour Economics.*(Vol. 51. No.1); pp. 1-23.

Bhagwati Jagdish (2001): 'Growth, Poverty and reforms', *Economic and Political weekly*, March 10, 2010; pp. 843-847.

Balakrishnana P (2010), '*Economic Growth in India: History and Prospect*, New Delhi: Oxford University Press.

Behera, Deepak Kumar (2012): 'Economic Growth and Employment Trends in India, 1983-2010: What does the Latest Employment Data Reveal'? *Indian Journal of Labour Economics*, (Vol. 55 No.2, 2012); pp. 265-279.

Bentley, J. H. (1999). Asia in World History. Education About Asia 4, (pp. 5-9).

Chandrasekhar, C P, Jayati Ghosh (2007) 'Recent Employment Trends in India and China: An Unfortunate Convergence'? Social Scientist, (Vol. 35, No. ¾ Mar. - Apr., 2007); pp. 19-46

Dasgupta.S; Singh.A (2007). 'Manufacturing, Services and Premature Deindustrialisation in Developing Countries: A Kaldorian Analysis in Mavrotas, George and Shorrocks, Anthony (eds.), Advancing Development: Core Themes in Global Economics, Palgrave MacMillan in association with the United Nations University', World Institute for Development Economics Research (WIDER); pp. 435-456.

Ezell.S; Atinson.S (2014).'The Indian Economy at a Crossroads' (Available at: http://www2.itif.org/2014-indian-economy-at-crossroads.pdf)

Economic Survey, Ministry of Finance, Department of Economic Affairs, Economic Division, Government of India (2015)

Feenstra, Robert C. (2004). "The Heckscher–Ohlin Model". 'Advanced International Trade: Theory and Evidence', *Princeton University Press*; pp. 31–63.

Frank, A. G. (1998). 'Reorient: Global Economy in the Asian Age'. Berkeley A: *University of California Press*.

Goldar.B.N. N (2014). 'Globalisation, Growth and Employment in the Organised Sector of the Indian Economy'. Working Paper WP 06/2014.*Institute for Human Development, 2014* ISBN: 978-81-88315-44-4.

Himanshu (2007). 'Recent trends in Poverty and Inequality: Some Preliminary Results', *Economic and Political Weekly*, February 10; pp. 497-531.

ILO (2009). 'Towards an Employment Strategy for India' (Available at: http://www.ilo.org)

ILO (1999).'Decent Work.International Labour Organisation'. Geneva

M.McCartney (2009). 'Political Economy, Growth and Liberalisation in India, 1991-2008 Routledge'.

Jha Praveen (2009). 'The Well Being of Labour in Contemporary Indian Economy: What's Active Labour Market got to do with it? Employment Sector', Employment Working Paper No.39, *ILO*

Kannan, K.P, and G. Raveendran (2009). 'Growth Sans Employment: A Quarter Century of Jobless Growth in India's Organised Manufacturing'. *Economic and Political Weekly*, (Vol. 44, No. 10 Mar. 7 – 13); pp. 80-91.

Kevin H. O' Rourke and Jeffrey G. Williamson (2002) 'When did Globalisation Begin?' *European Review of Economic History*, Vol. 6, (No. 1, April); pp. 23-50, Oxford University Press.

Mahendra Dev (2000). 'S Economic Liberalisation and Employment in South Asia: II', *Economic and Political Weekly*, (Vol. 35 No. 3 Jan. 15-21); pp. 135-146.

NCEUS (2007). Report on Conditions of Work and Promotion of Livelihoods in the Unorganised Sector. Ministry of Small Scale Industries.Government of India New Delhi.

NSSO (2006).Employment and Unemployment Situation in India 2004-05. Report No. 515(61/10/1)

NSSO (2014) Employment and Unemployment Situation in India July 2011-June 2012, NSS Report No. 554(68/10/1)

Papola, T S (2012); 'Employment Growth in the Post Reform Period, Keynote Paper on the Theme Employment in the Post-Reform India', *54th Annual Conference of the Indian Society of Labour Economics*- 20-22 December, 2012, Varanasi.

Nayyar Deepak (2006).'Globalisation, History and Development: A Tale of two Centuries *'Cambridge Journal of Economics*, (Vol. 30, No. 1, January), Oxford University Press.

Stiglitz, Joseph E. 'Globalisation and Its Discontents. New York: W.W. Norton, 2002. Print.

Shyam Sundar, K.R., (2010). 'Emerging Trends in Employment Relations in India', *Indian Journal of Industrial Relations,* (Vol. 45, April, No. 4), Changing International Industrial Relations.

Sharma, Alakh N: (2006). 'Flexibility, Employment and Labour Market Reforms in India', *Economic and Political Weekly*, May 27, 2006; pp. 2078-2085.

Roy Sumit (1997). 'Globalisation, Structural Change and Poverty: Some Conceptual and Policy Issues', *Economic and Political Weekly*, (Vol. 32, No. 33/34 Aug. 16-29); pp. 2117-2135.

Toye, John and Richard Toye (2003). 'The Origins and Interpretation of the Prebisch-Singer Thesis *'History of Political Economy*, (Volume 35, Number 3); pp. 437-467, Duke University Press.

Part - II
Globalisation Agriculture and Environment

Chapter - 8

Globalization and Sustainable Agriculture in India

Achiransu Acharyya

1. Introduction

In the last four decades there has been a radical restructuring of the scope and character of the production and distribution of agricultural products under globalisation. The characteristics of globalisation include the worldwide spread of modern technologies of production, particularly including in communications but also into farming, the agricultural supply sector and food processing. This involves money, production and trade as part of what has been termed 'the borderless world', and the networking of virtually all the world's economies, fostering ever-closer functional integration in world markets.

Globalisation has resulted in the rapid growth of world trade, internationalisation of production by multinational corporations and declining information and communications costs. The potential trade benefits for agriculture arise from the possibility of direct increased exposure of agriculture to international competition, the ability to access global markets and specialize in areas of comparative advantage which could yield high gains for the sector. Also, there are indirect effects of increased international trade on the growth of non-agricultural sectors changing the domestic demand for agricultural goods both quantitatively and qualitatively (Pingali and Khwaja, 2004). An often unrecognised consequence of globalisation is change in lifestyle including diets, particularly among the urban middle class, as a result of increased global inter-connectedness through travel and communications. Consumers in large, urban centres are more exposed to non-traditional foods as a result of their access to food retail outlets and marketing campaigns (Reardon, Timmer, et al., 2003). Large urban markets create the scope for the establishment of large supermarket chains, and they attract foreign investments and advertising from global corporations. Non-traditional foods are more accessible as a result of trade liberalisation and declining costs of transportation and communication (Chopra, Galbraith and Darnton-Hill, 2002).

A study on agriculture towards the year 2015 to 2030 by Food and Agricultural Organisation (FAO) indicates that the trends in international trade of foodstuffs, which have seen developing countries turn from net exporters to net importers of food commodities, are expected to continue in the future (FAO, 2002). In the 1960s, developing countries as a whole had an overall agricultural trade surplus of US$6.7 billion, but this gradually disappeared so that by the end of the 1990s trade was broadly in balance, with periodic minor surpluses and deficits. In the case of the least developed countries (LDCs) the deficit was much more pronounced, by end of the 1990s, agricultural imports were more than double their exports (FAO, 2004a). The outlook to 2030 suggests that the agricultural trade deficit of developing countries will widen markedly, reaching an overall net import level of US$31 billion (FAO, 2002).

Although globalisation has offered enormous opportunities it has also led to greater vulnerability of communities that are not adequately prepared to face its challenges. It has created turbulence, uncertainty, competitiveness, need for adaptation to change and timely adoption and absorption of technologies. Globalisation has affected the poor, particularly the rural people and small farmers having small land holdings. Moreover many of them have no access to information and other facilities that can help in enhancement of participation in economic development, improvement in productivity, income and living conditions.

Greater intensification of agriculture would be required in future to meet the demands generated by the growing population and increasing incomes. This will lead to significant environmental impacts like depletion of surface and underground fresh water resources, deterioration of soil and water quality, soil erosion, loss of biodiversity and even climate change.

Under the above circumstances, it is important to understand, especially for a country like India having the largest population in the world, how to adapt itself to a sustainable form of agricultural development for the future without harming the environment as also the future generation. Section 2 of this chapter tries to give a general and broad view of Indian agriculture and the problems faced by the sector. The rest of the sections discuss the various policies and technologies that can be used for a sustainable and environment friendly agricultural development taking advantage of globalisation and development of new technologies.

2. Agriculture in India: issues and challenges

So far as agricultural development in India is concerned it is very unique as compared to other countries. The most advanced as well as the most primitive kind of agricultural technologies are practiced here. On the one hand the most modern agricultural implements such as tractors and harvesting combines are used, on the other hand there are millions of farmers using bullock carts and ploughs. Diversity of soil and climatic conditions exist in the country leading to diversity of plant species and varieties of crops.

The major problems of Indian agriculture are fragmented farm lands, monsoon dependent irrigation in several areas, disruptive power-supply, increasing cost of farm inputs, non-availability of international quality seeds, exploitation of poor and illiterate farmers by intermediaries and lending institutions, lack of adequate information pertaining to what can be most useful and relevant in a given area and situation. Small farm holdings are one of the barriers to modernisation and automation of agricultural farms. There is an enormous fluctuation in the prices of agricultural commodities.

The increasing cost of agricultural inputs and comparatively low cost of agricultural products in the international market is creating a crisis situation for Indian agriculture. For instance it is cheaper to buy wheat from the international market than buy it from the Indian market. The constantly growing input cost of agriculture is affecting the small farmers and their families. The small farmers are increasingly under debt and under stress.

Moreover the growth in GDP over the last few years has not been reflective in the agricultural sector. Hence, the slow growth of agriculture remains a weak link in the overall Indian economy. Figure 1 uses the new gross domestic product (GDP) series, which was launched in January 2015, to plot the GDP growth and the growth of agriculture (including forestry and fishery), over the last few years. Figure 8.1 tells us very clearly that the overall GDP growth is much faster than the growth in agriculture on the whole.

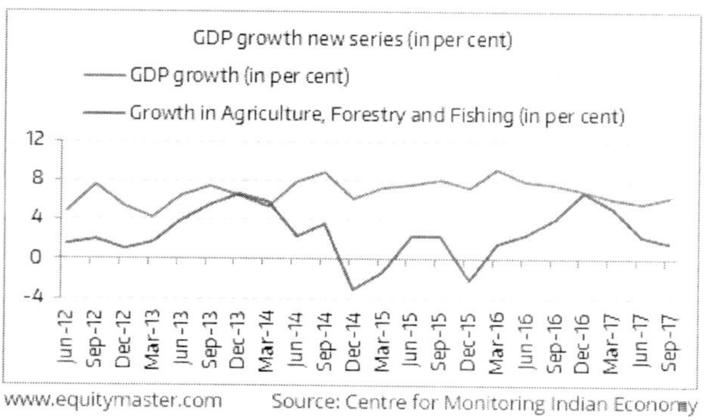

Figure 8.1. Growth of Agriculture with respect to GDP (new series)

The trouble is that the new GDP series has data starting from only June 2011. Given this, we have growth rates from June 2012 onwards. In order to look at periods before June 2012, we need to use the old GDP series. Figure 8.2 plots the overall GDP growth along with the growth in agriculture, forestry and fishing from 1999 to 2014.

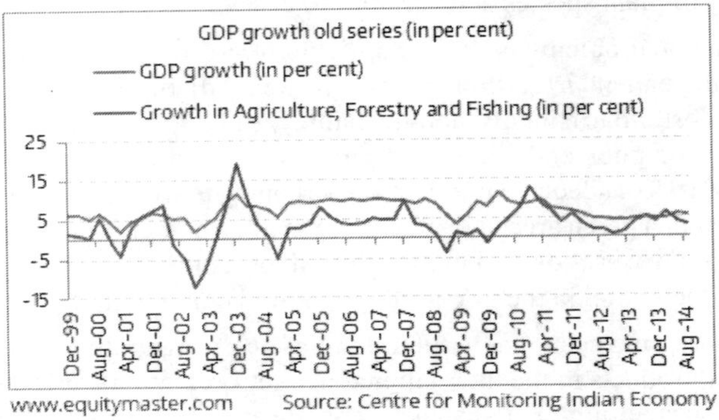

Figure 8.2: GDP growth (old series)

Figure 8.2 like Figure 8.1 clearly tells us that even as per the old GDP series, the GDP growth as a whole was much faster than the growth in agriculture, forestry and fishing. Of course, there were occasions (though not many) where the overall GDP growth was slower than growth in agriculture. The result of this slower growth has been the size of agriculture as a part of the overall economy has been shrinking over the years. This becomes clear from Figures 8.3 and 8.4. Figure 8.3 uses the new GDP series data, whereas Figure 8.4 uses, the old GDP series data.

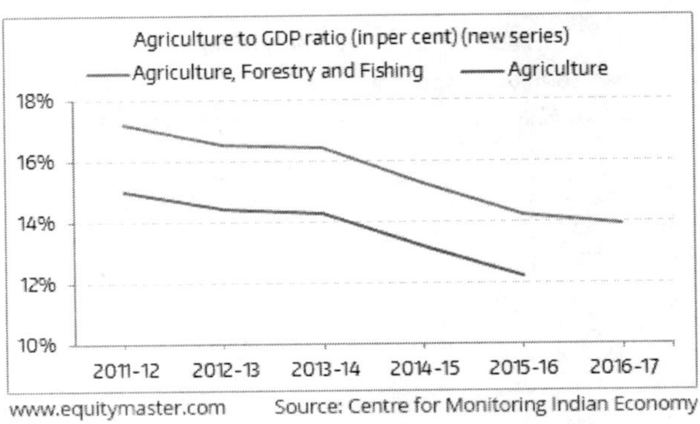

Figure 8.3. Agriculture to GDP ratio compared to overall GDP in India (new series)

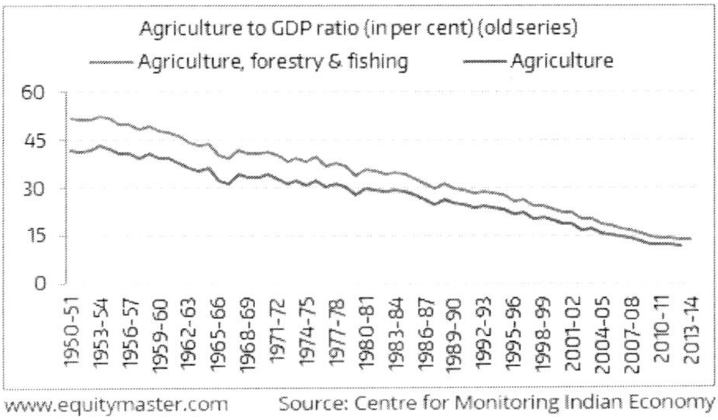

Figure 8.4. Agriculture to GDP ratio compared to overall GDP in India (new series)

What Figures 8.3 and 8.4 tell us very clearly is that the size of agriculture as a part of the overall economy (measured by the GDP) has shrunk rapidly over the years. This has happened because the overall GDP (i.e. the non-agriculture part of the economy) has grown at a faster rate.

As can be seen from Figure 8.4, in 1950-1951, agriculture formed more than 40 per cent of the economy. By now it is down to 12 per cent. This has happened as the average land holding on which farming is carried out has fallen over the years, as land has been divided across generations. The average size of the land farmed by the Indian farmer has fallen over the decades and in 2010-2011, the last time the agriculture census was carried out, stood at 1.16 hectares. In 1970-1971 it had stood at 2.82 hectares. This fall in farm size has made farming in many parts of the country, an unviable activity, leading to the size of agriculture as a part of the economy becoming smaller and smaller.

Table 8.1. Share of agriculture in rural economic output and employment over the years

Year	*Agriculture's share in the rural economic output (in per cent)*	*Year*	*Share in rural employment (in per cent)*
1970-1971	72.4	1972-1973	85.5
1980-1981	64.4	1983	83.6
1993-1994	57.0	1993-1994	78.4
1999-2000	51.4	1999-2000	76.3
2004-2005	38.9	2004-2005	72.6
2011-2012	39.2	2011-2012	64.1

Source: Changing Structure of Rural Economy of India Implications for Employment and Growth, Ramesh Chand, S. K Srivastava and Jaspal Singh, Discussion Paper, NITI Aayog, December 2017.

The trouble is that agriculture still employs a large portion of the workforce. While, its contribution to the overall economy has come down, a large number of people continue to remain dependent on income from agriculture as shown in Table 8.1.

As can be seen from Table 8.1 above, the share of agriculture in the rural economy has fallen from 72.4 per cent to 39.2 per cent, over the four-decade period between 1970-1971 and 2011-2012. During the same period, the proportion of people dependent on agriculture as a mode of employment has not come down at the same rate.

In 1972-1973, the share of agriculture in rural employment was 85.5 per cent. This came down to 64.1 per cent in 2011-2012. So, 64.1 per cent of the rural workforce produced 39.2 per cent of the rural economic output in 2011-2012. Hence, agriculture has many more people dependent on it, than is economically feasible.

It is clear from Table 8.1 that between 2004-2005 and 2011-2012, the proportion of people dependent on agriculture as employment has come down. This is a trend that would have continued. Even with that many more people continue to be dependent on agriculture than is economically feasible.

Due to low growth in agriculture, Indian agriculture is facing the critical challenge of feeding an escalating human population (i.e. 1.25 billion) under increasingly declining soil quality and changing climatic conditions. Moreover, the scope to increase the area of cultivation is limited. For example, the Indo-Gangetic plains have the most fertile soil in India and share around 13% of the total agricultural area of the country. However, it is undergoing severe land degradation due to soil erosion and nutrient depletion. Also, natural resources are already under severe pressure in India. India supports 18% of the human and 15% of livestock population of the world with only 2.2% of the world's geographical area, where only 46% of the land is cultivable.

Given that, agriculture in India is prominently monsoon-dependent, the vulnerability of agriculture has gone up due to erratic rainfall. Additionally, Indian agriculture is also threatened by shifting of farmers toward cash crop cultivation, withdrawal from agriculture (due to growing input cost and production insecurity under weather instability) and growing preference for meat consumption. Agriculture is the predominant mean of livelihood for about 60% of Indian population. Declining efficiency of agro-ecosystems coupled with the weather instability has worsened the living conditions for smallholding farmers, (having less than two hectares of farmland) and marginal farmers (having less than one hectare of farmland), and agricultural laborers, for whom occupational change is limited. Moreover, high fragmentation of these lands lead to reduced productivity due to increasingly growing cost of inputs and other reasons.

Agriculture in India, however, has a significant role in inclusive and sustainable development. For example, agriculture and allied activities constitute the single largest component (i.e. nearly 25%) of India's gross domestic product. It has tremendous importance in Indian economy as it provides employment to about two-thirds of the total work-force. Moreover, the share of agricultural products in exports is substantial accounting for about 15% of the export earnings. Having a weight of 57% in the consumer price index (CPI), any adversity in agriculture could have cumulative effects on the Indian economy. Therefore, growth in the agriculture sector directly correlates with the poverty eradication and employment generation. It is due to marginal attention given to agriculture in the past that the economic growth in India could not be inclusive.

Climate change may have a substantial impact on Indian agriculture, given that, rain-fed agricultural area constitutes about 60% of the net sown area, Indian agriculture is fundamentally dependent on the climatic stability. The Third Assessment Report of Intergovernmental Panel on Climate Change (2001) proposed the disproportionate impacts of climate change, with more upon developing countries and specifically on the resource-poor people within them. Further, it would exacerbate the inequities in the accessibility to food, clean water, health and other basic amenities. It is projected that change in climate due to global warming would lead to an increased variability in summer monsoon precipitation. Given that, agriculture in India is largely rain-fed, erratic monsoon precipitation would adversely affect the lives of majority of population. It would have serious implications for the farming communities in India and their ability to adapt to the impacts of climate change (Gadgil, 1995). The marginal and small holding farmers (which have least capacity to adapt, due to monetary reasons) would be severely affected by the adverse climatic conditions.

2.1 Green Revolution and its effects on Indian agriculture

The green revolution of the 1960s and 1970s which resulted in dramatic yield increases in the developing Asian countries is now showing signs of fatigue in productivity gains. Intensive agriculture practiced without adherence to the scientific principles and ecological aspects has led to loss of soil health, and depletion of freshwater resources and agro biodiversity(Redclift, 1989; Singh, 2000).

Hard-hit by successive droughts during 1958–1959, a new agricultural intensification strategy, popularly known as the Green Revolution technology was introduced to achieve self-sufficiency in food production. It resulted in a rapid growth in agricultural production, making India self-sufficient in food grain. However, it externalised the control of agro ecosystems leading to farmer's dependency on market based inputs such as fertilizer and pesticide (Altieri, 1999). For example, the introduction of high yielding variety seeds require frequent replacement due to the loss of vigor over time, contrasting with the traditional variety seeds which were adaptive to change in climatic conditions (Shiva, 1991).

Green Revolution thus changed the traditional pattern of cropping leading to environmental degradation which is evident from the fact that Punjab, the State with the greatest impact of green revolution is facing soil degradation in terms of soil infertility, erosion, water-logging, salinity, toxicity and alkalinity due to Green Revolution technology, which is threatening the region's food security (Srivastava et. al, 2016). Similar situation has been observed in the State of Haryana also (Singh, 2000).

It is therefore now widely evident that subsidized fossil-fuel supported present agricultural production cannot provide sustainability for the long run. A major drawback of Green Revolution technology appears to be the loss of biodiversity (Tilman et al., 1997; Hooper, 1998). Though with enhanced inputs, the major grain producing States such as Punjab and Haryana has now reached a plateau in agricultural output due to Green Revolution (Singh, 2000). Under the given circumstances, it is important therefore to rejuvenate soil health through sustainable practices with simultaneous increase in agricultural productivity to sustain the growing population in the country.

Along with the large scale soil degradation, the other problem facing the agriculture in the country is scarcity of groundwater as well as surface water.It is evident that water is important for agricultural growth and rural poverty alleviation.

Since independence, there has been a remarkable increase in water supplies for irrigation, through the building of large and medium surface irrigation schemes, and groundwater development which helped in the Green Revolution of the country. However, most of the major schemes for irrigation had been planned and implemented before more recent major advancements in hydro sciences. As a consequence, the efficiency of utilisation of water for irrigation has been extremely low in India, as in many other developing countries (Chaturvedi, 2000). The potential for adoption of water-saving micro-irrigation systems to improve water use efficiency in agriculture appears to be quite insignificant when compared to India's gross irrigated area (Kumar et al., 2008). On the other hand, the demand for water in agriculture is growing, both due to the increasing food grain needs of the growing population and the growing preference for water-intensive cash crops. The per capita demand for food grains is growing due to changing consumption patterns. While the average per capita demand for cereals for direct consumption has declined in the recent past, the demand for cereals for animal feed is increasing, owing to increased demand for animal products such as milk, beef, mutton, pork, poultry products, eggs and freshwater fish (Amarasinghe et al., 2007). In the urban and industrial sectors, the growth is more rapid, owing to the faster growth of urban populations and rapid industrialisation. By one estimate, the total water requirement for human and animal uses, industrial production and irrigated agriculture would be 104.50 million hectare metres in the year 2025. A comparison of water requirements and utilizable future supplies shows that, by the year 2025, the magnitude of scarcity would be 26.20 million hectare metres (Kumar, 2010). But the scarcity is not going to hit all regions uniformly. The naturally water-scarce regions would be hit adversely, as the demands for water from agriculture, industrial and urban sectors are quite high in these regions, while the renewable water resources available within the region are scarce. This is compounded by the demand for water for reducing environmental water stress in the rivers of these regions. In the absence of proper legal and institutional regimes under which water rights can be allocated among the competing uses, rights will be politically contested, leading to water conflicts (Kumar, 2010). Overuse of groundwater has led to various problems of arsenic contamination in ground water in Eastern India in the States of West Bengal, Bihar and Orissa problem of fluoride contamination in groundwater in the States of Rajasthan and Gujarat. Other than Arsenic and Fluoride contamination, groundwater in various States is contaminated with excessive iron, uranium and nitrate. (Acharyya, 2009, 2014a)

2.2 Impact of Climate Change on Indian agriculture

The Fourth Assessment Report of the Intergovernmental Panel on Climate Change (IPCC) (2007) has shown that by the end of this century, temperature increase is likely to be between 1.8 to 4.0 degree Celsius. This would lead to more frequent hot extremes, floods, droughts, cyclones and gradual recession of glaciers, which in turn would result in greater instability in food production. It is estimated that crop production loss in India by 2100 AD could be 10% to 40% despite the beneficial effects of higher carbon dioxide on crop growth. India could lose four to five million tonnes of wheat with every rise of one degree Celsius temperature. Dynamics of pests and diseases will be significantly altered (Aggarwal, 2008).

Also, due to climate change, India's hydro-climatic regime is expected to alter significantly over the course of the 21st century. Quite aside from the snowmelt impacts, parts of the Indo-Gangetic basin may also receive less rain than in the past. However, the rest of India, like much of Sri Lanka, is likely to benefit from greater, but more variable, annual precipitation.

According to IPCC (2007) most Indian landmass below the Ganges plain is likely to experience a 0.5 to 1 degree Celsius rise in average temperatures during 2020 to 2029 and a 3.5 to 4.5 degree Celsius rise during 2090 to 2099.

Many parts of peninsular India, especially Western Ghats, are likely to experience a 5 to 10 per cent increase in total precipitation (IPCC, 2007); however, this increase is likely to be accompanied by greater temporal variability (Acharyya, 2014b).

Throughout the subcontinent, it is expected that 'very wet days' are likely to contribute more and more to total precipitation, suggesting that more of India's precipitation may be received in fewer than 100 hours of storms – and half in less than 30 hours – as has been the case during recent decades. A combination of higher precipitation intensity, larger number of dry days in a year and increased frequency of extremely wet rainy seasons will also mean increased runoff.

Under the above circumstances of declining soil quality, low productivity, water crisis and imminent danger of climate change, it is important, especially for India, given its large population to feed, to follow a path of agricultural development which is sustainable and adaptive to climate change. Taking help of globalisation, India can use technology as well as human capital to mitigate the above mentioned problem. In the following Section we try to first define the notion of sustainability and then search for a road map to see whether globalisation and technical knowledge can bring in a sustainable form of development in Indian agriculture.

3. Sustainable Development of Indian Agriculture

The concept of sustainability, ever since it was propagated by the Brundtland Commission in 1987, has been under debate and is in a process of evolution. The basic criticism frequently is that the concept is too fluid to be defined. According to Pretty (1995), it is essential to identify: What is to be sustained? Till how long? And, for whom? Notwithstanding the debate, efforts have been made to define the sustainability of agriculture especially in the light of the contemporary discourse on growth (and trade), environmental damages, and livelihood (poverty reduction). For instance, OECD (2001) has defined sustainable development as a 'dynamic process, which focuses on the ability of an economy to improve human welfare in cost-effective ways through developing, combining and substituting resources in the production process. It is also a global concept, which recognizes that allowing flows of resources between sectors and economies through international trade can maximize production while reducing the pressure on fragile resources. What is also important is that the concept is multidimensional, encompassing economic, environmental and social aspects that could apply to a large extent, to the specific activities in agricultural sector' (OECD, 2001). A more simple definition, in the context of agriculture, would focus on the sustainability of production over an extended scale of time and space. This essentially would mean that crop production and economic gains would flourish over a long period of time, almost infinitely and globally. While this is a fairly workable definition, it is nevertheless, difficult to translate in terms of policies and actions at a global level. From the perspective of economics, sustainable agriculture would refer to a spectrum of the production system, which has a relatively moderate use of chemical inputs as compared to that associated with maximum yield, given the seed variety and the state of the agronomic practices adopted by a large number of farmers so that there is minimum damage to the environment and adaptable to climate change.

Prima facie, the relative neglect of the environment while talking of India's agricultural sector is a manifestation of the general apathy towards the issue and, also the perception that agriculture, as yet, is not a major contributor to environmental pollution or damages in the country. This kind of perception is often reflected in environmental policies and also in discussions at the various forums nationally as well as regionally. For instance, the strategy identified by the Ministry of Environment and Forest for meeting the objectives of the Tenth Five Year Plan, has a special thrust on promoting sustainable development. This is to be achieved by emphasizing the intrinsic linkage between environment management and socio-economic development through increased access to natural resources On a further note, the strategy mentions that 'while striving for the goal of increasing forest cover to 25 per cent by 2007, thrust will be given to increasing productivity and efficient management of resources besides other aspects (Khurana, 2003)

These kinds of policy statements reinstate the importance of resource access and utilisation for enhancing productivity in the sector. Thus growth in production continues to be the main thrust.Prima facie, there cannot be any denial of the fact that use of external inputs like irrigation–fertilizer–pesticides has brought negative externalities in terms of soil degradation, water logging, depletion of micro nutrients and soil structure, and contamination of ground water, etc. The pertinent issue however, is to draw the line of maximum tolerance level whereby (a) damages do not cross a limit of being irreversible; and (b) decline in land productivity does not become perpetual.

3.1 Globalisation and Sustainable Agricultural Development

Globalisation has offered immense opportunities for Indian farmers to export their agriculture products in world markets, concentrate on herbs and agricultural commodities that are in great demand in world markets including medicinal plants. Globalisation has brought greater awareness of opportunities and alternatives for farmers to enhance their incomes from farming. For example, by switching from subsistence farming to cash crop farming, Maharashtra's small farmers have gained an additional income per year (USAID, 2005). Hence globalisation is helping to bridge the technological gap and provide solutions to problems with the help of developed countries and international organisations.

Globalisation in the context of agriculture can best be discussed in the context of three components – improvement of productive efficiency by ensuring the convergence of potential and realised outputs, increase in agricultural exports and value added activities using agricultural produce, and finally improved access to domestic and international markets (Mahadevan, 2003).

Globalisation is likely to have a profound influence on food processing cottage industries and big industrial houses are likely to venture in the area of food processing for greater profitability through exports of such products that are in demand in international markets (Subhash, 2007).

Globalisation is also influencing the marketing of fresh agriculture produce. India has a middle class that have purchasing power equivalent to the whole of the Europe. This component of population is determining the imperatives and dynamics of new business environment in India. Merely transfer of information to farmers is not sufficient by itself. Farmers themselves must be able to make choices what is best for them and thoroughly understand what to do and how to do it to enhance their agriculture productivity and improve their economy.

Farmers should also make increasing efforts for learning new technologies and become information literate for surviving and thriving the knowledge intensive farming era. For constant access to latest agriculture knowledge someone from the farmer family must have access to the Internet facilities, knowledge of using the electronic information resources and be competent enough to make effective use of information technologies. The National Agriculture Policy lays emphasis on the use of Information Technology (IT) for achieving a more rapid development of Agriculture in India.

Efforts are being made at various levels to improve the information communication infrastructure in India. There is consistent growth of mobile phones in India. Because of fierce price competition, mobile phones is becoming one of the cheapest in the world and helping the rural India to get connected

Along with the challenge of imparting literacy to a large number of people, India has the additional challenge of imparting information literacy to a sizeable number of people including small farmers. These competencies will help the farmers to even independently access information of their interest and profitably use it for better functioning and performance. As important is development of information facilities for farmers, equally important is work environment of farmers because propensity to make use of information resources and urge to learn largely depend on the work environment, encouragement, elation, outcomes of hard work and time spent in the occupations they are engaged. It is not completely because of transfer of knowledge from Laboratory to Land that farmers are finding a way for doing something better, adopting and adapting agricultural technologies, they have been experimenting at their own level to improve crop varieties, animal breeds, irrigation methods and other farming practices. They have been sharing improved farm management practices and technologies with fellow farmers through informal communication systems and passing it on to their next generations.

3.2 Internet of Things (IOT)

Agriculture sector will have to be much more efficient and resilient to ensure global food security. Indian farmers are at great disadvantage in terms of size of farms, technology, trade, government policies, etc. Information and Communication Technology (ICT) can mitigate some of the problems of farmers. After the World Wide Web (of the 1990s) and the mobile Internet (of the 2000s), we are now heading to the third and potentially most "disruptive" phase of the Internet revolution—the "Internet of Things" (IOT) which is also known as "Ubiquitous Computing. The Internet of Things (IOT) is a worldwide network of intercommunicating devices. It integrates the ubiquitous communications, pervasive computing, and ambient intelligence. IOT is a vision where "things", especially everyday objects, such as all home appliances, furniture, clothes, vehicles, roads and smart materials, etc. are readable, recognizable, locatable, addressable and/or controllable via the Internet. This will provide the basis for many new applications, such as energy monitoring, transport safety systems or building security. This vision will surely change with time, especially as synergies between Identification Technologies, Wireless Sensor Networks, Intelligent Devices and Nanotechnology will enable a number of advanced applications. Innovative use of technologies is contributing to create a value proposition for stakeholders of IOT. Internet of Things will connect the world's objects in both a sensory and intelligent manner through combining technological developments in item identification ("tagging things"), sensors and wireless sensor networks ("feeling things"), embedded systems ("thinking things") and nanotechnology ("shrinking things").

IOT applications encompass diverse areas including agriculture, healthcare, retail, transport, environment, supply chain management, infrastructure monitoring etc. Applications in agriculture include soil and plant monitoring, greenhouse environment monitoring and control systems, monitoring of food supply chain, monitoring of animals, etc. Precision farming equipment with wireless links to data collected from remote satellites and ground sensors can take into account crop conditions and adjust the way each individual part of a field is farmed—for instance, by spreading extra fertilizer on areas that need more nutrients (Chui et al., 2010). The networking of things or physical objects must be cost effective and useful to the end users for acceptance and wide scale adoption of IOT. Global ICT Standardisation Forum for India has listed the potential benefits of IOT as: (i) Improved performance, visibility and scalability, (ii) Better and more cost effective service, (iii) Transparency of physical flows and detailed status information, (iv) Enhanced efficiency, accuracy, mobility and automation. The Accessible, Affordable, Interactive crowd sourcing platform for sustainable agriculture would provide a means for sharing information regarding traditional sustainable agricultural methods, techniques, tools, tips, etc. and allow interactivity and offline data entry for consolidated information upload.

Addressing the food security or water security with sustainable agriculture, the solution must provide supplementary information and services such as third-party agricultural, micro-finance services, etc. for farmers. It must also provide a centralised repository for a variety of information such as traditional sustainable farming techniques, crop diseases, etc. coming through various sources, allow interactive farming, easy access to users over various devices such as mobile phones, IVR, computers and kiosks in addition to providing multi-lingual support of traditional practices with modern value.

3.3 Climate Smart Agriculture (CSA)

So far as impact of climate change on Indian agriculture is concerned, over the last 100 years, an increase of 0.4degree Celsius in annual average surface air temperature has been recorded in the Indian subcontinent, and by the 2050s, average temperature is expected to rise by 2 to 4 degree Celsius (MEF, 2004) The spatial and seasonal variation in rainfall is also likely to increase in the coming decades (IPCC, 2014). Historical trends show a noticeable increase in mean temperature and large variation in monsoon rainfall in India (IPCC, 2001). Climate change is likely to reduce yields of most crops in long-term, and increased climatic variability could cause significant fluctuations in production in the short-run (Rao et. al., 2013). Recent studies on regional and global simulation models also indicate that a moderate increase in temperature will have significant negative impact on rice, wheat and maize yields in India (Aggarwal et al, 2009; Parry et al., 2004)

Under the above circumstances, it is extremely important for underdeveloped and developing countries of Africa and Asia to adopt measures under climate change so that the production of agriculture can be sustainably increased to feed the rising population of the country.

Climate-smart agriculture (CSA), as defined and presented by Food and Agricultural Organisation (FAO, 2013) tries to integrate the three dimensions of sustainable development (economic, social and environmental) by jointly addressing food security and climate challenges. It is composed of three main pillars: sustainably increasing agricultural productivity and incomes; adapting and building resilience to climate change and reducing and removing greenhouse gases emissions, where possible (FAO, 2013).

CSA is an approach to developing the technical, policy and investment conditions to achieve sustainable agricultural development for food security under climate change. The magnitude, immediacy and broad scope of the effects of climate change on agricultural systems create a compelling need to ensure comprehensive integration of these effects into national agricultural planning, investments and programs. The CSA approach is designed to identify and operationalize sustainable agricultural development within the explicit parameters of climate change (Ghosh and Acharyya, 2018).

CSA encourages sustainable development of agricultural systems through practices and approaches that achieve improved food security, increased resilience, and low carbon emissions development where possible and appropriate in the face of climate change (FAO, 2010a, 2013). In contrast to conventional agriculture management and planning, CSA is an effort to integrate climate change and agriculture development planning, specifically seeking out opportunities to link climate adaptation and climate mitigation efforts. Climate mitigation is any action taken to permanently eliminate or reduce the long-term risk and hazards of climate change to human life or property. The International Panel on Climate Change (IPCC, 2001) defines mitigation as "an anthropogenic intervention to reduce the sources or enhance the sinks of greenhouse gases" (IPCC, 2001). Climate adaptation refers to the ability of a system to adjust to climate change (including climate variability and extremes) to moderate potential damage, to take advantage of opportunities, or to cope with the consequences. The IPCC defines adaptation as the, "adjustment in natural or human systems to a new or changing environment. Adaptation to climate change refers to adjustment in natural or human systems in response to actual or expected climatic stimuli or their effects, which moderates harm or exploits beneficial opportunities." Various potential adaptation options exist to reduce moderate to severe climatic risks in agriculture. As per the guidelines of Food and Agricultural Organisation (FAO, 2010b), adaptation options that sustainably increase productivity, enhance resilience to climatic stresses, and reduce greenhouse gas emissions are known as climate-smart agricultural (CSA) technologies, practices and services

Thus the CSA approach tries to integrate the adaptation and mitigation of climate change to ensure holistic planning of agriculture taking the impact of climate change into account, maximizing multiple outcomes and minimizing tradeoffs in management of food systems (Lipper et al., 2014). CSA has gained considerable attention, especially in developing countries, due to its potential to increase food security and farming system resilience while decreasing greenhouse gas emissions (FAO, 2013, 2010a; Grainger-Jones, 2011). This is especially relevant to South Asia and Africa, where economic development depends on agricultural growth, which is also the most vulnerable sector so far as the impact of climate change is concerned (Rosenzweig and Parry, 1994; Vermeulen et al., 2012). Many agricultural practices and technologies such as minimum tillage, different methods of crop establishment, nutrient and irrigation management and residue incorporation can improve crop yields, water and nutrient use efficiency and reduce Greenhouse Gas (GHG) emissions from agricultural activities (Branca et al., 2011; Jat et al., 2014; Sapkota et al., 2015). Similarly, rainwater harvesting, use of improved seeds, Information and Communication Technology (ICT) based agro-advisories and crop and livestock insurances can also help farmers to reduce the impact of climate change and variability (Mittal, 2012; Altieri and Nicholls, 2017).

In general, CSA tries to integrate traditional and innovative practices, technologies and services that are relevant for particular location to adopt climate change and variability. The implementation of CSA technologies individually, or in a combination have substantial potential to reduce climate change impacts on agriculture.

Although CSA is an important step forward to achieve adaptive agriculture and land-based mitigation, its implementation is not straightforward. Questions remain about how a transition towards CSA could actually materialize (FAO, 2013). Such a transition requires not only new technical practices, but also new types of knowledge and modes of thinking, as well as new institutions and forms of organisation (Woodhill and Röling, 1998; Leeuwis and Aarts, 2011).

Due to the uncertain and dynamic nature of climate change impacts, a transition towards CSA requires innovation processes based on social learning (FAO, 2013). Most underscore the contextual and social nature of learning and the continuous reflexivity needed to reform social practices in the face of new risks. However, these theories pay different levels of attention to individual and collective learning, depending on their theoretical foundations (Blackmore, 2007).

Expanding on theories of social learning in the domain of community natural resource management, Muro (2008) identified the characteristics of co-creation of knowledge and reflection and recognition of others' perspectives and others' underlying goals and values as extremely important. He also emphasizes on the understanding of the complexity and interdependence, leading to at least partial convergence of goals through mutual agreement and collective or coordinated action. Indeed, community natural resource management literature posits collective action as an important outcome of social learning. This notion of collective action initially referred to institutional arrangements that facilitate coordinated management of common-pool resources (Ostrom and Gardner, 1994). Later, the terms social learning and collective action were also used for other shared pursuits. For instance, farmers' group formation and cooperation were considered crucial mechanisms to attain access to vital resources and markets (Meinzen-Dick et al., 2004; Markelova et al., 2009).

Stakeholder participation for social learning has also become a normative approach to attain sustainable agriculture and natural resource management (Reed et al., 2010; Muro and Jeffrey, 2008; Berkes, 2009). It may also be a valuable approach for implementing climate smart farming, which requires a continuous process of learning by doing. Several studies have cited the role of social learning in enhancing climate adaptation through collective action (e.g., Collins and Ison, 2009). In fact, continual learning through stakeholder participation may enhance group decision-making (Thorne, 2014) and provide technical as also socio-institutional mechanisms for managing complexity and uncertainty through incremental adjustment (Pahl-Wostl et al., 2007).

Presently, there are some evidences on how CSA can address the complex interactions between climate, social factors and food production at the community level. There is a growing body of CSA literature that calls for a need to research ways to integrate mitigation and adaptation in the food production practices of smallholder farming systems (Harvey et al., 2013; Lipper et al., 2014; Scherr, Shames, & Friedman, 2012). There is no one-size-fits-all approach to climate smart farming as temporal scale, geography, capacity, institutional factors, and technological innovations impede the integration of climate change goals in agriculture. A key challenge for scientists and governments, however, is to create policy based on limited scientific evidence that influences the knowledge, practices, and vulnerabilities of smallholder farmers in underdeveloped countries (IPCC, 2014). Practitioners and scientists are under immense pressure to explain how CSA interventions will work on the ground, which in turn can assist in the scientific validity of the approach. In particular, research into community-based processes that give rise to synergies and co-benefits, while minimizing conflicts of mitigation and adaptation practices is vital. While these terms have been used extensively (Smith & Olesen, 2010), the participatory processes underlying them are often ambiguous and based on very different assumptions of how smallholder farmers experience climate shocks and interact with agricultural landscapes.

Under the circumstances, empirical research can inform smallholder farmer of climate risks and landscape-suitable agricultural practices, technologies, and systems. Local institutions are vital to the design and implementation of climate change programs and policies in rural agrarian societies, and there is a growing literature to support this view. For example, National Adaptation Programs of Action has been successful in many developing countries as a result of local public, private, and civic institutions inventing and implementing a diversity of rural livelihoods mechanisms (Agrawal & Agrawal, 2008).

4. Public Policy for managing sustainable agricultural Development: The Road Ahead

Designing food and agriculture policy is substantially more complex in a globalised world than it was in a world of relatively closed food economies. While, chronic hunger and poverty continue to be daunting problems in much of the developing world, globalisation brings about new policy challenges both for countries well into the process of agricultural transformation and for countries at the low end of the transformation process. The traditional policy agenda for promoting agricultural growth and economic development needs to be redesigned and adapted to the new realities of an increasingly inter-connected global economy. The following are some of the areas of policy focus and re-direction.

4.1 Continued emphasis on enhancing food security and reducing poverty

Substantial progress has been made over the last decades in hunger and poverty reduction.. While the prospects for reducing the proportion of hungry are encouraging, the decline in the absolute number of hungry will be much slower and halving that number by 2020 is an unattainable goal in all regions of world, except East Asia. While "trickle down" from globalisation induced income growth can to some extent help alleviate poverty and food insecurity it will not be adequate without concerted efforts targeted at the neediest populations. For countries at the low end of the transformation process, concerted action towards enhancing food security especially through agricultural productivity growth is crucial in the quest for income growth and economic development. The same is true for low productivity regions in countries that are well into the process of agricultural modernisation.

Hunger and poverty reduction requires a twin-track approach which combines, (a) direct interventions and social investments to address the immediate needs of poor and hungry (social safety nets, conditional or unconditional cash transfers, health interventions, food and nutrition programmes) with (b) long-term development programmes to enhance the performance of the productive sectors (especially to promote agriculture and rural development), create employment and increase the value of the assets held by the poor (physical, human, financial). Coherence between policies and investments to increase productivity and economic efficiency and those in the social sectors improves the effectiveness of both (Pingali et al., 2006). Coherence is also needed between agriculture and trade policies in order to achieve an appropriate balance between food imports and domestic productivity growth.

Some argue that the benefits of low food prices are as easily accessed by trade as by investing in domestic agriculture (Sachs, 1997). This argument ignores the strong historical connection between domestic food production and consumption because of the difficulty and expense of transporting and marketing food staples in rural areas, far from ports and efficient transport links (Timmer, 2002).

Enhancing food security in the rural areas entails improvements in the productivity of smallholder agriculture. In the first instance, enhancing local food supplies contributes to improved household nutrition and thereby contributes to labour performance improvements. In the long term it broadens participation in market-led growth. Promoting sustainable use of natural resources, improving rural infrastructure, research and communications, facilitating the functioning of markets and enhancing rural institutions are integral parts of the strategy. Productivity-induced agricultural growth has a wider impact on rural areas through the strengthening of off-farm activities, rural employment and wages.

4.2 Re-orienting agricultural research and development priorities

Harnessing the best of scientific knowledge and technological breakthroughs is crucial as we attempt to "retool" agriculture to face the challenges of an increasingly commercialised and globalised agriculture sector. The primary objective of the research system remains to generate new technologies that sustainably improve productivity and farmers' income. Governments have a difficult task to perform: on one hand, continued food security needs to be assured for populations that are growing in absolute terms; on the other hand, research and infrastructural investments need to be made for diversification out of the primary staples. In responding to diversification trends, the research should not abruptly shift from an exclusive focus on one set of commodities to another set of commodities. The focus of research should be to provide farmers the flexibility to make crop choice decisions and to move relatively freely between crops and other agricultural enterprises (Pingali and Rosegrant, 1995).

Both substantial crop-specific research and system level research effort will be required to provide farmers the flexibility of crop choice. Crop-specific research includes increases in yield potential, shorter duration of cultivation, improved quality characteristics and greater tolerance to pest stresses. System-level research would include land management and tillage systems that allow for shifts of cropping patterns in response to changing incentives and farm level water management systems that can accommodate a variety of crops within a season. Also important at the system level is research on the carry over effect of inputs and management practices across crops, for instance, high insecticide and herbicide applications, or the effects of intensification in terms of prolonged water saturation, the buildup and carryover across crops of pest populations, rapid depletion in soil micronutrients and changes in soil organic matter could lead to reduced productivity of rice monoculture systems over the long term (Srivastava et al., 2016).

Modern science like Internet of Things (IoT) and Climate Smart Agriculture (CSA) can provide opportunities for enhancing input efficiencies and for developing more sustainable production systems. Modern science and technology can also help provide new impetus for addressing the age-old problems of yield improvement, production variability and food insecurity of rural populations living in marginal production environments. Whilst the real and potential gains from science and technology are apparent, it is also necessary to take into consideration the fact that research and technology development, such as biotechnology, are more and more in the private domain. Biotechnology holds great promise, but may involve new risks. In most countries, the scientific, political, economic or institutional basis is not yet in place to provide adequate safeguards for biotechnology development and application, and to reap all the potential benefits (FAO, 2004c). Similarly, the evolution of food chains has been led by the private sector with obvious benefits in terms of food quality, safety and food price reductions. However, there have been casualties as some farmers and firms have been marginalised. Countries at the low end of the agricultural transformation process have gained the least from the above developments. In this case the question becomes one of whether there are technical solutions and business models that can enable engagement of such marginalised groups and countries.

4.3 Creating an enabling environment for smallholder transformation

The challenges faced by smallholder agriculture should be seen in the context of the general trends that will influence the structure of agricultural production. Namely, the transformation of diets and rising import competition will contribute to the increasing commercialisation of the small farm sector. Governments ought to help create an enabling environment for smallholder commercialisation through infrastructure investments and institutional reform.

Rural infrastructure investments play a crucial role in inducing farmers to move toward a commercial agricultural system. The emphasis for public investments should be on improving general transport, communications, and market infrastructure, while allowing the private sector to invest in commodity-specific processing, storage, and marketing facilities. Accessible and cost-effective communication systems such as mobile telephones can help generate information and other market-related services. The Internet explosion and related technologies have drastically reduced exchange and search costs in many poor countries and may be highly indicative of the potential benefits to such countries (Bussolo and Whalley, 2002).

Efficient land markets and secure property rights are essential to capture agricultural growth (Binswanger et. al., 1993). Where land rights are secure, farmers have the greater incentive needed to invest in land improvements. Moreover, land ownership is an important source of collateral that can improve the credit status of farmers, leading to easier access to funding for inputs and so forth (Feder et al., 1988). Individual farmers and households need to be assured of "stable engagement" with other resources, such as water, water use rights that are flexible enough to promote comparative advantage in food staples and cash crops. Those rights must be matched by access to rural credit and finance and the dissemination of technology and good practices in water use (De Haen et al., 2003).

4.4 Reducing small farm transactions costs

Smallholder participation in commercial and vertically integrated markets is becoming an issue of major concern, especially in countries with rapidly modernizing agricultural systems. Because transaction costs vary over households and enterprises, commodities and regions, there is no single innovation or intervention, public or private, which can reduce them. However, there are a number of ways in which market entry by small farmers can be developed. These include contract farming, the development of farmer organisations for marketing, development of the supply chain for high value exports produced by smallholders through an appropriate mix of private and public sector initiatives and facilitating private sector provision of market information via improved telecommunications (Kydd et al., 2000).

The role of government is crucial in specifying property rights and enforcing contracts in order to promote specialisation and reduce the costs of market exchange (North, 2000). Moreover, government policy needs to create incentives and send signals that encourage private sector participation in developing rural economies. Before we target transactions costs as a remedy for increased small farmer participation we need to bear in mind two points. First, while a reduction in transaction costs should in principal allow for a greater number of farmers to trade, the ability to enter is not the same as the ability to stay. This is as much a function of other factors as it is of transaction costs. Therefore, interventions need to be cost-effective. Public money should not be spent in declining and non-competitive sectors. Second, transaction costs are household, commodity and location specific and are subject to constant change. Interventions aimed at targeted reductions in specific costs should not be in the public domain. Public sector interventions are best left for public good provision and institutional reforms to correct incomplete or absent markets. The reduction of transaction costs associated with the specificities of the food system is best left in the hands of the private sector.

4.5 Seeking complementarity between trade and domestic policy

Trade liberalisation can be a powerful tool to promote economic growth, however, low income countries, in order to benefit from trade reform, will need to enhance domestic competitiveness through policy and institutional reform (FAO, 2005). Liberalisation of domestic markets through removal of quantitative restrictions on trade, and opening up of economies to internal trade opportunities is often a key step in starting or accelerating the process of commercialisation. However, the opening up of markets also exposes producers to increased risk due to the greater short term volatility of world prices. Governments have historically intervened heavily in domestic markets to protect and stabilize the prices of agricultural commodities, with the result that domestic producer prices have varied substantially less than international prices. The relationship between diversification and risk is thus crucial in the context of trade and macroeconomic reform designed to align domestic prices more closely with international prices.

Many low-volume markets are associated with high-price volatility. This can be countered by measures to expand the market by lowering transaction costs, improving external linkages or providing storage and processing technologies. Effective rural financial institutions will also assist in risk spreading and in the sharing of the benefits of commercialisation more widely across the community and region.

Finally, in view of the continuing distortions on world markets, the least developed countries must be granted more "policy space" necessary to reduce poverty and hunger by developing their rural areas and agriculture. Trade liberalisation should go hand in hand with public support for improving agriculture productivity.

4.6 Establishing safety standards and regulations

Globalisation is increasing the "effective demand" for safe and healthy food. Government schemes to certify quality and safe food according to public regulations are required. This is important for domestic consumption and food safety, and even more so if a country wants to access foreign markets. If a country wants to export, it is necessary that an independent body will guarantee that the produce adheres to the required quality and safety standards (De Haen, et al, 2003). However, public systems to ensure food quality and safety suffer from lack of organisation and adequate funding. To the extent that developing country governments do not impose international-level standards, private standards are being implemented by the leading players in retail and food processing (Reardon and Farina, 2001).

4.7 Enhancing incentives for sustainable resource use

Public policy can play an important role in encouraging the sustainable use of natural resources. First, by correcting incentive-distorting policies that encourages unsustainable use of the resource base. Second, by identifying market based instruments for promoting the supply of environmental services through appropriate changes in agricultural production systems and land use. Government interventions in the cereals market, especially through output price support and input subsidies has long been providing farmers incentives for increasing cereal crop productivity, particularly the rice monoculture system, and the rice-wheat system in Asia (Acharyya, 2012).

Input subsidies that keep input prices low directly affect crop management practices at the farm level; they reduce farmer incentives for improving input use efficiency, which often requires farmer investment in learning about the technology and how best to use it. These policies have contributed to significant degradation of the agricultural resource base by creating soil fertility imbalances; disruptions in pest-predator ecology; salinity and waterlogging problems, and higher incidence of soil erosion.

With the progression towards global integration, the competitiveness of domestic cereal agriculture can only be maintained through dramatic reductions in the cost per unit of production. Technologies for more efficient use of fertilizers, pesticides, and water are available and could become worthwhile adopting as price distortions are removed. Increasing input use efficiency would also contribute significantly to the long-term sustainability of intensive food-crop production and help arrest many of the degradation problems mentioned above.

In addition to policy corrections, governments can play an important role in promoting (through payments, if necessary) eco-system conservation through changes in agricultural production systems that complements food and fiber production. Conservation tillage, agroforestry systems and climate smart farming are some of the many examples of agricultural production systems that can generate environmental benefits in the form of carbon sequestration, biodiversity conservation and watershed protection. The benefit of combining payments for the provision of public environmental goods such as soil carbon sequestration or watershed protection for the adoption of agricultural practices that can eventually lead to increased agricultural productivity is quite attractive. In some cases, however the adoption of the new agricultural practice could lead to a decrease in the returns to agriculture, in which case the payment for the public good component must be sufficient to compensate for such losses at a minimum (Lipper, et al, 2006).

Governments have a role to play in stimulating desirable land use change. In the process of economic development, as agricultural populations shrink and non-agricultural sectors grow, the potential for setting aside land for non-agricultural uses is high. Conversion of marginal agricultural lands to forests contributes to carbon sequestration, watershed protection and biodiversity conservation. For developing countries with similar conditions in the agricultural sector, national and international public sector support for land use changes that generate global environmental goods and services can be an important means of attaining sustainable resource use. Public policy to stimulate land use change is also warranted where the environmental costs of agricultural production outweigh the benefits. For example, the Chinese government has a goal of converting 14.6 million hectares of croplands on sloping lands to forest in order to reduce soil erosion that has serious economic impacts on land and water use efficiency (Lipper et. al. 2006). However, the successful incorporation of environmental services into the livelihoods of the poor via changes in either agricultural production systems or land use is dependent on the presence of enabling conditions such a property rights, food security and low transactions costs, as well as local and global recognition and willingness to pay for environmental goods and services.

4.8 Enabling income and livelihood diversification

It is important to start by recognizing that rural households, at all stages of development, rely on a diverse set of non-farm opportunities for earning incomes and sustaining food security and livelihoods. Higher agricultural productivity has contributed to the growth in rural non-farm and off-farm income earning opportunities through backward and forward linkages. Surveys of the rural non-farm literature indicate rural non-farm income represents on average 42% of rural income in Africa, 32% in Asia, 40% in Latin America and 44% in Eastern Europe (Davis, 2004; FAO 1998).

The diversity of income generating activities in the rural areas calls for policies with wider impact as opposed to sector specific policies: education and rural infrastructure such as communications, roads and electrification will have beneficial effects to a wide spectrum of rural activities (Winters et al., 2006). Public investments ought to be accompanied by policies that induce complementary flows of private investment.

Does the vertical integration of the food sector have a negative impact on rural non-farm employment opportunities? While empirical evidence on this question is not yet available, one could postulate that there will certainly be a change in the mix of activities. There could be a drop in small scale agro-processing and an increase in services and commerce. Finally, public investments made to create an enabling environment for non-farm employment will also be useful in preparing populations for exits from rural areas as economic development proceeds.

5. Conclusion

Agricultural growth has played a historically important role in the process of economic development. Evidence from industrialised countries as well as countries that are rapidly developing today indicates that agriculture was the engine that contributed to growth in the non-agricultural sectors and to overall economic well-being. Economic growth originating in agriculture can have a particularly strong impact in reducing poverty and hunger. Increasing employment and incomes in agriculture stimulates demand for non-agricultural goods and services, providing a boost to non-farm rural incomes as well. Trade liberalisation and global inter-connectedness pose new opportunities and challenges for developing countries like India. Since India is now well into the process of agricultural transformation and modernisation, it will benefit from exposure to globalisation trends. Past investments in rural infrastructure, productivity enhancing technologies, as well as market institutions, make them more responsive to global market signals. The transition will be pro-poor to the extent that production and post-harvest activities continue to be labor intensive and to the extent that there is an expansion in employment opportunities outside agriculture.

The transition process is by no means frictionless. Public policy needs to pay attention to inter-regional and intra-societal differences, particularly the prospects for small farm participation in commercialised markets. Also, the absorption of the rural poor in the industrial and service sectors has significant costs in terms of learning new skills and family dislocations that need to be addressed.

The most important issue for agricultural development in India is that it needs to be sustainable and eco-friendly in the long run so that pollution gets reduced and food for the future generation is secure. The role of government in promoting sustainable agriculture is extremely important. Through the use of global communication technology like IoT and providing incentives to farmers to produce ecofriendly products adaptable to climate change, the government can ensure sustainable agricultural development.

References

Acharyya, A. 2009 'Valuing Health Damages from Arsenic Contamination: A Willingness to Pay and Dose Response Approach' in Unai Pascual, Amita Shah and Jayanta Bandopadhyay edited Water, Agriculture and Sustainable Well-Being, Oxford University Press, New Delhi, Pages 1-25.

Acharyya, A. 2012. 'Sustainability of Groundwater in South Asia: Need for Management through Institutional Change', Nitte Management Review 6(2); pp. 28-38.

Acharyya, A. 2014a.'Valuing Health Damages from Arsenic Contamination in India and Bangladesh: Some Policy Prescriptions'. Journal of the Institution of Public Health Engineers, India, Volume 1, April, 2014, 65-73.

Acharyya A. 2014b 'Groundwater, Climate Change and Sustainable Well Being of the Poor: Policy options for South Asia, China and Africa', Procedia - Social and Behavioral Sciences, 157: 226 – 235. Elsevier

Acharyya Achiransu, Ghosh Madhusudan,. 2017. 'Climate Change Smart Farming Practices: A Review' in Kamal R. Gupta and V.B. Angadi edited Smart Farming: Problems and Prospects. Gaurang Publishing Globalize Private Limited, Mumbai, India.

Agrawal, A., &Agrawal, N. 2008.Climate adaptation, local Institutions, and rural livelihoods, IFRI Working Paper # W08I–6. Michigan: University of Michigan.

Aggarwal P.K., 2008. 'Global climate change and Indian agriculture:impacts, adaptation and mitigation', Indian Journal of Agricultural Sciences, 78(10), 911-919.

Aggarwal, P.K., Singh, A.K., Samra, J.S., Singh, G., Gogoi, A.K. Rao, G.G.S.N., Ramakrishna, Y.S., 2009. Introduction. In: Aggarwal, P.K. (Ed.) Global Climate Change and Indian Agriculture. Indian Council of Agricultural Research, New Delhi, India.

Aggarwal, P. K. and Rani, D. N. S. 2009, Assessment of climate change impacts on wheat production in India. In Global Climate Change and Indian Agriculture: Case Studies from the ICAR Network Project (ed. Aggarwal, P. K.), ICAR, New Delhi, pp. 5–12.

Altieri, M.A., 1999. The ecological role of biodiversity in agroecosystems. Agric.Ecosyst. Environ. 74, 19–31.

Altieri Miguel A. & Clara I. Nicholls.2017. "The adaptation and mitigation potential of traditional agriculture in a changing climate", Climatic Change 140 (1),pp: 33-45.

Amarasinghe, U. A., Shah, T., Turral, H., & Anand, B. K. 2007.. India's water future to 2025–2050: Business-as-usual scenario and deviations. Research report 123. Colombo, Sri Lanka: International Water Management Institute.

Berkes, F., 2009. Evolution of co-management: role of knowledge generation: bridging organisations and social learning. Journal of Environment and Management 90, 1692–1702.

Binswanger, H.P., Deininger, K. and Feder, G., 1993. Agricultural land relations in the developing world.American Journal of Agricultural Economics 75, 1242-8.

Blackmore, C., 2007. What kinds of knowledge, knowing and learning are required for addressing resource dilemmas? A theoretical overview. Environmental Science & Policy 10, 512–525.

Branca, G., McCarthy, N., Lipper, L. and Jolejole, M.2011. Climate-Smart Agriculture: A Synthesis of Empirical Evidence of Food Security and Mitigation Benefits of from Improved Cropland Management (Rome: Food and Agriculture Organisation of the United Nations (FAO),

Bussolo, M. and Whalley, J., 2003. Globalisation in developing countries: the role of transaction costs in explaining economic performance in India, Development Centre Working Papers. OECD Development Centre, Paris.

Chand, Ramesh., Srivastava S. K. and Jaspal Singh. Changing Structure of Rural Economy of India Implications for Employment and Growth and Discussion Paper, NITI Aayog, December 2017.

Chaturvedi, M. C. (2000). Water for food and rural development: Developing countries. Water International, 25 (1), 40–53.

Chopra, M., Galbraith, S. and Darnton-Hill, I., 2002. A global response to a global problem: the epidemic of overnutrition. Bulletin of the World Health Organisation 80, 952-8.

Chui, M., Loffler, M. and Roberts, R., 2010, The Internet of Things. McKinsey Quarterly, March, 2010. Global ICT Standardisation Forum for India. www.gisfi.org

Collins, K., Ison, R., 2009. "Jumping off Arnstein's ladder: social learning as a new policy paradigm for climate adaptation."Environmental Policy and Governance. 19(6), 358–373. John Wiley and Sons.Limited.

Davis, J., 2004. The Rural Non-Farm Ecnomy, Livelihoods and their Diversification: Issues and Options, Natural Resource Institute, Chatham, UK.

De Haen, H., Stamoulis, K., Shetty, P. and Pingali, P., 2003. The world food economy in the Twenty-first century: Challenges for international co-operation. Development Policy Review 21, 683-96.

FAO, 1998. The State of Food and Agriculture 1998: Rural non-farm income in developing countries, Food and Agriculture Organisation, Rome, Italy.

FAO, 2002. World agriculture: towards 2015/2030, FAO, Rome.

FAO, 2004a.Socio-economic analysis and policy implications of the roles of agriculture in developing countries, Research Programme Summary Report.Roles of Agriculture Project, FAO, Rome, Italy.

FAO, 2004b. The state of agricultural commodity markets, Food and Agriculture Organisation, Rome, Italy.

FAO, 2004c. The State of Food and Agriculture 2003-2004: Agricultural biotechnology, meeting the needs of the poor? Food and Agriculture Organisation, Rome, Italy.

FAO, 2005. The State of Food and Agriculture 2005: Making trade work for the poor. Food and Agriculture Organisation, Rome, Italy.

Food and Agricultural Organisation (FAO), 2010a. Climate-Smart Agriculture: Policies, Practices and Financing for Food Security, USA.

Food and Agriculture Organisation (FAO).2010b. Adaptation and Mitigation., Rome, Italy.

Food and Agriculture Organisation (FAO), 2013. Climate-smart Agriculture Sourcebook.

Food and Agriculture Organisation of the United Nations (FAO), Rome, Italy.

Feder, G., Onchan, Y., Chalamwong, Y. and Hongladarom, C., 1988. Land policies and farm productivity in Thailand, Johns Hopkins University Press, London.

Gadgil, S., 1995.Climate change and agricultrue – an Indian perspective.Curr. Sci.69, 649–659.

Grainger-Jones, E., 2011. Climate-Smart Smallholder Agriculture: What's Different? (No. 3), IFAD Occasional Paper (Rome).

Harvey, C. A., Chaco, M., Donatti, C. I., Garen, E., Hannah, L., Andrade, A., et al. (2013). Climate-smart landscapes: Opportunities and challenges for integrating adaptation and mitigation in tropical agriculture. Conservation Letters, 7(2), pp. 77–90.

Hooper, D.U., 1998.The role of complementarity and competition in ecosystem responses to variation in plant diversity. Ecology 79, 704–719.

IPCC.2001, Third Assessment Report.

IPCC, 2001. Climate Change 2001: Impacts, Adaptation, and Vulnerability. Cambridge University Press, Cambridge, UK.

IPCC, 2007, Fourth Assessment Report

IPCC, 2014. Climate Change 2014: Mitigation of Climate Change. Cambridge University Press, Cambridge, UK.

Jat, R.K., Sapkota, T.B., Singh, R.G., Jat, M.L., Kumar, M., Gupta, R.K., 2014. Seven years of conservation agriculture in a rice–wheat rotation of Eastern Gangetic Plains of South Asia: yield trends and economic profitability. Field Crops Res. 164, 199–210.

Khurana, I. (2003), 'Environment management in India: Policies, Practices and Future Needs', Shastri- Indo Canadian Institute, New Delhi.

Kumar, M. D., Patel, A., Ravindranath, R., & Singh, O. P. (2008).Chasing a mirage: Water harvesting and artificial recharge in naturally water-scarce regions. Economic and Political Weekly, 43 (35) 61–71.

Kumar, M. D. (2010). Managing water in river basins: Hydrology, economics and institutions. New Delhi, India: Oxford University Press.

Kydd, J., Poulton, C. and et. al., 2000. Globalisation, agricultural liberalisation, and market access for the rural poor, Wye College, Kent, UK.

Leeuwis, C., Aarts, N., 2011. Rethinking communication in innovation processes: creating space for change in complex systems. The Journal of Agricultural Education and Extension 17 (1), pp. 21–36.

Lipper, L., Thornton, P., Campbell, B.M., Baedeker, T., Braimoh, A., Bwalya, M., Caron, P., Cattaneo, A., Garrity, D., Henry, K., Hottle, R., Jackson, L., Jarvis, A., Kossam, F., Mann, W., McCarthy, N., Meybeck, A., Neufeldt, H., Remington, T., Sen, P.T., Sessa, R., Shula, R., Tibu, A., Torquebiau, E.F., 2014. Climate-smart agriculture for food security. Nature, Climate Change 4, pp. 1068–1072.

Lipper, L., Pingali, P.L. and Zurek, M., 2006. Less-favored areas: looking beyond agriculture towards ecosystem services, ESA Working Paper, forthcoming. Food and Agriculture Organisation, Rome, Italy.

Mahadevan, Renuka 2003. Productivity Growth in Indian Agriculture: The Role of Globalisation and Economic Reform. Asia Pacific Development Journal 10(2), 57-72.

MEF, India's initial national communication to the United Nations framework convention on climate change, Ministry of Environment and Forests, New Delhi, 2004.

Meinzen-Dick, R., DiGregorio, M., McCarthy, N., 2004.Methods for studying collective action in rural development.Agricultural Systems 82 (3), pp.197–214.

Markelova, H., Meinzen-Dick, R., Hellin, J., Dohrn, S., 2009.Collective action for smallholder market access. Food Policy 34, pp. 1–7.

Mittal, Surabhi. 2012. Modern ICT for Agricultural Development and Risk Management in Smallholder Agriculture in India. (CIMMYT), New Delhi, India.

Muro, M., Jeffrey, P., 2008. A critical review of the theory and application of social learning in participatory natural resource management processes. Journal of Environmental Planning and Management. 51 (3), pp. 325–344.

Narayan, Subhash., 2007. Govt. may hole out Rs 1,500 Crore subsidy for Mega Food Parks. Times News Network April 23, 2007, p1.

North, D.C., 2000. Revolution in economics. In: Menard, C. (Eds.), Institutions, Contracts, and Organisations: Perspectives from New Institutional Economics. Edward Elgar, Cheltenham, UK.

OECD, 2001.'Improving the Environmental Performance of Agriculture: Policy Options and Market Approaches', Paris, Cedex 16.

Ostrom, E., Gardner, R., et al., 1994.Rules, Games and Common-pool Resources. Michigan, USA. The University of Michigan Press, Ann Arbor.

Pahl-Wostl, C., 2002.Towards sustainability in the water sector – The importance of human actors and processes of social learning. Aquatic Sciences 64 (December (4)), pp. 394–411.

Parry, M. L., Rosenzweig, C., Iglesias, A., Livermore, M. and Fischer, G., Effects of climate change on global food production under SRES emissions and socio-economic scenarios. Global Environmental Change, 2004, 14(1), pp. 53–67.

Pingali, P.L. and Rosegrant, M., 1995. Agricultural commercialisation and diversification: Processes and policies.Food Policy 20, 171-85.

Pingali, P.L. and Khwaja, Y., 2004. Globalisation of Indian diets and the transformation of food supply systems, ESA Working Paper No. 04-05. FAO, Rome, Italy.

Pingali, P.L., Stamoulis, K. and Stringer, R., 2006. Eradicating extreme poverty and hunger: Towards a coherent policy agenda, ESA Working Paper No. 06-01.Food and Agriculture Organisation, Rome, Italy.

Pretty, J. (1995), 'Regenerating Agriculture: Policies and Practices for Sustainability and Self-Reliance', London: Earthscan Publications Ltd.

Rao, C. A. R. et al., 2013, Atlas on vulnerability of India agriculture to climate change. National Initiative on Climate Resilient Agriculture (NICRA), ICAR, Hyderabad, India.

Reardon, T. and Farina, E.M., 2001. The rise of private food quality and safety standards: Illustrations from Brazil. International Food and Agribusiness Management Review

4, 413-21.

Reardon, T., Timmer, C.P., Barrett, C. and Berdegue, J., 2003.The rise of supermarkets in Africa, Asia, and Latin America.American Journal of Agricultural Economics 85, 1140-6.

Redclift, M., 1989. The environmental consequences of Latin America's agricultural development: some thoughts on the Brundtland Commission report. World Dev.17, 365–377.

Reed, M, Evely, AC, Cundill, G, Fazey, IRA, Glass, J, Laing, A, Newig, J, Parrish, B, Prell, C, Raymond, C & Stringer, L 2010, 'What is social learning?' Ecology and Society 15(4).

Rosenzweig, C., and M.L. Parry, 1994: Potential impact of climate change on world food supply. Nature, 367, pp. 133-138.

Sachs, J., 1997. Nature, nurture, and growth. Economist June 14, 9-27.

Sapkota, T.B., Jat, M.L., Aryal, J.P., Jat, R.K., Khatri-Chhetri, A., 2015. Climate change adaptation, greenhouse gas mitigation and economic profitability of conservation agriculture: some examples from cereal systems of Indo-Gangetic Plains. Journal of Integrative Agriculture 14 (8), pp. 1524–1533.

Scherr, S. J., Shames, S., & Friedman (2012). From climate-smart agriculture to climate-smart landscapes. Agriculture & Food Security, pp. 1–12.

Shiva, V., 1991. The Violence of Green Revolution: Third World Agriculture, Ecologyand Politics. Zed Books.

Singh, R., 2000. Environmental consequences of agricultural development: a casestudy from the Green Revolution state of Haryana, India. Agric. Ecosyst. Environ.82, 97–103.

Smith, P., &Olesen, J. (2010). Synergies between the mitigation of, and adaptation to, climate change in agriculture. Journal of Agricultural Science, 148, pp. 543–552.

Srivastavaa, P., Singh R., Tripathi S., Raghubanshi S. A. 2016. An urgent need for sustainable thinking in agriculture – An Indian scenario. Ecological Indicators 67, 611–622.

Thorne, C., 2014. Geographies of UK flooding in 2013/4. Geography Journal 180 (4), pp. 297–309.

Tilman, D., Knops, J., Wedin, D., Reich, P., Ritchie, M., Siemann, E., 1997a. The influence of functional diversity and composition on ecosystem processes. Science277, 1300–1302.

Timmer, C.P., 2002. Agriculture and economic development. In: Gardner, B. and Rausser, G. (Eds.), Handbook of Agricultural Economics. Elsevier Science, Amsterdam, North Holland.

USAID (US Agency for International Development). 2005. Technology Broadens Farmers Markets. Available: http://www.usaid.gov/in/Pdfs/Farmer_Markets.pdf

Vermeulen, S.J., Campbell, B.M., Ingram, J.S.I., 2012. Climate change and food systems. Annual Review of Environmental Resources 37, pp. 195–222.

Winters, P., Carletto, G., Davis, B., Stamoulis, K. and Zezza, A., 2006. Rural income generating activities in developing countries: a multi-country analysis, Paper prepared for the conference "Beyond Agriculture: the Promise of the Rural Economy for Growth and Poverty Reduction," January 16-18, 2006. Food and Agriculture Organisation,

Rome, Italy.

Woodhill, J., Röling, N., 1998. The second wing of the eagle: the human dimension in learning our way to more sustainable futures. In: Roling, N.G., Wagemakers, M. A.E. (Eds.), Facilitating Sustainable Agriculture: Participatory Learning and Adaptive Management in Times of Environmental Uncertainty. Cambridge University Press, Cambridge, pp. 46–71.

Chapter - 9

Trends and Dimensions of India's Agricultural trade under WTO Regime

Mohd. Adil, Pragya Sharma

Abstract

Rapid globalisation created a need for liberalisation in all sectors of India including agriculture. In this paper, using secondary data we have analyzed the effects of GATT treaty viz. post World trade Organisation (WTO) regime's impact on Indian agriculture trade. An assessment of trade performance of Indian agriculture during pre and post WTO period has been made wherein we have compared the import-export pattern of several agricultural commodities and attempted to find the trends since 1990s.Further, the study attempts to add on to the existing literature by proving a picture of linkage between trade liberalisation in India and Agriculture under WTO regime. For the purpose of analysis, statistical tools of simple mean, Coefficient of Variation, Correlation Coefficient and Simple Regression Analysis have been used to derive a certain conclusion. Data analysis revealed that during 1995 to 2014 agriculture export has grown at a compound rate of 16.2 per cent whereas import has grown at the rate of 18.1 percent. Relatively larger growth rate of imports is a matter of concern for our economy. The paper concludes that there has been insignificant benefit to Indian agriculture in the post WTO regime as the trade balances in agriculture have been unfavorable. Exploring the reasons for such losses in Indian agriculture after WTO formation, the study suggests that lack of infrastructure, education, skills among farmers, lack of efficiency increasing technologies, inadequate credit facilities in this sector have decelerated the growth. Thus, there exists a need for formulation and implementation of structural reforms within agriculture sector so as to reap the benefits of global participation and competition.

1. Introduction

The world economy has been experiencing a progressive international economic integration since the last decade of the twentieth century. Certain events such as formation of WTO happened during 1990s which fostered the process of globalisation in all developing countries as well as in India. India signed the Uruguay Round Agreement on 15th April 1994 at Marrakesh and the agreement on agriculture (AOA) came into effect from January 1, 1995. This marked the dawn of a new era of agriculture trade policy in India. The basic aim of this Agreement was to liberalize agricultural trade by replacing physical controls with bound tariff rates while the overall objective was to provide a framework for the long-term reform of agricultural trade. But, in reality WTO formation and adoption of these agreements bought not much positive and significant impact on trade of developing countries.

2. Objectives and Methodology

In this paper, we have attempted to set up a theoretical as well as empirical linkage between formation of WTO and its impact on Indian agriculture trade. An assessment of trade balances, trade performance of Indian agriculture during pre and post WTO period has been made wherein we have compared the import-export pattern of several agricultural commodities and explored the trends since 1990s.For this purpose, we have collected data from on export-import of agro products from Ministry of Agriculture, Reserve Bank of India, Centre for Monitoring Indian Economy Pvt. Ltd. (CMIE) and Ministry of Commerce. Data analysis has been done using statistical tools viz. simple mean, Coefficient of Variation, Correlation Coefficient and Simple Regression Analysis.

Overall, the paper has been divided into *five* sections. Section 1 and 2 includes introduction and research methodology. Section 3 comprises literature review on WTO formation and its relationship with Indian agriculture trade pattern. Section 4 elaborates upon the trade scenario of agriculture products and commodities of India particularly showcasing its trends since 1995 and further making a comparison of pre and post WTO regime. The next section attempts to explore the prime reasons for changing pattern of trade in agriculture while the last section tries to sum up the findings and make policy recommendations.

3. Review of Literature: Formation of WTO and its Impact on Agriculture trade

Singh and Nandkeoliyar (2001) observed that the WTO agreement was likely to benefit the developing nations by bringing substantial gain in world trade and increased income from liberalisation, improved market access and export opportunities. They however pointed out loopholes in WTO commitments by stating that these commitments would favour the developed nations.

Podbury et.al (2001) in their study on "Agricultural export measures in WTO negotiations" have discussed the export measures in agricultural trade policy reform, application and reform of export subsidies, reforms in major export subsidizing countries misuse of food aid, export credits, and a four point plan for effective reform.

Chand, Ramesh (2005) in his research paper entitled "Post WTO agriculture trade and agenda for negotiation on agriculture" reviewed the performance of India's agricultural export and import during post WTO period by taking secondary data. In his paper he tried to figure out the main reason for favorable/adverse effect on agricultural trade and draw lessons for future negotiation on agreement on agriculture (AOA). He was of the view that there is a need to pay equal attention and commitment for India to adjust his own market and economy like other countries do. Moreover, there is a also need for Indian agriculture to utilize his all strength to compare with the global trade. However, he concludes that major threat for India is from import and adverse impact on export result from low level of international prices. At the end he suggested that India should adopt a path which brings reduction in domestic subsidies, particularly in developed countries because subsidies are the major factor for distortion and low level of International prices.

Kour, Sanmeet and Bhau, Priyanka (2013) in their research paper entitled "Impact of WTO on Indian agriculture using secondary data. The two variables that used in their study are agricultural growth and trade. They observed that WTO has made both positive and negative effect on Indian agriculture. Empirical evidences show that India's share in global agricultural export before WTO has increased but it has declined during post WTO period. They also observed that growth of India's agricultural import was more than export during post WTO period. However, their study suffers from certain limitation. The study has taken only two variables; agricultural growth and trade. The time period is also small from the point of view of long term analysis.

Miet, Maertens and Johan Swinnen, KU leuven (2015) asserts that the system of global agricultural and food trade is undergoing rapid processes of change, with important implications for economic development. In this paper they document and discuss these changes; including the rapid growth and structural change in agri-food trade, the increased consolidation in food supply chains, the proliferation of public and private food standards, high and volatile food prices, and increased vertical coordination in the chains. They investigate what the implications are of these changes for developing countries, for their participation in international agricultural trade as well as for economic development, income mobility and poverty reduction in rural areas.

4. Trade Scenario of Indian Agriculture

Agriculture trade has witnessed rapid changes and increase in India since 1995. Data and literature both suggest that Indian agriculture trade improvised after formation of WTO but our trade balances have remained negative, suggesting greater rise in imports. Table 9.1 shows values of export-import, their respective percentage share and trade balances of India.

Table 9.1: Imports and Exports of Agriculture commodities and trade balances of India from 1995-15

Year	*Exports (in Rs. Crores)*	*Imports (in Rs. Crores)*	*Trade Balance*	*Exports (%)*	*Imports (%)*
1995-96	106353	122678	-16325	28.6	39.4
1996-97	118817	138920	-20103	11.7	13.2
1997-98	130100	154176	-24076	9.5	11
1998-99	139752	178332	-38580	7.4	15.7
1999-00	159095	215529	-56433	13.8	20.9
2000-01	203571	230873	-27302	28	7.1
2001-02	209018	245200	-36182	2.7	6.2
2002-03	254913	296360	-41446	22	20.9
2003-04	293367	359108	-65741	15.1	21.2
2004-05	375340	501065	-125725	27.9	39.5
2005-06	456418	660409	-203991	21.6	31.8
2006-07	571779	881515	-309736	25.3	33.5
2007-08	655864	1012312	-356448	14.7	14.8
2008-09	840755	1374436	-533680	28.2	35.8
2009-10	845534	1363736	-518101	0.6	-0.8
2010-11	1136964	1683467	-546503	34.5	23.4
2011-12	1465959	2345463	-879503	28.9	39.3
2012-13	1634318	2669162	1034844	11.5	13.8
2013-14	1905011	2715434	-810423	16.6	1.7
2014-15	1465171	2134283	-669111	5	5.2
Mean	648404.9	964122.9	-248802	17.68	19.68
SD	577261.4	903276.4	387788.3	9.99	13.11
CV	89.03	93.69	-155.86	56.52	66.63

Source: (I) Hand Book of Statistics on Indian Economy, RBI, 2014-15.
(II) Economic Survey 2014-15.

From the above table, we may decipher that exports and imports have constantly risen but the share of imports has been higher. In 1995-96 exports were 28.6 per cent while imports stood at 39.4 per cent and in the years to follow, the situation has been same. Overall, the percentage agricultural export to total national exports has decreased from 28.6 per cent in 1995-96 to 2.7 per cent in 2001-02 due to larger increase in exports of non-agriculture commodities in the economy. This ratio has further come down to 0.6 per cent in 2009-10 owing to the global economic crisis. There were signs of slight improvement in 2013-14 wherein it increased to 16.6 percent. Checking out the fluctuations in imports and exports, one may conclude it is higher in case of exports; this is clear from the larger values of co-efficient of variation (C.V.). For agriculture export C.V. value is 89.03 per cent whereas for imports it is 93.69 percent.

The trade balance on agriculture account has shown continuous deficit in the post WTO era. This is definitely a matter of worry for India as India considered primarily being an agriculture dominant economy was supposed to reap the benefits of trade liberalisation but has not been in a position to do so. The Indian agriculture sector has not been in a position to compete the international prices of agricultural commodities. As a result, the trade deficit due to agriculture has increased by 41 times (from Rs.16325 Cr. to Rs. 669111 Cr.) in a span of 20 years in the post WTO period.

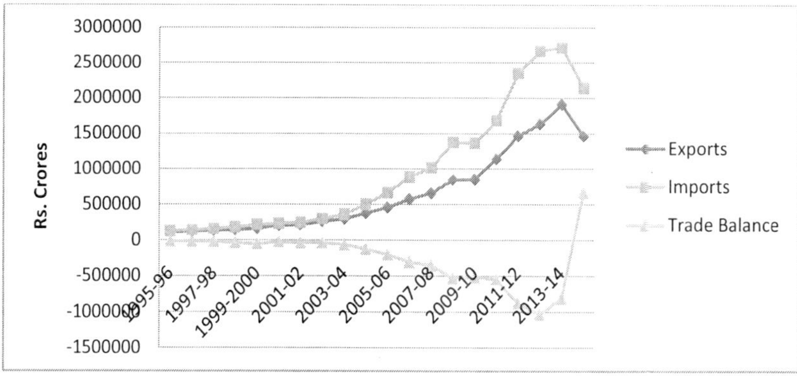

Source: Computed from data in Table 9.1.

Figure 9.1: Export, Import and Trade balances.

A graphical representation of data in table 9.1 has been depicted in Figure 9.1 which shows a clear picture of export-imports trends in Indian agriculture trade. Rising trade and declining trade balances is clearly portrayed through the graph.

From Figure 9.2 and 9.3, we have estimated the trade pattern over the period of twenty years during 1995-96 to 2014-15. The agriculture export has grown at a compound rate of 16.2 per cent whereas import has grown at the rate of 18.1 per cent over the same period. A larger growth rate for agriculture import is definitely a sign of concern. Both agricultural exports and imports growth have shown exponential growth rate over the year which is clear from the fitted curve. The goodness of fit R^2 is very high (more than 0.95) in case of

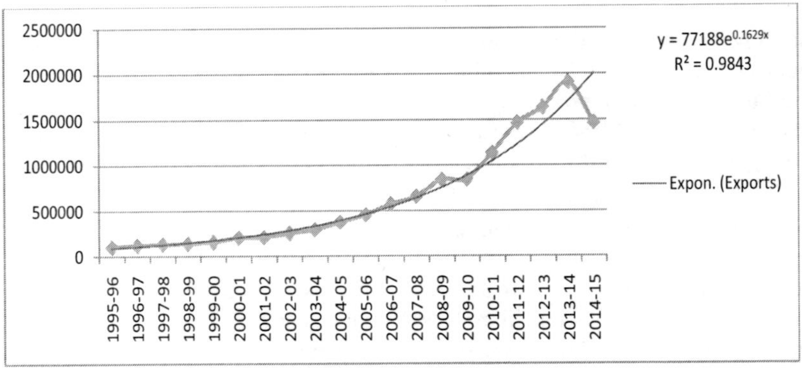

Source: Computed from data in table 9.1.

Figure 9.2 :Agriculture Exports.

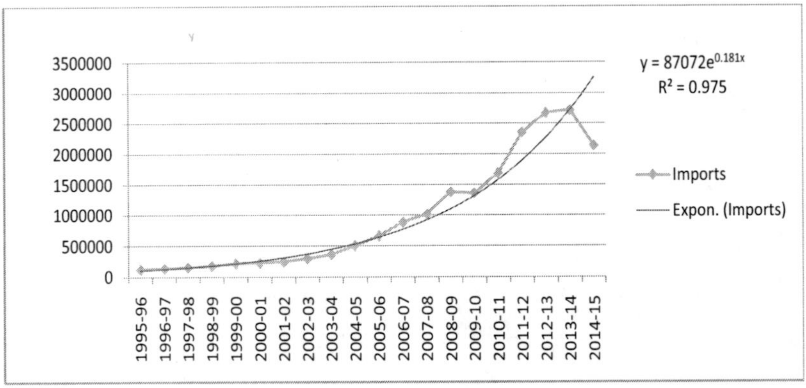

Source: Computed from data in table 9.1.

Figure 9.3: Agriculture Imports.

both exports as well as imports. Both exports and imports have shown large fluctuations over a period of 20 years in the post WTO period.

Using Cuddy-Della Valle Index[1] for variability measurement, we estimate that instability is 12.59 for agriculture exports whereas it is 16.23 for agricultural imports. This shows higher stability for exports in India. Therefore, the above findings prove that there has been a net loss to Indian agriculture in the post liberalisation era and under the WTO regime as the trade balances due to agriculture has shown a continuous deficit, a net burden to further widen the gap of an overall trade deficit. The adverse impact on Indian agriculture, which was feared by many in the country, seems to be well founded. The only matter of solace, though of very low degree, is that exports have shown lower degree of instability as compared to imports. Under the provisions of Agreement on Agriculture (AoA), India is unfavorably placed to exploit certain provisions of WTO. The international trading environment has not opened up to the extent predicted. The developed countries have managed to hold onto their position of the main cereal exports by delinking support to farmers from the market prices. Non-tariff barriers have been placed by the tariffs, but the effective level of protection has not declined. In view of the above, integration of Indian agriculture in the global trade a competitive trade scenario can be realised only by reducing domestic cost of production through measures which increase productivity and control procurement and distribution costs. The road to globalisation lies in productivity increases and not on the pre-supposed apprehensions regarding WTO.

In order to check the export pattern and level of diversification in trade of India, we have used Herfindahl and Gini-Hirschman Index. Table 9.2 represents the values obtained after using the indexes.

Table 9.2: Agriculture Export pattern of India and Herfindahl Index

Year	Agriculture Exports	Total National Exports	% of Agri. Exports to total Exports	H-Index[1]	G-H Index[2]
1995-96	20397.74	106353	19.18	0.192	0.037
1996-97	24161.29	118817	20.33	0.203	0.041
1997-98	24843.45	130100	19.09	0.191	0.036
1998-99	25510.64	139752	18.25	0.183	0.033
1999-00	25313.66	159095	15.91	0.159	0.025
2000-01	28657.37	203571	14.23	0.142	0.02
2001-02	29728.61	209018	14.22	0.142	0.02
2002-03	34653.94	254913	13.38	0.136	0.018
2003-04	37266.52	293367	12.7	0.127	0.016
2004-05	41602.65	375340	11.08	0.111	0.012
2005-06	49216.96	456418	10.78	0.108	0.012
2006-07	62411.42	571779	10.92	0.109	0.012
2007-08	79039.72	655864	12.05	0.121	0.015
2008-09	85951.67	840755	10.22	0.102	0.01
2009-10	89341.33	845534	10.57	0.106	0.011
2010-11	117483.6	1136964	10.28	0.103	0.011
2011-12	187609.3	1465959	12.8	0.128	0.016
2012-13	232041.1	1634318	14.2	0.142	0.02
2013-14	268469.1	1894182	14.17	0.142	0.02
Average				**0.139**	**0.020**

*Source** (I) Hand Book of Statistics on Indian Economy, RBI, 2014-15. (II) Economic Survey 2014-15.

1. Herfindahl Index – It is the sum of squared shares of each product in total export. A country with a perfectly diversified export portfolio will have an index close to zero, whereas a country which exports only one export will have a value of 1 (least diversified).
2. A country with a perfectly diversified export portfolio will have an index close to zero, whereas a country which exports only one export will have a value of 1.

Table 9.2 reveals that the level of diversification is high in Indian agriculture as the average values of Herfindahl index and Gini-Hirschman is 0.13 and 0.020 respectively. The range of these indexes is 0 to 1, wherein values near 0 represents diversification in exports while a value near to 1 shows low diversification. This clearly depicts that agrarian exports are not much focused upon and neither has their export increased over the stated time period, more specifically after formation of WTO.

Further, in order to check the growth of agriculture in India after WTO formation and liberalisation, a brief comparison of the production in India with some of the developing and developed countries in both pre-and post-reform periods on the basis of few indices viz. crop production index, food production index, livestock production index, cereal yield and agricultural productivity (depicted in table 9.3) has been done. The data shows that is far behind these countries in terms of several of these indices. Though the situation

Table 9.3: Agricultural output and productivity

	2004-06=100						*Cereal Yield (Kg/Hectare)*[4]		*Agriculture value added per worker (in $)*	
	Crop Pro. Index[1]		*Food Pro. Index*[2]		*Livestock Pro. Index*[3]					
	1990	*2009*	*1990*	*2009*	*1990*	*2009*	*1990*	*2009*	*1990*	*2009*
Australia	67.0	101.0	74.0	103.0	85.0	101.0	1,716	1,721	19,447	35,208
Canada	82.0	109.0	73.0	107.0	68.0	95.0	2,636	3,490	28,898	*44,619*
China	56.0	**116.0**	48.0	115.0	39.0	112.0	4,325	5,521	258	545
India	**73.0**	**113.0**	**71.0**	**114.0**	**62.0**	**115.0**	**1,891**	**2,537**	**357**	**489**
Japan	123.0	94.0	114.0	98.0	107.0	101.0	**5,846**	**5,852**	19,563	*48,794*
Sri Lanka	87.0	111.0	85.0	112.0	75.0	107.0	2,965	3,974	672	966
U.K.	104.0	102.0	107.0	101.0	107.0	99.0	6,171	6,957	19,880	25,681
U.S.	79.0	105.0	77.0	109.0	78.0	105.0	4,755	**6,988**	18,703	51,120
World	**70.0**	**122.2**	**70.0**	**123.0**	**74.0**	**120.3**	**2756**	**3568**	**781**	**992**

*Source** World Development Indicators 2004 & 2012.

1. Shows agricultural production for each period relative to the base period 1989-91. It includes all crops except fodder crops. The regional and income group aggregates for the FAO's production indexes are calculated from the underlying values in International Dollars, normalised to the base period 1989-91. The data in this table are three years average.
2. Covers food crops that are considered edible and that contain nutrients. Coffee and tea are excluded because, although edible, they have no nutritive value.
3. Includes meat and milk from all sources, dairy products such as cheese, eggs, honey, raw silk, wool and hides and skins.
4. Measured in kilogram per hectare of harvested land, includes wheat, rice, maize, barley, oats, rye, millet, sorghum, buckwheat, and mixed grains. Production data on cereals refer to crops harvested for dry grain only.
5. Refers to the ratio of agricultural value added, measured in constant 1995 U.S. dollars, to the number of workers in agriculture

has improved in the post liberalisation era, the growth rates of various indices during the same period if compared with China again shows a dissatisfying performance. China in the pre-liberalisation era had a value less than that of India in terms of the various indices; in the post liberalisation era due to a steep increase China has not only surpassed India but also many developed countries. One interesting feature is that despite India being called an agrarian economy for centuries, the above mentioned indices values are less in the country as compared to world average value

On the basis of above observations we are now in a position to say that on trade front our agriculture sector has not been favorable to us and it has not only shown a continuous deficit on trade account due to agriculture in the post WTO period but that deficit has increased gradually.

5. Reasons behind Unfavorable trade balances

According to World Trade Organisation (WTO) International Trade Statistics (2012) global export and import of agricultural and food products is US $1.66 trillion and US $ 1.82 trillion respectively while India's share stands mere at 2.07% and 1.24%. India used to be a net importer of food few years back but currently it produces 250 million tonnes (MT) of food grains, 100 MT of rice, 90 MT of wheat, 35 million bales of cotton, and more than 18 MT of pulses. This growth can be attributed to consistent investments in technology up-gradation, enhancement of irrigation infrastructure, encouragement of adoption of latest agricultural practices and provision of loans and disbursements to farmers. Up to some extent, foreign direct investment (FDI) inflows in agricultural sector have rendered immense support in increasing trade levels. But still, the trade deficits have not reduced. The basic challenges, which lie in this context, are low agriculture productivity, rural poverty and domestic food insecurity.

Trade balances have worsened because agricultural productivity per unit of land is still low. Productivity growth has also tapered off since 2001–02. India-wide productivity is, also, uneven (Gupta, undated).Marginal landholding size, insufficient irrigation facilities, inadequate credit support to farmers, high production costs make agriculture productivity and growth decline (Mundhe, 2015). Productivity levels in Indian agriculture are relatively low as compared to other developed and developing countries. India global ranking in terms of productivity in agriculture is quite disappointing. Excessive population pressure, inadequate social environment, land degradation and inability to use HYV seeds are some of the main causes of low agriculture productivity (Sreekanth et.al, 2017).

Though, sharp rise in food-grain production was seen during India's Green Revolution in 1970s and it enabled the country to achieve self-sufficiency in food-grains and stave off the threat of famine nut still much remained unanswered. Agricultural intensification during 1970-1980 was favorable with reference to employment and reduction in rural poverty levels but it could not bring growth in this sector. Agricultural growth in the 1990s and 2000s slowed down, averaging about 3.5% per annum, and cereal yields have increased only by 1.62% per annum in this period. Such a slow-down in agricultural growth became a major cause for concern for the policy makers and government. Even today, agriculture is the slowest developing sector and yields levels are unsatisfying. Rice yields in India are approx. one-third of China's and even worse off than countries viz. Vietnam, Indonesia etc. Similar situation prevails with reference to productivity and yield levels of other agriculture crops and commodities. This affects domestic production and consumption levels thereby making imports of primary products necessary and causing unfavorable trade balance.

Rural poverty is another challenge that poses a threat in increasing agriculture production/productivity thereby affecting trade. Rural development is still slow and non – inclusive. Moreover, there exist strong regional disparities wherein the majority of India's poor are in rain-fed areas or in the Eastern Indo-Gangetic plains. Though improvement has been made in this scenario wherein the number of persons classified as poor in rural population reduced by 40 per cent in 1990s and almost below 30 per cent during mid-2000, registering a fall of average 1 per cent every year (World Bank, 2017). Such high level of poverty among farmers is a grave issue as the entire agriculture cycle revolves around it.

Study by Aubron (2015) estimate that almost 30% of families make an incomefrom agriculture that is lower than the recently redefined national poverty threshold (32 rupees /person/day at the time of the study, according to the Planning Commission, 2014). NSSO (70 th round) and Ministry of Agriculture reports, state that almost 65 per cent of farmers belong to marginal category which in itself is a cause for exacerbated poverty as economies of scale cannot be achieved. Loans or subsidies granted by government and cooperatives are also not available to marginal landowners thereby affecting infrastructure setup. Lack of adequate machinery and infrastructure at farms prevents farmers to raise production and generate high yields.

6. Conclusion

Data analysis reveals that during 1995 to 2014 agriculture export has grown at a compound rate of 16.2 per cent whereas import has grown at the rate of 18.1 percent. Relatively larger growth rate of imports is a matter of concern for our economy. As far as trends of variation from mean with reference to exports and imports are considered larger values viz. 89.03 per cent for agriculture exports while it is 93.69 per cent for imports exist. Considering, data on farm production, cereal yield and agricultural productivity from 1990 to 2009, it is found that there has been a net benefit to our agrarian economy suggesting improvement with coming up of WTO regime. But this rise in production and productivity is not substantial as India lags behind many countries with reference to these indicators and agriculture sector would continue to suffer as trade diversification is occurring at a rapid pace.

Overall, we may conclude that there has been insignificant benefit to Indian agriculture in the post liberalisation era specifically under the WTO regime as the trade balances in agriculture depict continuous deficit. Though, it was expected that WTO formation would be extremely profitable for developing countries as it would increase income of farmers and lower production prices but however the situation turned to be different. Exploring the reasons for such losses in Indian agriculture trade after WTO formation, the study suggests that low agriculture productivity, farmer poverty, lack of infrastructure, lack of efficiency increasing technologies, inadequate credit facilities in this sector have decelerated growth. Therefore, there exists a need for formulation and implementation of structural reforms within agriculture sector so as to reap the benefits of global participation and competition.

References

A, Damodaran (2001), *"WTO Agriculture Agreement, Common Property Resources and Income Diversification Strategy",* Economic and Political Weekly Vol. 36, No. 38 (Sep. 22-28, 2001), pp. 3633-3642.

Ahmad, Rais (2009). "WTO *and Indian Agriculture- Opportunities, Problemsand Challenges"*. New Delhi: Mittal Publications.

Ahmad and Khan (2001), *"WTO challenges and opportunities - A case of Indian agriculture"*, National Bank News Review Mumbai 17(4): 8-19.

Auborn, C . (2015), "*Poverty and Inequlity in Rural India*" Open Edition journals, Echo geo (available at :http://journals.openedition.org/echogeo/14300#toctoln3)

B, Sheshagiri (2011), *Impact of W.T.O on Indian agriculture: Performance and prospects*, International Journal of Current Research 01/2011; Vol. 3:pp.066-070.

Deodhar Satish Y. (2006), "*WTO Agreements and Indian Agriculture: Retrospection and Prospects*", IIMA Working Paper # 99-11-06.

Government of India: Centre for Monitoring Indian Economy (Agriculture), (Various Issues), Ministry of Finance, Economic Division, New Delhi.

Government of India: National Accounts Statistics (various issues), Central Statistical Organisation. New Delhi.

Government of India (2013-14), "Agricultural Statistics at a Glance", Directorate of Economics and Statistics, Department of Agriculture and Cooperation, Ministry of Agriculture, New Delhi.

Government of India (2014-15), Economic Survey, Ministry of Finance, Department of Economic Affairs, Economic Division, New Delhi.

Gupta, D. (undated), "India's Lagging Sector: Indian Agriculture in a Globalising Economy", Working paper, University of Canberra (available at: https://crawford.anu.edu.au/acde/asarc/pdf/papers/2008/WP2008_05.pdf)

Mundhe,F.(2015), "Agricultural productivity in India: trends during five year plans", Business and Mangement Review, Vol. 5, No. 4.

Podbury T, I Roberts, A. Tielu, and B. Beutre. ABARE (2001), *"Agricultural export measures in WTO negotiations",* Australian bureau of agricultural and resource economics Research Report 01.12, RRRDC publication no. 01/134. Canberra: ABARE.

Sharma, Devinder (2000). "Indian Farmers Not Benefiting from W.T.O. Agreement". *Third World Network Features*. Date retrieved 30 Aug 2009 Available at: http://www.twnside.org.sg/title/2099.html

Sing S.R. and Nandkeoliyar (2001): "*WTO: Its effects on the Indian Economy*", in G.K. Chadha (ed.), 'WTO and Indian Economy', New Delhi, Deep and Deep publications Private Ltd.

Chapter - 10

Globalization and Water: the Dynamics of Privatization and Water Markets

Raina Ghosh

Abstract

Semantics behind the Washington Consensus have given rise to free market shibboleths which find market as a 'solution' to efficiently manage scarce resources. According to Scholte[1], the analytical lynchpin for understanding social change in the contemporary world is provided by the intuitive concept of 'globalisation' that renders the best entry point for such an enquiry. For the water sector, this has translated into a corporate theft of 'blue gold', within informal or formal institutional arrangements; interestingly made possible, courtesy the increasing mediation of public opinion by the State as well as the supra national institutions, backed by the advent of globalisation, that has successfully woven the imagery of 'safe drinking water' as a precondition for healthy living. The alarming imposition is that, its provision is not solely a State responsibility anymore, inviting newer players in the supply side of the drinking water sector.

1. Introduction

The crux of the paradigmatic shift in the water sector policies is to be understood in the light of the broader economic thinking in the era of globalisation, allowing the primacy of the social sector provisioning to be replaced by a central focus on the 'markets'. This reinstates the changing role from 'welfare' to a 'neoliberal state' as neoliberalism emerged as a radical anti-Keynesian movement that sought to dismantle major Keynesian institutions and policies and viewed the former entity as a part of the 'problem' that should be subject to the neoliberal 'solution' (Kus, 2006)[2].

However, the narrative of this change unfolds under the initiative of the supra-national institutions advocating for the demand responsive approaches in water sector thereby packaging the water reforms as a sugar-coated welfare enhancing scheme. The seemingly neutral, technical policy provisions are in fact deeply political because they entail far-reaching redistributions of water and of water rights, water power and water based profits (Boelens and Zwarteveen, 2005, 2010)[3].

The rational choice paradigm of neoliberalism clinging on to the language of efficiency, utility maximisation and private property rights intends to turn the 'backward' water delivery and management institutions into more efficient 'modern' ones drawing on its inspirations from the 'neo-liberalist utopian dreams' to pave the way for an unequivocal celebration of market forces and private ownership. These are justified on grounds of looming water crisis and by constructing the 'new moral political project' of instillation of fear about health if one is not consuming 'safe water', delivered through prior treatment processes. The construction of the larger economic cum social imaginary resting on the ideas that scarcity hinders the economy's potential growth and more specifically in case of water – posing a threat for the very human existence, makes it convincing enough for the public to attest for the market mechanisms to be favoured, to operate at the earliest. Locally and practically this translate into efforts to build 'unconscious and uncritical habitual modes of thought of ordinary citizens, useful for the governing regime which is ruling the country on behalf of the domestic and corporate interests' (Sood & Baruah, 2017:1).

Bakker[4] identifies neoliberalism as a heterogeneous and contested political project, consisting of an 'interaction of two processes of transformation-privatisation and commercialisation which are concerned with the reorganisation of water allocation, with resources and assets that used to be publicly owned being made available for private ownership and for idle capital to invest in and speculate with'. Implicitly making water resources, land (for further ground water exploitation) and other services available to the market at 'very low or zero cost' and putting them to the centre of profitable use goes behind the very essence as well as the economics of Harvey's 'accumulation by dispossession' [5] that characterise 'water privatisation' as part and parcel of such larger on-going processes of capitalist transformation. The utopian project thus skilfully etches out a theoretical design for the reorganisation of international capitalism or to re-establish the conditions for capital accumulation through economic deregulation as well as institutional devolution to create competitive markets, encashing on the 'scarcity' as an opportunity to enter the market or expand it for more surpluses. Moreover, the riveting fact is that despite the call for the withdrawal of the state in providing public utilities and services, the implicit idea of neoliberal governance is to use the state machinery for legal, administrative and social measures to facilitate private entrepreneurs and 'appropriate functioning of markets', making the deregulation associated with globalisation- a sort of re-regulation in its creation of new governing structures and discourses that sustain neoliberalism (Harvey,

2005: 19; 2007[6]; Boelens and Zwarteveen, 2010: 45[7], Peck and Tickell, 2002[8]; Castree, 2008 [9]).

Understanding the dynamics of social change that is inevitably associated with the institutionalisation of these ideas brings to fore the conflicting interests of the irreconcilable economic classes which have their basis in the structure of the society. Using the dialectical method to interpret the superstructural manifestations of the structural contradictions, it is evident how these conflicts spell out in the water sector in terms of the tensions between the market forces and its players, that treat water as an economic good versus the consensus of viewing water as a basic human right when at the superstructural realm, commercialisation of water supply across globe, posits the 'blue gold' as 'an increasingly vital component in the relentless quest of capital for new sources of accumulation', creating newer 'enclosure of the commons' - an objective of state policies (Swyngedouw, 2005: 87[10]; Luxemburg, 2003[11]).

The chapter aims to sketch out the dynamics of water privatisation in the rural drinking water sector in India whereby it intends to introspect the various dimensions that have shaped up the interplay between State and Non-State actors regarding issues of provision of potable water for people. The objectives are –

(i) To trace the overall policy trajectory that provides the backdrop behind the emergence of Water markets in the drinking water sector
(ii) To review the changing role of the State associated with such developments

1. Methodology

The paper attempts to engage with critical policy analysis of the existing water policies, inspecting the three fundamental elements – contexts, texts and consequences, considering the three National Water Policies of 1987, 2002 and 2012 as the cut-off periods. Through textual deconstruction of the policy clauses, their tactics of language and a temporal trend analysis of the national and international drinking water sector programmes, it tries to bring out the meanings associated with them in the neoliberal regime, allowing a conceptualisation of the changing role of state, located within the broader context of globalisation.

2. A Look back at the Policy Landscape

A look back at the international and national milestones and policies in the water sector, illustrates before us the journey unfolded so far and how brilliantly the policy texts have paved the way for the unravelling of privatisation and advent of water markets even in case of rural drinking water.

2.1 Phase 1. Before 1987: The early laws of the land

In case of hydraulic civilisations such as India, water rights have been mostly understood in terms of riparian rights since ancient times. These rights were primarily customary rights over water resources enjoyed by the communities and subject to mutual settlements. At the domestic level, colonial legislation first focused explicitly on the regulation of water for economic reasons, commercial interests; for instance, through the development of legislation concerning irrigation and navigation (Cullet, 2007: 1).

Otherwise water law in India closely associated with the land policies. India Easements Act of 1882 granted '*every landowner with the right to collect and dispose, within his own limits, all water under the land and on the surface*'. As a consequence of this law, owner of a piece of land has been allowed to dig wells and extract water based on availability and his discretion without any legal liability for any damage caused to water resources as a result of over-extraction. Interestingly, the focus on drinking water in India comes much later in the country, in the form of the Bhore Committee on hygiene which pointed out that causes behind the low status of health in India was primarily because (among other reasons), totally inadequate provision of protected water supply and drainage', recommending the safe supply of water to cover 90% of India's population in a time frame of 40 years, ie. by 1989 (Bhore Committee Report, 1946 : 11).

In the absence of any comprehensive water law in the colonial phase, the state could only exert its explicit control in the post-independence era, following the declaration of water as a State subject (Entry 17 of List II ie. State List, 7th Schedule) under Article 246 of the Indian Constitution in 1950.The Constitution also mandated through Article 47, conferring the duty to the State to provide safe drinking water in order to raise the standard of living in the country and improve public health conditions. Thus the focus on drinking water supply was more of a ramification of the alarming concern on 'hygiene' borne out of the escalating morbidity, mortality rates in the country. The post-Independence era saw the translations of the then relevant nation building perspectives backed by Nehruvian socialist, nationalist ideals in the structure and design of welfare and development projects undertaken by the State (National Rural Drinking Water Supply program of 1969, Accelerated Rural Drinking Water Supply Programme of 1972–73, Minimum Needs Programme etc.)

3. Rationale behind the inception of NWP

The need for national water policies was raised in the Mar del Plata Action Plan (following the United Nations Water Conference, held in Mar del Plata, Argentina in March 14-25, 1977) which made sure, there is a commitment on behalf of the national governments to 'provide all people with water of safe quality and adequate quantity and basic sanitary facilities by 1990, according priority to the poor and less privileged and to water scarce areas' while Part B of the recommendations for action, framed provisions for each country to establish 'goals for 1990 which match as far as possible the global targets'.

During the 1960s and 1970s, international and national efforts focused on the achievement of coverage figures (Nicol, 2000) with a **strong footing on qualitative assessment of water meant for provision**, bringing to the fore, a comprehensive lens of viewing water supply issues along with sanitation facilities. Although, it was long back in 1954 that Water Supply and Sanitation were brought under the purview of the Central Public Health and Engineering Organisation (CPHEO) of the Ministry of Works and Housing, Government of India, **'Rural Sanitation Programme'** in India had been receiving consistent attention ever since the formulation of the **Centrally Sponsored Rural Sanitation Programme (CRSP)** in 1986 and subsequent inclusion of Rural Sanitation in the **Minimum Needs programme (MNP)** in 1987. These were given a series of institutional backing through the setting up of a multi-donor partnership programme called Water and Sanitation Programme (WSP) launched by UNDP and World Bank in 1978, the WHO Guidelines on the Drinking Water Quality, 1983-'84, 1st Edition, nationally - the establishment of a separate Department of Drinking Water Supply in 1980 and **National Drinking Water Mission** in 1986 under the MoRD and most importantly, in compliance with the spirit imbibed by the proclamation of the **International Drinking Water Supply and Sanitation Decade between 1980-1991**[12], during which *'member states would assume a commitment to bring about a substantial improvement in the standards and levels of services in drinking water supply and sanitation by the year 1990'*. This decade coincided with the 6th and 7th FYP (1980-'85, 1985-'90) in India and led to the formulation of a 'common set of technical guidelines for the rural drinking water sector, established nationally and applied across different state governments in the early 1970s' (Joshi, 2002). The nuances in language of technical guidelines (Joshi, 2004: 8), underpinned the state's increasing priorities towards **quality provisions than quantity concerns.** These were –

- ***Complete coverage** for all **no-source problem villages** and partially covered villages*
- Water supply to be provided within the stipulated norms of **40 lpcd within a maximum distance of 1.6km or at an elevation of 100m** in the hilly regions.
- **Priority of safe water provision** where the existing supply sources exhibit health- harming characteristics.

3.1 1987 : Formulation of the National Water Policy

The National Water Policy (NWP) adopted in September 1987 recognised water as a ***'basic human need;** a precious national asset and one of the most crucial elements in development planning'* (1.1, 1.8, NWP, 1987), something that is repeatedly acknowledged in the national policy documents to follow. The stress on the need for an integrated and environmentally sound management approach in the planning, development and conservation of a **'scarce'** resource like water to cater to the increasing **demands** from rural society made the economic thinking behind it more evident. Interestingly, keeping a separate sub-section on **'water rates'**, the policy called for the promotion of **conservation awareness** about the ***'efficient utilisation'*** of the *'scarce resource'* through ***'education, regulation, incentives and disincentives'*** andimposition of **water rates for surface and ground water, *'adequate to cover the annual maintenance and operation charges and a part of the fixed costs'*** (although that should be***'rationalised with due regard to the interests of small and marginal farmers')*** *(11. Water Rates; 15. Conservation of Water; 21.Conclusion, NWP, 1987)*

Phase 2. Between 1987 and the Revision of Policy in 2002

Pushing the slogan '**Some For All Rather Than More For Some',** the 1990 Global Consultation on safe Water and sanitation, New Delhi Statement preceded the ill famous Dublin Statement of 1992 and was significant for heralding the ideological battle regarding the role of the State as it provisioned the Government's roles to become that of **'promoters and facilitators'** reasserting the failures of the supply-led approaches of Government programmes of 1980s, as it highlighted the need for a focus on education, training, social mobilisation, **decentralisation of service delivery and community involvements.**

3.2 Changing Perspectives: Right to Water – recognition in India

Economic liberalisation marks the year 1991 as the milestone in India's economic history for the reforms initiated thereafter. But for the water sector in India, 1991 marked a different milestone altogether as the then existing legal framework concerning water got complemented by a human rights dimension with Supreme Court recognizing that, **right to life 'includes the right of enjoyment of pollution free water and air for full enjoyment of life',** implied in Article 21 (right to life) as per *Subhash Kumar v. State of Bihar, 1991*. A watershed in the history of evolution of global water policies has been the **Dublin Statement on Water and Sustainable Development,** issued by the **International Conference on Water and the Environment** (IWCE, held in Dublin, Ireland on 26-31st January 1992) that created major fault lines in policy trajectories so far. Principles 1-3 recognised the ***'vulnerability'*** and ***'finite'*** nature of fresh water as a resource whose management requires a participatory approach involving *'users, planners, policy makers at all levels'*. However, these were far outweighed by the impact generated by its **fourth principle** acknowledging that ***'water has an economic value in all its competing uses and should be recognised as an economic***

good'. The argument put forward vouched for a clear cut deviation from the role assigned to the State so far, dictating a trade off for one's basic right - to have access to clean water and sanitation at an affordable price, for achieving efficient and equitable use, encouraging conservation and protection of water resources and the fact that ***'past failure to recognize the economic value of water*** *has led to wasteful and environmentally damaging uses of the resource'*. Winpenny (1994: 18) argued that this new approach to valuation would increase water supply coverage and **encourage private investment as 'low prices depress the profitability of investment in the water sector'**. World Bank and later the Washington Consensus encashed upon the economic valuation of the resource which was eventually to become the core of the emerging consensus and changing paradigm of viewing water (or other environmental resources per se) as an 'economic good', whereby State's role was expected to shrink with the advent of free-market capitalism, legitimising the commoditisation of resources and justifying scope for its privatisation (Finger and Allouche, 2002 ; Mehta, 2010). The Dublin Principle on water as an economic good, Phillip Cullet[13] argues, has been the single most important change to water policy, leading to a **focus on demand management** and **increases in water use efficiency**, for such **economic connotations usually privilege certain types of meaning and beliefs** into cultural and public good aspects that makes it easier to defend the massive gap in access to water supply and sanitation that has persisted till today.

4. Millennium Declaration – Foundation stone for the future developments goals

Building upon the events like Earth Summit, 1992 (Rio de Janeiro), the First World Water Forum of 1997, followed by the Marrakech Declaration in 1997, 1999- Protocol on Water & Health, United Nations General Assembly adopted the United Nations Millennium Declaration at the UN Millennium Summit (Resolution A/res/55/2) in New York, 2000, which set out the future developmental pillars in the form of 8 Millennium Development Goals (MDGs). With respect to access to drinking water and sanitation, through the set target 7.C of the MDGs, States committed themselves to "*halving, by 2015, the proportion of people without sustainable access to safe drinking water*", thereby laying the international policy and service level benchmark for the countries worldwide. By the Johannesburg Targets adopted at the 2002 World Summit on Sustainable Development, States committed themselves to the additional target of "*halving, by the year 2015, the proportion of people who do not have access to basic sanitation.*" An important event in the global arena concerning water, took place in November 2002 — with the adoption of the ***General Comment No.15, on the 'Right to Water' by the Committee on Economic, Social and Cultural Rights (CESCR),*** presenting a continuum between the provisions formulated in human rights language and other provisions formulated in a regulatory language.

Article 1.1 stated that –

> *"The human right to water is indispensable for leading a life in human dignity; a prerequisite for the realisation of other human rights".*

Comment No.15 also defined 'right to water' as the **right of everyone**, to **sufficient, safe, acceptable** and **physically accessible** and **affordable** water for personal and domestic uses.

Phase 3. Need for a Revision: NWP, 2002 and the period till 2012

A review of the 1987 policy was initiated with the publication of a revised National Water Policy-2002, which in line with the developments made at the larger international level '*underscored the need for the utmost efficiency in water utilisation and a public awareness of the importance of its conservation*', given the inevitable increase in '*demands for water for diverse purposes*', due to expansion of growth and economic activities in the period concerned, bearing the potential threat to make a scarce resource like water '*even scarcer in future*' *(1.7, NWP, 2002)*. Stress was also laid on the need to monitor quality of water, maintenance of water resources, specially the physical and financial sustainability of existing facilities, to bring about *improvements in existing technologies, innovation of new technology base* resting on science and technical training through a '*multi-sectoral, multi-disciplinary and participatory approach*. Taking cue from the earlier version of NWP, the World Bank recommendations of its 1998 review, the policy of 2002 extended the argument for '*a need to ensure that the* ***water charges for various uses*** *should be fixed in such a way that they* ***cover at least the operation and maintenance charges*** *of providing the service initially and* ***a part of the capital costs*** *subsequently*' and as a **major digression from its welfare approach,** encouraged **wherever feasible, various combinations of *'private sector participation*** *in planning, development and management of water resources projects*' promoting their potential in *'introducing innovative ideas, generating financial resources and introducing corporate management and improving service efficiency and accountability to users'.(11. Financial and Physical Sustainability; 13. Private Sector Participation, NWP, 2002).*

In various aspects, the 2002 policy reflected the provisions made by the 73rd and 74th Constitutional Amendment Act to **decentralise power** and pave way for **local governance** in rural and urban areas by **involving Water Users' Associations, local bodies such as municipalities and *gram panchayats*** *(12. Participatory Approach to Water Resources Management, NWP, 2002).* But the exposition of utmost importance, carrying the impressions of the predominant shift in policy legacy during that phase, is interpreted from clause 22, stating '*there is an* ***urgent need of paradigm shift*** *in the emphasis in the* *management of water resources sector; from the* ***present emphasis on the creation and expansion of water resources infrastructures*** *for diverse uses, to the need to give* ***greater emphasis on the improvement of the performance*** *of the existing water resources facilities'* and the 'optimal, economical and equitable use' of the resource, bearing its implications on the changing priorities of allocation of funds and in outlining the guidelines to improve the performance of this sector. To conclude, the policy mandates the **formulation of a State Water Policy,** backed with an operational action plan within two years, also sanctioning provisions for the periodic revision of National Water Policy '*as and when need arises'*.

The Swajal project of 1996, **piloted by World Bank in UP as a Sector Reform Programme in 67 districts across 26 states** was scaled to the **Swajaldhara Programme, initiated on 25th December, 2002,** that emphasized the need for taking up of community based rural water supply programs and initiate reform initiatives in rural drinking water sector, upholding the principles of **'decentralisation and participation'** as mandated by the 73rd Constitutional Amendment Act, reflecting the market ideals as promoted by the World Bank. The Swajaldhara guidelines also suggested that water users have to take up partial responsibility for the capital cost of new drinking water infrastructure and full responsibility for operation and maintenance, **reinforcing the notion that water is an economic good and that all water services must be based on the principle of (full) cost-recovery**. This was a **demand-driven**, integrated approach to rural water supply and sanitation requiring partial (10%) capital cost recovery and 100% O&M financing by users. The guidelines meant to foster a **change in the role of the government from direct service delivery to that of facilitating activities**, largely undertaken by people themselves, proposing the **progressive withdrawal of the state** from the provision of the fundamental right to drinking water.

The stress on water quality, the emphasis on the need to provide 'safe drinking water' through technology based water treatment plants and the projection of water-related services as determined by economic principles continued at the international front with the **Bonn Charter for Safe Drinking Water, framed by the International Water Association in September 2004,** assigning the goal to provide ***'good, safe water which has the trust of consumers'***, the publication of the **WHO Revised Guidelines for Drinking Water Quality, 3rd Edition** revising its earlier guidelines to focus on the prevention of microbial and chemical contamination of drinking water supplies through the **use of a comprehensive risk assessment and risk management approach that encompasses all steps in water supply from catchment to consumers, called Water safety plans (WSPs)**.

5. 'Water for life' Decade

With a goal to promote efforts to fulfil 'long term sustainable international commitments' (Millennium Declaration, the Johannesburg Plan of Implementation of the World Summit for Sustainable Development and Agenda 21) made on water and water-related issues, 'in terms of both quantity and quality and measures to improve sanitation', by 2015, the United Nations General Assembly in December 2003, proclaimed as per the General Assembly **Resolution A/RES/58/217**, the period 2005-2015 as the **'International Decade for Action 'Water for Life'**[14].

The decade also saw the recognition of the ***'right to clean water services'*** the UN General Assembly Resolution (Resolution 64/292) on the ***'Right to Water and Sanitation'*** on July28th, 2010 explicitly recognising the '***human right to water and sanitation'***, acknowledging that '***clean drinking water and sanitation are essential for the realisation of all other human rights'***— all of which provided the legal basis of rights through the decadal developments of right to water and sanitation in the field of international human rights and humanitarian law.

In the Indian context, the decade witnessed the launching of the **National Rural Drinking Water Quality Monitoring and Surveillance Programme** in February 2006, envisaging institutionalisation of community participation for monitoring and surveillance of drinking water sources at the grassroots level by Gram Panchayats and Village Water and Sanitation Committees, followed by checking the positively tested samples at the district and state level laboratories; followed by the upgradation of the former ARWSP to NRDWP (National Rural Drinking Water Program that brought under it all rural submissions. In 2010, Department of Drinking water and Sanitation was set up and the NRDWP operationalised as per the Strategic Plan 2010-2022, ensuring that *'all citizens living in rural areas have access to safe, clean water for drinking, cooking, and other domestic needs* ***with the intention of eventually providing piped water to every rural household.'***

Phase 4. National Water Policy 2012 and beyond

On June 7, 2012, the Ministry of Water Resources published its Draft National Water Policy 2012 (NWP) seeking to address issues such as the scarcity of water, inequities in its distribution and the lack of a unified perspective in planning, management and use of water resources which was adopted by the National Water Resources Council on August 9, 2012.

The Preamble to the policy and its draft, brought to fore the '***low public consciousness*** *about the overall scarcity and economic value of water results in its* ***wastage and inefficient use***', asserting that the *'objective of the National Water Policy is to take cognizance of the existing situation,* ***to propose a framework for creation of a system of laws and institutions and for a plan of action with a unified national perspective'***. It pointed out that the ***'principle of equity and social justice*** *must inform use and allocation of water'* which needs to be managed as a ***'common pool' community resource*** *held, by the state,* ***under public trust doctrine*** *to achieve food security, support livelihood, and ensure* ***equitable and sustainable development for all'*** - clauses that draw the background behind the provisions outlined by the Acts of 2013 and 2016.

6. National Water Law and Draft national Water Framework Bill, 2013, GOI, MoWR

In the spirit of the precedence set by the European Water Framework Directive of 2000, the South African National Water Act of 1998 and so on, this law incorporates all major legal pronouncements by the Supreme Court with reference to water such as the **Public Trust Doctrine** and the recognition of the **right to water, the principle of subsidiarity** as explicated in the 73rd and 74th Constitutional amendments.

Formally defined to be *a 'bill based on the emphasis laid by the* National Water Policy (2012), adopted by the National Water Resources Council on the need to evolve **a National Framework Law** it recognizes water as a ***limited*** *natural resource that has to be protected and preserved for generations'* through *'continuous and cohesive action',* translating into the Act of 2013. It unambiguously lists down the definitions pertaining to water resources sector including terms that are often come across in water resources management literature and specifically in the national water policy documents like – 'common pool resources', 'community-based institutions', 'corporatisation', 'livelihood', 'pre-emptive needs', 'participatory management', 'principle of differential pricing', , 'privatisation', 'public trust' etc. *[2.Definitons.(iv), (v), (vi), (xiii), (xviii), (xix), (xxii), (xxii), (xxii), (xxiv), Draft National Water framework Bill, 2013].*

Interestingly, on one hand it identifies water as a '***common pool resource of the community*** *and shall be managed, protected and preserved as such* ***by community based institutions'***, **held by the state as a trustee for the benefit of all *'in public trust for the people'***, obliging it to *'protect water resources'* and affirming that this responsibility to the state as public trustee ***'shall remain even if some of the functions of the state in relation to water are entrusted to any public or private agency'*** *[Clauses (4), (5), Chapter II, Basic Principles for Water Management].* On the other, the Act prioritises allocation of water for the drinking water and sanitation, food securi2ty, as livelihood-support for the poor, exempting it from the *'principle of differential pricing'* while making sure that for other uses, *'water shall increasingly be subjected to allocation and* ***pricing on economic principles to ensure its development costs, efficient use and reward conservation'*** with prior '*consultation with all stakeholders'*, through '*independent statutory Water Regulatory Authority, set up by each State' [Clause(6), Chapter II, Basic Principles for Water Management].*

Legitimising the basic rights to water, the Act avers that *'every individual has a* ***right to a minimum quantity of potable water*** *for essential health and hygiene and within easy reach of the household'* which *'shall not be less than 25 litres per capita per day'*, complying with the quality standards set by the Government and ***'despite corporatisation or privatisation of water' services*** **shall remain** ***'the State's responsibility to ensure the people's right to water'****.[Clause 4.(1) and (3), Right to Water, Chapter III, Rights to Water, Preservation of Water Quality and Water Pricing, Draft National Water Framework bill, 2013]*. The concept of determination of water charges on a ***'volumetric basis, reviewed periodically to meet equity, efficiency and economic principles'*** based on the *'principle of differential pricing'*, compulsion to *'ensure conformance to the Service Level Benchmarks for water supply, sanitation* and the practice of regular *'water audits to sensitize communities for reduction of nonrevenue water'* are also notified in the Act. *[Clause (6). Water Pricing, ; Clause 13.(1), (2 and (3), Urban Water Management, Chapter III, Rights to Water, Preservation of Water Quality and Water Pricing, Draft National Water Framework bill, 2013]*.

7. Draft National Water Framework Bill, 2016

A revision to the earlier 2013 Act, the National Water Framework Act, 2016 adds on to the previous set of directives of 2013, new definitions like 'full cost recovery pricing', 'water footprint', 'water for life' *[2. Definitions.(i), (z).(aa,), Chapter I. Preliminary, Draft National Water framework Bill, 2016]* and the terms of pricing whereby *'water as a part of water for life as defined herein,* ***shall not be denied to anyone on the ground of inability to pay'*** *[Clause 22.1.(a) Water Pricing and Water Regulators Chapter V. Planning for Water Security, Draft National Water framework Bill, 2016]*. Acknowledging its commitment to the United Nations Sustainable Development Goals to be attained by 2030, it conceives the ***'Right to Water for Life'*** for every person, **regardless of, among others, caste, creed, religion, community, class, gender, age, disability, economic status, land ownership and place of residence** complying with the standards set by *'The Manual of the Central Public Health and Environmental Engineering Organisation, Bureau of Indian Standards specifications or standards adopted by the appropriate government as modified or revised from time to time'[3. Right to Water for Life, Clause.3.(1), (2). Chapter I. Preliminary, Draft National Water framework Bill, 2016]*. Insisting for the **convergence of all water sector schemes (14,),** it advocates for the preparation of ***'Water Security Plans'*** at the *'lowest possible administrative level'* that would be *'valid for a period of five years'. [Clause 14, Chapter III Basic Principles, Clause.15, (2), Chapter V : Planning for Water Security, Draft National Water framework Bill, 2016] and the 'conservation, protection, regulation and management'* of groundwater as per the ***'Model Bill for the Conservation, Protection, Regulation and***

***Management of Groundwater, 2016'** [Clause 18, Chapter V : Planning for Water Security, Draft National Water framework Bill, 2016].*

2015 marked the initiation of the era of sustainable development as per the UN Agenda for Sustainable Development (2016-2030) held on 25th September 2015, listing out 17 goals to be achieved by 2030. Goal 6 of the 17 SDGs stated that by 2030, universal and equitable access to safe and affordable drinking water for all needs to be achieved. The SDGs, together with the provisions of Paris Climate Change Conference have led to the UN Water GLAAS, 2017 (Global Assessment of Sanitation and Drinking Water) and the UN General Assembly Resolution forthe **Proclamation of International Decade for Action, "Water for Sustainable Development (2018-2028)"**, promising further developments in the water sector.

8. Critical Policy Review: Changing Role of the State

Besides stage-crafting 'water' as an economic good, water reforms through policy reversals have implied an important shift in terms of the rights of control over and access to water, recasting the perspectives of looking at water from a public trust thing to the introduction of water rights and the possibility to trade water entitlements. The novelty introduced by the reforms is that water rights are now created in favour of water users (Cullet, 2007:7) expediting the trading process of the entitlements.

Endorsements for decentralisation in decision-making to the lowest level and participation of 'all stakeholders' have been based on the crafted as well as perceived inability of the state to deliver appropriate services, thus proclaiming the role of the state from that of a 'service provider' to that of a 'regulator'. The other attributes added on to water through such characterisation is that its services should be based on the principle of (full) cost-recovery, making water users pay at least for the operation and maintenance charges linked to the 'supply' of water - seen by the Asian Development Bank as the first instrument for conserving water[15].

Tracing back the role of the state in this entire policy spectrum, it is seen that in the initial years after independence, the state was a dominant entity in rendering the social sector services to the people. Skocpol calls this 'explanatory centrality of the states as potent and autonomous organisational actors', whereby 'impulses shaping the major policies and actions within the state' were thought to be outcomes of what Miliband calls the state's conception of national interest, as a trustee of nation's normative aspirations.

Sudipta Kaviraj describes this phase as the ideational revolution within the Indian State that carried with it significant transformatory potential (Kaviraj, 1997) but this was soon punctuated by exogenous shocks in the global water arena, that were harbingers of massive changes to follow. The critical juncture brought about substantial changes in policy ideas within the Indian State conforming to the then significant prescriptions of deregulation and globalisation in the liberalisation phase. The Eighth Five-Year Plan period thus forced the State to admit that 'under-performance of the rural water supply sector is likely to continue unless there is a fundamental reform of the service arrangements' and an explicit warning that the State will not be able to provide necessary expansion of services to a growing population' (GoI, 1997). In the same spirit, Swajaldhara guidelines were announced in December 2002 as 'non-negotiable reform principles, which supersede all earlier guidelines' (GoI, 2003) only to arrive at the Eleventh Plan (2007-2012) where despite acknowledging the basic right to water, approach to pricing water was further, highlighted. The emphasis now was on flexible cost sharing arrangements between the Centre, State, and Local Governments, Markets and User Communities. In the years to follow, the Governments at the Centre have taken up the projects like JNNURM, Swachh Bharat Mission that have created backdoor favouring of corporate entities to run business encashing on the country-wide reforms drive. Be it the coalition or right at the Centre, the State slowly has got into the role, similar to Poulantzas's Neo-Marxian view of defining the State as a 'relatively autonomous entity', enjoying its autonomy from the dominant economic class even though it acts on behalf of it, safeguarding its interests.

9. Structure of the market

Based on the information available in the online blogs and websites of various companies in the water purification industry in India, a rough estimate of the water purifier market is outlined (since practically no data is available on the extent of privatisation of the market). This takes into account only the market in the rural sector as a proxy to the overall privatisation that has taken place in the water sector. The companies have found the opportunity lucrative enough to encash on the narrative of 'safe drinking water consumption' to penetrate the rural markets with their home based solutions in the form of low-priced water filters which are often non electric in nature and come with a decent amount of storage facilities.

Types of Purification Models:

(a) Centralised water treatment facilities as the case of urban areas
(b) Point of use water purifiers
(c) Community water systems

Types of Business models:

1. Outright Sale: Here the water company sells the water system to the government, NGO or CSR. Often the village panchayat (local government) owns and operates the plant either directly or through a jointly constituted committee. Revenue generated through the sale of purified water (typically at INR 2-5 for 20 litres) is used to fund

operations. Often these systems are maintained poorly as the revenue does not cover the necessary operating costs.

2. Sale and Maintenance: This model is similar to the previous one in which the system is sold outright, usually to the government. However, in this case, the water company continues to service and maintain the system for a fee. Generally, these continue to operate well although the price is higher (e.g. INR 4-7 for 20 litres) because the professional water company is being paid to properly maintain these units.
3. Franchise: Here the water company identifies a local entrepreneur who contributes part of the initial system cost. The entrepreneur operates the system and shares part of the profit with the water company. In this model too water is sold at a higher rate (INR 6-10 for 20 liters) to recover the initial capex cost (most of which is borne by the water company).

Table 10.1: Major Market players for sale of Non-Electric Storage Filters customised for rural households with low purchasing power and lack of electricity facilities.

Brand Name/ Price	*Mother Corporate Group*	*Technology Used*
Aquasure (rural specific brand) Rs. 1499 to 20,999/-	Eureka Forbes; Shapoorji-Pallonji Group	Particulate, sediment filter, carbon block, UV,UF,ROTechnology replaceable cartridge 'AquasureAmrit with Kitanu Magnet' at 449/-
Pureit Rs. 2000/- (variants : 1200/- to 16000/-)	Hindustan Unilever Limited	Chlorine discharger kit replaceable after 1500L at 365/-
Swach & Swach Smart (Rs. 999 & 749/- introductory prices, now 1349 to 3200/-) Takes off from Sujal	Tata (Tata Chemicals, TCS, Titan Industries)	Silver Nano technology, Rice husk ash; replaceable cartridge with 3000L shelf life costs 299/-
Sujal (2000-2003) piloted among NGOs, Distributed in Tsunami affected rural districts of South India, 2004	Tata	Basic water filter
Other players include: Voltas Water Solutions, Kent UF Gravity water filters (Kent RO Systems Limited, Ion exchange India Ltd – 'Srijal Purifier' with Zero-B resin technology.		

In addition to the home based solutions mentioned, community purifier systems have been setup in many of the rural districts with the help of microfinance or seed finding financing the establishment of these projects. A full-fledged financial market revolving around this demand driven water purification industry has evolved in recent years drawing on the policy trajectory discussed so far. This shows the extent of proliferation of the water market in areas where the state has failed to provide adequate and water supply of safe quality.

Microfinance and Water:

- **Water-Credit**, an innovative program launched byWater.org which addresses this issue by providing small loans to households for the purchase of water filtration systems.
- In another such initiative, **Milaap**, a **Unitus Seed Fund** portfolio company has tied up with **Guardian, a microfinance institution, and Yunus Social Business Fund,** to provide micro loans people in Tamil Nadu for building water connections and toilets in their homes.
- **Spandana Sphoorty** Financial Ltd. started off with this model in Neemuch and Ujjain district, MP involving a weekly repayment amount similar in both areas Rs 43 ($0.95) per week for 25 weeks, Rs 39 ($0.87) per week for 17 weeks .
- Monthly repayment plan Rs 250 ($5.60) per month for 6 months, plus upfront payment of Rs 250 started by **Pragati Seva Sanstha under the umbrella org ACCESS in Andhra Pradesh.**

Investment firms in the water sector –

- **Aavishkar** –Mumbai based, equity investments in social enterprises. Investment in Waterlife.
- **Acumen –** Raises Charitable donations for investments, in India has invested in Water Health International, Guardian and Spring Health.
- **Avantage Ventures** – Asia based social investment company with offices in Hongkong and Beijing, invested in Piramal-Sarvajal which franchises their proprietary filtration equipment to local entrepreneurs who then operate the machines and sell water at a minimum cost.
- **Matrix Partners** -Investment in Waterlife.
- **Sandi group** –Washington based company investing in Aquakraft,
- **Unitus Seed Fund** investing in many of the water projects operating in the districts shown in map.

10. Conclusion

Policies and international agreements have laid down targets and goals for the water and sanitation sector to achieve by 2030 and some even before that. However, some of the greatest barriers that the States face today are related to financing of development schemes and to bear the capital costs of increasing the coverage status in rural areas to ensure safe drinking water for all. Moreover the donor organisations backing such social sector programs have talked the language of neoliberal policies encouraging private players to take part in the service delivery mechanism and ensure cost recovery of it.

Although this study fails to validate the actual extent of privatisation and the current size of the water market with details of its players and structural elements, the paper substantiates the fact that policy documents and the actions taken up by the supra national donor organisations have provided the incentive to the companies for seeking profit in this 'life- saving' business.

The riveting fact is that the water business has set its strong footing in the rural drinking water sector taking advantage of the utopian imageries of 'safe water' created by policies so far and that too in areas which are official statistics wise found to be having pretty high treated water supply facilities by the State. The huge business potential given India's unmet demands by the State makes key themes - equipment supply, public private partnerships for water supply and distribution, water treatment plants and water EPC (engineering, procurement and construction) business and integrated water resource management for utilities – the building blocks of establishing increased private control in this sector.

References

Achterhuis, H., Boelens, R., & Zwarteveen, M. (2010). Water property relations and modern policy regimes: neoliberal utopia and the disempowerment of collective action. Out of the Mainstream: Water Rights, Politics and Identity, London: Earthscan, 27-56.

Bakker, K. J. (2003). A political ecology of water privatisation.Studies in political economy, 70(1), 35-58.

Barlow, M., & Clarke, T. (2002). *Blue gold: The fight to stop the corporate theft of the world's water*. The New Press.

Barlow, M. (2010, August). The global water crisis and the commodification of the world's water supply. In *International Forum on Globalisation*.

Castree, N. (2008). Neoliberalising Nature: The logics of deregulation and reregulation. Environment and Planning A, 40(1), 131-152.

Cullet, P. (2007). Water law in India: overview of existing framework and proposed reforms. Geneva: International Environmental Law Research Centre.

Harvey D (2007) A Brief History of Neoliberalism. Oxford: Oxford University Press.

Kus, B. (2006). Neoliberalism, institutional change and the welfare state: The case of Britain and France. International Journal of Comparative Sociology, 47(6), 488-525.

Luxemburg, R. (2003). The accumulation of capital. Routledge

Peck, J., & Tickell, A. (1994). Jungle law breaks out: Neoliberalism and global-local disorder. Area, 317-326

Rosegrant, M. W., & Binswanger, H.P. (1994). Markets in tradable water rights : potential for efficiency gains in developing country water resource allocation. World Development, 22(11), 1613-1625.

Scholte, J.A.(2005). *Globalisation: A critical introduction.* Palgrave Macmillan.

Section 37 and Section E, Asian Development Bank, Water for All – The Water Policy of the Asian Development Bank (2003).

Swyngedouw, E. (2005). Dispossessing H2O: The contested terrain of water privatisation. Capitalism Nature Socialism, 16(1), 81-98.

Zwarteveen, M., Roth, D., & Boelens, R. (2005).Water rights and legal Pluralism. Liquid Relations: Contested water rights and legal complexity, edited by Dik Roth, Rutgerd Boelens and Margreet Zwarteveen, 254-268.

Notes

1. Scholte, J.A.(2005). Globalisation: A critical introduction. Palgrave Macmillan.
2. Kus, B. (2006). Neoliberalism, institutional change and the welfare state: The case of Britain and France. International Journal of Comparative Sociology, 47(6), 488-525.
3. Zwarteveen, M., Roth, D., &Boelens, R. (2005).Water rights and legal Pluralism. Liquid Relations: Contested water rights and legal complexity, edited by Dik Roth, Rutgerd Boelens and Margreet Zwarteveen, 254-268.
4. Bakker, K. J. (2003). Apolitical ecology of water privatisation.Studies in political economy, 70(1), 35-58.
5. Accumulation by dispossession refers specifically to practices that operate and evolve through the violent expulsion of peasants through land privatisation, the conversion of common property rights, the suppression of alternative and indigenous forms of production and consumption, and the appropriation of natural resources (Harvey, 2003)
6. Harvey D (2007) A Brief History of Neoliberalism. Oxford: Oxford University Press.
7. Achterhuis, H., Boelens, R., &Zwarteveen, M. (2010). Water property relations and modern policy regimes: neoliberal utopia and the disempowerment of collective action. Out of the Mainstream: Water Rights, Politics and Identity, London: Earthscan, 27-56.
8. Peck, J., & Tickell, A. (1994). Jungle law breaks out: neoliberalism and global-local disorder. Area, 317-326.
9. Castree, N.(2008). Neoliberalising nature : the logics of dereulation and reregulation. Environment and Planning A, 40(1),131-152.
10. Swyngedouw, E. (2005). Dispossessing H2O: The contested terrain of water privatisation. Capitalism Nature Socialism, 16(1), 81-98.
11. Luxemburg, R. (2003). The accumulation of capital. Routledge
12. As per the General Assembly Resolution 34/191 of 18th December 1979 and Resolution 25, entitled International Drinking Water Supply and Sanitation Decade, 39th July 1980 adopted by World Conference of the United Nations Decade for Women: Equality, Development and Peace.
13. Cullet, P. (2007). Water law in India: overview of existing framework and proposed reforms. Geneva: International Environmental Law Research Centre.
14. Resolution adopted by the General Assembly on 23rd Dec 2003, Fifty-Eighth session, Agenda Item-95, [on the report of the Second Committee (A/58/485)] 58/217. International Decade for Action, "Water for Life", 2005-2015
15. Section 37 and Section E, Asian Development Bank, Water for All – The Water Policy of the Asian Development Bank (2003).

Chapter - 11

Collective Action for Common Property Resource Conservation as an Antidote to the Destruction of Adivasi Livelihoods being Wrought by Globalization

Rahul Banerjee

Abstract

The need for collective action for the management of common property resources and the importance of this for both livelihood promotion and climate change mitigation have come to be universally acknowledged now as an antidote to the ravages wrought by the commercial and extractive processes unleashed by Globalisation. However, given the political and economic forces that tend to atomize societies and discourage collective action, invariably such action needs to be catalyzed by outside agents. Social activists have performed this role very well in a number of situations. The present paper is a case study of one such situation in which social activists have helped a Bhil Adivasi community in Alirajpur district of Madhya Pradesh to organize themselves in small collectives to husband their common property resources very effectively.

1. Introduction

The present article aims to evaluate the importance of collective action in bringing about social, economic and environmental benefits to the Bhil Adivasis in Alirajpur district through the two organisations Khedut Mazdoor Chetna Sangath (KMCS) and Dhas Gramin Vikas Kendra (DGVK). While the first is a trade union the latter is an NGO. The two organisations have worked in tandem, the first to conduct political campaigns to secure the rights of the Adivasis and the second to implement development programmes to improve the natural resource base. Decentralised and participatory development has been acknowledged as a major desideratum for tackling Adivasi deprivation (Sharma, 2001). With the award of the Nobel Memorial Prize in Economic Sciences to Elinor Ostrom in 2009 even mainstream economics has come to acknowledge the importance of collective action for the management of common pool resources (Ostrom, 1990). This has also gained in importance because of the benefits in terms of mitigation of climate change and provision of ecosystem services that such communitarian natural resource management can achieve and so reverse the destruction of environment that accelerated economic activities due to globalisation (IISD et al, 2003).

Nevertheless the Adivasis being mostly illiterate and economically poor lack the capacity to counter the centralised governance apparatus that tends to increase their deprivation. Consequently they need to be guided in their attempts to secure justice and development by trained activists who can formulate appropriate strategies and supervise their implementation. Thus, this chapter by critically evaluating such an intervention where activists have played a significant role in organizing the Adivasis to take advantage of laws and policies that are beneficial to them and brought about visible improvement in their situation will yield valuable pointers towards future design of Adivasi development programmes.

The present chapter, however, is a case study of a specific successful intervention in a small area and the main limitation is that the conclusions from it can only be taken as indicators and cannot be generalised. For general validity a host of such case studies are required of many more activist interventions over different Adivasi areas. Moreover, the respondents of the study are all beneficiaries of the process being studied and the investigator is one of the activists so there is an inherent favourable bias which will tend to play down the negative aspects of the process and especially the role of the activists who have initiated and mentored it.

2. Methodology of Study

The three villages of Chhoti Gendra, Attha and Bari Sirkhiri, which form the first milli-watershed (defined as being of size between 1000-10000 ha area) at the headwaters of the Kara River, have been chosen in a purposive manner for the case study as this watershed is the best example of the work done by KMCS in Alirajpur district since 1982. These villages have 105, 223 and 96 households respectively.

First a baseline information survey was done of the villages to assess the socio-economic, infrastructural, environmental and gender situation in the village. This was followed by a random sample survey of fifty male and fifty female persons, each from a separate household, chosen from these three villages or in other words a sample of 100 households from a total of

324 households or 30% which is a statistically valid proportion. A questionnaire was administered to the respondents that had questions regarding the economic and political status prior to the mass organisational and development processes initiated by the activists in collaboration with the people, the obstacles that have been overcome, the failures and the present status of the villagers and.

The baseline survey and the household questionnaire was also administered to 15 men and 15 women from thirty households of a control village Gatha which is outside this watershed but has the same agro-ecological and broad socio-economic characteristics as the survey villages but which has not been active in the KMCS. This has been done to test the difference in perspectives between members and non-members of the organisation and compare the development process and results. Group discussions were also conducted in all the villages to assess the status of implementation of the Scheduled Tribes and Other Traditional Forest Dwellers (Recognition of Rights) Act 2006 hence forward referred to as FRA. Secondary sources like forest and revenue department and Panchayat records and literature have also been researched. The data has been analyzed and the inferences drawn are presented below.

3. Geographical Characteristics

The watershed is part of the Jhabua Hills agro-climatic zone of Madhya Pradesh and is situated in the Vindhya Ranges bordering on the River Narmada. The main features are given in Table 11.1.

Table 11.1: Geographical Characteristics

Mid Latitude	$22^{0}02$
Mid Longitude	$74^{0}17$
Avg Ht. abv. MSL	500 m
Rock Structure	Banded Gneisses
Soil	Clay & Sandy loam
Rainfall	900 mm
Avg PET	2100 mm

The area is underlain with fractured banded gneisses and so there is good percolation of the rainfall into the aquifer. The deep aquifer is not very productive but the phreatic aquifer does support well irrigation. The soils are mostly sandy loam and of low soil depth with poor N, P, K characteristics. There are some patches of clayey soil of medium depth on the banks of the river. The terrain is sloped from the ridge line to the river with 5% slopes near the river and rising to a steep 20% near the ridgeline.

The rainfall is moderate and the precipitation takes place mainly in about 40 rainy days from mid-June to mid-September. The potential evapo-transpiration is very high at 2100 mm and so the rainfall evaporates quickly and soil moisture is low leading to water stress in the kharif season and lower yields in years of less rainfall. The map based on Survey of India Toposheet is given in Figure 11.1 below.

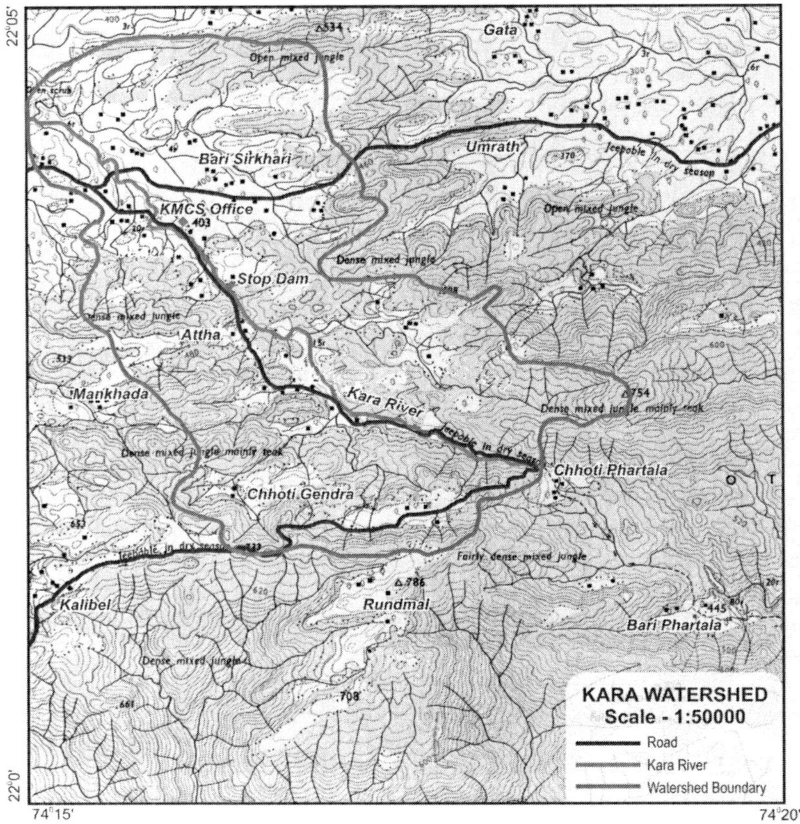

Figure 11.1: Map of Kara River Watershed.

The watershed is located about 48 kms by road from the district town of Alirajpur with the nearest market village being at Chhaktala 13 kms away. The road to Chaktala is now being macadamised under the Pradhan Mantri Gram Sadak Yojana. The nearest railway station is at Dahod which is 70 kms from Alirajpur. Thus the watershed is in a very remote location. The map shows that the watershed had dense mixed jungle consisting mainly of teak and other species like dhavra, salai, tinis, sisam, kher, mahua, tendu and sajar in the early 1970s when the survey was conducted. However, by the late 1980s this had become denuded due to commercial logging by the forest department and encroachments for farming by the Adivasis who found their livelihoods being eroded due to this deforestation. The actual land use for the years 1989 and 2009, as surveyed by Dhas Gramin Vikas Kendra is given in Table 11.2 below.

Table 11.2: Landuse Change in the Study and Control Villages 1989 - 2009 (Ha)

	Chhoti Gendra		*Attha*		*Bari Sirkhiri*		*Gatha*	
	1989	*2009*	*1989*	*2009*	*1989*	*2009*	*1989*	*2009*
Total Land	392.51	392.51	430.96	430.96	267.61	267.61	303.54	303.54
Res. Forest Dense*	0	87.0	0	78.0	0	38.0	0	0
Res. Forest Open	128.0	48.0	113.0	45.0	32.0	22.0	44.0	22.0
Res. Forest Degraded	17.0	0	37.0	14.0	42.0	12.0	37.0	54.0
Res. Forest Encroached	37.0	47.0	49.0	62.0	7.0	9.0	14.0	19.0
Non Agri. Land	3.11	3.87	4.32	5.04	4.67	5.22	4.17	5.09
Pastures	2.73	3.24	3.46	3.21	3.43	2.76	3.26	2.45
Cultivable Wastes	3.56	1.14	5.46	2.23	6.18	3.24	3.67	2.26
Waste	2.34	2.56	4.81	5.86	3.26	4.13	4.38	4.13
Agricultural Land	198.77	199.70	250.91	252.62	169.07	171.26	193.06	194.55

*More than 40% crown cover

Source: Records of Dhas Gramin Vikas Kendra.

The villages are all very small in size with the study watershed villages together having a total area of 1091.08 hectares. To better understand the comparative landuse changes that have taken place over two decades from 1989 to 2009 in the study watershed and the control village the data above have been presented as a proportion of the total land in Table 11.3 below.

Table 11.3: Comparative Changes in Landuse from 1989-2009 (% of Total Land)

Land Use Category	*Study Watershed*		*Change*	*Control Village*		*Change*
	1989	*2009*	*(%)*	*1989*	*2009*	*(%)*
Total Land	100.0	100.0	0.0	100.0	100.0	0.0
Res. Forest Dense	0.0	18.61		0	0	0.0
Res. Forest Open	25.02	10.54	-57.88	14.50	7.25	-50.00
Res. For. Degraded	8.80	2.38	-72.92	12.19	17.79	45.95
Res. For. Encroach.	8.52	10.81	26.88	4.61	6.26	35.71
Non Agri. Land	1.11	1.30	16.78	1.37	1.68	22.06
Pastures	0.88	0.84	-4.26	1.07	0.81	-24.85
Cultivable Wastes	1.39	0.61	-56.51	1.21	0.74	-38.42
Waste	0.95	1.15	20.56	1.44	1.36	-5.71
Agricultural Land	56.71	57.15	0.78	63.60	64.09	0.77

Source: Dhas Gramin Vikas Kendra.

The most significant change over the past two decades in the study watershed is in the increase in dense reserved forest area from 0 to 203 hectares constituting at present 18.61% of the total area. This has resulted from the equally significant reduction of open and degraded reserve forest by 57.88%

and 72.92% respectively due to conservation efforts on the part of the inhabitants. This is in stark contrast to the control village where there has been no increase in dense reserve forest area and instead open reserved forest has been degraded leading to its reduction in area by 50% and the increase in the degraded reserved forest area by 45.95%. The increase in reserved forest area that has been encroached for cultivation too is more in the control village as compared to the study watershed.

4. Socio-Economic Characteristics

The demographic characteristics of the villages are as given in Table 11.4 and 11.5 below.

Table 11.4: Population by Caste and Gender of Study Watershed and Control Village

Caste	*Gendra*			*Attha*			*Sirkhiri*			*Gatha*		
	Hhds	*Popu.*		*Hhds*	*Popu.*		*Hhds*	*Popu.*		*Hhds*	*Popu.*	
		Male	*Fem*		*Male*	*Fem*		*Male*	*Fem*		*Male*	*Fem*
Bhilala	104	277	275	220	618	603	94	519	502	109	304	299
Hindu	0		0	3	7	7	0	0	0	0	0	0
Muslim	1	3	2	0	0	0	2	7	6	0	0	0

Source: Dhas Gramin Vikas Kendra.

Table 11.5: Educational Distribution by Age-Group and Gender (%)

Age-Group (years)	*Gendra*			*Attha*			*Sirkhiri*			*Gatha*		
	Prop of Total	*Education*		*Prop of Total*	*Education*		*Prop of Total*	*Education*		*Prop of Total*	*Education*	
		Male	*Fem.*		*Male*	*Fem.*		*Male*	*Fem.*		*Male*	*Fem.*
0 - 5	14.1	-	-	15.2	-	-	13.8	-	-	14.7	-	-
6 - 12	23.7	38.4	19.1	22.3	43.3	25.2	24.8	40.7	21.4	22.8	29.3	13.4
13 - 17	15.1	23.2	11.6	13.4	29.5	16.8	14.7	20.1	8.8	15.4	23.2	8.5
18 - 59	43.9	14.4	7.3	46.4	17.1	8.4	43.1	11.2	5.4	44.7	9.3	4.6
> 60	3.2	0.0	0.0	2.7	0.0	0.0	3.6	0.0	0.0	2.4	0.0	0.0

Source: Dhas Gramin Vikas Kendra.

The Bhilala Adivasis are the dominant residents of the area and the overall sex ratio is fairly good at 977 per thousand. The average household size is 6.3 which is a bit on the high side and this adversely affects the per capita availability of agricultural land which is only 0.24 ha. More than 50% of the population is aged less than 17 years and it is also evident that life expectancy beyond 60 years is very limited.

The young population is mostly not going to school and this is even more so in the case of girls whose enrolment is half that of boys. Even the low rate of enrolment at the primary level decreases drastically at the middle and higher levels. This is primarily due to the lack of good educational facilities in the area. There is a government middle school in Attha village while there are government primary schools and education guarantee schools in the hamlets of the villages. However, the number of teachers appointed is much less than what is required and their calibre and training is also of a poor standard leading to a high drop out rate. Some students from the area study in residential schools run by the government in Chhaktala, Sondwa or Alirajpur. Some students study in the residential school run by the KMCS in Kakrana village on the banks of the Narmada River.

This poor educational status of the people is reflected in their occupation. An overwhelming 95.7% of the populations are cultivators or agricultural labourers. There are only three people from the area in permanent government service. There are five more in contract service as Panchayat secretaries and teachers. One person practices as a quack in addition to being a cultivator. Since there is no medical sub-centre in the area this quack is the main provider of instant medical care. Thus, agriculture forms the main source of livelihood for the people and since this is not sufficient to provide sustenance in most cases given the low per capita availability of land and low soil and terrain quality of this land there is substantial seasonal migration as will be detailed later.

5. Land Distribution

Table 11.6: Land Distribution

Village	*Landholding Category*											
	Landless		*Marginal 0-1ha*		*Small 1-2ha*		*Semi -Med. 2-5 ha*		*Medium 5-10 ha*		*Large > 10 ha*	
	Hhd	*Area*	*Hhd*	*Area*	*Hhd*	*Area*	*Hhd*	*Area*	*Hhd*	*Area*	*Hhd*	*Area*
Gendra	5	0	29	23.73	49	89.24	22	86.73	0	0	0	0
Attha	8	0	88	41.25	121	197.20	6	14.17	0	0	0	0
Sirkhiri	4	0	24	17.32	52	89.70	16	63.24	0	0	0	0
Gatha	4	0	26	21.71	68	129.02	11	43.82	0	0	0	0

Source: Dhas Gramin Vikas Kendra.

The biggest category of households are small farmers with one to two hectares of landholding constituting just a little more than 50% of the total households. There are very few landless households and these are mostly the non-Adivasis who are traders. The households in the semi-medium farmer category also are only about 15 % of the total households while those in the marginal farmer category constitute about 25% of the total households. As noted earlier there is very little agricultural land with the residents. However, the distribution is fairly equal and there are no medium and big landholdings at all and there is no leasing of land. This is a factor in the success of communitarian collaboration for natural resource management in the study watershed. Even though the control village also has fairly equal land distribution there are other factors that prevented communitarian collaboration there as will become clear later.

6. Land Quality

The land in the study area and in the control village is mostly hilly with thin sandy loam soils and most of it is not suitable for agriculture. Traditionally the Adivasis used to practice shifting cultivation here and take advantage of the richness of organic manure in the early stages before shifting to another location. However, that came to an end after independence as this area was declared a reserved forest. The situation with regard to quality of agricultural land is given in Table 11.7 below where the various parameters have been expressed as a proportion of the total land in percentage. The parameters have been rated by the respondents according to the accepted understanding in the area regarding land quality. This is the understanding that comes into play when land has to be subdivided between heirs on the death of a landholder and so it is quite rational.

Table 11.7: Agricultural Land Quality (% of Total Land)

Village		*Slope*			*Soil Fertility*			*Soil Depth*			*Soil Erosion*		
		Steep	*Mod*	*Low*	*Good*	*Med*	*Bad*	*Deep*	*Med*	*Low*	*High*	*Med*	*Low*
Gendra	1989	22	55	23	5	34	61	0	13	87	44	48	8
	2009	22	23	55	16	55	29	10	34	56	22	24	54
Attha	1989	17	42	41	13	46	41	0	26	74	22	63	15
	2009	17	22	61	21	64	15	8	57	35	17	31	52
Sirkhiri	1989	19	57	24	8	41	59	0	14	86	31	53	16
	2009	19	32	49	19	59	22	7	54	49	19	30	51
Gatha	1989	21	56	22	11	45	44	0	16	84	53	41	6
	2009	21	56	22	2	34	64	0	14	86	61	34	5

Source: Dhas Gramin Vikas Kendra.

Clearly the land quality has improved considerably in the study watershed while it has deteriorated in the control village. This has resulted from the communitarian cooperation in soil and water conservation that has taken place over the past two decades in the study watershed as opposed to the control village where this has not occurred.

7. Investment in Soil and Water Conservation

The KMCS organised the villagers in the study watershed into small groups of ten to twelve farmers each who then pooled their labour and cooperated with each other to perform their agricultural operations together and also undertake soil and water conservation activities. This was in fact a revival of a traditional labour pooling system called Dhas from which the name of DGVK is derived. This system had fallen into disuse because the intrusion of the market economy and the destruction of the natural resource base had destroyed community institutions. Considerable effort was expended to revitalize this system and it has paid rich dividends. Apart from this external funding was also sourced on two occasions for soil and water conservation work through the sister NGO, DGVK. The additional work done in soil and water conservation in the two decades is given in Table 11.8 below as the proportion of the total land covered through such work.

Table 11.8: Investment in Soil and Water Conservation (% of Total Land)

Village	*Bunding & Levelling*	*Gully Plugs & Boulder Checks*	*Farm Ponds*	*In situ Composting*
Gendra	32	31	5	23
Attha	23	32	0	26
Sirkhiri	25	29	7	24
Gatha	3	6	6	0

Source: Dhas Gramin Vikas Kendra.

A major feature of the cooperative soil and water conservation work is the equal participation of women in it. This has not only empowered women within the traditional Bhil society which is highly patriarchal but has also given them a greater say in household affairs. A picture of women working on a gully plug to create a new farm in Gendra village is shown in Figure 11.2 below.

Figure 11.2: Women working on a Gully Plug in Gendra Village

8. Investments in Forest Conservation

The KMCS organisation began with the problem of ensuring access to the encroached farms of the Adivasis in the reserved forest and as a solution to this problem very early on it was decided to protect the remaining forest area and prevent it from degradation. This was done to counter the claim of the forest department that the Adivasis were destroying the forest. Consequently in all the hamlets of the study watershed social protection of the forests to ensure their regeneration was undertaken with small groups patrolling them by turns. The fodder generated from such protection is cut and bought by the members at the end of the monsoon season and the money thus generated is kept in a fund for carrying out plantation work. This forest protection has considerably increased the availability of fodder, firewood and non-timber forest produce in the study watershed and this has especially benefited the women and children who are the main collectors of forest products. Greater fodder availability has facilitated goat and buffalo rearing and so increased the supplementary incomes from animal husbandry which provides an insurance against livelihood shocks to the Adivasi households. A survey done in the study villages by the youth has shown that there are as many as 63 species of trees, 8 varieties of vegetables, 7 varieties of grasses, 10 varieties of fruits and 29 varieties of herbs. The landscape in the control village is barren by contrast and there the forest product availability is low. The picture of the regenerated forest in Attha village is shown in Figure 11.3 below.

Figure 11.3: Regenerated Forest in Attha Village

9. Irrigation and Water Availability

The intensive soil and water conservation work and the forest conservation have together ensured that both natural and artificial recharge in the watershed has increased considerably and so the Kara river in now perennial flowing throughout the year. This enhanced water availability combined with the availability of electricity and diesel for pumps has meant that there is considerable irrigation in the watershed whereas earlier there was none. The soil and water conservation work has also ensured the greater availability of soil moisture and so double cropping has become possible even without irrigation. The egalitarian distribution of land has ensured that the water is equally distributed. Such is the water flow in the stream that even after triple cropping in the watershed the stream does not dry up even in summer as shown in Figure 11.4 below. In contrast even though there is some irrigation in the control village it is much less and achieved only through well irrigation.

Figure 11.4: A Farmer drawing water from the Kara River in Summer

The irrigation (proportion of total land) and water availability in summer (proportion of households) are shown in Table 11.9 below.

Table 11.9: Irrigation (% of Total Land) and Summer Water Availability (% of Hholds)

Village	*Groundwater*	*Nala*	*Tank*	*Water Availability in Summer*		
				Good	*Med*	*Low*
Gendra	11	16	8	90	10	0
Attha	14	21	7	93	7	0
Sirkhiri	13	19	9	92	8	0
Gatha	11	0	0	5	15	80

Source: Dhas Gramin Vikas Kendra.

Even though there is some irrigation from wells in the control village the respondents said that the water was not sufficient and so the yields were low. They could not grow wheat and instead had to grow gram which is less productive. Water availability for domestic and livestock use in summer is a serious problem in this village as they have to rely only on two handpumps as the others go dry.

10. Migration

The low per capita resource endowment in the area means that agriculture and animal husbandry alone cannot provide complete livelihood support to the people. In the absence of any non-farm employment opportunities in the area members from all households in the area have to migrate seasonally to Gujarat to supplement their incomes by working on farms and construction sites. However, the amount of migration from the control village is much more in terms of the number of members migrating and the duration for which they have to migrate due to agriculture and animal husbandry being less productive there as a consequence of a degraded natural resource base.

11. Reasons for Better Community Mobilisation and Availability of Natural Resources

The initial resource endowment and socio-economic conditions in the study watershed and the control village were similar and yet the KMCS struck roots in the former while it did not succeed in the latter. The main reason is that in Gatha village the traditional Patel and some of his cohorts did not want their influence to be reduced due to communitarian mobilisation and vehemently opposed this. The forest department staff and other government functionaries too supported the Patel as their interests lay in continuing the status quo. The rest of the people in the village could not muster up the courage to overcome this opposition. In Gendra, Attha and Sirkhiri villages too there was initial opposition to the mobilisation process but here a section of the people braved the opposition and even went to jail fighting for their rights and established the organisation. Once the organisation was established and natural resource conservation work began the benefits began to flow and this acted as a reinforcing factor in the continuation of the process. The respondents said that crucial factor here was the knowledge and perseverence of the activists who continually supported them in their efforts to mobilise and undertake rights based actions and developmental works. This helped them to overcome their handicap in adjusting to a modern system which was unfamiliar to them.

12. Comparison of Role of KMCS and Government

There has been little investment in the development of the region by the government. As mentioned earlier there are no medical facilities and the educational institutions are not functioning properly. With regard to economic development there has not been much investment apart from electrification as the roads have still not been macadamised under the Pradhan Mantri Gram Sadak Yojana. The investments made through various schemes from 2006-07 when the NREGS became functional in the Panchayats in the area are as given in Table 11.10 below. Gendra Panchayat includes the village of Phartala also which is not part of the study. Sirkhiri Panchayat includes the village of Gatha which is the control village.

Table 11.10: Panchayat Investments 2006 - 2009 (Rs Lakhs)

Panchayat	*NREGS*			*12th Finance Commission*			*Basic*			*Indira Awaas Yojana*		
	06-07	*07-08*	*08-09*	*06-07*	*07-08*	*08-09*	*06-07*	*07-08*	*08-09*	*06-07*	*07-08*	*08-09*
Gendra	7.11	11.86	12.74	1.09	1.87	1.45	0.64	0.86	0.83	0.55	0.67	0.73
Attha	8.22	17.49	11.56	1.36	2.28	0.80	0.75	1.03	1.40	0.25	0.74	0.96
Sirkhiri	8.01	10.93	11.76	1.21	1.54	1.11	0.63	0.76	0.91	0.34	0.51	0.77

Source: Panchayat Records.

The main investment is through the MGNREGS and before the initiation of this scheme there was very little development work being done by the Panchayats. The MGNREGS too does not function properly despite continuous monitoring by the KMCS members. The main problem is the delay in payment of wages which can sometimes take as much as a year. The payment of wages in Sirkhiri village was held up because the people had unearthed a defalcation of funds by the Sarpanch and complained about it. This deters the people from demanding work and working under this scheme as they find it more profitable to migrate to Gujarat instead. The MGNREGS faces a major problem in that the staff for the implementation of the programme has to be provided by the State Governments. In most cases the State Governments are unable to provide adequate staff to manage such a big programme and so demands for employment are processed slowly as are the payments once work is done. The net result is that the amount of work generated is very low.

Thus, the KMCS has acted as a catalyst in mobilising the people for their rights and entitlements in the face of a government bureaucracy which is both inefficient and oppressive. The main contribution has been in channelising the communitarian energy into cooperative natural resource conservation work over a period of two decades to bring about huge improvements in the sustainability of the natural resource base and also improve their earnings from agriculture and animal husbandry.

The exercise of rigorously evaluating the investments made and incomes generated is a complicated one and should be done by an independent investigator and so has not been attempted as part of this study. However, the positive effects of this investment can be seen when the study watershed is compared with the control village. The laws and policies that favour Adivasis are not implemented primarily because they are not aware of these provisions. The activists of the KMCS by raising their awareness in this regard have brought about a positive transformation.

13. Implementation of The Scheduled Tribes and Other Traditional Forestdwellers (Recognition of Rights) Act (Popularly known as the Forest Rights Act or FRA)

The FRA has been plagued with problems right from the beginning. Even though the Act was passed in 2006 it took another year for the Rules to be framed and passed by parliament. Even after that the Madhya Pradesh government was very tardy in setting in motion the process for application and verification of the rights of the Adivasis. The KMCS had to organize a mass rally in Alirajpur town on 12th October 2009 to get the process started. Thereafter the Village Forest Rights Committees were constituted and the process of rights verification and distribution of rights deeds begun. The whole process has been plagued by the recalcitrance of the Forest Department and so even now only about half the claims have been resolved. The KMCS is continually monitoring the process and has through applications filed under the RTI Act been able to garner documented evidence of violation of the FRA by the district administration.

14. Conclusion

The KMCS and DGVK have together used the favourable legal provisions to ensure that the Bhils of Alirajpur are able to secure their rights and entitlements and gain justice from the modern economic and political systems that govern this country. In conclusion a critical assessment of this process of community mobilisation will be undertaken within the evaluation framework for institution building for successful common pool resource management proposed by (Ostrom, 1990) as follows -

1. Group boundaries are clearly defined.
2. Rules governing the use of collective goods are well matched to local needs and conditions.
3. Most individuals affected by these rules can participate in modifying the rules.
4. The rights of community members to devise their own rules is respected by external authorities.
5. A system for monitoring member's behavior exists; the community members themselves undertake this monitoring.
6. A graduated system of sanctions is used.
7. Community members have access to low-cost conflict resolution mechanisms.
8. For CPRs that are parts of larger systems: appropriation, provision, monitoring, enforcement, conflict resolution, and governance activities are organised in multiple layers of nested enterprises.

The first principle is very important and the KMCS was able to inspire the Adivasis to assert their identity and clearly demarcate their sovereignty over their habitats. The laws and rules for utilisation of the forests were that laid down by the government and administered by the Forest Department and were not matched to the local needs and conditions in violation of the second principle above. The KMCS succeeded in mobilising the people through regular meetings and trainings to stand up for their rights against the forest department staff and design their own rules for governing the use of the collective natural resources.

A section of the people initially braved the opposition of the traditional Patels who were agents of the Forest Department and even went to jail fighting for their rights and established the organisation. Once the organisation was established and natural resource conservation work began, the benefits began to flow and this acted as a reinforcing factor in the continuation of the process and so later even the Patels, who were initially opposed to the process, later became a part of it.

The mobilisation process resulted in a fairly strong people's organisation spread over a large area of fifty villages and hence the KMCS members were able to ensure that the Forest Department was forced to allow the villagers to manage their common resources according to their own rules The monitoring of the forests as well as the soil and water conservation work is done by the members themselves and that is why the system has worked very well for over two decades. The members of the KMCS have developed a system of sanctions beginning with fines for small infringements of the rules and going up to ostracism for more serious violations and this is administered by the people themselves. The traditional community conflict resolution mechanisms of the Bhil Adivasis have also been revived and these are also working very well.

The final principle is the most important as far as community mobilisation on a large scale is concerned. Unless the government ensures a participatory framework of rulemaking and monitoring at several levels it is difficult for a small organisation to build up a larger movement of conservation.

Since the government through the forest department and police has actively opposed the people's mobilisation it has taken place only in about fifty villages in Alirajpur district and it is difficult to expand its reach. The laws and policies that favour Adivasis discussed in detail in the beginning are not implemented primarily because they are not aware of these provisions and the Government is not serious about them. The KMCS and the DGVK by raising the awareness of the Adivasis in this regard have brought about a positive transformation in Alirajpur. This unique combination of Trade Union and an NGO, by synthesising social activism and development intervention, has improved the situation of the Bhil Adivasis by creatively using the favourable legal provisions for Adivasis.

The PESA Act was a first step in the direction of preserving and promoting Adivasi culture and thus ensuring a saner world involving more sustainable resource use and equitable inter-personal relations than the one we are living in (Rahul, 1997). The KMCS has relied on the inherent Adivasi culture and synergised it with developmental efforts to improve the lives of the Adivasis who are its members. The passage of the National Rural Employment Guarantee Act, The Scheduled Tribes and Other Traditional Forestdwellers (Recognition of Rights) Act and the Right to Information Act in 2006 has considerably enhanced the effectiveness of the PESA Act. Many Adivasi mass organisations have conducted long drawn campaigns which have resulted in the enactment of the FRA which complements the Fifth Schedule and nullifies the historical injustice done to the Adivasis through the implementation of the Indian Forest Act. The KMCS has leveraged the provisions of this Act too. Thus, despite its limitations, the mobilisation process described above has ensured justice for the Bhil Adivasis of Alirajpur and provided them with a better livelihood situation. This fight has at the same time made a significant contribution to mitigation of Climate Change and so is an effective antidote to the ravages being wrought by globalisation. It is a fight to save the earth.

References

Aurora, G S (1972): *Tribe-Caste-Class Encounters: Some Aspects of Folk-Urban Relations in Alirajpur Tehsil,* Administrative Staff College, Hyderabad.

Banerjee, R (2007): *Struggles of the Bhil Indigenous People in Jhabua for Access to Water,* Dams, Rivers and People, 5:3, South Asia Network of Dams, Rivers and People, Delhi, 2007.

——————— (2008): *The Decline and Fall of the Bhil Adivasi Homeland: A Tale of Two Worlds,* The India Economy Review, Vol 5, 30th September, 2008.

Banerjee, S (1984): *India's Simmering Revolution,* Zed Publications, London.

Baviskar, A (1995): *In the Belly of the River: Adivasi Conflicts over Development in the Narmada Valley,* Oxford University Press, Delhi.

Bose, N K, (1971): *Adivasi Life in India,* National Book Trust, Delhi.

Deliege, R (1985): *The Bhils of Western India: Some Empirical and Theoretical Issues in Anthropology in India,* National, Delhi.

GOI, 1996, *Concurrent Evaluation of Integrated Rural Development Programme(IRDP) - A Report,* Government of India, New Delhi.

Hardiman, D (1987): *The Bhils and Sahukars of Eastern Gujarat,* in R Guha (ed) *Subaltern Studies V: Writings on South Asian History and Society,* Oxford University Press, Delhi.

International Institute for Sustainable Development (IISD), International Union for Conservation of Nature andNatural Resources (IUCN) and Stockholm Environment Institute (SEI) (2003): *Livelihoods and Climate Change:Combining Disaster Risk Reduction, Natural Resource Management and Climate Change Adaptation in a New Approach to the Reduction of Vulnerability and Poverty,* International Institute for Sustainable Development, Canada.

Mahapatra, L K, *Adivasi Development in India: Myth and Reality,* Vikas Publishing House, Delhi.

MPHDR (2008): *Fourth Madhya Pradesh Human Development Report 2007*, Govt. of Madhya Pradesh, Bhopal.

NCAER (National Council of Applied Economic Research), 1963, *Socio-Economic Conditions of Primitive Tribes in Madhya Pradesh,* New Delhi.

Ostrom, E (1990): *Governing the Commons: The Evolution of Institutions for Collective Action*, Cambridge University Press.

Petras, J & Veltmeyer, H (2001): *Globalisation Unmasked: Imperialism in the Twenty-first Century,* Zed Books, New York.

Rahul, 1997, *Reasserting Ecological Ethics: Bhils' Struggles in Alirajpur*, EPW Vol.30 No. 3.

Shah, M, Banerji, D, Vijayshankar, P S & Ambasta, P (1998): *India's Drylands: Adivasi Societies and Development through Environmental Regeneration*, Oxford University Press, Delhi.

Sharma, B D (2001): *Adivasi Affairs in India: The Crucial Transition,* Sahayog Pustak Kutir Trust, Delhi.

Singh, K S (1983): *Adivasi Movements in India Vol II*, Manohar, Delhi.

Varma, S C (1978): *The Bhil Kills,* Kunj Publishing House, Delhi.

Chapter - 12

Need for Developing System of Integrated Environmental and Economic Accounts to Address Sustainable Development Goals

Maniparna Syam Roy

1. Introduction

The focus of all developing nations is on building up "Green Economy" which signifies human well-being and social equity together with reducing environmental risks and ecological scarcity. The challenge of sustainable development in developing countries is to consider the cause of green economy - raising the standard of living but with due consideration to resource use and environmental impact. The UN Sustainable Development Summit, 2015 adopted on25th September, 2015 seventeen sustainable development goals for "Transforming Our World: the 2030 Agenda for Sustainable Development" to take actions for ending poverty, protecting the planet and ensure safety and security to all. Out of all these integrated, indivisible set of global SDGs, SDG- 1 (on poverty), SDG -2 (on food security), SDG- 6 (on water and sanitation), SDG -7 (on energy), SDG -8 (on economic growth), SDG- 9 (on infrastructure), SDG- 10 (on reduction of inequality), SDG -11 (on cities and human settlements), SDG -12 (on sustainable consumption and production), SDG -13 (on climate change), SDG -14 (on oceans and seas) and SDG - 15 (on biodiversity) are particularly important to the case of preservation of environmental resources and the optimal use in the appropriate manner. Climate change has been impacting public health, food and water security, migration around the world. Action on climate change will drive sustainable development and vice versa.

Therefore, the indicators of sustainable development are to be chosen in such a way so as to reflect the realities of economic growth and development.

The conventional national income accounting (SNA) or the Gross Domestic Product (GDP) cannot be a complete indicator of sustainable development because it deals only with changing stock and flow of manmade capital but not of natural capital such as land, water, air, forest etc., and of its depleting stock as used up through its present economic activities. System of National Accounts has been defined as a statistical compendium showing the expenditures and income of the nation on an annual basis (Kadekodi, 2004). It consists of a coherent, consistent and integrated set of macroeconomic accounts, balance sheet and tables based on a set of internationally agreed concepts, definitions, classifications and accounting rules. The accounting is entirely done on the commodities which are valued in terms of the market prices.

Continuous effort to find the right indicator as appropriate signaling mechanism of sustainable development, green accounting emerged as one of the possible indicators of sustainability. Appropriate quantification of natural asset would help in the assessment of stock and flow. So representation of development processes through indicators of sustainability can provide a reasonable tool for policy making and monitoring of implementation. Natural resources or natural capital are like the man-made capital and the accounting of the resources will be in the line of capital formation i.e. generation of natural capital must be added whereas the degradation must be subtracted to arrive at a net value.

Environmental accounts provide a way to measure total wealth and monitor changes as possible indicator of sustainability. Thus, greening the accounts or creating the environmentally adjusted GDP can generate an indicator that can guide the nations to consume without impoverishing itself. The principal concern of sustainability and of environmental accounting is the impact of ill-informed social choices on inter-generational equity. It is a valuable tool as it has the potential to provide an insight into the impact of human activities on the environment and their subsequent effect on human welfare.

Considering green accounting as an appropriate indicator, research started worldwide as how go to about with this resource accounting. In 1993, SNA included a satellite account which is primarily based on the environmental-economic accounting. Following this, the United Nations also published a handbook of National Accounting: Integrated Environmental and Economic Accounting. After the publication of SEEA, several developed and developing countries tried experimenting with the implementation on environmental accounting. A revised version of this Handbook was built later upon a wide consultation process that concluded in 2002. It has been issued in 2003 by the United Nations, the International Monetary Fund (IMF), the Organisation of Economic Cooperation and Development (OECD), the European Commission and the World Bank.

The System of Integrated Environmental and Economic accounting (SEEA) of UN, 2003 aimed at integrating environment and social dimensions in the accounting framework at least through satellite system of accounts following the capital approach to sustainable development. The satellite system of natural resource account is a modified system of income accounting showing environmental related sectoral activities separately along with their physical account flow changes valuation and possible link to main SNA. The System of Integrated Environment and Economic Accounting (SEEA) are primarily created with the intention to expand conventional national economic accounts in order to better reflect interactions between the market economy and the natural environment.

This chapter is a unique attempt to understand the problems faced while attempting to account the natural resources with respect to developing countries. Lacks of documentation leading to data gaps make the accounting a much more difficult task. But the prospect of this study is that it can be used by policy maker for monitoring development pathway on sustainable development direction. This study provides the methodology and if updated from time to time lead to revision of policies based on the findings, addressing the priorities on a periodical basis. However, further improvement should also be in the agenda of the development planners.

The paper considers accounting of Water for the state of West Bengal, one of the important states of India. The paper has been put forward in the following way:

Section 1 concentrates on the how we have proceeded on the accounting of water resources, the problems encountered while accounting and what are the important highlight points that came out from the study.

Section 2 suggests some policies based on the problems faced that may be considered for better accounting practises.

2. Section 1

While accounting for Water Resources, it must be highlighted that the Government of India has also come up with the National Water Mission 2009 under the National Action Plan on Climate Change to create a general consciousness of the need to use water in the most sustainable manner in view of its scarcity and assess the impact of climate change on water.

Following the various approaches suggested for natural resource accounting, we have developed water account in a manner that is consistent with SEEAW (UN 2003, 2006). United Nation Statistical Division (2006) contributed significantly in preparing the Integrated Environmental and Economic Accounting for Water Resources. (SEEAW). The SEEAW was developed in support of SEEA (2003) with special focus on water resources.

The SEEAW has primarily focussed on the satellite system of accounts – the account links data on water to economic accounts through a shared structure, set of definitions and classifications. Apart from the UN SEEAW, we have reviewed other contributions which attempted the development of water accounts. ESCAP (Volume II), 1997 Chapter 4 provides the description of the water account prepared for Republic of Korea where water quality and quantity of ground water, surface water have been discussed. It also discusses how to connect water quality with sectoral activities such as activities relating industry, household, transport and agriculture in order to bring about policy outcomes. Lange, Hasan and Jiwanji(2003) mainly concentrated on the flow accounts in the preparation of water accounts for the state of Botswana, Namibia and South Africa as there are insufficient data for the preparation of asset or stock accounts.

This will enable policy makers' tomonitor the physical accounts. Further, the economic analysis enables the policy makers to make a more informed choice regarding allocation of water to different economic activities. Additionally, the water flow accounts can be combined with economic models to find out the impact of alternative water policies.

The SEEAW has been the most useful tool in support of integrated water resource management by providing the information system to feed knowledge into decision making. The water account prepared on the basis of SEEAW helps in improving water efficiency, understanding the impact of water management by all users of the economy, linking water availability and its use which is particularly important in situation of water stress, providing a standardised information system and thus allows to fill up inconsistencies as well as data gaps and hence ultimately may lead to more efficient and consistent data collection system as well as getting stake holders involved in decision making.

The basic water accounting structure shows that water resources accounts can be broadly divided into two purposes — quantity account and quality account. Both these types of accounts can be further subdivided into stock/ asset account and flow accounts. Water Flow Accounts measures the flow of water by detailed economic activities and households. The flow accounts are presented both in physical and monetary forms. Stock Account is prepared with the objective to analyze how the stocks of water at the beginning of the accounting period is affected by the flow of water between the environment and the economy and ultimately arrive at the stock of water at the end of the accounting period. The UN's SEEAW, 2006 has been taken as a satellite system of SNA based on the SEEA-2003 framework. It comprises five categories of accounts: Physical water supply and use tables, Hybrid and economic accounts, Asset accounts, Quality accounts, Valuation of water resources.

1.1 Physical water supply and use tables

This category consists of physical supply and use tables which provide information on the volumes of water exchanged between the environment and the economy (abstractions and returns) and within the economy (supply and use within the economy) as well as the emissions by industry and households.

1.1.1 Hybrid and economic accounts

The hybrid accounts bring in together the supply and use tables with the economic accounts. The name hybrid originates from the combination of different types of units of measures in the same category of accounts.

1.1.2 Asset accounts

Asset accounts measure the stock at the beginning and end of the accounting period and record the changes in the stock during the period of consideration. The increase and decrease in the stock due to natural causes such as precipitation, evapo-transpiration, inflows and outflows) and changes due to human activities are also considered.

1.1.3 Quality accounts

The quality accounts are generally the asset accounts which try to account for the change in the quality of the stock of water over the period of consideration.

1.1.4 Valuation of water resources

Finally this account is to put a price considering it as a commodity and an economic good.

In spite of limited data availability, we have considered all the accounts in this study, tried to find out the major bottlenecks while executing natural resource accounting for a developing nation.

The physical water accounts can be disaggregated by source of water i.e. the supply side of the water resource account and users of water or the demand side of the economy. Initially we have considered these two sides of the account separately and then clubbed them together. In this context we must also know the stakeholders associated with the water resources in our state:

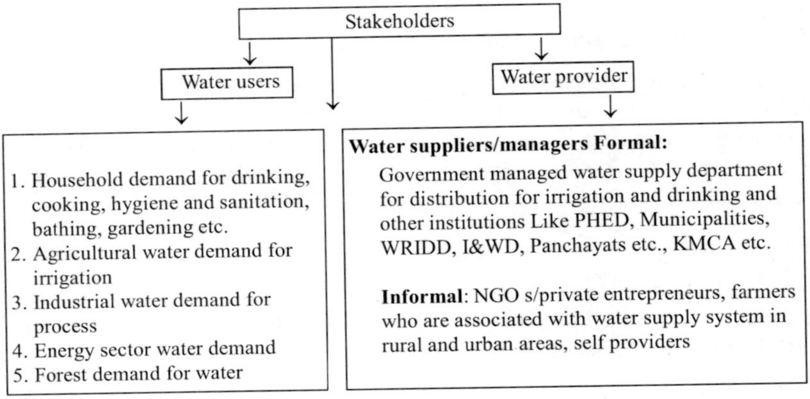

Figure12.1: Stake holders associated with Water Resource in West Bengal.

The physical supply and use table consists of physical supply and use tables which information on the volumes of water exchanged between the environment and the economy (abstractions and returns) and within the economy (supply and use within the economy) as well as the emissions by industry and households. The water supplying sources can be classified into natural and institutional sources. The most important natural sources are ground water and surface water. From the demand side, water can be used directly or indirectly. Direct use of water includes water used for agriculture, manufacturing, services, hydro- electric power generation, human consumption and sanitation, recreation and navigation. Indirect uses include and support of ecosystem health.

We have considered the amount of surface and ground water basin and sub-basin wise in order to know about the status of supply from these two principal sources. Due to the limited data availability, we could collect data corresponding to two time points 1995, 2004 for ground water but data for surface water is available for a single time point 2002. We have also taken population figures for 1991 and 2001(census figures) to get an idea of the population they are catering to. One interesting observation is that ground water availability in the districts of West

Bengal is more that the total ground water resource availability of Ganga basin. Since the data is collected from two different sources, there must be some gap and lack of coordination among the different departments and record keeping organisations or it may be due to the reason that district boundary and the basin boundary are not completely comparable. Moreover, we found that ground water availability is increasing in 2004 with comparison to 1995. This is not in conformation with the reality. In course of personal interactions with the Central Ground Water Board, it was learnt that the methodology adopted for 1995 differed from the one adopted in 2004. The 1995 methodology did not incorporate some of the variable.

Table 12.1: Total Availability Status in West Bengal

River Basins	*District*	*Sub basin*	*Area (sq km)*	*Population 2001*	*Population 1991*	*Ground water availability '95 (mcm)*	*Ground water availability' 95 (mcm)*	*Surface water*
Ganga								
Damodar, Bankura Silabati, Kasai		Darakeswar,	6882	3192695	2805065	1270.48	1899.26	2060
Damodar, Ajay, Bagirathi, Barakar	Burdwan		7024	6895514	6050605	2634.28	3032.95	1840
Dakshin Dinajpur Tangon		Atrai, Punarbhaba,	2219	1503178	1230608		871.2	1550
Uttar Dinajpur		Mahananda	3140	2441794	1897045	1235	1536.86	3310
Rupnarayan, Damodar, Hoogly	Howrah		1467	4273099	3729644	220.79	333.3	960
Hoogly, Damodar, Hooghly Mundeshwari		Darakeswar,	3149	5041976	4355230	1387.97	1526.4	590
Ganga, Mahananda, Kalindi, Tangan	Malda		3733	3290468	2637032	880.87	723.79	2140
Ganga, Mayurakshi Murshidabad Dwaraka		Jalangi, Bhairab,	5324	5866569	4740149	1783.8	2270.38	540
Ganga, Churni, Jalangi	Nadia		3927	4604827	3852097	1423.29	1955.11	-270
North 24 Parganas Kalindi, Raimangal		Ichmati, Bagirathi,	4094	8934286	7281881	1081.81	1955.11	1910
Hoogly, Matla, Bidyadhari, South 24 parganas Thakuran, Saptamukhi		Raimangal,	9960	6906689	5715030	NA	NA	1860
Ajoy, Mayurakshi Brahmani	Birbhum		4545	3015422	2555664	1432.62	1526.12	1460
Kolkata		Hoogly	185	4572876	4399819		NA	250
SUB TOTALS(% indicate percentage of Total) Percentage of total Ganga and Subarnarekha			**55649 (71.50%)**	**60539393 (75.5%)**	**51249869 (75.28%)**	**13350.91 (63.18%)**	**17630.48 (64.23%)**	**18200 (35.67%)**
						116.14%*	**153.37%***	**28.20%**

River Basins	*District*	*Sub basin*	*Area (sq km)*	*Population 2001*	*Population 1991*	*Ground water availability' 95 (mcm)*	*Ground water availability' 95 (mcm)*	*Surface water*
Ganga								
	Darjeeling	Mechi, Mahananda, Balason, Tista, Jaldhaka	3149	1609172	1299919	430.05	469.57	5780
	Jalpaiguri		6227	3401173	2800543	2928.46	2372.59	11300
	Cooch Behar	Tista, Torsa, Jaldhaka, Radiak	3387	2479155	2171145	1472.33	2085	6420
SUB TOTALS (% indicate percentage of Total) Percentage of total Ganga and Brahmaputra			**12763 (16.4%)**	**7489500 (9.34%)**	**6271607 (9.21%)**	**4830.84 (22.86%)**	**4927.16 (17.95%)**	**23500 (46.06%)**

River Basins	District	Sub basin	Area (sq km)	Population 2001	Population 1991	Ground water availability' 95 (mcm)	Ground water availability' 95 (mcm)	Surface water
Ganga								
Ganga/ Subarnarekha								
Purba Medinipore		Kasai, Rupnarayan, Hoogly, Kalghai					743.41	3270
Kasai, Paschim Subarnarekha, Medinipore Rupnarayan			3149	9610788	8331912	2282.28	3444.47	2360
Subarnarekha, Puruliya Kasai, Damodar			6259	2536516	2224577	665.48	701.47	3680
SUB TOTALS (% indicate percentage of Total)			**9408**	**12147304**	**10556489**	**2947.76**	**4889.35**	**9310**
Percentage of total Ganga and Brahmaputra			**(12.08%)**	**(15.15%)**	**(15.50%)**	**(13.95%)**	**(17.81)**	**(18.25%)**
Total			**77820**	**80176197**	**68077965**	**21129.51**	**27446.99**	**51010**
			100%	**100%**	**100%**	**100%**	**100%**	**100%**

Source: Estimated using data from Statistical Abstract 2002-03, 2005, West Bengal Pollution Control Board, 2009, Central Ground Water Board Report, 1995, 2006.

*Note: The observed counter-intutive result may be due to two reasons. One, the district boundary and the basin boundary are not completely comparable. Secondly, we tried to compile and collate data from various sources. Ground water availability in selected districts of West Bengal is more than that of the total ground water resource availability of Ganga basin. This is surprising. We could not correct it as it is outside the purview of the study. But we want to state that the data on basin wise availability and ground water position is taken from different sources and thus there might be some anomaly in reporting, measurement differences or may be other reasons. At best what we can conclude is data management with coordination of the different departments is needed so as to ensure reliability in the data structure.

Table 12.2: River basin wise per capita availability

River Basins	District	Sub basin	per capita'95 (cubic m)	per capita'04 (cubic m)
Ganga				
	Bankura	Damodar, Darakeswar, Silabati, Kasai	1187.309	1240.1
	Burdwan	Damodar, Ajay, Bagirathi,Barakar	739.4765	706.6841
	Dakshin Dinajpur	Atrai, Punarbhaba, Tangon		1610.721
	Uttar Dinajpur	Mahananda	1948.739	1984.959
	Howrah	Rupnarayan, Damodar, Hoogly	316.5959	302.6609
	Hooghly	Hoogly, Damodar, Darakeswar, Mundeshwari	454.1597	419.7561
	Malda	Ganga, Mahananda, Kalindi, Tangan	1145.557	870.3291
	Murshidabad	Ganga, Mayurakshi ,Jalangi, Bhairab, Dwaraka	490.2378	479.05
	Nadia	Ganga, Churni, Jalangi	299.3928	365.9443
	North 24 Parganas	Ichmati, Bagirathi, Kalindi, Raimangal	410.8568	432.6154
	South 24 parganas	Hoogly, Matla, Bidyadhari, Raimangal, Thakuran, Saptamukhi	Na	Na
	Birbhum	Ajoy, Mayurakshi, Brahmani	1131.847	990.2826
	Kolkata	Hoogly	Na	Na
Brahmaputra/Ganga				
	Darjeeling	Mechi, Mahananda, Balason, Tista, Jaldhaka	4777.259	3883.718
	Jalpaiguri		5080.608	4019.963
	Cooch Behar	Tista, Torsa, Jaldhaka, Radiak	3635.1	3430.604
Ganga/ Subarnarekha				
	Purba Medinipore	Kasai,Rupnarayan, Hoogly, Kalghai		
	Paschim Medinipore	Kasai, Subarnarekha, Rupnarayan	1223.556	1021.548
	Puruliya	Subarnarekha, Kasai, Damodar	1953.396	1727.358

Another observation is that there is no uniform pattern of distribution of ground water and surface water. Some of the districts such Burdwan, Hoogly, Murshidabad, Nadia, Paschim Medinipore, ground water is greater than the surface water availability. Thus the policy makers need to be careful regarding the decision regarding the conventional district levels planning or the basin-wise plans which are being proposed in the context of Nation Action plan for Climate Change.

The supply side accounting has also considered another important yardstick– the per-capita availability of water. Accounting for water based on per-capita availability gives us an indication that whether the present endowment of water resource can support the existing population and their associated economic activity.

Note, here:

SAFE

absolute scarcity-less than 500m^3/person/year
less than 1000m3/person/year-water scarcity starts
Between 1000m3/year and 1667m3/year -water stress

Source: Author's estimate, colour code as per the range given Water Resource and its Quality in WestBengal, West Bengal Pollution Control Board, 2009

The per capita water availability in the state calculated on basis of the population shows absolute scarcity in five districts Howrah, Hoogly, Murshidabad, Nadia and North 24 Parganas. Only 5 districts Darjeeling, Jalpaiguri, Puruliya, Cooch Behar and Uttar Dinajpur are safe with respect to water availability. Popular perception that Darjeeling is water scarce is not reflected since Darjeeling is water abundant with respect to natural water supply but water scarce with respect to institutional sources. So we can say that policy makers need to pay due attention to issues like human settlement planning based on water availability, water demand management and also institutional management for proper resource planning. But we could not calculate per capita availability positions for South 24 Parganas and Kolkata since Ground Water estimation are not available for these districts.

Moreover, as evident from the per capita water availability, there is scarcity of water in terms of natural water supply. This gives us an indication that we have exceeded the carrying capacity in some districts within the state at districts such as Howrah, Hoogly, Murshidabad, Nadia and North 24 Parganas. They all suffer from absolute water scarcity. Thus appropriate planning is necessary to address these areas as well as make proper planning for the areas which are in water stress situation or are somewhat safe for sustainable water management. In the next section we take up the supplying institutions that are responsible for water supply in the state.

If we now consider the water supply scenario in West Bengal, we find that it is managed by the Panchayat in rural areas and municipalities in urban area, who plan, design and execute most of the water supply schemes. However, for piped water supply schemes, the PHED continues to play primordial role in planning, designing and executing the schemes and then hand over to the concerned Panchayat and the Municipality after a period of run. However, the water for Irrigation is managed by two departments – Water Resource Investigations & Development and Irrigation and Water Ways Departments. In case of command area of less than 2000 hectares, the irrigation is done by surface water lift or by ground water lift by Water Resource Investigation & Development Department. But in case of command area of more than 2000 hectares, it is managed by the Irrigation and Water Ways Department. The Central Government also plays an important role by coordinating and harmonizing the standards. Apart from this, the NGOs (both national and international) have played a significant role in the sector in India over the past three decades.

The supply side of any model can be best understood if we can get a demand side scenario picture as well. From the demand side, water uses in West Bengal can be categorised into – Domestic use of water, Industrial use of water, demand for water for the energy sector, water demand for forests in West Bengal and last but most important water for agriculture or irrigational water demand.

Table 12.3: Percentage of Water Use to Total Water availability

Sectors	*Water Use 2001 (in mcm)*	*Percentage of Total 2011*	*Water Use 2011 (in mcm)*	*Percentage of Total 2011*
Domestic	1980.83	1.88	2270.98	2.02
Forest	23447.95	22.27	23447.95	20.88
Agriculture	73671	69.96	73671	65.60
Energy	3600	3.42	8300	7.39
Industry	2600	2.47	4610	4.11
Total	**105299.8**	100	**112299.9**	100

Source: Calculated on basis of the information available based on Water Resource and its Quality in WestBengal, West Bengal Pollution Control Board, 2009.

Comparing the two years with respect to water demand by sectors we present the following for better visual representation and understanding:

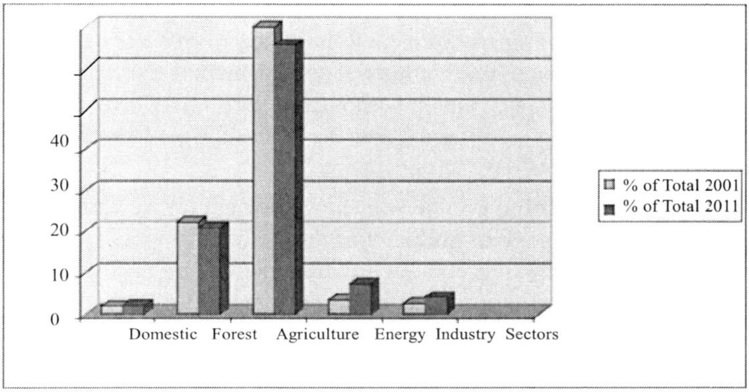

Figure 12.2 Sector-wise water use percentage 2001 and 2011.

We can see that the agricultural sector claiming a significant portion of the total water use 5(almost 70%), which is expected to fall by 4% in 2011 because of competing demand by the other sectors. The demand for water for domestic, energy and industry is expected to increase by small percentage and therefore comparing the sector wise water use percentage for the two years, we have seen that agriculture and forest sector will have to sacrifice their share of water use in order to support other sectors. Thus, taking the overall supply demand position, we come across the following situation.

Table 12.4: Water Demand and Supply situation along with deficit and surplus

Water Suppy Demand Position 2001 (in mcm)	*Demand*	*Supply*	*Deficit/ Surplus*
Ground Water	11647.38*2	27446.99	15799.61
Surface water	NA	51010	NA
Total	102699.78	78456.99	-24242.79

Source: Estimated on basis of above Table.

Therefore we see that is a deficit if we compare the demand and the supply situation. The ground water and the surface water are only meeting part of the demand. It is not known how the demand is meted with. It may be that we are over-extracting the ground water to unsustainable levels i.e. rate of extraction is more than what can be regenerated or it may that we are using water which does not satisfy the required standard level for consumption.

In case of environmental resources another important part is considering the emission resulting from the pollutants discharged and accordingly accounting for it. The emissions accounts provide the description in terms of pollutants resulting from production and consumption of the waste water flows. Sources of pollution are classified in point source and non-point source emissions. Point source emissions include emissions from waste water treatment plants, power plants, and other industrial establishments. Non points sources (or diffuse) of pollution are sources without a single point of origin or a specific outlet into a receiving water body. For the state of West Bengal, we do not have much data on waste water generation.

We will mainly try to collate whatever information we can collect with reference to the discharge of pollutant of the different sectors or waste water generation that are released without any treatment . The difference between gross emission and net emission is also important in this connection. Gross emission are the pollutant released by an activity assessed at that point where waste water leaves that activity site(example household release of waste water) whereas net emission is waste water directly discharged into water resource. The gross and net emission coincides when waste water is directly released into the water body.

For the state of West Bengal we do not have much data on waste water generation. From the little information that we can gather we present below the waste water generation position of the domestic sector which is one of the major sectors contributing to waste water.

Table 12.5: Domestic Wastewater Generation and Treatment in West Bengal 2001

State	*Wastewater Generation MLD*	*Wastewater Treatment MLD*	*Untreated Waste-water Discharge MLD*
West Bengal	2113	372	1741
India	22903	5942	16961

Reference: www.indiastat.com downloaded on 12.10. 2010.

Waste water generated is much higher than treated. This has very important policy implications.

Since we donot have much data on sector wise waste water generation we try to calculate it based on personal communication with the West Bengal Pollution Control Board as to the approximate waste water generation as a percentage of total water use. We have taken the water demand of the different sectors in the previous chapter as a proxy of water use though we know that the entire water demand cannot be meted as there is a deficit in water supply. We have taken that both the domestic sector as well the industrial sector generates 80% of the water used as wastewater.For agriculture, forest, the percentage of waste water to total water use is taken to be 0 as water percolates back to the soil and we do not get any discharge as waste water. For the energy sector the percentage of waste water generation to use is not available. These are very important if environmental service and payment for environmental service becomes a policy issue and incentive design to drive sustainable development action.

Table 12.6: Sectorwise emission of waste water

Sectors	*Total Water Use 2001 (in mcm)*	*Waste Water Generation (in mcm)*
Domestic	1980.83	1584.664
Forest	23447.95	0
Agriculture	73671	0
Energy	3600	NA
Industry	2600	2080
Total	105299.78	3664.664

Source: Estimated on the basis of the above Tables and approximate estimates provided by WBPCB

Therefore, we have seen the supply –use table as well the emission account which are basically physical quantity based accounts. In the next section we will try to provide some insights to economic water account following the hybrid accounting structure.

The Hybrid account aims to inter link the physical information on the different aspects of use and supply with the conventional system of National accounts. The hybrid account helps to decide upon possible tradeoffs that may be entertained for efficient water utilisation and to ensure optimum possible outcome with regard to the water resource. This account is also necessary for implementing polluter's pay principle as the users in most cases do not bear the full cost of water being supplied to them and are generally borne by the government.

Hybrid account or Hybrid supply use table try to interlink the physical and monetary information related to water. However, monetary information with regard to a resource which is almost treated as a "freegood" is difficult to obtain specially in our state.We have tried to collate whatever small information is available to prepare this account so as to get some indicators of the impact of water resource on the economy and vice versa. A standard hybrid account will consist of two parts: one part is based on supply where as other part is based on demand.

We have tried to gather all possible monetary information of water supply to different sectors. On the basis of personal communication with the Water Investigation and Development Department we tried to access information on the different irrigation techonologies that are used in West Bengal and the associated cost of supplying water through those technologies. We have come to know that irrigation in West Bengal is either through ground water or surface water.

Further while discussing with WRIDD, we came to know though there is wide variation in the cost of installation of these different technologies and operation, the operation cost is Rs 320/hac for supplying 2 cm irrigation water if the operation and maintenance is carried out at the farmer's end after installation by the Government agencies. The cost of supplying irrigation water in West Bengal is Rs 1.60/kl of water. Since we know the water demanded for the agricultural sector from the physical account, we use that as the total amount of water being used in the agricultural sector. Multiplying the total water use with the cost associated with water supply, we get the monetary assessment of supplying water in agricultural sector i.e. Rs 117873.6 million.

For industries, we have got from the ASI data, the total quantity of water purchased by different industries and the value associated with that quantity of purchase. Since we donot have current data availability we have taken the 1994-95 data.We have seen that for the year 1994-95, the quantity of water purchased is 11032 million litres i.e. 11.03 mcm. But for 2001-02, water demand is 2600 mcm, thus the cost of water for the Industrial sector is Rs 8805820.5Thus we form the following water table which has both the physical as well as monetary account within the same table:

Table 12.7: Hybrid Account 2001 having water demand as well as value

Sectors	*Domestic*	*Forest*	*Agriculture*	*Energy*	*Industry*
Water Use (mcm)	1980.83	23447.95	73671	3600	2600
Money value of water (Rs'000)	0	0	11783600	na	8805821
Gross capital formation	na	Na	Na	na	Na

Note : value =the cost of water use.

Information on gross fixed capital formation for water related infrastructure represent investment in fixed capital related to water. In case of household, it is installation of pumps, wells etc, whereas, in case of agriculture, development of irrigation related infrastructure etc. But such data are not available at such detailed level. These can be constructed through field based survey which we have not tried here but can be taken as future research agenda.

Some derived indicators which may be useful to analyze the sector-wise productivity of water are:

1. Water Use Intensity by sector provides information about efficiency of water use. Thus policy makers can use this as a decision taking indicators as to the allocation of water use.
   Water Use Intensity = Volume of water used/ value added (cubic m/ million Rs)
2. Water Use Productivity is a concept similar to capital productivity or labour productivity which measures how much value added is

generated by one unit volume of water. It is the reciprocal of water use intensity and defined as

Water Use Productivity = Value added/ Volume of water used (may be calculated over periods)

We have proceeded to develop this in two parts. We have derived the physical water intensity by linking the production of major agricultural crops and industrial production with the water use. The following table has shown the water intensity of the different crops and industries in quantity terms.

Table 12.8: Water Use Productivity of major crops and Industries

Agriculture	*Production*	*Unit*	*Water Used (in mcm)*	*Water use productivity (water quantity /unit of physical production)*
Rice	14884	in thousand tonnes	173.50	85.78
Pulses	167.3	in thousand tonnes	4.14	40.38
Oilseeds	556.8	in thousand tonnes	9.89	56.27
Cereals	159.4	in thousand tonnes	204.97	0.78
Total fibres	7947	in thousand bales of 180 kgs each	14.50	547.78
Tea	188081	in thousand kg	0.22	827093.23
Industries				
Distillery	29400	kilolitre alchohol	4.29	6853.15
Steel	3142000	tonne	706.95	4444.44
Sugar	425	tonne	0.001	664062.5
Textile	20434	100 kg	0.20	100000

Source: Author's estimate based on data from Statistical Abstract 2005 and West Bengal Pollution Control Board, (2004): Air Quality Status of West Bengal – A State of Environment Report

The agricultural water productivity is calculated based on data of agricultural production and area. Taking the water requirement of the various crops into consideration we have multiplied that with the area under crop production we get the water use of the different crops. Dividing that by their corresponding production level we calculate the water productivity. The total volume of water used in the industries was known and dividing by their corresponding production level, we get the water productivity of the respective industries.

But, the problem with this type of productivity calculation is that different commodities are measured in different units and therefore it is difficult to compare across industries.

Therefore we have also tried to calculate water productivity in terms of a single unit i.e. we intended to calculate the productivity in monetary terms. Since we do not have data on value added by each sector, we have used the sectoral contribution to the gross domestic product and tried to find the productivity of water in terms of its value.

Table 12.9 : Value of Water Productivity

	2003-04 (Rs Crores) GSDP at current prices	*Water use (in mcm)*	*Water Productivity*
Agriculture	40143.24	73671	.54
Manufacturing	37574.45	2600	14.45

Source: Author's estimate based on Table and Statistical Abstract 2005.

Results shown in the above table are very simplistic and care needs to be taken as they are very aggregates. Food security and its weightage are not taken into consideration. Value addition by agriculture sector might not be representing the true value due to subsidy in the system. So quick policy recommendations like allocation decision of water by water productivity cannot be built based on such simple parameters.

Next, we have attempted on the asset account which tries to link the abstraction and discharge of water with information on the stock of water resource in the environment so as to assess the effect of current level of abstraction and discharge on the stock level. The asset account considers abstraction of water, water returns, precipitation, inflow and outflow, evapotranspiration and other volume changes associated with the stock account. Thus the Asset account will consider – opening and closing stock for the period under consideration, changes due to human activities such as abstraction and return and changes due to natural processes i.e. flow of water within the economy and the environment and transfer of natural resource within the environment. A schematic representation of asset account is shown below:

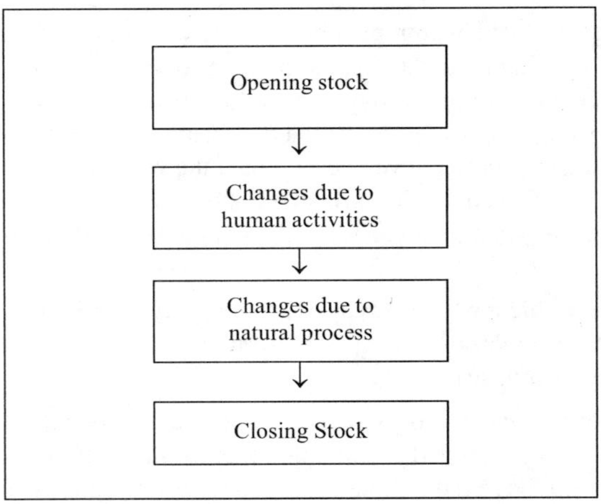

Source: UN, 2006.

The changes due to human activity in the asset account represent the supply and use table and are therefore the link between the flow account and the stock account.

On the onset, we will first show the changes in volume due to natural processes for the different districts as shown below:

Table 12.10: Accounting if water stock change is due to natural processes

Districts of West Bengal	*Average rainfall (mcm)*	*INFLOW estimated runoff received from upstream (mcm)*	*Estimated mean Evapo-transpiration (mcm)*	*OUTFLOW estimated runoff leaving district (mcm*	*INFLOW receipt from/donation to other region*	*Within region storage*	*Changes in volume due to natural process*
Bankura	10647.8	13347.8	6492.5	17503	500	334.5	834.6
Burdwan	11235.6	45537.2	6056.1	50716.7	915.4	434.4	1349.8
Cooch Behar	11080.7	44175.6	2341.4	52914.9	0	62.9	62.9
Dakshin Dinajpur	4278.8	18644.6	1781.7	21141.7	0	93.3	93.3
Darjeeling	8665.5	16253	2361.1	22557.4	0	0	0
Howrah	2481.7	67363.9	1150	68695.7	4.1	77.9	81.9
Hooghly	5194.8	65281.6	2909.1	67567.3	211.6	247.6	459.2
Jalpaiguri	19154.5	32564.6	5220.9	46498.2	0	16.5	16.5
Malda	6401.5	553213.7	2856.2	556759.1	0	156.2	156.1
Murshidabad	8268.2	561884.1	5209.7	564942.5	42.1	286.8	329
Nadia	6312.7	48248.7	4407.4	50154	0	125.5	125.5
North 24 Parganas	6891.1	50325.2	3407	53809.4	0	231.7	231.6
South 24 parganas	17216.4	81034.5	11517	86734.1	0	243.6	243.4
Purba Midnapore	8141.8	76677.6	4042.7	80776.6	0	165.3	165.4
Paschim Midnapore	15421.3	3607.9	9240.9	9788.3	314.7	320.1	634.8
Purulia	9434.2	9598.3	4982.1	14050.3	-681.6	1005.9	324.4
Uttar Dinajpur	7557.7	16858.3	2569.5	21846.5	0	132	132
Birbhum	6941.7	4497.4	3816.3	7622.8	185.4	417.7	603.1
Kolkata	314.6	50069.6	60.6	50323.6	0	0	0
West Bengal	165640.6	598562.8	80422.2	683781.4	1491.6	4351.9	5843.3

Source: WBPCB 2009.

Thus we get an idea of the changes in volume that takes place due to natural processes. From table we can see district wise changes due to rainfall, average inflow and outflow of water, potential evapotranspiration taking place in that region as well as othe storage changes. Collating all these information we try to create an asset account.

The preparation of asset account is a difficult task. Till then, we tried on accounting of water resources considering the capital theory where natural resource is taken as any other capital. We have constructed capital account for a single year 2009 (as presented in the table 4.26 and therefore cannot account for the changes in stock over time.

Table 12.11: Water Asset Account of West Bengal

ASSET ACCOUNT (in mcm) 2009	*TOTAL*
OPENING STOCK	27446.99
GROUND WATER	51010
SURFACE WATER	78456.99
TOTAL WATER	102699.78
CHANGES DUE TO HUMAN ACTIVITIES	
Abstraction	
Return	
CHANGES DUE TO NATURAL PROCESS	
Precipitation	165640.6
Inflow	598562.8
from upstream	1491.6
from other territories	80422.2
Evapotranspiration	
Outflow	683781.4
to downstream	
to other territories	4351.9
other volume changes-storage	133741.11
CLOSING STOCK	

Source: Author's estimate based on tables above and West Bengal Pollution Control Board, '2009.

Table above gives us important information as to the changes in stock both due to changes in natural flow as well as human intervention. It may be noted that these accounts if prepared over time, can give proper indication of the changes in the resource –base and therefore result in appropriate policy intervention.

Apart from this quantity aspect, there is also a quality aspect associated with water. Water pollution has worsened due to increased household and waste water discharge which have destroyed the quality of water in the rivers as well as the drinking water sources. Again, the quality of river beds may have been polluted with heavy metals. Water Quality account does not have a direct link to the economic accounts, as changes in quality cannot be attributed to economic quantities using linear relationship. The quality account was attempted with reference to both surface water as well as ground water. In surface water, we have accounted the quality taking determinants like BOD, DO and Total Coliform.

In spite of data scarcity as to the quality of different surface water bodies in the districts of West Bengal we have tried to prepare the quality accounts for surface water body by gathering information from few sources. Comparing these standards with the reported quality on water, one can get an idea of the condition of the quality of surface water resources in the state.

Table 12.12 : Surface Water Quality Account of West Bengal

District	*Measured at*	*Rivers*	*BOD 2005*	*BOD 2004*	*DO 2005*	*DO 2004*	*Total Coliform 2005*	*Total Coliform 2004*
Burdwan								
Birbhum								
Bankura	Rajgram	Dwarkeshar		1.9		7.18		1284
Midnapore	Ragamati	Kasai		1.65		7.07		1125
Howrah	Howrah (Shibpur)	Bhagirathi Hoogly	3.52	2.14	5.05	5.31	430833.3	320000
	Uluberia	Bhagirathi Hoogly	2.50	5.95	5.63	5.59	232666.7	581666.67
Hoogly	Srirampore	Bhagirathi Hoogly	2.58	2.95	6.58	6.72	115833.3	305000
24 Parganas (N)	Palta	Bhagirathi Hoogly	3.09	2.03	6.55	6.57	123333.3	110500
	Dakshineswar	Bhagirathi Hoogly	3.98	3.28	5.51	5.51	2416667	810833.33
24 Parganas (S)	Diamond Harbour	Bhagirathi Hoogly	1.89	1.66	6.36	5.97	22000	54500
Kolkata	Garden Reach	Bhagirathi Hoogly	2.75	2.92	5.25	5.52	256666.7	430000
Nadia		Churni		2		4.92		Na
Murshidabad	Berhampore	Bhagirathi Hoogly	1.98	1.69	7.27	6.57	37833.33	23166.67
Uttar Dinajpur								
Dakshin Dinajpur								
Malda	English Bazar	Mahananda		1.02		5.84		20421
Jalpaiguri Darjeeling Kooch Behar	Siliguri	Teesta		1.39		8.48		17087
Purulia								
West Bengal								

Source: Based on West Bengal Pollution Control Board, 2009 and www.westbengalstat.com

From the above table we find that in Dakshineswar, Uluberia, Howrah(Shibpur) , the BOD level for either of the two years is higher than 3mg/l cannot be used for drinking even with conventional treatment or for outdoor bathing. For DO, water quality is more acceptable at least with outdoor bathing and consumption with conventional treatment . The total coliform count is unacceptably high in all the monitored areas and is therefore a matter of serious concern.

Therefore we can say that the surface water quality is West Bengal need to be taken care of. Dumping of domestic waste, industrial waste in the river water without proper treatment is one of the principal reasons. Appropriate mechanism for proper treatment of the waste water needs to be ensured in order to protect the surface water resource for sustainable development.

In case of ground water, in addition to these determinants, we have two other concern areas, the Arsenic and the Flouride affected areas. Presence of arsenic above the level of .05 mg/l or 50ìg/l is said to be contaminated. Eight districts in West Bengal are Arsenic affected. South 24 Parganas, North 24 Parganas, Nadia, Murshidabad, Malda are highly affected, whereas the rest 3 districts Bardhaman, Hoogly and Howrah are moderately affected. Fluoride concentration over and above 1mg/litre is said to be fluoride affected. Seven districts in West Bengal are fluoride affected. We have accounted for ground water quality taking all these considerations.

Table 12.13: Table showing Ground water quality of West Bengal

Ground Water Quality							
District	*Stations*	*DO (mg/l)*	*BOD (mg/l)*	*TC (MPN)*	*Arsenic Affected Blocks/ Municipality*	*Max Concentration of Arsenic(mg/l)*	*Flouride affected blocks*
Burdwan	Asansol	7.25	0.25	120	2	.28 (Dkshin Block : Purbasthali II)	9
	Durgapur	2.15	0.3	296			12
Birbhum							
Bankura							
Midnapore	Haldia	2.775	1.025	169.5			
Howrah	Domjur	0.375	0.35	NA	2	0.09 (Shantinagar Block : Balliyjaga)	1
Hoogly	Rishra	1.6	1.325	5.5	1	0.6 (Abdulpur Block : Abdulpur)	
	Dankuni	1.15	0.85	11			
24 Parganas (N)	Barasat	1.55	1.225	6	19/7	1.40 (Shidalaya Block : Basirhat I)	1
24 Parganas (S)					10	3.20 (Ramnagar Block : Baruipur)	4
Kolkata	Tangra	0.825	0.3	8			
	Topsia	0.2	0.425	300			15
	Dhapa	0.35	0.25	13			
	Garia	0.6	0.5	2			
Nadia	Kalyani	2.45	0.8	2	13/1	1.16 (Mohisbathan Block : Karimpur II)	
Murshidabad					15	1.85 (Makrampur Block : Beldanga I)	
Uttar Dinajpur							
Dakshin Dinajpur							
Malda					5	1.43 (Mohanpur Block : Kaliacham II)	
Jalpaiguri							
Darjeeling							
Kooch Behar							
Purulia							
West Bengal							
1. Arsenic level **2.** Fluoride level	0.06 - 0.10 (Safe limit 0.05 mg./litre) 1 - 1.46 (Safe limit 1 mg./litre)						

Water Account with respect to both quantity and quality

Finally we consider the flow account for water resources with respect to both quality as well as quantity in the following table, we get some interesting results.

Table 12.14 : Accounting Water Resources considering both quantity and quality

Districts of West Bengal	*Quantity Account*	*Quality Account*	
	per capita water availability	Arsenic affected Districts	Fluoride affected Districts
Bankura	1240.10		Fluoride
Burdwan	706.68	Arsenic	
Cooch Behar	3430.60		
Dakshin Dinajpur	1610.72		Fluoride
Darjeeling	3883.72		
Howrah	302.66	Arsenic	
Hooghly	419.76	Arsenic	
Jalpaiguri	4019.96		
Malda	870.33	Arsenic	Fluoride
Murshidabad	479.05	Arsenic	
Nadia	365.94	Arsenic	
North 24 Parganas	432.62	Arsenic	
South 24 parganas	NA	Arsenic	Fluoride
Purba Midnapore			
Paschim			
Midnapore	1021.55		
Purulia	1727.36		Fluoride
Uttar Dinajpur	1984.96		Fluoride
Birbhum	990.28		Fluoride
Kolkata	NA		
West Bengal			

Note: Colour Codes Used in Table Represent

Safe

Absolute scarcity-less than 500m^3/person/year

Less than 1000m3/person/year-water scarcity starts

Between 1000m3/year and 1667m3/year -water stress

Three districts in West Bengal are safe with respect to both quantity as well as quality. They are Cooch Behar, Darjeeling and Jalpaiguri. The districts which are in absolute water scarcity also suffers from the problem of arsenic contamination in ground water. These aspects are of serious policy consideration.

UN SEEAW does not have any standard format for valuation of water resources. Valuation of water is at an experimental stage. But while valuing water they considered it to be treated as any other products. The need to treat water as an economic good has been recognised as an essential component of sustainable water management. Efficient and equitable allocation of water takes into account the value of water used by competing end-users in the present generation, the allocation of resources between present and future generations and the degree of treatment of wastes discharged to water or other activities that affect water quality. Water valuation can also be used to set water pricing policy in the design of instruments to achieve better use of the resources.

Since we have based our study entirely on the secondary data source without considering any primary survey, in this section we use monetary value as available in the literature (Roy et al. 2004). The study has tried to find out value of drinking water quality using averting expenditure behaviour of households for drinking water quality. Averting expenditure i.e. expenditure on purification methods are taken as proxy measurement of production cost of drinking water quality and, the estimated average expenditure is Rs 168.72 per month per household. Based on previous socio economic study in the context of Kolkata city we know that an average daily consumption of 2.43 litres for drinking purpose. Then assuming an average family size of 4 persons, we can say that for an average monthly consumption of 291.6 litres/month, the cost of drinking quality water is Rs 168.72. Roy, 2008 estimated using household health production function the value of arsenic safe water for a representative household at around Rs. 297-Rs 336 depending upon the income class to which they belong. Based on estimates provided by Roy, 2008, the monthly welfare gain of reduction of 1ìg of Arsenic from 1 litre of water is Rs.0.49

These valuation of water quality are not found using uniform method . But they all are showing some proxy estimates for water quality if various kinds. So we apply these to arrive at some monetary accounting for water looking into district wise specificities.

Table 12.15: Rural and Urban Population associated with risk of Arsenic

Districts of West Bengal	*Number of rural household*	*Number of urban household*	*% of population at risk*	*No of rural household at risk*	*No of urban household at risk*
Burdwan	862458	518415	0.31	2674	1607
Howrah	399845	438390	5.12	20472	22446
Hooghly	665263	355355	0.68	4524	2416
Malda	580336	49580	20.48	118853	10154
Murshidabad	991967	137626	24.64	244421	33911
Nadia	736063	207588	21.67	159505	44984
North 24 Parganas	802407	995407	12.18	97733	121241
South 24 parganas	1080318	233773	13.51	145951	31583

Source: Calculation based on Statistictal Abstract, http://www.cgwb.gov.in/ accessed on 10.12.2008

We now try to estimate the welfare gain of reduction of arsenic for the different districts of West Bengal which are exposed to the arsenic contamination. We already have noted that 8 districts are arsenic affected. They are Burdwan, Howrah, Hoogly, Malda, Murshidabad, Nadia, North 24 Parganas and South 24 Parganas. But the entire population of these districts are not exposed to the threat of arsenic. On basis of the percentage of population exposed to the risk of being affected by arsenic contamination we try to figure out the households who may be exposed to the risk in the following table.

Since we know that the benefit of reducing arsenic in water to safe limit 50ìg/l differs on basis of income class we divide the households into poor and non-poor based on rural and urban poverty ratio.

Based on these above assumptions, we try to estimate the monthly welfare gain of the two groups – poor and non-poor for the rural and urban areas. We will mainly concentrate on the arsenic affected areas and the population at risk.

Table 12.16 : Monthly Welfare gain for reduction in arsenic concentration to safe limit 50ìg/l

Districts of West	*Welfare gain Rural*	*Welfare gain Rural Non*	*Welfare gain Urban*	*Welfare gain Urban Non*
Bengal	Poor (Rs)	Poor (Rs)	Poor (Rs)	Poor (Rs)
Burdwan	170594.1	643272.122	91796.78	396162.9
Howrah	524838.2	5616283.52	100304.8	6577671
Hooghly	310534.5	1069074.79	92801.9	635644.7
Malda	14136829	22803338.4	225174.7	2816695
Murshidabad	37876209	39113075.3	5646922	5080105
Nadia	15193794	33942712.3	2344295	11288154
North 24 Parganas	4732006	24843997.3	4069610	32411206
South 24 parganas	13172016	31704314.4	902002.8	8582765

Table above shows the monetary gain associated with arsenic reduction. The huge gain as shown above justify any installation of arsenic removal plants and therefore a more sustainable water supply situation in future.

We have seen that water account is one of the efficient indicator and therefore can help the policy makers for appropriate policy formulation to ensure a sustainable development pathway. But it may be noted that if this water account is updated from time to time it can give clear representation as to whether our march towards better tomorrow is at all sustainable.

2. Section 2

The second part is the most crucial one which summarizes the main problems encountered while accounting for the water resources and therefore has important policy implications.While preparing the water quantity account, the first and foremost problem that we encountered is with respect to data availability. In case of surface water, we were unable to find data on two time points and therefore cannot compare whether there is any change in the volume over the years. Another important observation is that while comparing ground water availability with respect to both replenishable ground water as well as net water availability for the two years 1995 and 2004, there is an increasing trend for almost all districts. But ground water availability is not increasing in reality. In this context, personal communication with the line departments was made and it was learnt that the methodology adopted for 1995 differed from the one adopted in 2004. The 1995 methodology did not incorporate some of the variable. So the methodology of assessing the supply of water position is crucially important as it may alter people's perception and, therefore, decisions regarding water use.

Another interesting observation is that ground water availability in the districts of West Bengal is more than the total ground water resource availability of Ganga basin. The observed counter-intutive result may be due to the fact that the district boundaries and the basin boundaries are not completely comparable or it may be due to the fact that the data is collected from two different sources, the anomaly in reporting may be due to lack of coordination among the different departments and record keeping organisations. To address this issue, a task force with experts in this area needs to come up to resolve this problem.

While accounting for the water resources, we have also seen that for some of the districts such Burdwan, Hoogly, Murshidabad, Nadia, Paschim Medinipore, ground water is greater than the surface water availability. So the proposed basin –wise planning in the context of National Action Plan on Climate Change may not always be suitable and may, therefore, face barriers while implementing. There may arise a conflict between the conventional district levels planning with the basin-wise plans. The policy makers must , therefore, consider these issues by careful planning before going for any decisions regarding the consumptive use of ground water and surface water.

The per capita water availability calculated on basis of population and resource availability gives us the indication of water abundance or scarcity with respect to the different districts. Thus, policy makers need to pay due attention to issues like human settlement planning based on water availability; otherwise water stress and scarcity situation will aggravate.

Another important point is with respect to piped water supply in rural areas; we find that most of the districts have less than 50% access with respect to piped water supply. But this is not at par with the sustainable development objective. For this, the Government needs to come forward along with the community mobilisation. As studies have shown, non recovery of water charges act as major barrier for providing access to piped water to households.

Water users are one of the important stake holders in the water resource scenario. And therefore, policies focussing on users form an integral part of water resource management. In our state, water is not priced to the level that it should be. Domestic users do not have to pay any price for water use. Thus, wastage of water can be reduced to increase water use efficiency commensurate with NWM 's goal. First and foremost, what is needed is awareness that unnecessary water use may lead to scarcity in future and an unsustainable growth path. For that we need policy makers to use different flora of media to promote this awareness. But promoting awareness requires evidence and that a standardised water account is needed for designing awareness building modelling system for improving the situation.

We have also seen that given the current level of water resource availability, water demand from domestic, industrial and energy sector will increase reducing the water availability for agriculture and forest. Less water for agriculture implies less production and thus increasing population may face food scarcity in future. Since we are already in a state of water deficit, the situation may become worse in future, if not properly addressed. In view of this, optimum utilisation of the available water resources should be planned to the maximum possible extent. Basin wise, sub basin wise, district wise water use plans must be formulated and coordinated for best results.

Apart from this, both conventional and unconventional methods should be explored such as rainwater harvesting including roof-top rain water harvesting, inter basin transfers, artificial recharge of ground water etc.

When we come to the emission account, we found that there is no concrete information as to the discharge of water by the different sectors and whether any part of this water is being treated. Therefore, the West Bengal Pollution Control Board needs to address this area as to how much water is being discharged by the household sector and the industrial units. There must also be a standardised information pattern of the different crops and their probable water use and their associated waste water discharge.

Therefore, with respect to the water use and supply, the policy makers needs to come up with a format as follows which is consistent with the UN SEEAW. However, we could not come up with a format like this due to data unavailability. But we feel it can be tried out as next research project in coordination with all water using and supplying agencies. This will take some time but will be useful.

Table 12.17: Water Account format

	Agriculture	*Domestic*	*Manufacturing*	*Others*	*Total Use*
Within economy					
Reuse					
Waste water to sewerage					
To the environment					
Irrigation					
Lost in transport					
Treated waste					
Untreated waste water Total Supply					
Consumption					

This will help the different water use partners to be aware and change their use pattern to improve efficiency.

While considering the water quality, we found that the quality of Water in West Bengal is also a cause of severe concern. Eight districts in West Bengal are Arsenic affected. South 24 Parganas, North 24 Parganas, Nadia, Murshidabad, Malda are highly affected, whereas the rest 3 districts Bardhaman, Hoogly and Howrah are moderately affected. Seven districts in West Bengal are fluoride affected. And for these districts special precautions are needed to supply safe water to the population. Thus, ground water in these zones must be extracted from the safe zone of the aquifer or surface water may be used instead. If water is supplied from the ground water bed, then treatment plants should be utilised for removal of these chemical compounds. Water testing is also required from time to time so as to analyse the water quality. Apart from this, awareness building is also needed so that people in these areas know about the after- effects of using this water.

Another interesting observation is that that district which suffers from water scarcity also faces the problem of arsenic contamination of ground water. Thus, for these districts such as Howrah, Hoogly, Murshidabad, Nadia and North 24 Parganas simultaneous measures to address both quality and quantity are needed urgently to counter this alarming situation.

So now, forming an appropriate State Water Policy is the need of the hour since development and management of water is primarily a state subject for systematically developing, harnessing and adopting suitable approach for sustainable water use in the state. But the policy will not be a uniform one. It must be district-wise water policy addressing issues like demand management, human settlement, institutional supply management etc. Moreover, suitable measure must be taken to ensure proper treatment of waste water with a view to restoring the water quality of the river/water bodies. Promoting recycling and recycled of treated waste water is also needed.

India is an important signatory to the Declaration of Sustainable Development Goals (SDGs) at the Sustainable Development Summit, 2015 and also at the Paris Agreement on Climatic Change Conference, COP 21. The SDGs are now to be reached by the world in general and India in particular with reference to the country's obligation under COP 21. India will only be able to reach its target if all the state contributes in a sustainable way in the growth trajectory of the country. And therefore the issue of sustainable development considering the resource base becomes vital to ensure that the resources are being used optimally.

With such framework the resource situation can be understood which will try to make alter people's perception about resource use, arrest unnecessary misuse in some cases and help in better management of the resources. These local attempts will help in global climate change management and ensure a sustainable future for all.Additionally, it will take care of the the SDG Summit, 2015 that all Member States should develop national responses to the overall implementation of this Agenda and conduct regular and inclusive reviews of progress at the national and sub-national levels which are country-led and country-driven.

References

Cooper, Christine and Thomson, Ian: The Social and Political Roles of National Accounting in Simon, Sandrine and Proops, John,(2000): Greening the Accounts, Edward Elgar, USA

Economic and Social Commission for Asia and Pacific, (1997): Accounting and Valuation of Environment, Volume I

Economic and Social Commission for Asia and Pacific,(1997): Accounting and Valuation of Environment, Volume II

Government of India, Ministry of Water Resources, 2004-05: Annual Report.

Government of India, National Action Plan on Climate Change, 2009

Government of India, National Environmental Policy, 2006

Government of India, National Water Policy, 2002

Chapter - 13

An Empirical Analysis of Ability-biased Technical Change with Environmental Constraints

Saheli Das, Meeta Keswani Mehra

Abstract

Technical change is a major driving force for economic growth and development. During the past 25 years there has been an acceleration of technical change that has favoured skill bias of labour force. Although individual skills are captured through educational level, in the long-run what matters is the un-observable ability inherent in an individual. Due to this individual ability-differentiation, technological change even affects the efficiency levels of workers among skilled labour force that may even have the same level of education differentially. At the same time, climate change is happening with simultaneous change in economic growth. This is affecting skilled and unskilled labour force differentially with respect to their adaptation or coping capacities. Climate change is happening mainly due to anthropogenic activities. This paper attempts to empirically capture the simultaneous effects of skill-biased technical change and environmental quality change on different economic variables like, within-group and between-group wage inequalities, income distribution, economic welfare etc. through the channel of individual ability-differentiation. Ability-biased technical change along with environmental quality change affects developing countries more than developed ones due to different economic constraints, such as geographical conditions, natural resource constraints, capacity for innovation, labour structure, institutional constraints, political situations etc. The empirical analysis shows that environment-friendly ability-biased technical change improves economic welfare for all the countries of the world. However, ability-differentiation affects economic welfare differentially for developed and developing countries with respect to income distribution. Specifically, ability-differentiation via income inequality improves economic welfare for developing nations, whereas it declines economic welfare for developed nations. Finally, it is shown that temporal convergence or divergence of a developing country vis-a-vis a developed country due to the simultaneous effects of ability-biased technical change and environmental quality change.

Introduction

In the last two decades United States (US) and other advanced economies, like the Organisation for Economic Co-operation and Development (OECD) countries, have experienced rapid skill-biased tech-nological progress and rising wage inequalities, both within[3] and between[4] groups with a simultaneous environmental quality change. This environmental quality change is mainly due to anthropogenic activities (Gradus and Smulders (1993)). The contemporaneous phenomenon of increasing wage inequalities is largely induced by information and communication technologies (ICTs), which tend to be work mainly through skill-biased technical change. However, over the past 50 years, wage inequality has evolved in a cyclical fashion (Goldin and Katz (1998), Autor and Katz (1998)). Recent literature on skill-biased technical change has focused on the role of unobserved inherent ability or skills mainly for the evolution of wage inequality during the ICT boom. On the one hand, inherent ability would affect workers' efficiency to produce (Acemoglu (1999)), to absorb new skill-specific technologies (Eicher (1996), Gouldand Weinberg (2001)) or to adopt new technologies (Galor and Tsiddon (1997), Galor and Moav (2000)). On the other hand, residual wage inequality[5] could be explained not only by higher wage volatility and instability due to partial transfer of skills across sectors (Aghion and Violante (2000), Violante (2002)), but also by increasing returns to inherent ability within multiple sectors (Gould (2005)). In addition, different groups within a country are differentially impacted due to climatic variations (Acemoglu and Dell (2009)), largely due to disparities in their skills and coping capacities. That is, labour efficiency could potentially be affected by environmental quality as well as technological improvement. It is this additional channel of change in economic welfare that forms the motivation for this research.

There exists a large and distinct body of literature that captures the effects of technological improvement on skill-differentiated labour force both theoretically and empirically, by only including the observable factor of skill, i.e., educational attainment, while only few works support ABTC (as a part of SBTC frameworks) or the unobserved ability differentiation. Moreover, while DTC theory does capture the endogenous economic growth process with environmental constraints (see Acemoglu and Hemous (2012)), there is no such literature in SBTC theory with environmental constraints. In this milieu, our paper aims to analyze the interface between endogenous growth theory (with thrust on ability-biased technological progress) and economics of climate change in an increasingly technology oriented world.

In this paper, we have performed an empirical analysis of comparison between two types of economies, developing and developed, by considering Crifo (2008)'s model as the basic analytical framework. In the aggregate we have data for 62 countries over the time period 1995-2015, where 39 are developed economies and 23 are developing economies. In the Crifo (2008)'s model, there are three types of workers: high-ability workers (who are all educated) and ordinary-ability educated workers, both of which form skilled work force, and then there are uneducated or unskilled workers. All of these workers, even uneducated workers are also employed in job market. Each of these types of workers have different efficiency levels to adopt any type of technical and environmental change, such that high-ability workers are assumed to have the capability to adopt any type of change, while both ordinaryability educated and unskilled workers have a negative effect on their efficiency levels due to any such change, as they have to spend much more time than the high-ability workers to adapt to any change. This negative effect is called the erosion effect. Depending on this type of labour structure, we first calculate both within and be-tween group inequalities by calculating the income levels of three types of workers by assigning primary, secondary and tertiary educational attainment to unskilled, ordinary-ability educated workers and high ability workers respectively. We also calculate both within and between group educational attainment ratios to capture the skill differentiation through education. We next proceed with a two-stage estimation analysis. In the first stage, we determine both within and between group ability differentiations respectively by estimating within and between group income inequalities using panel random effect model. For this estimation we include economic growth, some environmental indicators (environmental vulnerability index, growth of air pollution PM2.5, emission of CO_2, growth of CO_2 emission, pollution index), within and between group educational attainment ratios, and interactions of economic growth and environmental indicators with educational attainment ratios as independent variables. Next, we estimate economic welfare for the whole economy and for developing and deveĺoped economies individually, by using the widely utilised PCSE (panel corrected standard error) model, by including gross fixed capital formation as aggregate economic investment, some environmental indicators (namely, environmental vulnerability index, emissions of CO_2, growth of CO_2 emissions and pollution index), both inequalities and the interactions of environmental indicators and inequalities with educational attainment ratios and ability differentiations as independent variables. For welfare estimations, we exclude the growth of air pollution PM 2.5 as an environmental indicator since it does not affect economic welfare directly and significantly at the macro aggregate level of economies. A comparison of the estimated economic welfare levels of developing and developed economies reveals that through the period of time 1995-2015, developing economies are found to converge with developed economies on account of environment friendly ability biased technical change; the only exception being Kazakhstan.

In what follows, a review of literature on the subject is presented.

1. Literature Review

The trend in the US wage structure of increasing wage premium along with increasing skill supply can be confirmed by looking at Figure 13.1 shows the relationship between college premium and relative supply of college skills over the time period 1939-1996, taking the data from March CPSs and 1940, 1950 and 1960 censuses.

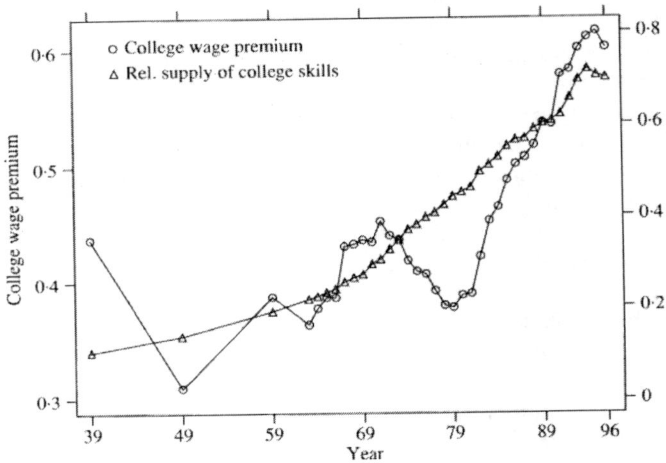

Source: Acemoglu (2002)

Figure 13.1: U.S. Wage Structure, 1939-1996

The standard explanation for the US wage pattern over the past 60 years can be found in the phenomenon of Directed Technological Change (DTC), first introduced by Daron Acemoglu in 1998. The key effect of DTC is that a rise in the relative supply of skilled workers improves the technologies used by skilled workers. The main focus here is on how DTC is affecting the wage and employment structure through different channels, like the elasticity of substitution between two intermediate goods, one produced by skilled labour and another produced by unskilled labour, elasticity of substitution between skilled and unskilled labour, opening of trade, technological progress with different types of property right enforcement, selection of labour force according to the job, creation of skill specific jobs etc.

We know skills are two dimensional – education and ability – where the latter is generally unobservable. Acemoglu (1998), Acemoglu (1999), Acemoglu and Zilibotti (2001), Acemoglu (2002), Acemoglu(2003b) mainly showed how DTC was affecting economic welfare through different channels, by onlyincluding the observable factor of skill, i.e., the educational level. In SBTC stream, the unobservable quality of skill or ability has been captured, mainly by Galor and Moav (2000).

Galor and Moav (2000) examined the wage inequality, within and between groups, by defining the threshold level of ability. Here, the supply of efficient units of labour depended on their respective abilities. They showed that, given the increase in exogenous technological growth rate, the supply of efficient skilled workers increased, and that of unskilled workers decreased, i.e., the threshold value of ability decreased. Thus, a monotonic increase in the rate of technological progress increased both the wage inequality, within and between groups. Also, the average wage of skilled workers increased (along with an increase in their relative supply) due to technological progress, but the average wage of unskilled workers decreased, despite a decline in their relative supply in the aggregate labour force. Later, they endogenised technological growth, as a monotonic positive linear proportion of skilled workers in the economy, and again derived similar results.

Galor and Moav (2000) explained endogenous technical change without considering the incentives in the growth promoting sector explicitly, and also provided an explanation for the cyclical trend between wage inequality, and skill supply along with a monotonous increase in skill supply. But, Crifo (2008) explained endogenous technical change as the result of resources devoted to R&D. Also, he distinguished between skilled and unskilled workers by accounting for both, the level of skill and education attainment, along with the ordinary ability workers. As SBTC increased the returns to the more productive workers, firms found it profitable to save relatively less productive workers among the high skilled labour force, and increased their demand for the most productive workers. Thus, as a result, there arose a discouragement effect to attain higher education for the ordinary skilled workers. This result, in turn, adjusted the supply of skilled workers downwards, with ordinaryability ones choosing to become less educated, and the relative wages of the high ability workers increased with a lower relative supply of high skilled workers. This led to higher inequality within the educated workers' group. Further, due to SBTC, there was an erosion effect. This erosion effect entailed that, the number of efficiency units of labour supply of both unskilled and ordinary ability workers declined with a rise in the rate of technological progress, but not the number of efficiency units of labour supply by high-ability workers. Thus, together the erosion and discouragement effects arising due to SBTC caused the non-monotonic cyclical relationship between wage inequality and skill supply through oscillatory technological transition. This procyclical trend between wage inequality and skill supply can be depicted through Figure 13.2. In Figure 13.2, wage differential and relative skill supply in logarithms are taken along the vertical axis and year is taken along the horizontal axis.

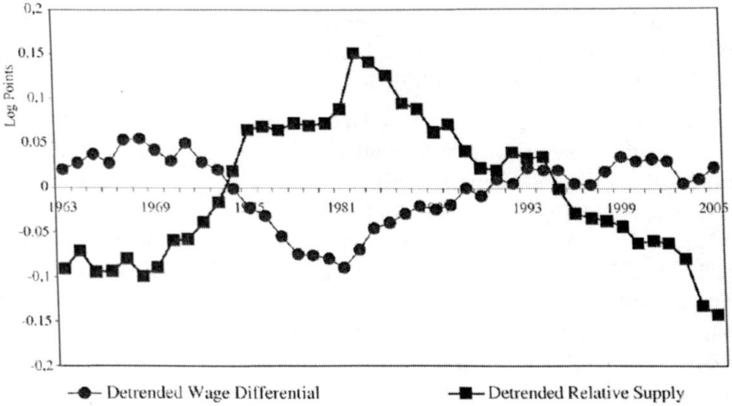

Source: Autor, Katz, and Kearney (2005)

Figure 13.2: Detrended College-High School Wage Differential and Relative Supply in the U.S.

Figure 13.2 shows that, during 1963-1970 and 1990-1995, the relative skill supply and wage inequality appeared to move in the same direction. However, the period 1970-1981 depicted an increase in the college-high school relative supply parallel to a college-high school wage differential while both the periods, 1981-1990 and 1995-2005 exhibited a reverse trend, i.e., a decline in the college-high school relative supply together with an increase in the college-high school wage differential. Further, after fifteen years of continuous rise, the relative skill supply started decreasing in the 1980s, with a significant expansion in the growth rate of Gross Domestic Product (GDP), and the wage inequality (1980-1985), followed by a decline in the relative skill supply (1985-1990). Hence, the period with a decline in the relative skill supply was preceded by an acceleration in the growth rate, and in the wage inequality (mainly within-group, followed by between-group).

It has long been observed that there exists a trade-off between environmental degradation and long term economic growth rate, derived by correlating the level of income to the indicators of environmental quality like, air pollution, water pollution etc., the so-called Environmental Kuznets Curve (EKC)[6] hypothesis (see for example, Grossman and Krueger (1991), Grossman and Krueger (1995), Dell and Olken(2008), Dell (2009)).

The survey articles by Xepapadeas (2005), Brock and Taylor (2005) and Ricci (2007) provided a comprehensive review of existing theoretical and empirical research related to the link between economic growth and environmental quality, as also the direction for future research. They focused on how the development of clean technologies and abatement of emissions would impact economic growth and its sustainability. The idea of technical change models was that these could be biased towards some specific sectors in the economy. Depending on that, this bias could be used to redirect technological improvement to cleaner sectors vis-a-vis the dirty sector or vice-versa.

Utilizing the DTC framework propounded by Acemoglu (1998), Smulders and de M. Nooij (2003) developed an endogenous growth model in which energy was an essential input. They modelled innovation as a rational investment behaviour driven by profit maximisation, where energy-related innovation was much worse than other types of innovations, and found a fall in economic growth if the energy share was close to its steady state level along the energy conservation path.

Again using Acemoglu (2003a) framework, Maria and Valente (2008) analyzed an economy where natural resource was owned by the economic agents used in the production. They showed that a steady state would exist in the presence of a non-renewable natural resource used in the production under the decentralised equilibrium. While Grimaud and Rouge (2008) and Acemoglu and Hemous (2012) (hence forth referred to as AABH model) utilised the idea of the equilibrium bias of technical change and for-malised different conditions, channels and policy directions through which sustainable growth could be achieved.

Grimaud and Rouge (2008) proposed a framework of welfare analysis in a decentralised economywhere the consumption good was produced with two resource inputs: one a non-renewable resource, which was polluting and another being labour resource, a non-polluting one. They tried to show the effects of three associated economic policy tools: a tax on the polluting resource and two research subsidies on environmental quality. They found that the quantity of research was not changed; however, the quality of research was changed in the direction of 'green'[7] research from 'grey'[8] research. In the short-term, the environmental policy was grey-biased, and while in the long-term, it was green-biased.

Acemoglu and Hemous (2012) provideda more generalised production structure in the comparisonwith Grimaud and Rouge (2008). They integrated the models of DTC and environmental policy by explicitly bringing out the market size effect. They showed the effects of DTC with environmental constraints by using 'dirty' and 'clean' inputs in the final good production. They found three distinct results. First, when the inputs were sufficiently substitutable, long run growth could be sustainably achieved using temporary policy intervention. Second, a delay in policy intervention would become costly, and lastly, use of an exhaustible resource in dirty input production helped the switch to clean innovation. Thus, with a high elasticity of substitution between the clean and dirty inputs, optimal environmental regulation could be achieved by an immediate switch of R&D resources to clean technology, followed by a gradual switch of all production to clean inputs. With respect to the degree of substitution in all the cases, optimal policy included a carbon tax, but research subsidies were even more important to DTC.

To find empirical support, Aghion and Reenan (2012) tested the path dependency in auto industry innovation distinguishing between dirty and clean patents using firm level panel data across 80 countries over several decades and showed that firms were more likely to innovate in clean technologies if they had been previously exposed to clean technologies. Greaker and Heggedahl (2012) introduced long-lived patents into the AABH model and found that the research subsidy for clean technologies became less important than the carbon tax. While under different informational constraints on the behaviour of economic agents, Bondarev and Greiner (2013) compared the models with exogenous and endogenous technical change as well as directed and undirected endogenous technical change using non-linear model predictive control technique. They showed that endogenous technical change yielded lower environmental damages than exogenous technical change with fully informed agents, and a green growth scenario would generate a smaller temperature increase that went along with less output and lower welfare in the case of DTC.

To the best of our knowledge, there is no literature that studies the relationship between environmental quality and economic growth with respect to ability biased technical change. Most of the work discussed in the above literature captures the effects of technological improvement on skilled and unskilled labour force by only including the observable factor of skill, i.e., the educational level, while only few works support the Ability Biased Technical Change (ABTC, as a part of the SBTC frameworks). Although, DTC theory does capture the endogenous economic growth process with environmental constraints, there is no research work on SBTC theory with environmental constraints (see Acemoglu and Hemous (2012)). Thus, in this respect, this paper proposes an improvement over the earlier SBTC frameworks.

3. Data and Methodology

In this paper, we attempt to validate the findings of the Crifo (2008)'s model by empirically finding evidence of both DTC and ABTC, with key focus on ABTC with environmental constraints. For testing the effect of environmental degradation, we utilize air pollution indicators, namely,

PM 2.5 air pollution, CO_2 emission, environmental vulnerability index, and pollution index. Further, GDP growth (annual %) is used as an indicator of economic welfare, while within group[9] and between group[10] educational attainment ratios are utilised as indicators skill-differentiation with respect to education. Further, within-group and between-group inequalities are estimated from efficiency wages (per worker) of unskilled, ordinary skilled and high-skilled group of workers by using the data for labour force with different educational level (primary, secondary and tertiary), labour productivity with different educational level and labour incomes.

We examine the simultaneous effects of technological progress, i.e., economic growth and environmental degradation on income inequalities through education by utilizing Panel Corrected Standard Error (PCSE) model due to its better estimation procedure (see Beck and Katz (1995)). Next, the effects of environmental degradation and income inequalities, working through both education and individual ability differentiation, on economic welfare across 62 countries over the time period 1995-2015 are estimated. Finally, we present the convergence or divergence results for 23 developing countries as a group with respect to 39 developed countries over time by defining a dummy variable (d). The dummy variable d takes value one for developed countries and zero for developing countries, i.e.,

d	=	0;	8 developing countries
	=	1:	8 developed countries

Here the characterisation of the countries as developed or developing is made according to the World Bank Country and Lending Groups. The effects of environmental degradation and income inequalities, working through education and ability differentiation on economic welfare, are captured by the interactions of environmental degradation and income inequalities with both educational attainment ratios (within and between) and ability differentiations (within and between), predicted as the spatial error terms from the inequality (within and between) regressions individually. These interaction terms are the most significant feature of this study, as there is known significant effect of environmental change on human health (or efficiency) (see Haines and Corvalan (2006), McMichael and Hales (2006), Boselloand Tol (2006)). Thus, affecting human efficiency indirectly, environmental change or air pollution isfound to impact educational outcomes (see Miller and Vela (2013)).

3.1 Data Description

The dataset used in this study consists of the following variables, obtained from select sources described below:

GDP growth (annual percent) as an indicator of economic welfare, collected from World Bank databank;

PM 2.5 air pollution (mg=m^3), population exposed to levels exceeding WHO guideline value (per-cent of total) as an indicator of environmental degradation, collected from World Bank Databank;

CO_2 emissions (kt) as an indicator of environmental degradation, collected from World Bank data-bank;

Environmental Vulnerability Index as an indicator of environmental degradation, collected from ND-GAIN, i.e., Notre Dame Global Adaptation Initiative (organised by Climate Change Adaptation Program of the University of Notre Dame's Environmental Change initiative, i.e., ND-ECI);

Pollution Index as an indicator of environmental degradation, collected from NUMBEO (organised by BBC, TIME, Forbes, Business Insider, Financial Times, Investopedia, SFGate, The New York Times, The Economist, The Week, The Sydney Morning Herald, The Age, The Independent, the guardian, The Telegraph, ABC, China Daily, People's Daily, Fox News, Wired, USA Today, The Vancouver Sun, The Washington Post);

Labour income (as a share in GDP) to calculate income inequalities, collected from International Labour Organisation (ILO);

GDP (constant 2011 international dollars in PPP) to calculate labour income or wage, collected from World Bank databank; per unit efficiency wage of high-skilled workers per unit efficiency wage of ordinary skilled workers

Labour productivity[11] to calculate income inequalities, collected from International Labour Organisation (ILO);

Labour force with primary, secondary and tertiary education (per cent of total) to calculate labour productivity with respect to educational attainment, collected from World Bank databank;

Employment to population ratio (per cent of total, modeled ILO estimate) to calculate total employment, collected from World Bank databank;

Total population (number of person) to calculate total employment and educational attainment, collected from World Bank databank;

Educational attainment, at least completed primary, lower secondary, upper secondary, post secondary and short cycle tertiary (per cent of total, in cumulative) to calculate educational attainment ration for within and between groups, collected from World Bank databank;

Gross fixed capital formation (per cent of GDP) as an indicator of investment, collected from World Bank databank.

We calculate income inequalities by using the above mentioned variables as,

$$\text{Within-group inequality} = \frac{\text{per unit efficiency wage of skilled workers}}{\text{per unit efficiency wage of unskilled workers}}$$

and, Between-group inequality = $\frac{\text{per unit efficiency wage of skilled workers}}{\text{per unit efficiency wage of unskilled workers}}$

where, per unit efficiency wages are determined as,

Per unit efficiency wage of high-skilled workers = $\frac{\text{total employment}}{\text{labour force with tertiary education}}$

labour income or wage,

Per unit efficiency wage of ordinary-skilled workers = $\frac{\text{total employment}}{\text{labour force with secondary education}}$

* labour income or wage,

Per unit efficiency wage of unskilled workers = $\frac{\text{total employment}}{\text{labour force with primary education}}$

labour productivity *
* labour income or wage.

We define educational attainment ratios for within and between groups so that by regressing inequalities on economic growth, all environmental variables, educational attainment ratios and interactions of variables with educational attainment ratios, ability differentiations for within and between groups can be determined by using the prediction procedure of unobserved errors terms. Now, we define educational attainment ratios as,

Educational attainment ratio for within-group =

$$\frac{\text{educational attainment for skilled workers}}{\text{educational attainment for unskilled workers}}$$

and, Educational attainment ratio for between-group =

$$\frac{\text{educational attainment for ordinary-skilled workers}}{\text{educational attainment for high-skilled workers}}$$

where, educational attainment for different skilled workers are determined as,

Educational attainment for high-skilled workers = (total educational attainment at least short cycle tertiary[12]+ total educational attainment at least post-secondary) * (total population),

Educational attainment for ordinary skilled workers = (total educational attainment at least upper sec-ondary + total educational attainment at least lower secondary) * (total population),

Educational attainment for unskilled workers = (total educational attainment at least primary) * (total population).

We considered that high skilled workers acquire highest education (at least completed secondary), ordinary skilled ones acquire education lower than high-skilled (secondary) and unskilled workers have minimum level of primary education. One can consider a higher level of education as educational attainment for high skilled workers than what we considered, as there are higher levels of education than short cycle tertiary. However, we consider upto short cycle tertiary level of education so that there will not be too large a gap between educational levels of high skilled workers and ordinary skilled workers and the unobserved ability can be captured easily. For a higher level of education than short cycle tertiary education, it may possible that both educational skill and ability skill become inextricably linked.

The specification of the data are as follows:

Welfare = Economic welfare (annual percent) GFC =

Gross fixed capital (percentage of GDP)

EVul = Environmental vulnerability index[13]

ECO_2 = CO_2 emission (kt)

EPM = PM2.5 air pollution (mg=m^3)

PI = Pollution index

INE_w = Within-group inequality

INE_b = Between-group inequality

EAR_w = Within-group educational attainment ratio

EAR_b = Between-group educational attainment ratio

$GECO_2$ = Growth of CO_2 emission (kt)

GEPM = Growth of PM2.5 air pollution (mg=m^3)

3.2 Methodology

This section provides a step-wise description of the methods used in this study.

1. Decision making about one-way or two-way error component regression model depending on the unobservable factor, which may occur spatially or over time. Most of the panel data applications utilize a one-way error component model where the only unobservable disturbance factor is the individual effect. In our model also, the individual effects, i.e., ability differentiation are unobservable and the time effects, i.e., technological improvement are observable through economic growth over time. Thus, in our estimation we use the one-way error component regression model due to the only unovseravble factor is ability differentiation across individuals.
2. Check stationarity of all variables by using two unit-root test, namely, Levin-Lin-Chu (LLC) test (Levin and Chu (2002)) and Harris-Tzavalis (HT) test (Harris and Tzavalis (1999)). Although LLC is the most popular unit-root test, for small T and large N it

gives a less powerful t-statistic due to the assumption of asymptotic T, rather than fixed. Since our data set also consists of small T and large N, we mostly consider the unit-root results of the HT test.

3. Regress economic growth, all environmental degradation variables, educational attainment ratios and the interactions of educational attainment ratios with economic growth and all environmental degradation variables on income inequalities by using both panel fixed effect model and panel random effect model.
4. Run the Hasuman test (Hausman (1978)) to determine which is a better specification – fixed effect or random effect – for the data set.
5. Check for the problems of contemporaneous correlation, auto-correlation and heteroscedasticity by using the Friedman's test (Friedman (1937)), Wooldridge test statistic and Wald test statistic respectively.
6. Estimate income inequalities by Panel Corrected Standard Error model where PCSE models are similar to White's heteroscedasticity-consistent standard errors for cross-sectional estimators, but are better because they take advantage of the information provided by the panel structure of the data (see Beck and Katz (1995)).
7. Calculate the predicted spatial error term using post-estimation procedure of panel fixed/ random effect model depending on which is more suitable and would yield the unobserved ability differentiation across countries in the form of the error terms.
8. Regress all environmental degradation variables, income inequalities and their interaction with educational attainment ratios and ability differentiation as predicted above, along with country dummy by using panel fixed/ random effect models.
9. Repeat steps no. 3, 4, and 5 for the above regression mentioned in step no. 8.
10. Repeat step no. 8 by using PCSE model for developed and developing countries individually by defining the value of the dummy variable as 1 for developed and 0 for developing respectively.
11. Predict the value of the dependent variable, i.e., economic welfare for developed and developing countries respectively.
12. Trace the convergence or divergence paths of developing countries' welfare with respect to the developed countries' welfare levels by a graph.

3.3 Empirical Results

This sub-section summarizes the empirical results of our analysis. We start with the unit-root tests by checking for the stationarity of all the variables. If any variable is non-stationary, then first difference of that variable in level is taken and the unit-root test is performed again. Further, we proceed with the estimation procedure in a step-by-step fashion as discussed in the foregoing sections, and present the convergence or divergence for the developing countries with respect to the developed countries over the period of analysis which is from 1995 to 2015.

3.3.1 Unit-Root Results

In this section, the results of both the Levin-Lin-Chu (LLC) and the Harris-Tzavalis (HT) unit-root tests are presented. The null hypothesis for both the unit-root test is that panel contains unit-roots. For HT test, we make an adjustment for time T for small sample and for LLC test, the optimal lag is included according to AIC (Akaike Information Criterion). Here unit-root test are performed in levels and the first-difference for the differenced variables, wherever needed.

The unit-root test results are shown in Table 13.1. The stationarity depends on the p-value. If p-value of any variable is less than 0.01, we cannot accept the null hypothesis of non-stationarity and thus, the variable is considered as stationary at 1% level of significance, and on the contrary, if p-value of any variable is greater than 0.01, we should accept the null hypothesis of the presence of unit-root in the panel at 1% level of significance and then the variable is considered as non-stationary. Trends are also included in unit-root tests for some variables that display some trend over the time period. From the table one can see that,

For the unit-root tests, trends are considered for the variables EVul, ECO_2, EPM, INE_w in both LLC and HT tests, and for the variables INE_b, EAR_w, EAR_b in only HT test.

Welfare, GFC, EVul, INE_b, EAR_w, EAR_b are stationary, i.e., in I(0) or level at both 1% and 5% level of significance according to both LLC and HT tests, as the p-values are less than 0.01 and 0.05 respectively.

EPM is non-stationary at both 1% and 5% level of significance according to both LLC and HT tests, as the p-values are greater than 0.01 and 0.05 respectively. EPM is in I(1).

ECO_2 and PI are stationary at both 1% and 5% level of significance according to only LLC test. These two variables are non-stationary according to HT test, as the p-values are greater than 0.01 and 0.05 for HT test.

INE_w is stationary at both 1% and 5% level of significance according to HT test, but non-stationary as per LLC test since the p-values are greater than 0.01 and 0.05.

The HT unit-root test is the most appropriate unit-root test for our panel data set since our data contain fewer time periods and more cross-sectional units. Thus, we consider INE_w as a stationary variable and

Table 13.1: Unit-Root Results

Variables	*Tests*	*Statistic*	*p-values*	*Remarks*
Welfare	LLC	16:5098	0.0000	Stationary
	HT	0.3402	0.0000	Stationary
GFC	LLC	7:5228	0.0000	Stationary
	HT	0.7726	0.0000	Stationary
EVul	LLC	4:8226	0.0000	Stationary
	HT	0.5644	0.0002	Stationary
ECO_2	LLC	3:3415	0.0004	Stationary
	HT	0.7326	0.9971	Non-stationary
EPM	LLC	0.7041	0.7593	Non-stationary
	HT	0.9521	1.0000	Non-stationary
PI	LLC	5:2492	0.0000	Stationary
	HT	0.9756	1.0000	Non-stationary
INE_w	LLC	10.7686	1.0000	Non-stationary
	HT	0.4813	0.0000	Stationary
INE_b	LLC	12:0335	0.0000	Stationary
	HT	0.0318	0.0000	Stationary
EAR_w	LLC	8:6147	0.0000	Stationary
	HT	0.0373	0.0000	Stationary
EAR_b	LLC	7:4858	0.0000	Stationary
	HT	0.1482	0.0000	Stationary
$GECO_2$	LLC			
	HT	0.0173	0.0000	Stationary
GEPM	LLC	6:4554	0.0000	Stationary
	HT	0.6727	0.0000	Stationary

Table 13.2: Fixed vs. Random Effect for Inequality Regressions

Inequality	*Prob>chi²*	*Remarks*
INE_w	0.0333	Random Effect
INE_b	0.0165	Random Effect

ECO_2 as a non-stationary variable. On the contrary, we consider PI as a stationary variable[14], as per the LLC test results, since PI is an index. Again for ECO_2, the LLC test shows stationary and the HT test shows non-stationary. So, we consider both the results and include both ECO_2 and $GECO_2$, i.e., the first difference of ECO_2 in our model estimation.

Thus, we proceed with our estimation in a step-by-step manner, the results of which are discussed below. The variables included in our analysis are Welfare, GFC, EVul, ECO_2, $GECO_2$, EPM, PI, INE_w, INE_b, EAR_w, EAR_b.

3.3.2 Results of Inequality Regressions

We first regress inequalities (within and between) on economic welfare, all environmental degradation variables, both within and between educational attainment ratios and the interactions of economic welfare and environmental variables with both educational attainment ratios at 99% confidence interval by using both panel fixed effect and random effect models. Next, we perform the Hausman specification test for fixed effect versus random effect model for both types of inequality variables. The results of Hausman test are presented in Table 13.2. It shows that, for both within and between inequality regressions, the Prob>chi^2 value is greater than 0.01. Thus, we should accept the null hypothesis of random effect over fixed effect and hence, and a panel random effect model is estimated for inequality estimation.

Now, we know that estimates may be biased and we may get least robust standard error due to the presence of contemporaneous correlation or cross-sectional dependence, auto-correlation, heteroscedasticity, multicollinearity etc. So we need to check for the presence or absence of these problems. We perform the Friedman's test to check for contemporaneous correlation problem and the Wooldridge's test for auto-correlation problem. Table 13.3 displays the results of the presence or absence of such problems in our inequality estimations. The results show that, for both within and between inequality regressions, the Prob values are greater than 0.01 for Friedman's test and also, the Prob>F value is greater than 0.01 for Wooldridge's test. Thus, we should accept the null hypotheses of no contemporaneous correlation and no auto-correlation respectively at 1% level of significance.

Table 13.3: Presence of Different Problems In Inequality Regressions

Inequality	*Prob. of Friedman Test*	*Prob.>F of Wooldridge Test*
INE_w	0.7310	0.0830
INE_b	0.9986	0.6123
Remarks	No contemporaneous correlation	no auto-correlation

Although there do not exist problems of contemporaneous correlation and auto-correlation in our model, there may be others like, heteroscedasticity[15], sample selection bias, multicollinearity (as environmental vulnerability, emissions of CO_2, growth of CO_2 emissions, emissions of PM2.5 are correlated with pollution index)[16] etc. To address these problems, we rely on the use of PCSE estimation first and then regress the significant independent variables from PCSE model on both the inequality variables respectively by using panel random effect model, so that we can get the predicted spatial error, i.e., u_i from both the inequality regressions. These spatial error terms actually represents the unobserved qualitative factors that may affect economic welfare. One of the most important unobservable qualitative factor that is almost constant over time is the individual's inherent ability differentiation. So, once we regress all the significant independent variables (from PCSE regressions) on both within and between inequalities, we get the unobserved within (u_w) and between (u_b) ability differentiation respectively. In the estimation technique, the decision of being a significant independent variable depends on the z-value. If the z-value of any estimated independent variable is greater than or equali to 2, then one can say that the independent variable affects the dependent variable significantly. By doing this, we can get the most likely predicted values of the spatial error terms by including the most significant independent variables. In our case, the specific form of the model that is estimated is:

$INE^s = a + b{:} Wel\,f are + b\,{:}W\,EAR + c\,{:}EVul{:}$

$+c_2{:}EVulEAR_b + d_1{:}GEPM + d_2{:}GEPMEAR_b$

$INE_{it}^{s=u}$

$+ f_1{:}GECO_2 + g_1{:}PI + g_2{:}PIEAR_b$

$+h_1{:}EAR_w + h_2{:}EAR_b + u^s_{it};$

and,

$= a_2 + b_1{:}Wel\,f are + b_2{:}W\,EAR_w + c_1{:}EVul{:}$

$+c_2{:}VulEAR_b + d_1{:}GEPM + d_2{:}GEPMEAR_b$

$+e_1{:}ECO_2 + e_2{:}ECO_2EAR_w + e_3{:}ECO_2EAR_b + f_1{:}GECO_2$

$+ f_2{:}GECO_2EARw + f_3{:}GECO_2EAR_b + g_1{:}PI$

$+h_1{:}EAR_w + h_2{:}EAR_b + u^s_{it}{}^{=u}{:}$

The results of the within group inequality estimation using PCSE is given in Table 13.4 below. The above results can be interpreted as follows:

Although welfare is not directly affecting within group inequality significantly, it works significantly through between group educational attainment as skilled workers are getting more education due to ABTC.

Both within and between group educational attainment ratios affect within-group inequality negatively and significantly. In presence of ABTC, due to discouragement effect, i.e., the negative incentive to acquire education for ordinaryability workers as hiring high ability workers is always profitable for firms, if the ordinaryability workers don't acquire education and only high ability workers do, in that case within group educational attainment ratio increases. But, the net efficiency income decreases for high-ability workers as they have to spend some time from their work for attainment of education. As a result, within-group inequality decreases. Further, when more and more oridinary ability workers acquire education for economic development, then the aggregate educational attainment level of skilled workers increases and thus it increases between group educational attainment ratio. As a result, the gap between net efficiency income between ordinary ability and high ability workers, within skilled work force declines. Thus, within group inequality also declines.

Table 13.4: Within-Group Inequality Regression

Indept. Variables	*Coeff.*	*z-value*	*P>jzj value*
Welfare	0.008978	0.38	0.701
EAR_w	0:00592373:18	0.001	
EAR_b	0:01040185:03	0.000	
$W EAR_b$	0.0003334	4.13	0.000
EVul.	9.828256	8.33	0.000
$EVulEAR_b$	0.0444827	5.15	0.000
GEPM	0:16614682:82	0.005	
$GEPMEAR_b$	0:00277316:23	0.000	
ECO_2	2:05e 07	3:16	0.002
ECO_2EAR_w	2:48e 09	3.04	0.002
ECO_2EAR_b	4:33e 09	5:94	0.000
$GECO_2$	4:14e 06	2:41	0.016
PI	0:00090582:06	0.039	
$PIEAR_b$	0.0000111	2.85	0.004
cons.	0:6899724	2:55	0.011

Environmental vulnerability directly as well as indirectly, through education, affects within group inequality positively and significantly. More the environmental degradation, higher is the vulnerability to adopt any change, requiring faster innovation towards sustainable economic growth, which in turn raises within group inequality.

Growth of air pollution PM2:5, emissions of CO_2, growth of emissions of CO_2 and pollution index affect within group inequality directly as well as indirectly, through education negatively and significantly. These negative effects may be due to the policies and institutions moving towards more eco-friendly ABTC, where a part of ABTC helps lower inequality through educational attainment.

The emissions of CO_2 through within group educational attainment and pollution index through between group educational attainment impact within-group inequality positively and significantly, similar to the environmental vulnerability.

The results of between group inequality estimation using PCSE is given in Table 13.5.

Table 13.5: Between-Group Inequality Regression

Indept. Variables	*Coeff.*	*z-value*	*P>jzj value*
Welfare	0:04962511:58		0.115
EAR_w	0:01923431:62		0.106
EAR_b	0.005402	1.31	0.190
$W\ EAR_w$	0.001733	1.38	0.168
EVul.	15.24988	12.16	0.000
$EVulEAR_b$	0:02419691:39		0.165
GEPM	0:14391251:87		0.062
$GEPMEAR_b$	0.0009313	1.50	0.133
ECO_2	3:94e 07	3:37	0.001
ECO_2EAR_w	2:10e 06	1.79	0.073
ECO_2EAR_b	2:38e 06	3.20	0.001
$GECO_2$	6:13e 06	1.79	0.074
$GECO_2EAR_w$	5:73e 07	1:67	0.096
$GECO_2EAR_b$	2:60e 08	1:77	0.076
PI	0.0015598	2.80	0.005
cons.	2:539973	8:95	0.000

These results can be interpreted as follows:

Although welfare declines between group inequality as the coefficient is negative, it rises inequality through educational attainment due to ABTC. These effects are statistically insignificant as the z-values are less than 2.

Within group educational attainment ratio lowers between group inequality whereas, between group educational attainment ratio raises between-group inequality, though these effects are statistically insignificant. Such effects are may be due to the fact that, in presence of ABTC, due to discouragement effect, it may possible that ordinaryability workers don't acquire education and thus within group educational attainmnet ratio increases. As a result, the aggregate income of skilled workers decreases and thus, between group inequality declines. Further, as more and more ordinary ability workers acquire education, between group educational attinment ratio increases with a simultaneous increase in the aggregate income level of skilled workers. As a result, between group inequality rises.

Environmental vulnerability, growth of CO_2 emissions and pollution index directly affect between group inequality positively and significantly for EVul and PI, while for $GECO_2$ this effect is almost significant as it is closer to 2. Also, the growth of PM2:5 air pollution and CO_2 emissions through educational attainment raises between group inequality significantly. Thus, with a rise in environ-mental degradation, between-group inequality rises.

However, the growth of air pollution PM2:5 and CO_2 emission affects between group inequality negatively and significantly. These negative impacts are may be due to the policies and institutional movement towards more eco-friendly ABTC, where a part of ABTC is lowering inequality. Similarly, environmental vulnerability and growth of CO_2 emissions through educational attainment lowers between group inequality although these effects are statistically insignificant.

Thus, after estimating of the inequality regressions with PCSE model, as presented above, we estimate the inequality regressions by panel random effect model (including the same independent variables as in PCSE method) to predict the most likely random error components u_w and u_b. After getting the predicted values of the spatial random error components from the two inequality regressions, we continue with the economic welfare regression in the next section.

3.3.3 Results of Welfare Regressions

Similar to the inequality regression estimation, we first regress economic welfare on gross fixed capital formation as aggregate investment of the economy, all environmental degradation variables, both within and between inequalities, both within and between educational attainment ratios, both within and between ability differentiation ratios, a country specific dummy d (defined previously) and the interactions of all environmental degradation variables and two inequalities with both educational attainment ratios and ability differentiation ratios at 99% confidence interval by using both panel fixed effect and random effect models. Next, we perform Hausman specification test for fixed effect versus random effect model. The result of Hausman test is presented in Table 13.6. The result shows that, the Prob>chi^2 value is less than 0.01. Thus, we cannot accept the null hypothesis of random effect over fixed effect and hence, a panel fixed effect model has to be performed for further welfare estimation.

Table 13.6: Fixed vs. Random Effect for Welfare Regression

Economic Welfare	*Prob>chi^2*	*Remarks*
Welfare	0.0000	Fixed Effect

We know that due to the presence of some problems, like contemporaneous correlation or cross sectional dependence, auto correlation, heteroscedasticity, multicollinearity etc. the estimates may be biased and the standard errors may be least robust. So, we need to check for the presence or absence of these problems. Again, we repeat the Friedman's test to check for contemporaneous correlation and the Wooldridge test for auto correlation for welfare model estimation. We also perform the Wald's test[17] to check for presence or absence of heteroscedastic errors in the welfare model. Table 13.7 contains the results of the presence or absence of such problems in our welfare estimation. The results show that the Prob value for Friedman's test is less than 0.01, the Prob>F value for Wooldridge's test is less than 0.01 and also, the Prob>chi^2 value for Wald's test is less than 0.01. Thus, we cannot accept the null hypotheses of no contemporaneous correlation, no-auto-correlation and homoscedasticity at 1% level of significance. Thus, due to the presence of all of these problems, we continue the estimation of our welfare regression by using PCSE model for its better capability to produce more reliable standard errors than other estimation procedures. Now, at first we estimate the welfare regression for the whole

Table 13.7: Presence of Different Problems In Economic Welfare Regression

Economic Welfare	*Prob. of Friedman Test*	*Prob.>F of Wooldridge Test*	*Prob.>chi^2 of Wald Test*
Welfare	0.0000	0.0000	0.0000
Remarks	Contemp. correlation	Auto-correlation	Heteroscedasticity

economy, i.e., for the full data set of 62 countries and then we estimate the welfare regression for 23 developing countries and 39 developed countries separately. Further, we calculate the linear predictions individually for developing and developed countries by using post estimation techniques. Next, we demonstrate the possibility of convergence or divergence for the developing countries vis-a-vis the developed countries graphically.

The specific form of welfare regression model is estimated as:

$$Wel\ f\ are^{W} = a_3 + b_1{:}GFC + c_1{:}EVulU_w + d_1{:}ECO_2it$$

$$+e_2{:}GECO_2EAR_w + e_3{:}GECO_2EAR_b + e_4{:}GECO_2U_b$$

$$+ f_1{:}PIEAR_w + g_1{:}INE_w + g_2{:}INE_b + g_3{:}INEEAR_w$$

$$+g_4{:}INEEAR_b + g_5{:}INEU_w + g_6{:}INEU_b + h_1{:}d + u^{l}_{it} ;$$

and results using PCSE for the whole economy is given in Table 13.8.

Table 13.8: Welfare Regression For Whole Economy

Indept. Variables	*Coeff.*	*z-value*	*P>jzj value*
GFC	0.2106642	4.75	0.000
$EVulU_w$	1:017744	3:90	0.000
ECO_2	1:65e 06	5:52	0.000
ECO_2U_w	4:63e 07	3.37	0.001
ECO_2U_b	9:13e 07	5:44	0.000
$GECO_2$	0.0000573	6.50	0.000
$GECO_2EAR_w$	3:16e 06	3:96	0.000

(Contd...)

$GECO_2EAR_b$	6:41e 08	2:50	0.012
$GECO_2U_b$	0.0000157	3.68	0.000
$PIEAR_w$	0.0001072	1.71	0.088
INE_w	0.1071753	1.34	0.181
INE_b	0:11891771:74	0.082	
$INEEAR_w$	0.0035276	1.00	0.317
$INEEAR_b$	0.000441	1.56	0.119
$INEU_w$	0.0131399	2.18	0.029
$INEU_b$	0.014455	1.27	0.204
d	1:2031663:530.000		
cons.	0:5589357	0:50	0.615

The results from welfare regression can be interpreted as follows:

GFC has a positive significant effect on economic welfare. Thus, higher the investment in the economy higher will be the economic welfare.

Environmental vulnerability through within group ability differentiation lowers economic welfare significantly. From Table 13.4 it has been seen that, environmental vulnerability directly as well as indirectly increases inequality. So one can say that, as inequality rises, economic welfare declines. Thus, rising environmental degradation through ability differentiation lowers economic welfare.

Emissions of CO_2, directly as well as indirectly, through between-group ability differentiation, affect economic welfare negatively and significantly. This effect may be due to the fact that, between group ability differentiation cannot be captured easily, as in both the skilled and unskilled labour force, ordinary ability workers exist simultaneously. However, CO_2 emissions through within group ability differentiation improve economic welfare. Such effect may be due to the presence of ABTC, as within group ability differentiation, i.e., ability differentiation between high ability and ordinary ability workers can be captured easily and aslo high-ability workers can cope quickly with any change, high ability workers can handle the situation of increasing CO_2 emission quickly and thus increase economic welfare.

Growth of CO_2 emissions directly as well as indirectly, through between-group ability differentiation, significantly improves economic welfare. Similarly, pollution index through educational attainment has an almost significant (as the z-value is closer to 2) and positive effect on welfare. However, the growth of CO_2 through educational attainment significantly reduces economic welfare whcih is a natural case. The positive effects may be due to the fact that, in the long run between group ability differentiation can be captured over time and then the ordinary ability educated workers along with high-ability workers can manage the situation of increasing growth of CO_2 emission as well as increasing overall pollution level (captured by pollution index). This helps to increase economic welfare through the movement of the economy towards eco-friendly ABTC.

Within-group inequality has a positive and between-group inequality has negative effects on eco-nomic welfare, though these effects are statistically insignificant as the absolute z-values are less than 2. However, both within and between-group inequalities improve economic welfare through educational attainment and ability-differentiation due to the skill-biasness of ABTC, where the effect working through within-group ability-differentiation is found to be significant.

The country specific dummy variable d has a significant negative effect on economic welfare. The dummy variable actually captures the effect of the movement of associated factor from d = 1 to d = 0, i.e., movement of the economy from developed to developing nations. Thus the negative effect shows that, moving from a developed to developing country affects economic welfare adversely.

After welfare estimations for the entire sample of countries, we continue with the estimation by categorizing the data set into developed and developing countries separately. Thus, the specific form of the model for developing countries is estimated as:

$$\begin{aligned} Welfare^{UD} = {} & a_4 + b_1{:}GFC + c_1{:}EVulEAR_w + c_2{:}EVulU_w i \\ & + e_1{:}GECO_2 + e_2{:}GECO_2U_w + f_1{:}PIEAR_w + f_2{:}PIU_w \\ & + f_3{:}PIU_b + g_1{:}INE_w + g_2{:}INE_b + g_3{:}INEEAR_w \\ & + g_4{:}INEEAR_b + g_5{:}INWU_w + g_6{:}INEU_b + u^2_{it}\,; \end{aligned} \tag{4}$$

and the results of estimating economic welfare for the developing countries are given in Table 13.9.

The results for welfare estimation of developing countries can be interpreted as:

GFC affects economic welfare positively and significantly, as is also true for the entire sample.

Emissions of CO_2 directly as well as indirectly, through educational attainment and ability-differentiation significantly distort economic welfare due to more pollution. Similarly, environmental vulnera-bility through within-group educational attainment and ability-differentiation and pollution index through between-group ability-differentiation affect welfare negatively, where the effect of environmental vulnerability through ability-differentiation only is found to be statistically significant.

Growth of CO_2 emissions has significant positive direct and indirect effect on economic welfare, where the latter works through ability-differentiation. Again, pollution index affects economic wel-fare positively, working through within-group educational attainment and ability-differentiation, may be due to the movement of the economy towards eco-friendly ABTC, as explained in Table 13.8.

Within-group inequality improves welfare for the developing countries, whereas between-group inequality lowers it significantly.

Table 13.9: Welfare Regression For Developing Economies

Indept. Variables	*Coeff.*	*z-value*	*P>jzj value*
GFC	0.2071168	3.43	0.001
$EVulEAR_w$	0:5042884	1:05	0.294
$EVulU_w$	1:055716	3:14	0.002
ECO_2	4:05e 06	3:08	0.002
ECO_2EAR_w	2:21e 06	3:22	0.001
ECO_2U_w	2:36e 06	3:02	0.002
$GECO_2$	0.0000746	4.94	0.000
$GECO_2U_w$	0.0000251	2.94	0.003
$PIEAR_w$	0.0026988	2.19	0.028
PIU_w	0.0016891	2.12	0.034
PIU_b	0:00073081:76	0.079	
INE_w	0.0847156	0.81	0.419
INE_b	0:32008323:49	0.000	
$INEEAR_w$	0:00030240:00	0.996	
$INEEAR_b$	0:00151031:46	0.144	
$INEU_w$	0.0159107	1.87	0.061
$INEU_b$	0.0624211	3.56	0.000
cons.	0.0815816	0.05	0.957

Both within and between-group inequalities, through educational attainment, affect the welfare of developing countries negatively. However, both the inequalities improves economic welfare of the developing countries through ability-differentiation due to ABTC.

Next, the specific form of model of economic welfare for developed countries is estimated as:

$$Wel\ f\ are^{D} = a_5 + b_1{:}GFC + c_1{:}EVulEAR_w + c_2{:}EVulU_w it \quad (5)$$

$$+e_1{:}GECO_2 + e_2{:}GECO_2U_b + f_1{:}PI + g_1{:}INE_w$$

$$+g_2{:}INE_b + g_3{:}INEEAR_w + g_4{:}INEEAR_b + g_5{:}INEU_w + g_6{:}INEU_b + u^3_{it};$$

and the results of welfare estimation for developed economies are given in Table 13.10.

Table 13.10: Welfare Regression For Developed Economies

Indept. Variables	*Coeff.*	*z-value*	*P>jzj value*
GFC	0.2328869	3.95	0.000
$EVulEAR_w$	0:3091126	1:88	0.060
$EVulU_w$	1:955493	3:44	0.001
ECO_2	2:66e 06	4:69	0.000
ECO_2U_w	1:32e 06	3.72	0.000
ECO_2U_b	5:83e 07	3:03	0.002
$GECO_2$	0.0000316	6.97	0.000
$GECO_2U_b$	0.0000179	4.10	0.000
PI	0.0016863	1.80	0.073
INE_w	0.0778274	0.44	0.659
INE_b	0.1715276	1.47	0.142
$INEEAR_w$	0.0554837	2.04	0.042
$INEEAR_b$	0.0006939	2.70	0.007
$INEU_w$	0:013629	0:28	0.780
$INEU_b$	0:0585257	3:35	0.001
cons.	2:677987	1:94	0.053

The empirical results for the developed country group can be interpreted as follows:

GFC has significant positive effect on economic welfare for developed economies also, which is more generally true as well.

Emissions of CO_2 directly as well as indirectly, operating through between-group ability-differentiation, affect the welfare of the developed economies negatively and significantly. Similarly, environ-mental vulnerability lowers economic welfare through within-group educational attainment and ability-differentiation significantly as increasing pollution reduces economic welfare.

However, the growth of CO_2 emissions and pollution index directly improve economic welfare of the developed countries significantly. Also, CO_2 emissions, operating through within-group ability-differentiation, and the growth of CO_2 emissions, working through between-group ability-differentiation, affect economic welfare positively and significantly may be due to the movement of the economy towards eco-friendly ABTC.

Both within and between-group inequalities promote welfare for the developed economies perhaps due to the innovation towards new technologies, though these effects are statistically insignificant as the z-values are less than 2.

Inequality through educational attainment significantly improves the welfare of the developed economies due to ABTC. However, inequality through between-group ability-differentiation declines economic welfare significantly as higher between-group ability-differentiation leads to a higher distortion in income distribution.

Thus it has been seen that, the effects of CO_2 emission through within-group ability-differentiation and both within and between-group inequalities directly and indirectly through educational attainment ratios and ability-differentiation affect economic welfare of developing and developed countries differently. Due to the movement towards eco-friendly ABTC, high-ability workers can cope with any environmental change, like CO_2 emission quickly and increase economic welfare in developed countries compared to developing countries as there must be more number of high-ability workers in developed countries than in developing ones.

Again, for the inequality effects it has been seen from Tables 13.9 and 13.10 that, within-group inequality does not matted as such due to its statistical insignificance, similar to the effect for the whole economy (see Table 13.8). However, between-group inequality significantly affects economic welfare adversely for developing nations as it creates economic distortions with respect to distributional aspects. However, between-group inequality improves economic welfare for developed nations, which may be due to the faster technological improvement in developed nations, although this effect is statistically insignificant. Further, inequality through educational attainment and ability-differentiation respectively decreases and increases economic welfare for developing countries, whereas for developed countries it increases and decreases economic welfare respectively. These varied effects are may be

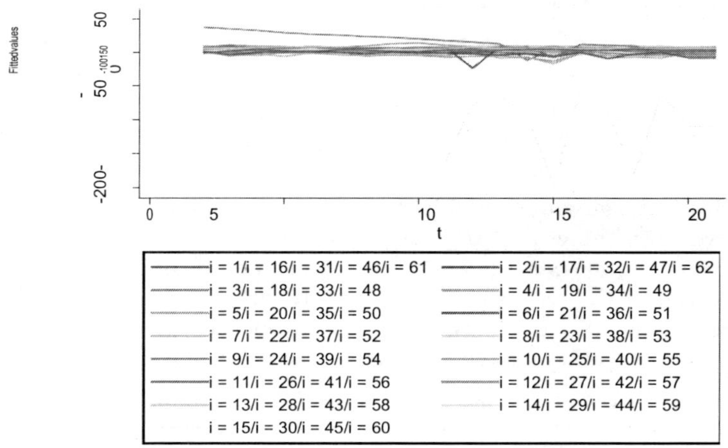

Figure 13.3: Overall Economic Welfare of All Developing Countries for the Time Period 1995-2015

due to the fact that, for developed countries what matters ultimately in the long-run is individual inherent ability. So any kind of inequality due to ability-differentiation is not good for them in the long-run as they already reached at some targeted level of economic developement. Whereas, inequality due to educational attainment captures the capability to cope with the short-run effects of technological improvements, which increase economic welfare as a result of technological improvement. However, for developing countries also ability being the main factor which matters ultimately in the long-run, any kind of inequality due to ability-differentiation is good for them in the long-run as they have to catch the targeted level of economic development at which developed countries are already there. Whereas, inequality due to any kind of difference in educational attainment is not good for developing countries, which leads to the need of an equal education for all within the economy for its development.

After estimating developing and developed economy individually, we make the linear prediction of the welfare of two economies. The overall predicted economic welfare for the developing and developed economies are shown by Figure 13.3 and Figure 13.4 respectively. Then, we present the convergence or divergence paths for the developing economy vis-a-vis the developed economy over the time period 1995-2015 in Figure 13.5. In Figure 13.5, the red triangles, connected by blue lines represent the linear predicted values of economic welfare of developing countries, and the blue circles, connected by red lines represent the linear predicted values of economic welfare of developed countries.

As can be seen, over the time period 1995-2015, developing countries in general are found to almost converge to the developed countries due to eco-

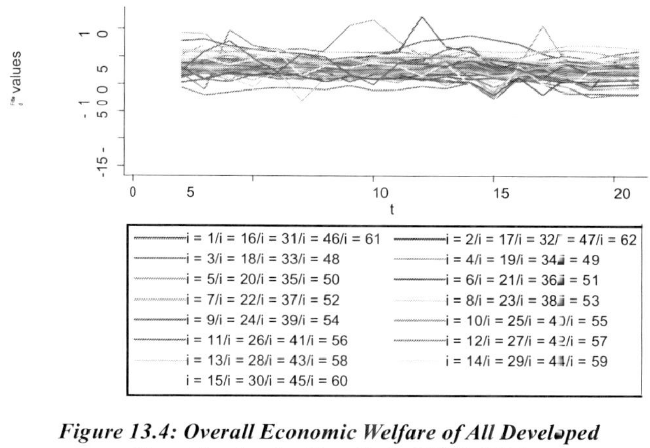

Figure 13.4: Overall Economic Welfare of All Developed Countries for the Time Period 1995-2015

friendly ABTC supported by educational attainment and inherent ability-differentiation except one. By comparing Figure 13.3 and Figure 13.5, we can see that this odd-one country is the 8th developing country, which is Kazakhstan

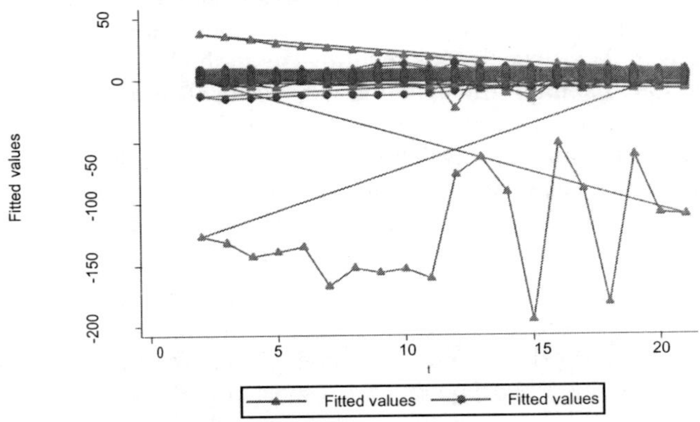

Figure 13.5: Convergence or Divergence of Economies over the Time Period 1995-2015

in our sample. Some reasons for this economic backwardness that can be offered are: poor labour market structure, lower capacity for investing more in R&D sectors, poor environmental conditions, all of which may not be supportive for a higher growth trajectory.

4 Conclusion

The present paper validates the existence of a trade-off between economic growth and environmental degradation and its implications on income distribution and economic welfare through ability-differentiation for 62 countries, among which 23 are developing countries and 39 are developed countries over the time period 1995-2015. To begin with, we check the stationarity of all the variables, economic growth, gross fixed capital formation, environmental vulnerability index, emissions of CO_2, PM2.5 air pollution, pollution index as environmental indicators, both within and between-group inequalities, both within and between-group educational attainment ratios by using LLC and HT tests for further estimation proce-dures, where PM2.5 air pollution and emission of CO_2 comes out as a non-stationary series respectively according to both LLC and HT tests and according to only HT test. So we make them stationary by taking their first difference. Since income inequalities are occurring due to educational attainment and ability-differentiation, where ability-differentiations are unobservable factors, we first regress income inequalities on economic growth, environmental indicators (environmental vulnerability index, growth of PM2:5 air pollution, CO_2 emission, growth of CO_2 emission and pollution index), educational attainment difference, and the interactions of economic growth and environmental indicators with educational attainment individually by using panel random effect model, and then we obtain the unobserved factors, ability-differentiations as the predicted time-fixed residuals. Using these predicted time-fixed residuals as ability-differentiations in the next economic welfare regression using panel corrected standard error model, along with other significant independent variables, gross fixed capital formation as aggregate economic investment, environmental indicators (environmental vulnerability index, CO_2 emission, growth of CO_2 emission and pollution index), both types of inequalities, and the interactions of environmental indicators and inequalities with education attainment difference and ability-differentiation, we validate the existence of a trade-off between economic growth and environmental degradation and the distortion of economic welfare due to a rise in income inequality. In the estimation of economic welfare, the growth of air pollution PM2:5 does not affect economic welfare significantly. Further, we show empirically that in general environmental degradation, working through environmental vulnerability index and CO_2 emissions, lowers economic growth due to ability-biased technical change, which is usual; whereas environmental degradation through pollution index and a positive growth of CO_2 emissions raises economic growth even in the presence of ability-biased technical change. This may be due to the movement of technological progress towards eco-friendly technology. Again, economic welfare decreases as a result of the distortion in economic distribution for only developed economies, whereas income inequalities improve economic welfare through ability-differentiation for developing countries, may be due to the fact that, developed countries already reached to a targeted level of economic development and developing countries have to catch the developed ones over time. Finally, we show that through out the period of time 1995-2015, developing countries are almost converging to the developed ones, except Kazakhstan which has the lowest economic welfare as per the measure used by us.

References

Although we check the estimation procedure by considering PI as non-stationary variable. The first difference of PI, i.e., GPI is again found to be non-stationary according to HT test, i.e., PI is in I(2) and, thus, we take the difference of first difference and that becomes stationary. We continue the estimation procedure with difference of first difference of PI variable, i.e., G2PI, but the results are not significant. Thus, we exclude that variable from our estimation procedure.

Between-group educational attainment ratio is calculated as addition of tertiary and secondary to primary educational attainment.

EKC shows the inverted U-shaped relationship between environmental degradation and per capita income.

'Green' research represents eco-friendly technological improvement.

'Grey' research represents technological improvement which degrades environmental quality like, pollution generated from production.

Indices and ratios do not have any unit.

Labour productivity is calculated as output per worker (GDP constant 2011 international dollar in PPP).

Short cycle tertiary educational attainment indicates acquiring tertiary level of education for a short time period. It is not so high level of tertiary educational attainment.

There is no such test for heteroscedasticity with panel random effect models.

Wald's test of heteroscedasticity is applicable for panel fixed effect model. That is why we cannot use this test for the earlier income inequality regressions as for those regressions panel random effect model is used.

We take environmental vulnerability, CO_2 emissions and PM2.5 air pollution individually to show the short-term effects and pollution index to show long-term effects. Since pollution index is a combination of all environmental pollutants, there must have collinearity between pollution index and other environmental variables considered. Although there is mul-ticollinearity problem, we estimate our models by including pollution index as a independent variable since it gives more appropriate results over the results of estimation by excluding pollution index.

Within-group educational attainment ratio is calculated as the ratio of tertiary to secondary educational attainment.

Chapter - 14

Globalisation and Groundwater Management: Challenges in Indian Agriculture

Pragya Sharma, Sanatan Nayak

Abstract

Globalisation paved way for increased international trade which has indirectly played role in natural capital depletion and degradation. Focusing specifically on trade of agro commodities and water stress, Hoekstra and Chapagain (2008) mentioned that many water resource problems are inter linked with international trade.Working in similar context, using data from various secondary sources, analysis of export pattern of India and its impact on groundwater resources of the country has been done in this paper. Since globalisation period, country's share in total export of water intensive crops viz. rice, sugarcane, cotton, soybean, wheat has been substantially high and so has been the increase in groundwater abstraction.

Data analysis show that groundwater use splurged in 1980s and currently 89 per cent of groundwater is extracted for irrigation (Suhag, 2016). Further, the study connotes that states viz. Punjab, Rajasthan, Madhya Pradesh, Maharashtra, Karnataka, Tamil Nadu and Uttar Pradesh which produce higher quantity of water-guzzling crops have groundwater development of more than 50 per cent which is definitely not a positive sign. Therefore, increased production of such crops for meeting trade demands poses to be a challenge in groundwater management. Thus, the study suggests that for trade liberalisation should not be done on the cost of water resource base depletion. For this adoption of water-efficient technologies in agriculture, farmer awareness and community management of groundwater is sine-qua-non.

1. Introduction

Agriculture withdraws the majority of water all across the globe from rivers, lakes, and particularly underground. With rapid globalisation and rising consumption levels water abstraction has risen. United Nations has estimated that the global demand for food is expected to increase by 70% by 2050 which would invariably affect global agricultural water consumption and increase it by 19 percent. Such water consumption projections could be much higher if crop yields and the efficiency of agricultural production do not improve dramatically. In such a scenario, agriculture trade also needs to be conducted in a sustainable manner without putting stress on water resources of any country. But, in reality, this is not being done and a developing country like India seems much concerned about economic growth while compromising its water resource base.

Objectives and Methodology

Working in the above mentioned context, using data from various secondary sources viz. Minor Irrigation Census, Agriculture Census, Ministry of Agriculture had attempted to establish a link between rising trade levels of water intensive crops and increasing groundwater depletion/ degradation in the country. Further, it explores socio-economic challenges which globalisation has posed for groundwater management in agriculture sector in India.

Broadly, the study consists of *four* sections. Section I covers up the introduction, objectives and methodology. The next section deals with overview of literature on agriculture trade and its linkage with water resources. Section III briefly discusses the dynamics of trade and impact on groundwater development at macro and micro level in India. The conclusion and suggestions regarding changes in food trade patterns and groundwater management are covered in the last section.

2. Review of Literature: Agriculture Trade and Water Resources

Trade in exchange of goods and services results in exchange of water in virtual form. According to Hubacek (2007) "importing water-intensive goods from one water-scarce region to another doesn't solve the problem of water scarcity, it just shifts the pressure to other regions". Scholars have attempted to account water footprints and trade flows of agrarian products as they are comparatively more water intensive and account for around 70% of global freshwater withdrawals (UNESCO, 2014). The largest share (76%) of the virtual water flows between countries is related to international trade in crops and derived crop products. It has also been estimated that 15% of the world's agricultural water use is for export products (Chapagain and Hoekstra, 2008). Specifically, water-intensive cereal grains like wheat, rice and corn account for 27 percent; meat production 22 percent; and dairy 7 percent. Focusing on the linkage between agriculture trade and its impact on water resources, literature suggests that unsustainable trade patterns have exacerbated water stress. Several examples of such relationship have been showcased by Hoekstra and Chapagain (2008) in their study on international trade dynamics and affect on water resources. They mentioned that in Morocco, water abstraction for irrigating export crops has increased foreign exchange but it is being done at the cost of lowering the water table of the Souss Aquifer. A similar problem is reported in the Rufiji-Ruvuma sub-system in East Africa. Kehl (2013) gave few more examples of such linkage wherein he concluded that arid parts of Egypt, Turkey and Eastern Europe, including the Aral Sea region produced large quantities of water-intensive cotton and exported it to Asia and Europe. Such inefficient trade is a function of short-term economic planning for rapid growth, perverse water and energy subsidies, and myopic use of methods exceeding ecological limits. Subsidized water in Uzbekistan is being over exploited to produce cotton for export, water depletion and degradation has been witnessed in Thailand with rise in irrigation of rice for export. Similar studies in Indian context by Goswami and Nishad (2015) reveal that India is poised to lose its entire available water supply within 500 years if the current food export policy continues. Jha & Rabindran (2011) indicate that trade liberalisation has resulted in an increase in exports from industries that are more water and air pollution intensive relative to less pollution-intensive ones. Landefeld & Sekhri (2013) carried out a study on trade in agricultural commodities during 1999-2005 and found out that trade promotion led to increased abstraction of water. According to an estimate of the International Water Management Institute, the current patterns of extraction in India could lead to a 25 per cent decline in food production by 2025 (Seckler et al, 1998). Such findings are of great concern as India extracts the largest amount of groundwater in the world, almost twice as much as the United States. Around 60 per cent of Indian agriculture is sustained by groundwater. Between 1980 and 2010, water tables declined by more than 12 meters in many parts of India, and the depletion rates have been accelerating since 2000 (Rodell at al., 2009; Sekhri, 2012). According to the satellite-data-based study conducted by NASA, the rate at which aquifers are being mined in India is unsustainable (Rodell at al., 2009). Decline in water tables would threaten food/ water security and would also affect the ability to mitigate droughts. Concerns about changing precipitation patterns due to global warming have made sustaining groundwater reserves even more critical. Thus, from a policy perspective, understanding how groundwater can be used in a sustainable manner for various agricultural purposes is necessary. Within any country the overuse of groundwater by one set of users can undermine the resource base for all.

3. Globalisation, Agriculture exports and Groundwater Development in India

Globalisation can either lead to conservation or depletion of natural resources that are used in the production of traded goods. In this context, we have tried to focus upon the current main irrigation ingredient viz. groundwater that is utilised in producing agro products. The onset of globalisation bought about a revolution in agriculture wherein a significant shift in irrigation source was witnessed. Farmers got access to underground blue gold viz. groundwater which was easy and flexible to extract through installation of pumpsets and this lead to increase in well or tubewell based irrigation.

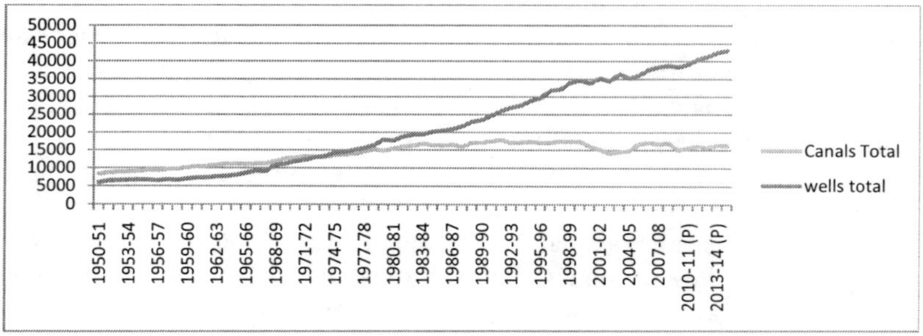

Source: Ministry of Agriculture, various issues (www.Indiastat.com)

Figure 14.1: Net Area Irrigated by Source from 1950-2016 (in 000'hectates)

Figure 14.1 shows that net area irrigated by canals was higher than irrigated by wells till 1974 but thereafter more specifically after 1980s the gap between two irrigation sources widened. Data on net irrigated area by source reveals that prior 1980s wells were not the major irrigation source but their quantum has increased considerably. Currently, 89 per cent of the groundwater is extracted by irrigation sector (Suhag, 2016). Rapid globalisation, rising food consumption needs, decentralised availability of groundwater, easy access, and cheap electricity has made groundwater a likeable resource. Area irrigated by wells in 1950 was 5978'000 hectares while by canals it was 8295'000 hectares. In 1974, a shift in source of irrigation is witnessed, where wells (14229) take over canal (13514) irrigation. Currently (2014-15), majority of the area is irrigated through wells i.e. 42960'000 hectares while canal irrigation is stuck at 16182'000 hectares. Similar rising levels of groundwater usage are witnessed in all parts of the globe. A new study by researchers from the University College London, International Institute for Applied Systems Analysis, Columbia University's Climate Research Centre and NASA's Goddard Institute of Space Studies has found that the use of groundwater has increased exponentially (Economic Times, April 8, 2017). In 2000, non-renewable groundwater accounted for 20 per cent of the world's irrigation and is expected that in the next ten years ground water depletion increased 22 per cent. This jump in use of non-renewable groundwater in the first decade of the 21st century was powered by China, which registered a 102 per cent increase in groundwater depletion, along with the United States (31 per cent) and India (23 percent).

Considering agriculture trade, the same study estimates that almost 11 per cent of global non-renewable groundwater withdrawn for irrigation is used to produce crops that are traded on the international market. Two-thirds of the exported crop that uses non-renewable groundwater is produced in three countries Pakistan (29 per cent), United States (27 per cent) and India (12 per cent). The crops which contribute the most to trade of non-renewable groundwater are rice (29 per cent), wheat (12 per cent), cotton (11 per cent), maize (4 per cent) and soybeans (3 per cent). Checking out the export pattern of these water intensive crops in India, we see that the trade liberalisation has promoted their trade which on one hand is positive but on the other it has compromised upon our groundwater levels as depicted by rising groundwater development.

India is major exporter of water guzzling crops such as sugarcane, rice, soybean and cotton. Currently, India is world's largest exporter of rice, second largest exporter of cotton and third largest of sugar. It is also amongst top five exporters of soybean. Analysing the export quantity of these crops since the

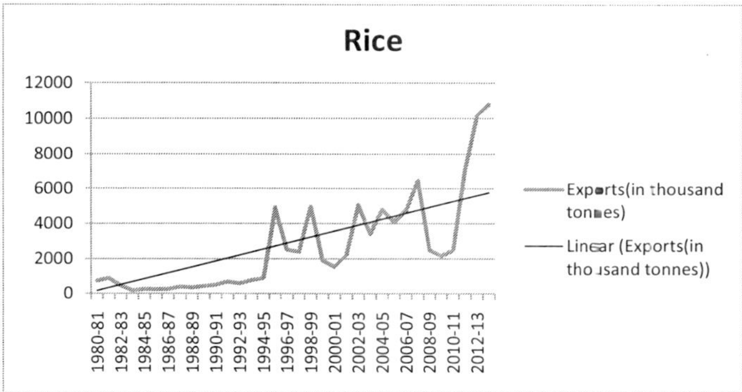

Figure 14.1: Source: I) www. Indiastat.com II) Ramakrishna & Degoankar (2016)

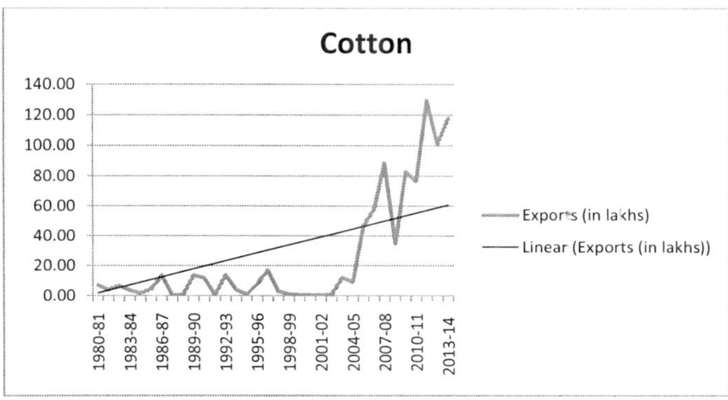

Figure 14.2: Source: Ministry of Agriculture (various issues)

onset of globalisation till 2014, we see a continuous rise. Trend lines fitted in every graph show an increasing trend with reference to all crops. Considering rice, we estimate that there have been high fluctuations since 1990s. Figure 14.2 shows that the export quantity of rice remained constant till 1990-91 but increased thereafter and reached 4914 thousand metric tonnes (MT) in 1995 from 727.35 thousand MT in 1980. In 2013-14, the export of rice stood at a higher number of 10775.95 thousand MT.

Cotton is one of most water-intensive commodity and India's share in its export is one of the highest. The quantum of cotton exports did not increase initially after 1980 but a rise in its trade is witnessed after 2005 when suddenly exports surged to 47 lakh bales and since then an increasing trend is observed with 117.92 lakh bales as of 2013-14. Similar picture is seen with reference to Sugar and Soybean exports. A constant rise in sugar exports is observed from the data. India exported 2000 tonnes of sugar in 1990 while the number is 26.85 lakh MT in 2013-14. In case of soybean export, constant rise has been registered with exports being mere 107 thousand MT in 1980, 1180 thousand MT in 1991, 2097thousand MT in 2000 and 3252 in 2013. From these figures, we may state that increase has been fast during the early phase of globalisation while it has been gradual in the later phase.

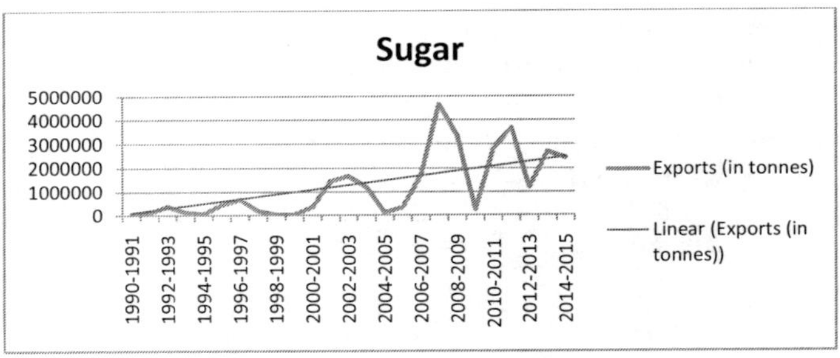

Figure 14.3: Source: Ministry of Agriculture (various issues)

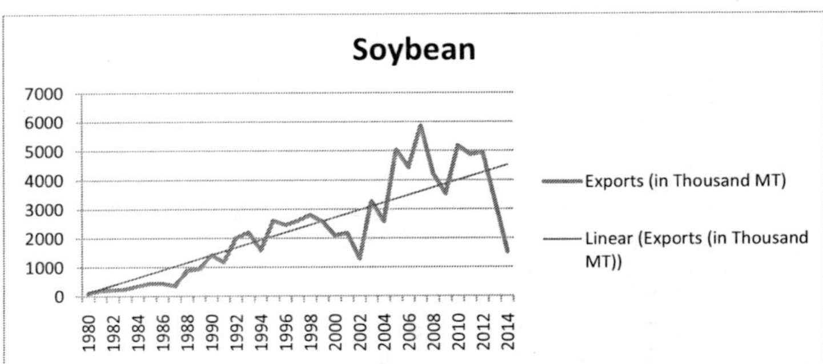

Figure 14.4: Source: Ministry of Agriculture (www.Indexmundi.com)

From above graphical representations, one may conclude that exports of water-intensive commodities have increased significantly since globalisation. But, from this analysis we may not clearly state whether their trade has affected groundwater depletion. For this purpose, we tried to establish a link between production of water-intensive crops/commodities, area under irrigation of principal crops and groundwater development.

Table 14.1: State wise Ranking of Major States producing Water Intensive (as of 2016)

Crop	*Rank 1*	*Rank 2*	*Rank3*	*Rank 4*
Rice	Andhra Pradesh	Punjab	Orissa	Tamil Nadu
Sugarcane	Maharashtra	Uttar Pradesh	Karnataka	Tamil Nadu
Cotton	Gujarat	Maharashtra	Andhra Pradesh	Karnataka
Soybean	Madhya Pradesh	Maharashtra	Rajasthan	Karnataka

Source: (I) Open Governance Centre, Indian Institute of Management, Bengalaru
(II) Status paper on Sugarcane (2014-15), Directorate of Sugarcane Development
(III) Cotton Corporation of India (2016)
(IV) Soyabean Processors Association of IndiaDatabank (2016)

Table 14.1 represents the rank wise order of highest producer states of various crops. In case of Rice, we see that Andhra Pradesh is the largest producer followed by Punjab, Orissa and Tamil Nadu. Among these states, Punjab and Tamil Nadu have high levels of groundwater development, 172 and 77 per cent respectively. The situation is different in Andhra Pradesh and Orissa because the availability of groundwater is comparatively low due to hydrogeological conditions and share of surface water usage in irrigation is also high in these areas. With reference to Sugarcane, data reveals that Maharashtra and Uttar Pradesh are top producers. Both these states have groundwater development of more than 50 percent. Maharashtra has 53 per cent while Uttar Pradesh has 74 percent. Stories of water crisis in both these states are also not uncommon, be it the water stress in Latur district or groundwater depletion in western districts of Uttar Pradesh. Considering cotton production, statistics divulge that Gujarat, a groundwater stressed region having groundwater development of almost 70 percent, is the biggest producer. Gujarat's water plight is also not hidden, Columbia Water Centre (2012) mentions that the groundwater situation is extremely serious over there and the future of agriculture in North Gujarat seems gloomy. It is the alarming rate of groundwater use in state in agriculture which has lead to creation of groundwater markets, passing of groundwater bill, reducing subsidies on energy and implementation of feeder-segregation policies in agriculture sector. In case of soybean production in India, Madhya Pradesh is the leading producer followed by Maharashtra, Rajasthan and Karnataka. All these states extract huge amount of groundwater for irrigation purposes and have groundwater development of 64, 53, 137 and 77 per cent respectively. Rajasthan is already a water stressed state so there is a need to consider production of water –

Table 14.2: Area irrigated under Principal Crops (2013-2015) and Groundwater development (in percentage, 2011)

States	Rice		Wheat		Sugarcane		Cotton		Maize		GW Dev
	2013-14	2014-15	2013-14	2014-15	2013-14	2014-15	2013-14	2014-15	2013-14	2014-15	2015
Andhra Pradesh	4356	3809	8	6	192	177	2389	2540	1006	995	45
Bihar	3131	3268	2009	2188	258	256	NA	NA	732	714	44
Chhattisgarh	3802	3809	103	98	9	19	NA	NA	111	122	35
Gujarat	788	785	1442	1146	174	204	2519	3010	461	423	67
Haryana	1228	1287	2499	2592	102	101	536	647	9	8	133
Himachal Pradesh	74	68	358	400	2	2	NA	NA	293	300	71
Karnataka	1340	1296	209	197	420	450	662	869	1377	1340	64
Kerala	200	198	NA	NA	2	2	NA	NA	0	0	47
Madhya Pradesh	1930	2153	5380	5560	73	111	514	574	868	1132	57
Maharashtra	1613	1547	1097	895	937	1048	4192	4192	1001	1059	53
Orissa	4180	4166	1	1	14	10	124	127	95	92	28
Punjab	2851	2894	3512	3514	89	94	446	420	130	126	172
Rajasthan	146	168	2810	3318	5	6	393	487	927	904	137
Tamilnadu	1726	1830	NA	NA	313	263	152	186	345	342	77
Uttar Pradesh	5982	5869	9839	9846	2228	2228	NA	NA	767	712	74
Uttarakhand	253	262	348	348	104	102	NA	NA	25	25	57
West Bengal	5514	5386	332	335	17	18	NA	NA	129	150	40
All-India	**44136**	**43855**	**30473**	**30969**	**4993**	**5144**	**11960**	**13083**	**9066**	**9258**	62

Source: Directorate of Economics and Statistics, Ministry of Agriculture and Farmers Welfare.

intensive crops in such regions. Setting up another linkage of water-intensive crops/ commodities with groundwater development we assess the area under irrigation of principal crops. Table 14.2 has been made so as to depict this relationship.

From Table 14.2 one may assess that states wherein sugarcane, rice, cotton and wheat is grown more has a higher level of groundwater development. In Uttar Pradesh, wheat, rice and sugarcane are the principal crops, thus, groundwater development is more than 70 percent. Tamil Nadu has majority of the area under irrigation of rice, a high water requirement crop leading to groundwater development of 77 percent. Gujarat, highly groundwater stressed region is engaged in cotton production with an area of 3010 mha under its irrigation. Analysis of data of State-wise irrigated area under different selected crops shows that the main States contributing to irrigated area under rice are Uttar Pradesh, Andhra Pradesh, West Bengal, and Punjab. Irrigated area under wheat was concentrated in the States of Uttar Pradesh, Punjab, Madhya Pradesh, Rajasthan and Haryana. Sugarcane had the highest irrigated area in Uttar Pradesh having its share as more than 40 per cent in the total irrigated area under this crop in the country. Sugarcane is one of the most water consuming crop. Therefore, Uttar Pradesh needs to consider growing of sugarcane at such huge level with rising groundwater. This scenario depicts that globalisation is also somewhere a cause of rising groundwater stress in India. As the country exports huge amount of water-intensive agro products, the production of such commodities has been increasing. Farmers also earn better incomes in producing these high return crops so they lack incentive for abstaining from its production. Apart from it, high subsidies in power and other agriculture setup also promote excessive use of groundwater in agriculture posing a threat towards groundwater management.

4. Conclusion

The study findings suggests that India's food trade policy seems to be bit flawed if we assess the scenario with reference to water resources particularly groundwater. The data represented above shows that share of groundwater in irrigation has significantly risen since contemporary globalisation. Though, directly one may not blame globalisation for groundwater depletion but indirectly with rising quantum of trade of water-intensive crops and commodities we are able to conclude so. Macro and micro level data of area under irrigation of principal crops and largest producer states of rice, sugarcane, cotton, and soybean reveal that states which produce more of these crops viz. Madhya Pradesh, Gujarat, Punjab, Rajasthan, Tamil Nadu, Karnataka and Uttar Pradesh all have more than 50 per cent groundwater development and the situation is precarious in Punjab and Rajasthan where ratio of groundwater availability to its abstraction is as high as 172 and 137 per cent respectively. Thus, giving us an idea that production and trade of such water demanding crops has increased after globalisation and this poses a challenge in groundwater management in water stressed country like India. Several countries viz. USA, China etc. have started to strategically manage their trade but India still seems to be impassive towards the growing water stress as a result of trade in water intensive products. It is expected that if the current trade policies patterns continue and business-as-usual approach in groundwater use follows then India is set to face catastrophic events very soon. Environmental concerns especially with reference to water resources need to be addressed in trade agreements so as to protect exploitation of natural capital by developed countries. Further, as it not feasible to completely stop trade of water-intensive crops, therefore, adoption of water-efficient technologies in agriculture, farmer awareness and community management of groundwater are few viable solutions.

References

Chapagain, A. K. & Hoekstra, A. Y (2008), The global component of freshwater demand and supply: an assessment of virtual water flows between nations as a result of trade in agricultural and industrial products, *Water Int.* 33, pg. 19–32.

Columbia Water Centre (2012), Gujarat, India (available at: http://water.columbia.edu/research-themes/water-food-energy-nexus/water-agriculture-livelihood-security-in-india/gujarat-india/)

Central Ground Water Board (2011), Dynamic Groundwater Resources of India, Technical Report.

Cotton Corporation of India (2016) http://cotcorp.gov.in/current-cotton.aspx?pageid=4.

Economic Times (2017), *How one item in your shopping cart could deplete groundwater,* epaper, April 08(http://epaperbeta.timesofindia.com/Article.aspx?eid=31818&articlexml=HOW-ONE-ITEM-IN-YOUR-SHOPPING-CART-COULD-08042017009031.

Fraiture, C., Cai, X., Amarasinghe, U., Rosegrant, M.& Molden, D. (2004), Does International Cereal Trade Save Water? The Impact of Virtual Water Trade on Global Water Use, *Comprehensive Assessment Research Report 4*, International Water Management Institute, Colombo, Sri Lanka.

Goswami.P, Nishad, S.N (2015), Virtual water trade and time scales for loss of water sustainability: A comparative regional analysis, *Scientific Report 5.*

Jha. S, S. Rabindran (2002), Environmental Impact of India Trade Liberalisation, *Cornell University International Colloquium on S75 Years of Development Research.*

Ministry of Agriculture data (various issues) accessed from www.Indiastat.com

Open Governance Centre, Rice exports in India, *IIM Bangalore* (http://opengovernance-india.org/tmhmjzc/top-rice-producing-states-in-india)

Rodell, M., Velicogna, I. and J. Famiglietti (2009), Satellite-based estimates of groundwater depletion in India, *Nature*, Vol. 460, pp. 999-1002.

Seckler, D., Amarasinghe, U, Molden, D., De Silva, R., and R. Barker (1998), World water demand and supply 1995 to 2025: Scenarios and issues, *Research Report* No. 19, International Water Management Institute.

Sekhri, S. (2011), Public Provision and Protection of Natural Resources: Groundwater Irrigation in Rural India, *American Economic Journal*, Applied Economics, Vol. 3(4), pp. 29-55.

Sekhri, S. (2013, a), Wells, Water, and Welfare: Impact of Access to Groundwater on Rural Poverty and Conflict, *Working Paper*, University of Virginia.

Sekhri. S, P. Landefeld (2013), Agricultural Trade, Institutions, and Depletion of Natural Resources, *Virginia Economic Online paper 405*, University of Virginia (available at: http://people.virginia.edu/~ss5mj/Agtrade_water.pdf)

Singh, D. and A. Singh (2002), Groundwater Situation in India: Problems and Perspective, *Water Resources Development.*

Suhag, R. (2016), Overview of Groundwater in India, *Report submitted to PRS* (available at:http://www.prsindia.org/administrator/uploads/general/1455682937~~Overview%20of%20Ground%20Water%20in%20India.pdf)

Status paper on Sugarcane (2014-15), Directorate of Sugarcane Development

Soyabean Processors Association of India (SOPA) Databank (2016), http://www.sopa.org/statistics/soybean-production-by-state/

Part - III

Globalization and other Social Aspects

Chapter - 15

An Empirical study on Higher Education under Globalisation in India

Dr. L. Clement Baskar

Abstract

This paper examines the present status higher education under globalisation in India, especially in Tamil Nadu. It also discusses the major challenges that the globalisation brought to higher education. In the higher education segment of India substantial improvement is possible in both quantitative and qualitative terms post globalisation. The major objective is to make an attempt to identify the any significant impact on higher education due to globalising higher education. Advanced Statistical tools were used to analyse the data for this research paper.

1. Introduction

Higher education in the beginning of the 21st century has become increasingly important. From the highly industrialised countries of the Organisation for Economic Co-operation and Development (OECD), to the so-called transitional countries that are moving from centralised to market economies, to the middle and low income countries, higher education is seen nearly everywhere as an underpinning to democratic civil societies, an engine of economic growth, and a policy instrument for the advancement of individual economic mobility and social justice.

In spite of this universally recognised importance for higher education it seems everywhere there is a gap between the demand and supply for financial aid. The gap between demand and supply for financial aid arises due to flat or declining governmental budgets in support of higher education and is manifested by overcrowded institutions, deteriorating physical plants, declining faculty-student ratios, increasingly demoralised and distracted faculty, and in many countries higher fees, and greater student debt loads.

Before independence the growth of higher education in India was very less and diversification in areas of studies was very limited. Since independence, the number of institutions has increased significantly. Under this circumstance, higher education in India is viewed as a long-term social investment for the promotion of economic growth, culture, social cohesion, equity and justice. The Government of Tamil Nadu has shown keen interest to strengthen the higher education system in the State in response to its demands. Education not only has an impact on the human development and economic growth, but is the fundamental requirement for democracy. Through education, people become more responsible and informed citizens, and can voice their concerns and issues in political system of their society. It is an essential element for democracy and eradicating poverty. It also helps people in improving productivity, thus playing greater roles in economic life and earning a better livelihood for themselves and the society.

Under these circumstances it is relevant to have a brief study on present status of higher education under the globalisation in Indian and in particular with Tamil Nadu State.

1.1 Financing of Higher Education: An International Comparison

The most standard and popular indicator used to measure finances for education is the per cent of Gross National Product (GNP) devoted to education, though some of the limitations of this indictor are well known. According to the Human Development Report 2014, the Human Development Index Rank for India is 135which come under the Medium Human Development Countries. Public expenditure on education is referred to the total public expenditure (current and capital) on education, expressed as per cent of GDP. The public spending on education as per cent of GDP was 4.4 per cent. In comparison with other countries, many countries spend more than 6 per cent, some more than 8 per cent and a few more than 10 per cent on educations. Some of the countries, which spend more than 4 per cent of GDP on education, are even economically poorer than India.Suchcountries, for illustration, are Poland (5.1per cent), Costa Rica (6.2per cent), Jamaica (6.1per cent), Maldives (8.7per cent), Cuba (12.9per cent), Kenya (6.7per cent), Ethiopia (4.7per cent), Saudi Arabia(5.6per cent), and Botswana (7.8per cent).India had set a long time ago a target of six per cent of GNP to be spent on education. This target still eludes, and may continue to elude in the near future.

1.2 Financing of Higher Education in India

According to Tikal (2002) financing education in an economy can be measured in terms of adequacy, equity and efficiency of funds. In 1960s, in terms of adequacy, investment in education in any economy was used to be judged in terms of international comparisons particularly with reference to the share of education in GNP and the share of education in the government budget. Later adequacy of the financial resources was judged in terms of physical targets, that is, enrollment (ratios). Since 1980s, equity of measure was considered, besides considerations for quantitative expansion (e.g., provision of schools), and improvement in quality (e.g., increasing the number of trained teachers). These have exerted considerable influence on public financing of education. In respect of equity, the equality in outcomes cannot be ensured, but equality in inputs, that is, equality in opportunities, can be ensured. According to educational planners and researchers equity has been related to equality in educational opportunities of regional, caste and gender groups of population measured in terms of literacy, enrolment and number of institutions.

There are two aspects relating to efficiency, efficiency of investment made in education, and cost effectiveness. The former is measured in terms of labour market outcomes, essentially rates of return to education, which refer to the overall or labour market efficiency of investment in education, while the latter, viz., cost effectiveness refers to efficiency of investment made in educational outcomes such as number of pass-outs, survival and transition rates, etc. The labour market efficiency is also referred to as external efficiency and measures on cost efficiency as internal efficiency. While cost effectiveness analysis explains how efficiently the resources are being used to produce the given output in the schools while rate of return analysis shows how efficient is the overall investment in education. In the case of India, the level of financing of education cannot be regarded adequate based on any of the above criteria.

Table 15.1: Budgeted Expenditure on Education by Education Department and Other Departments (Revenue + Capital + Loan and Advances)

(Rupees in Crores)

	Actual (2012-13)	*Revised Estimates (2013-14)*	*Budget Estimates (2014-15)*
	Expenditure on Education	*Expenditure on Education*	*Expenditure on Education*
	Total (%)	*Total (%)*	*Total (%)*
Centre	89757.60 (6.36)	101594.26 (6.39)	122489.34 (6.82)
State/UTs	282922.86 (18.90)	340034.78 (18.48)	393203.29 (17.79)
Total (Center + State/Uts)	372680.46 (12.82)	441629.04 (12.87)	515692.62 (12.87)

Source: Analysis of Budget Expenditure on Education 2012-13 to 2013-14, MHRD. GoI.

Table 15.1 shows the budget expenditure on education by education department and other department subject to Centre and States/ Union Teritarries in India since2012-13 to 2014-15. From the table it is understood that the increase in budget expenditure is very less, that is, 0.05 from 2012-13 to 2013-14 and nil from2013-14 to 2014-15. The time series data on GRE and Public Expenditure on Education as % of GDP is presented in Table 15.2.

Table 15.2: Comparison on GRE and Public Expenditure on Education as % of GDP

Year	*GER in Higher Education of All Level of Students (in Lakhs)*	*Public Expenditure on Education as % of GDP*
1950-51	4.0	0.64
1960-61	10	1.48
1970-71	33	2.11
180-81	48	2.98
190-91	49	3.84
2000-01	86	4.28
2005-06	143	3.34
2006-07	156	3.48
2007-08	172	3.40
2008-09	185	3.56
2009-10	207	3.95
2010-11	275	4.20
2011-12	292	4.17
2012-13	296	12.82
2013-14	226	12.87
2014-15	316	12.87

Source: 1. National Institution for Transforming India, Government of India
2. All Indian Surveys on Higher Education, MHRD.
3. Annual Report 2015-16, MHRD.
4. Analysis of Budget Expenditure on Education, MHRD. GoI.
5. http://aishe.nic.in/aishe/viewDocument.action?documentId=204

Table 15.2 reveals that the increase in public expenditure on education as percentage of GDP for a decade, from 2005-06 to 2014-15, was approximately three times of 3.34% (2005-06), that is, 12.87% (2014-15) while the Gross Enrolment Ratio was one and half times increase for the same period.

1.3 Ministry of Human Resource Development

The Ministry of Human Resource Development (MHRD) declared that the Gross Enrolment Ratio (GER) for Higher Education in India increased to 24.5 per cent during 2015-16. This is a positive step toward increasing the rate of literacy in the country. Only a decade ago, that is during the period 2004-5, the GER for higher education in India was only 10 percent. The ministry said that the quantum jump in GER over the last decade was an indication of improvement in registration of students in higher educational institutes.

The Central Government has launched various initiatives to improve the quality of education in institutes of higher education. The HRD ministry launched National Institute Ranking Framework (NIRF) in 2015. NIRF released its first ranking list in 2016 and is set to release the ranking list for 2017 in April this year.

In the Twelfth Five Year Plan a new scheme called Rashtriya Uchchatar Shiksha Abhiyan (RUSA) was launched. RUSA seeks to promote equity, access, and excellence in state higher education system. This scheme supports upgrading autonomous colleges to universities, clustering colleges to form a university, setting up of new professional colleges in unserved and underserved areas and providing grant to colleges and universities to help them improve their infrastructure.

Table 15.3: Level-wise Enrolment in Higher Education 2014-15

Level	*All Categories*			*SC*			*ST*		
	Male	*Female*	*Total*	*Male*	*Female*	*Total*	*Male*	*Female*	*Total*
Ph.D.	70	48	118	NA	NA	NA	NA	NA	NA
M.Phil.	14	19	33	NA	NA	NA	NA	NA	NA
P.G.	1867	1986	3853	NA	NA	NA	NA	NA	NA
U.G.	14467	12705	27172	NA	NA	NA	NA	NA	NA
PG Diploma	121	94	215	NA	NA	NA	NA	NA	NA
Diploma	1788	720	2508	NA	NA	NA	NA	NA	NA
Certificate	74	86	170	NA	NA	NA	NA	NA	NA
Integrated	87	55	142	NA	NA	NA	NA	NA	NA
Higher Education Total	18488	15723	34211	2504	2102	4607	894	747	1641

Source: MHRD, GoI. (http://mhrd.gov.in./statist)

NA: Not Available

Scholarship is boon for students belonging to the weaker sections of the society, who are unable to pursue their education for some reason or the other. Scholarship is an incentive as well as encouragement for students, who are talented, but do not have the means to study further. There are a variety of scholarships – merit-based, need-based, student-specific, career-specific and college-specific.

The Ministry of Human Resource Development, Department of Higher Education offers National Scholarship and also facilitates in the nomination process for the External Scholarships offered by various countries, to the meritorious and eligible students.

1.4 The National Scholarships are

1. Central Sector Scheme of Scholarship for College and University Students
2. Special Scholarship Scheme for Jammu & Kashmir
3. Scheme for Scholarship to Students from Non-Hindi Speaking States for Post Matric Studies in Hindi

1.5 The External Scholarships are:

1. Commonwealth Scholarships for United Kingdom and New Zealand
2. Scholarships offered by China, South Korea, Israel, Japan, Italy, Mexico, and Sri Lanka.
3. Agatha Harrison Memorial Fellowship

The Ministry also issue No Obligation to Return to India (NORI) Certificate required by Indian Immigrants in Canada, USA, Singapore, etc. In addition, the Ministry also implements Central Scheme of Interest Subsidy for Education Loans (CSIS).

1.6 Tamil Nadu State Government

According to the statement of Minister for Higher Education (2014), Tamil Nadu, till now, only students from affluent sections of the society could afford to travel and study in overseas institutions. But, Late Chief Minister Jayalalithaa was keen that the opportunity of studying in leading foreign institutions should be given to the students of 62 government colleges in the State, he said.

Fourteen postgraduate students of government colleges in the State have been selected to go to London in a month to study for a semester in reputed educational institutions there, said P. Palaniappan, Higher Education Minister. A salient aspect of the recently launched Study abroad programme was that of those qualified for it, 13 were women. The selected second-year postgraduate students would be sent abroad in the third semester. The selection was based on a screening test. The State government will bear the expenses that works out to Rs. 15 lakh per head, the Minister said.

The programme has become feasible following the MoU signed between the Tamil Nadu State Council for Higher Education and the British Council to facilitate the deserving postgraduate students of the government colleges to have a brief stint in leading U.K. institutions for enriching their academic skills. This is the first of its kind programme in the State.

1.7 Definitions

Study Abroad Programs are for experiential education[1]. Picture the world as your classroom with each destination a new interactive textbook where instead of reading, you are experiencing history, art, culture, fashion, food and the arts in real time. Maybe you have travelled overseas and had a taste of exploring a foreign city, a sandy beach, or a historical landmark. If you are looking for countries to study abroad and another opportunity to travel, to discover, learn, understand and connect with new people, studying abroad is a great option.

Study abroadis a defined for the purpose of this study as a period of time where a student engages in an educational activity through an institution of learning or organisation for schooling/ (or) college in a foreign country.

1.8 Statement of the Problem

Higher education goes beyond the classroom and gains in intellectual content to also educate students in a variety of skills, values, and dispositions. Students have opportunities to become aware of themselves and the world. They develop personal values and skills that will shape their identities for the future. However, previous research on the effect of study abroad on the identity development of students is very limited.

1.9 Objectives of the Study

- To examine the impact of globalisation on higher education
- To evaluate the correlation and regression analysis to test the relationships/degree among variables taken for the study.

1.10 Limitations

This study looked only at a scheme of Study Abroad Programme undertaken by the Tamil Nadu state for students who study in Government Arts and Science Colleges. And the other students who are undergoing the similar programme were not were not included in this study. These students were participated in a one semester study abroad programme.

2. Literature Review

The study abroad programmes have not been extensively researched. But previous research on study abroad experience has reported positive impacts on students' overall development during study abroad.

In this section literatures are provided as a background on current trends in study abroad and the various models for study abroad programs. Brief reviews of the research conducte2d on study abroad are provided.

2.1 Data on Study Abroad

Open Doors reports are annual reports on international education published by the Institute of International Education. Funding for Open Doors reports is made available by funds from the U.S. Department of State's Bureau of Educational and Cultural Affairs (Open Doors, 2005). During the 2003-2004 academic year, 191, 321 American college students participated in study abroad programs according to Open Doors 2005. This is an increase of 9.6percentage from the 2002-2003 academic year. The majority (65.6percentage) of those students are female. Of the students who study abroad, 38percentage participate in a one-semester study abroad. Thirty six point two per cent of students who study abroad are of junior standing. The dominant trend in study abroad programs for American students is to spend their abroad period in Western Europe, although this is slowly shifting to include Latin America.

The proportion of students who study abroad in Europe has decreased to 60.9 percentage from 62.9 percentage in 2002-2003. As of November 2005, the top five destinations for study abroad were; United Kingdom (16.8 percentage), Italy (11.5 percentage), Spain (10.5 percentage), France (7.5 percentage), Australia (7.2 percentage).

The regional breakdown of host countries is as follows:

Europe: 60.9 percentage, Latin America: 15.2 percentage, Asia: 6.9 percentage, Multiple Regions: 5.5 percentage, Oceania: 7.4 percentage, Middle East .5 percentage, Africa: 3.0 percentage, North America: .6 percentage (Open Doors, 2005).

2.2 Issues Facing Study Abroad

Currently, only about one per cent of American undergraduate students participate in study abroad programs (Wheeler, 2000). Participation in study abroad is growing, but many students do not take advantage of the opportunity and benefits of study abroad. College student may not participate in study abroad for many reasons including students having to take a "break" in the academic cycle of the home institution, the transferability of courses taken at the host university to the students' degree programs, and enrolment costs and associated travel expenses incurred by students enrolling in study abroad programs (Sowa, 2002).

Study abroad is viewed by some as being elitist, or only available to those students who are of the upper class, because of the financial implications to students (Stryker, 1997). Studying abroad is often much more expensive than a semester or year at the student's home institution. Additionally, students who are able to take advantage of special tuition discounts in their US institution, such as Western Undergraduate Exchange at Montana State University, could potentially be excluded from studying abroad because these programs may have a requirement that students maintain continuous enrolment at the their home institution in order to receive the benefit. There are an increasing number of affordable study abroad programs as well as a number of scholarships available for students who want to study abroad. In addition, federal legislation (1992 Reauthorisation of the Higher Education Act of 1965) was passed allowing students to use their financial aid package toward study abroad programs sponsored by American institutions (Hoffa & Pearson, 1997). This option is making study abroad a more affordable option for many students. Issues that threaten personal health and safety for students studying abroad may also limit participation. It is important that students follow the US Department of State guidelines for safety abroad and use good judgment in protecting themselves (Scharman, 2002). Students may also need to obtain the proper inoculations as advised for their region of study (Scharman, 2002). Guidance is available to students on which vaccinations and precautions to take prior to studying abroad by the student health service on most campuses. Students must also execute good judgment and make healthy decisions while abroad to protect their health.

2.3 Variables Affecting Study Abroad Outcomes

Research shows that many factors may affect the result of a participant's study abroad experience. These include: the age and maturity level of the student, year in school, student's major, length of stay in the host country, level of openness to new cultures and ideas, skills in the host country's/culture's language(s), and student expectations regarding the experience and characteristics of the overseas institution attended (Kaufmann, et al., 1992; Martin &Rohrlich, 1991; Thomlison, 1991). The student's familiarity with the host culture and previous experience in travelling to foreign countries may also influence the outcome of a study abroad experience (Kaufmann, et al., 1992). The larger the difference between the host and home cultures, the greater the change that can potentially occur within the student (Douglas & Jones-Rikkers, 2001).

2.4 Student Development and Study Abroad

The body of research conducted on students that have studied abroad and their developmental outcomes is limited. There have been very few studies conducted in recent years and even fewer in the past, that have measured the outcomes and issues relating to identity development and the acquisition of the values associated with study abroad. The few studies that do exist have found that the study abroad experience can be a beneficial component to undergraduate education. The results suggest a positive impact on a student's development through the following outcomes: increased desire to participate in extracurricular activities, new desire to learn foreign languages, loss of competitiveness, and increased involvement in international activities (Kaufmann, et al., 1992). Researchers suggests that it may be easier for students to experience and be open to change while engaged in a study abroad program because they are away from their normal peer group including their family and friends (Kaufmann, et al., 1992; Meara, 1994). Students do not have the pressure of being held to their normal behavior and can feel free to experiment with new belief systems and to experience new ideas and culture (Kaufmann, et al., 1992). New peer groups that students interact with while participating in study abroad make up a special support network. The students can go through changes together in a non-threatening, change-friendly environment (Kaufmann, et al., 1992).

Study abroad may be viewed as a form of experiential education. Experiential education is defined as learning through experiencing or doing (Hopkins, 1999). A student's non-academic experience, such as weekend travel or relationships developed with new friends or host family, may count for as much benefit as his or her academic experiences (Hopkins, 1999). Students who study abroad have the opportunity to experience learning by doing, experiencing a culture not only on paper, but three dimensionally using all of their senses. Students often state of their experiences abroad that they learned how much they actually knew and how to apply the skills that they have developed during their education (Christie &Ragans, 1999).

One criticism of study abroad states that there is little to be gained from short term (less than six months) experience. According to the literature, for a true immersion to take place, at least one year of residence must be experienced. This gives the students ample time to become acclimated to the culture and to begin to view their experiences as members of that cultural community (Kaufmann, et al., 1992).

2.5 Educational Attainment and Study Abroad

Students on study abroad develop an understanding of other cultures, societies, and traditions. They improve their ability to discuss international issues and gain knowledge of other countries' political systems. Students also become more knowledgeable about international affairs because of time spent abroad (Gray, Murdock, & Stebbins, 2002; Kaufmann, et al., 1992; Sowa, 2002). Gaining language skills, considered at one time to be the primary purpose of study abroad, is a large component of a student's educational attainment while abroad. Students who study abroad in non-English speaking countries have improved skills in speaking a foreign language (Cummings, 2001). Many researchers believe that language acquisition is the largest benefit in the realm of educational attainment for study abroad. Students have reflected that the language skills that they have obtained during study abroad are the most valuable aspect of their experience (Kaufmann, et al., 1992).

2.6 Attitudes and Values and Study Abroad

Study abroad experiences affect a wide range student attitudes and values (Kaufmann, et al., 1992; Meara, 1994). The list of values gained during study abroad includes enhanced cross-cultural understanding, better understanding of American culture, altruism, better understanding of personal relationships, leadership ability, increased levels of self-esteem, and higher levels of self-confidence (Kaufmann, et al., 1992; Sowa, 2002). Additionally, students that have participated in study abroad are more prepared to assist others in need and have a better understanding of other cultures following their experiences abroad (Sowa, 2002). Students feel empathy toward values and cultures other than their own, and they express an increased desire to experience other cultures (Gray, Murdock, & Stebbins, 2002). Additionally, an overseas experience helps one to better understand him or herself and to become more mature (Holland, 2003).

2.7 Identity Development and Study Abroad

Having an experience far from home helps the student to become more individualistic compared to levels he or she displayed prior to study abroad. Study abroad allows the student the opportunity to begin to view his or her country and his or her self away from the home environment and the influences of personal cultural bias (Holland, 2003). Through experiences abroad, students develop an appreciation and better understanding of their own cultures, and increase in self-reliance and self-confidence (Juhasz& Walker, 1987; Sowa, 2002). Experiences encountered by students during study abroad have a significant impact on the student's sense of self (Rabinowitz, 1994). Students that have studied abroad generally have increased self-confidence, self-esteem, and respect for others because they have been pushed outside of their comfort zones in experiencing new and different ways of living and different attitudes regarding daily life (Gray, Murdock, & Stebbins, 2002; Juhasz& Walker, 1987). They have been encouraged to become more reflective in their thinking (Sowa, 2002).

2.8 Higher Education System in India

India's higher education system is the third largest in the world[2], next to the United States and China. The main governing body at the tertiary level is the University Grants Commission, which enforces its standards, advises the government, and helps coordinate between the centre and the state. Accreditation for higher learning is overseen by 15 autonomous institutions established by the University Grants Commission (UGC).As per the latest 2011 Census; about 8.15 percentage (68 millions) of Indians are graduates, with Union Territories of Chandigarh and Delhi topping the list with 24.65 percentage and 22.56percentage of their population being graduates respectively. Indian higher education system has expanded at a fast pace by adding nearly 20, 000 colleges and more than 8 million students in a decade from 2000-01 to 2010-11. As of 2016, India has 799 universities, with a break up of 44 central universities, 540 state universities, 122 deemed universities, 90 private universities, 5 institutions established and functioning under the State Act, and 75 Institutes of National Importance which include AIIMS, IIT's and NIT's among others. Other institutions include 39, 071 colleges as

Government Degree Colleges and Private Degree Colleges, including 1800 exclusive women's colleges, functioning under these universities and institutions as reported by the UGC in 2016. Colleges may be Autonomous, i.e. empowered to examine their own degrees, up to PhD level in some cases, or non-autonomous, in which case their examinations are under the supervision of the university to which they are affiliated; in either case, however, degrees are awarded in the name of the university rather than the college.

The emphasis in the tertiary level of education lies on science and technology. Indian educational institutions by 2004 consisted of a large number of technology institutes. Distance learning and open education is also a feature of the Indian higher education system, and is looked after by the Distance Education Council. Indira Gandhi National Open University is the largest university in the world by number of students, having approximately 3.5 million students across the globe.

Some institutions of India, such as the Indian Institutes of Technology (IITs), National Institute of Technology (NITs), Indian Institute of Science, Indian Institute of Science Education and Research (IISERs), Indian Institutes of Information Technology (IIITs), Indian Institutes of Management (IIMs), International Institute of Information Technology (IIIT), University of Mumbai and Jawaharlal Nehru University have been globally acclaimed for their standard of education. The IITs enroll about 8000 students annually and the alumni have contributed to both the growth of the private sector and the public sectors of India. However, India still lacks internationally behind universities such as Harvard, Cambridge, and Oxford.

The National Policy on Education-1986, revised in1992 (NPE) states that in Higher Education in general and Technical Education in particular, steps will be taken to facilitate inter-regional mobility by providing equal access to every Indian of requisite merit regardless of his origins. As a result there is positive growth in respect of higher education institutions as well as enrolments.

Table 15.4: Overview Growth of Higher Education System

Name of Institutions/Enrolment	*2010-11*	*2011-12*	*2012-13*	*2014-15*
Universities	621	642	665	760
Colleges	32974	34852	35829	38498
Institutions	11095	11126	11443	13707
Enrolment (in lakh)	275	292	296	316
Enrolment in Distant mode (in lakh)	33.14	3415	35.25	38.12

Source – Various UGC Annual Reports

Figures / estimation based on AISHE & UGC back years data

AICTE Annual Report 2011-12// Statistics of Higher and Technical Education

The above Table 15.4 shows that there is good growth in Universities, Colleges and Institutions.The enrolment between 2010-11 and 2014-15 indicates that Higher Education system is on righttrack. There is phenomenal growth of 5524 colleges during the period of 2010-11 and 2014-15. During the same time enrolment figures were increased by 41 lakh.

Indian higher education is in need of radical reforms. A focus on enforcing higher standards of transparency, strengthening of the vocational and doctoral education pipeline, and professionalisation of the sector through stronger institutional responsibility would help in reprioritizing efforts and working around the complexities.The rise of IT sector and engineering education in India has boxed students into linear path without giving them a chance to explore and discover their passions. Concerted and collaborative efforts are needed in broaden student choices through liberal arts education.

2.9 Globalisation and Its Impact on Higher Education in India

Globalisation has a multidimensional impact on the system of higher education in India[3]. It has underlined the need for reforms in the educational system with particular reference to the wider utilisation of information technology, giving productivity dimension to education and emphasis on its research and development activities because education is an important investment in building human capital. The higher education system in India suffers from acute paucity of funds, lack of autonomy, burden of affiliation. On the other hand the effect of globalisation on education brings rapid developments in technology, communication and knowledge economy.

2.9.1. Globalisation and economic reforms in India have yielded significant changes in the role of state and restructuring of social welfares education, employment, agriculture and health system. In higher education it was always the monopoly of middle class and elite groups of the society.

2.9.2. Privatisation of higher education- There has been an increasing trend towards privatisation of higher education in India. The quality and content of the education are industry oriented due to privatisation. In this day age of globalisation and privatisation with competition and to meet the new challenges of the 21st century higher education should be radically transformed. India is required to set up a chain of educational institutions which are accredited, globally acceptable. We should also keep in mind that quality can come only from quality teachers and quality infrastructure, under quality leadership.

2.9.3. Women education- Women literacy rate has grown over the three decades. Women education plays a very important role in the overall development of the country and improving the quality of life at home and outside.

2.9.4. Commercialisation- Impact of globalisation is commercialisation of higher education due to which self financing courses have been introduced which has deprived many from getting higher education especially in countries like India where illiteracy still prevails and education is a dream to many. The existing policy of globalisation of higher education is motivated by profits rather than social justice or the policy of the government. Its goals therefore are to meet the demands of the market.

2.9.5. Teacher education- In the global society today the aspects of rapid change, lifelong learning, flexible routes of learning and the use of technology have a major impact on all the areas of teacher education. Major steps to be taken qualitative expansion, value based, competency based and ICT based teaching learning.

2.9.6. Knowledge- The impact of globalisation on higher education is the transition to a knowledge society towards universities as knowledge-centres.

2.9.7. Skill- Higher education is seeking ways to meet the demands and challenges put forth by globalisation. Higher education today is expected to produce skilled and trained workforce who can compete in this global market.

2.9.8. Education policies- Globalisation also impact the education policies on higher education in India. In the last two decades Indian government has formed various committees, commission and also different kinds of economic bodies came to existence like NAAC.

2.9.9. Entry of Foreign Universities- Foreign Direct Investment (FDI) is important tool of globalisation. As government lack of funds FDI is allowed into higher education. The foreign universities is expected to bring the quality infrastructure in teaching, research as well as physical infrastructure This will attract large scale foreign investments into India and also to an extent reverse brain drain. However, the government will have to create a level playing field for all institutions and also ensure that other factors are considered. Their entry should also increase the qualities in research areas and so on, rather than focus on undergraduate programs.

2.9.10. Communication- The effects of globalisation on education bring rapid developments in technology and communications. It changes the role of students and teachers and producing a shift in society from industrialisation towards an information-based society.

2.9.11. E-learning- People with disability get benefit from globalisation only if they endowed with knowledge, skills, capabilities and rights needed to pursue their basic livelihoods. The introduction of technology into the classroom is changing the nature of delivering education to students is gradually giving way to a new form of electronic literacy, more programs and education materials are made available in electronic form, teachers are preparing materials in electronic form; and students are generating papers, assignments and projects in electronic form. Video projection screens, books with storage device servers and CD rooms as well as the emergence of on-line digital libraries are now replacing blackboards. Even exams and grades are gradually becoming available through electronic means and notebooks are starting to give way to laptops. Also, students can be examined through computer managed learning systems and do tutorial exercises on a computer rather than in a classroom.

2.9.12 Impact of Globalisation on Higher Education- Education sector is undergoing constant changes under the effects of globalisation[4]. Rapid developments in technology and communications are seen. Changes in school systems across the world ideas, values and knowledge are changing the roles of students and teachers, and producing a shift in society from industrialised to an information-based society. It effect is reflected on culture and brings about a new form of cultural imperialism. The rise of a global society, driven by technology and communication developments are shaping children, into global citizens "Education is becoming a lifelong learning and training process, developing transferable skills and knowledge that can be applied to competitive markets where knowledge and information is being traded as a commodity.

3. Tamil Nadu State: Ensuring Quality of Higher Education

The Gross Enrolment Ratio (GER) is a statistical measure used in the education sector to determine the number of students enrolled in school at different grade levels (like elementary, middle and high school) and examine it to analyze the ratio of the number of students who live in that country to those who qualify for the particular grade level.The GER at national level is 13percentage and for Tamil Nadu it is higher at 18percentage. The aim of TN Govt. is to make it as 21percentage by 2017 and 25percentage by 2025[5].These objectives are achieved through: Concrete Road map through '*Vision 2023, 12th Five Year Plan, Policies and Announcements'*.

3.1 Twelfth 5-Year Plan Objectives (Technical and Professional Education)

- Improving physical infrastructure
- Strengthening quality of education
- Strengthening training and quality of faculty
- Promoting research orientation
- Strengthening finance of higher education institutions.
- Improving ICT infrastructure
- Bringing governance reforms

3.2 Study Abroad Programme in Tamil Nadu

It is a scheme undertaken during the Year 2012-13. The Hon'ble Chief Minister's pioneering 'Study Abroad Programme' for academically bright but economically deprived post–graduate students studying in Government Arts and Science Colleges, to study one semester overseas, is being carried out through Tamil Nadu State Council for Higher Education[6]. The Study Abroad programme funded by the Tamil Nadu State Council for Higher Education (TANSCHE), Department of Higher Education, Government of Tamil Nadu (India). In the first phase, a Memorandum of Understanding was signed between TANSCHE and British Council in the presence of the Hon'ble Chief Ministerof Tamil Nadu to send 25 students to study their third semester and five teachers to study special courses in select universities in the United Kingdom. 25 students and five faculty members have been selected through a rigorous process based on criteria, specially framed by an expert selection committee. Edge Hill University, Birmingham University, Nottingham University and two Colleges – Royal Halloway College and King's College affiliated to London University have been selected for this purpose. Students and faculty members will study in United Kingdom between September 2013 and January 2014. The entire expenditure for the Study Abroad Scheme is borne by the State Government @ Rs.15 lakhs per student / faculty candidate.

3.3 Beneficiaries of Study Abroad Programme: Poor Students

There are complaints now that many colleges do not show keen interest in the Tamil Nadu Government scheme for economically weaker students[7]. In this scheme the poor students are sent to foreign countries to pursue higher studies. The professors state that since many colleges do not show keen interest in this programme, the poor students miss this rare opportunity. The last date for the year 2015-2016 to enrol in this scheme is over but more than 40 Government Colleges have not submitted the applications. The study abroad programme is a fully funded scheme of Tamil Nadu State Government. It is a unique programme to support students from Government Colleges and Universities especially from the lower economic and social background from across Tamil Nadu to study one semester in the UK. Tamil Nadu government will fund 25 postgraduate students in Physical, Natural Sciences, Social Sciences, Humanities, Business, Computer Sciences, IT, Management from public funded state universities to spend one semester at an UK university starting September 2015. In addition, Tamil Nadu Government will also fund 5 faculty members to spend a semester in the UK University either doing a CPD or faculty development programme or a short research project.

This programme is undertaken by The Higher Education sector of Tamil Nadu. The circular will be sent to all government colleges during the month of March. The colleges should select the best student and send his application to Tamil Nadu Higher Education department. The selected students will be sent to British Council to undergo IELTS training. If they are selected they will be sent to UK for further studies. So far 50 poor students and 10 professors have been benefited under this program.

3.4 Government of India:Subsidy on Educational Loan for Overseas Studies

The Ministry of Minority Affairs is implementing a scheme, 'PadhoPardesh' to provide Interest Subsidy on Educational Loans for overseas studies for students belonging to minority communities' from the current year (2014-15)[8]. Under this scheme, interest subsidy is awarded to pursue approved courses of studies abroad at Master's and Ph.D. levels with the objective to provide minority students better opportunities for higher education and enhance their employability. The interest subsidy is provided for the period of moratorium (course period, plus one year or six months after getting job, which ever is earlier). To be eligible, students should have availed loan under the Education Loan Scheme of the Indian Banks Association (IBA) and the annual family income should not exceed Rs. 5.00 lakh. State/UT-wise No. of applications received under PadhoPardesh-Interest Subsidy on Educational Loans for overseas studies during the last three years and the current year-2014-15. All over the 25 states number of applications received was 813. The highest number of claim received from the state of Kerala 325, and from Tamil Nadu 85. Fund allotted for the year 2014-15 was Rs. 4 Crore and released for the purpose was Rs. 3.50 Crore as on 27/02/2015. Number of students benefited was 573.

3.5 NSDL e- Governance Infrastructure Limited

National Securities Depository Limited (NSDL) is an Indian central securities depository based in Mumbai. It was established on 8 November 1996 as the first electronic securities depository in India with national coverage based on a suggestion by a national institution responsible for the economic development of India.[9] Vidya Lakshmi is a first of its kind portal for students seeking Education Loan. This portal has been developed under the guidance of Department of Financial Services, (Ministry of Finance), Department of Higher Education (Ministry of Human Resource Development) and Indian Banks Association (IBA).The portal has been developed and being maintained by NSDL e- Governance Infrastructure Limited. Students can view, apply and track the education loan applications to banks anytime, anywhere by accessing the portal. The portal also provides linkages to National Scholarship Portal.

3.6 The Salient features of the scheme are as under:

- The scheme envisages loans up to Rs.7.5 lakh for studies in India and up to Rs. 15 lakh for studies abroad.
- For loans up to Rs. 4 lakh no collateral or margin is required and the interest rate is not to exceed the Prime Lending Rates (PLR). For loans above Rs. 4 lakh the interest rate will not exceed PLR plus 1 percent.

- The loans are to be repaid over a period of 5 to 7 years with provision of grace period of one year after completion of studies
- Repayment of an education loan is deductible under section 80E of the Income Tax Act.

Equitable Access to quality higher education has been a concern of the University Grants Commission[10]. To this purpose the Commission, besides encouraging colleges and universities to provide for liberal financial support to the meritorious but needy students, has also been instrumental in educational loan scheme. The Reserve Bank of India (RBI) has issued guidelines in this regard to all commercial banks. A large number of banks have already launched educational loan schemes. Since the rules, regulations, eligibility conditions, repayments and interests rates etc are revised by the banks from time to time in keeping pace with the changing capital market conditions, students and parents are advised to thoroughly check the terms and conditions of educational loan scheme on offer at the time of application.

3.7 Feedback of Study Abroad Programme

A sample of feedback obtained from a student as well as a faculty who were selected under this scheme from Tamil Nadu[11].

Ms SangeethaManokaran, Student of Bharathi Women's College, Chennai has been selected for the Study Abroad Programme to do her third semester of Masters degree in Mathematics at the Royal Holloway University of London. She expressed her views as, "I will utilize this golden opportunity optimally to build my Career. The papers that I'm going to study in UK are completely application Oriented. So, I'm looking forward to know the applications of mathematics. I believe that it will expand my employability prospects and I'm expecting a great cultural exchange too. In future, I will pursue research work in papers which I learn in UK and surely I will contribute my best to the society's welfare. Thanking our Honourable CM and other officials for everything".

Dr. T. Jayasudha, Associate Professor of English, Bharathi Women's College, Chennai, who has been selected under this scheme, expressed that the Study Abroad Programme has been a historical milestone in the history of higher education in India with respect to equity, affordability and accessibility to the socio-economically disadvantaged students of government colleges. The initiative by the Honourable Chief Minister is not only going to change the next generation and their future prospects, but also provide opportunities for faculty members to upgrade their professional skills on par with the international academicians and enable to launch Tamil Nadu into the global league. As an awardee of the fellowship, it has provided me an opportunity to collaborate with peers from Nottingham and develop suitable strategies for implementation in the government college environment. Adaptation and using international benchmarking (Common European Framework of Reference) to design, develop and produce language teaching/learning material are the prime objective of the research work that I propose to carry out during my stay there. There has been a demand-supply mismatch with regard to employability vs jobs ratio. The need to tailor the courses to cater to the immediate professional needs of the learners is imperative. Peer observation and the application of theoretical models in real classroom teaching in native speaker's contexts would throw light on glocalising the theory for the local teaching contexts to reap the expected results. The TANSCHE-BC interface has been a platform to empower me to use the state-of-the-art techniques and technology for language teaching. I'm looking forward to a rewarding experience which will give me enough strategies to share through workshops as a trainer once I'm back in India. I heartily thank the Tamil Nadu government for launching this innovative project and opening it to faculty members too.

4. Analysis

Using time series data on Gross Enrolment Ratio (GER) and Public expenditure on Education for India correlation and regression analysis are conducted to test the objectives. The results are discussed below.

4.1 An analysis of Regression

The Regression Model is, $Y= \beta_0 + \beta_1 X + U$

Where Y= Dependent Variable

X= Independent Variable

β_0= intercept

$\beta_{1=}$ slope, and

U= random error term.

4.2 Assumption of the Model

Linear regression assumes thatthe relationship between two variables is linear, and the residuals (defined as Actual - predicted) are normally distributed.

4.3 Interpretation of Regression line

The output shows (table 15.7) the parameters of β_0 and β_1 respectively. Hence the model is rewritten as $Y_{GER} = 71.01208 + 14.1226\ X_{PE} + U$.

Where $Y_{GER=}$ GER in Higher Education of All Level of Students (in Lakhs)

X_{PE} = Public Expenditure on Education as % of GDP

β_0= 71.01208, and

$\beta_{1=14.12126}$

Therefore, one can predict GER in Higher Education of All Level of Students (in Lakhs) given Public Expenditure on Education as % of GDP using this linear function between the two variables. Furthermore, under the heading "parameter estimates" are columns labeled "standard error", "t value," and "Pr> |t|" (Table 15.7). The t values and the associated p-value test the hypothesis that the parameter is 0.0447. In this case the p-value is 0.0270; therefore we can conclude that the Public Expenditure on Education as % of GDP has a significant linear effect on GER in Higher Education of All Level of Students (in Lakhs).

Table 15.5: Analysis of Variance

Source	*DF*	*Sum of Squares*	*Mean Square*	*F Value*	*Pr > F*
Model	1	35251	35251	6.21	0.0270
Error	13	73839	5679.94452		
Corrected Total	14	109090			

Table 15.6: R-Square Value

Root MSE	75.36541	R-Square	0.3231
Dependent Mean	134.20000	Adj R-Sq	0.2711
Coeff .Var.	56.15902		

Table 15.7: Parameter Estimates

Variable	*DF*	*Parameter Estimate*	*Standard Error*	*t Value*	*Pr > |t|*
Intercept	1	71.01208	31.96875	2.22	0.0447
Public Expenditure on Education as % of GDP	1	14.12126	5.66838	2.49	0.0270

4.4 Checking assumptions

Linear regression assumes thatthe relationship between two variables is linear, and the residuals (defined as Actual - predicted) are normally distributed. These can be check with scatter plot and residual plot (Fig. 1 and Fig. 2) as shown below.

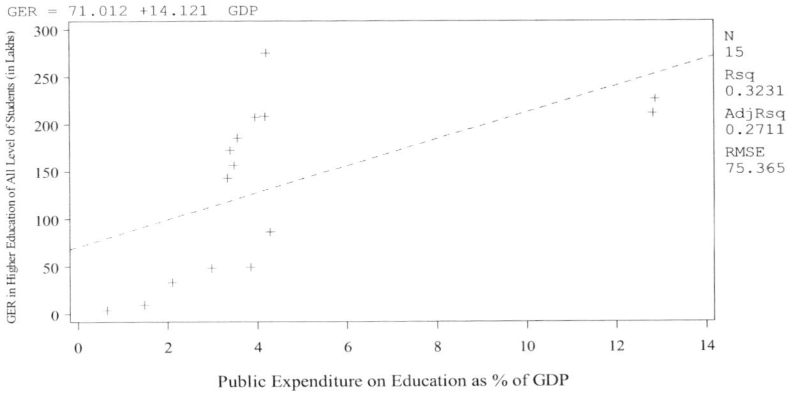

Figure 15.1: Budgeted Expenditure on Education by Education Departments and other Departments (Revenue + Capital + Loan and Advances) Regression - GDP ON GER and residual plots

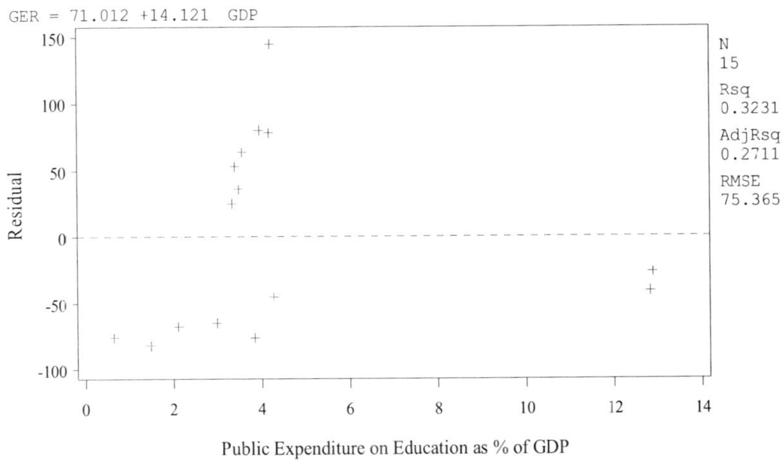

Figure 15.2: Budgeted Expenditure on Education by Education Departments and other Departments (Revenue + Capital + Loan and Advances) Regression - GDP ON GER and residual plots

4.5 An analysis of the correlation

Correlation analysis is a method of statistical evaluation used to study the strength of a relationship between two, numerically measured, continuous variables (e.g. height and weight). This particular type of analysis is useful when a researcher wants to establish if there are possible connections between variables. It is often misunderstood that correlation analysis determines cause and effect; however, this is not the case because other variables that are not present in the research may have impacted on the results.If correlation is found between two variables it means that when there is a systematic change in one variable, there is also a systematic change in the other; the variables alter together over a certain period of time. Depending upon numerical value the correlation said to be either positive or negative. Correlation coefficient value ranges between +1 and -1. The zero value indicates the no correlation among variables.

Table 15.8

Simple Statistics						
Variable	*N*	*Mean*	*StdDev*	*Sum*	*Minimum*	*Maximum*
GER in Higher Education of All Level of Students (in Lakhs)	15	134.20	88.27	2013	4.00	275.00
Public Expenditure on Education as % of GDP	15	4.47	3.55	67.12	0.64	12.87

Table 15.9

Pearson Correlation Coefficients, N = 15 Prob > |r| under H0: Rho=0		
	GER in Higher Education of All Level of Students (in Lakhs)	***Public Expenditure on Education as % of GDP***
GER in Higher Education of All Level of Students (in Lakhs)	1.0000	0.5685 0.0270
Public Expenditure on Education as % of GDP	0.5685 0.0270	1.0000

4.6 Interpretation of the correlation

Table 15.8 and Table 15.9 are given some descriptive statistics on the variables in the variable list along with acorrelation matrix. The correlation is the top number and the p-value is the second number. In this data, "GER in Higher Education of All Level of Students (in Lakhs)" and"Public Expenditure on Education as % of GDP" is moderately correlated with a correlation 0.5685 (with a pvalueof 0.0270). The small p-value (at a significant level of 0.05) suggests the correlation is significant. The matrix is symmetric along the diagonal line.

5. Conclusion

Globalisation is expected to have a positive influence on the volume, quality and spread of knowledge through increased interaction among the various states. The world is becoming increasingly globalised, and international experience is one of the most essential components of highereducation in the 21 century. The global number of students who study abroad continues to rise with an annual increase of 10%. There were almost 5million international students in 2014. The Organisation for Economic Co-operation and Development (OECD) has projected that, with demographic changes, the international student population is likely to reach 8 million by 2025. The United States, the United Kingdom, Germany, France, and Australia are the most popular host countries for internationalstudents. Half of all international students study in these five countries.This paper concludes that the higher education under globalisation has a positive impact. In Tamil Nadue under the scheme of 'Study Aboard Programme'higher education is globalised in recent past. And this paper found that it has a positive impact on beneficiaries.

Reference

1. American Association to Advance Collegiate Schools of Business. (2012). AACSB, Tracking the Trends in Globalisation, *BizEd.*
2. Bhawya Sachdeva Mukhi, Dr. Robin Anand, International Journal of Engineering Technology, Management and Applied Sciences www.ijetmas.com November 2015, Volume 3, Special Issue, ISSN 2349-4476 218.
3. Black, H. Tyrone, and David L. Duhon. (2006). Assessing the Impact of Business Study Abroad Programs on Cultural Awareness and Personal Development, *Journal of Education for Business,* 81 (3).
4. Carlson, Jerry S. & Widaman, Keith F. (2002). The Effects of Study Abroad During College on Attitudes toward Other Cultures. *International Journal of Intercultural Relations*, 12 (1).
5. Dwyer, Mary M. (2004). More is Better: The Impact of Study Abroad Program Duration. *Frontiers The Interdisciplinary Journal of Study Abroad.*
6. Gardner, Philip, Linda Gross, and Inge Steglitz. (2009). Translating Study Abroad Experiences for Workplace Competencies, *Peer Review,* 11 (4).
7. Higher Education Department; Policy Note 2013 – 2014; Demand No. 20; Government of Tamil Nadu 2013
8. Pramod Kumar Naik Dr. Globalisation and its Impact on Higher Education in India, International Journal of Humanities and Management Sciences (IJHMS) Volume 3, Issue 6 (2015) ISSN 2320–4044 (Online)
9. Policy Note: 2012-13, Higher Education Government of Tamil Nadu
10. Press Information Bureau, Government of India Ministry of Minority Affairs, March 2015
11. UGC Educational Loan (2017)
12. https://nsdl.co.in/about/milestone.php
13. https://www.britishcouncil.in/tamil-nadu-study-abroad-programme
14. https://www.studyabroad.com/worldwide#jumpToListings 1/10
15. https://en.wikipedia.org/wiki/Higher_education_in_India
16. http://www.livechennai.com/detailnews.asp?newsid=18374

Notes

1. https://www.studyabroad.com/worldwide#jumpToListings 1/10.
2. https://en.wikipedia.org/wiki/Higher_education_in_India.
3. Dr. Pramod Kumar Naik, Globalisation and its Impact on Higher Education in India, International Journal of Humanities and Management Sciences (IJHMS) Volume 3, Issue 6 (2015) ISSN 2320–4044 (Online)
4. Bhawya Sachdeva Mukhi, Dr. Robin Anand, International Journal of Engineering Technology, Management and Applied Sciences www.ijetmas.com November 2015, Volume3, Special Issue, ISSN 2349-4476 218.
5. Policy Note: 2012-13, Higher Education Government of Tamil Nadu.
6. Higher Education Department; Policy Note 2013 – 2014; Demand No. 20; Government of Tamil Nadu 2013.
7. http://www.livechennai.com/detailnews.asp?newsid=18374
8. Press Information Bureau Government of India Ministry of Minority Affairs, March 2015.
9. https://nsdl.co.in/about/milestone.php
10. UGC Educational Loan (2017).
11. https://www.britishcouncil.in/tamil-nadu-study-abroad-programme

Chapter - 16

Gender Inequality in India after a quarter century of Globalisation

Dr. Shobana Karthikeyan

Abstract

Globalisation has impacted everyone's lives. The shrinkage of time and distance has delivered different results to different stakeholders. There may be huge differences in the effects of globalisation to developed countries as opposed to developing countries. Similarly men and women need not necessarily gain equally from globalisation. This study investigates the payoffs to Indian women from 25 years of globalisation. This study looks at education-related changes, employment-related changes and few social issues. Results show that the globalisation has delivered a mixed bag of results to Indian women. While on the one hand, the literacy levels of women has gone up, it can be noticed that women only pursue selective courses. Courses like engineering, law, management etc are chosen by the men with a notable exception of humanities and medicine. The proportion of the working age women has gone down from 34.8 in 1990 to 26.8 in 2015. This could probably be attributed to the increasing time both urban and rural women spend on domestic activities. Also the percentage of seats held by women in the parliament has slowly and marginally increased over the years. India is still home to huge number of serious atrocities against women. While India has taken few steps in the positive direction, India has a long road to be travelled in the area of gender inequality.

Introduction

Globalisation has altered various aspects of people's everyday lives. The shrinkage of time and distance has brought about rapid unrecognizable changes to the economic landscape such as making available a whole new platter of job opportunities in new sectors, quicker and more efficient means of transportation, cross-national migration of people in search of better jobs and life-styles, the proliferation of electronic gadgets and other devices redefining the ways in which people communicate and commute and the ways businesses and economies are organised and operated. The Indian economy embraced liberalisation in 1991 with a wide set of reforms, thereby changing the economic landscape of the nation opening up the economy to a new world of opportunities.

Presently India has presently completed a little over quarter century of being a part of the globalised world. The economic consequences of the Indian globalisation experience can be summarised as being quite favourable. Since 1991, the Indian GDP has more than quadrupled, and the foreign exchange reserves has gone up by about 330 times. In the last two decades, India has halved the share of its population living in poverty and the overall literacy has gone up from 52.2% in 1991 to 74.4% in 2011 (Census of India, 2011, a). While there are many overall positive highlights of globalisation, it is equally important to examine if the benefits of globalisation have reached the entire population, i.e., all sections of people in the economy, or if they have been limited to a chosen few beneficiaries.

Of specific interest to the author is the study of the effect of globalisation on Indian women. After two and a half decades of globalisation, it is important to understand whether there have been any positive payoffs for Indian women or not. Have Indian women been able to capitalize on this huge opportunity which hitherto did not exist? Or have they been kept out of the race due to the traditional power dynamics in Indian families that has held Indian women captive within their households? A very recent report, the World Economic Forum's (WEF) Global Gender Gap Index places India at the 108th spot, behind neighbouring countries such as China and Bangladesh. A few of the major reasons for this ranking is due to the very low participation of women in the economy, high wage differentials and the high proportion of unpaid household work that is done by women. The WEF ranking of India, in a way, serves as a wake-up for us to look at gender inequality issues with greater seriousness.

This research paper aims to understand the socio-economic status of Indian women in the country. In order to do that the researcher compares few key statistics across various time periods, viz, at the time of globalisation till the most recent data available for the same. This enables the researcher to draw conclusions about the present socio-economic status of Indian women and the pay-offs, if any to Indian women.

The paper is organised as follows. First, the author deals with the primary causes of gender inequality in the economy. This section deals with a short explanation on how gender inequality, which starts in the social sphere gathers momentum and ultimately results in economic negative outcomes. The second section of the paper presents a brief review of extant literature. The third section deals with how certain specific statistics related to women have behaved in the past two and a half decades post globalisation. Published statistics from 1991 to the most recent time period is used in studying three important changes – education-related, employment-related changes that have taken place and few social issues of the Indian society. The final section deals with the conclusion of the study and provides directions for future research in this area.

Manifestation of Gender Inequality in the Economy

Gender inequality manifests in three levels in the economy. Gender inequality manifests much before the girl child is actually born. Inequality starts right at the point where families and societies traditionally prefer the male child to the female child. Prolonged such preferences for the male child, practices such as female foeticide and infanticide – practices still rampant across the country leads to a very unhealthy sex ratio skews the natural sex ratio of the country. Added to this is the problem of unequal gender roles and relations (Bradshaw and Castellino, 2013) which excludes women from gaining access to basic services such as healthcare, education, access to resources such as land, credit and business services. This lack of exposure to education and any other empowerment tools snowballs into negative economic outcomes such as low labour market participation, job segregation, wage inequality, besides others (UNCTAD, 2004). This process of excluding women from eventual economic freedom is depicted in Fig. 16.1.

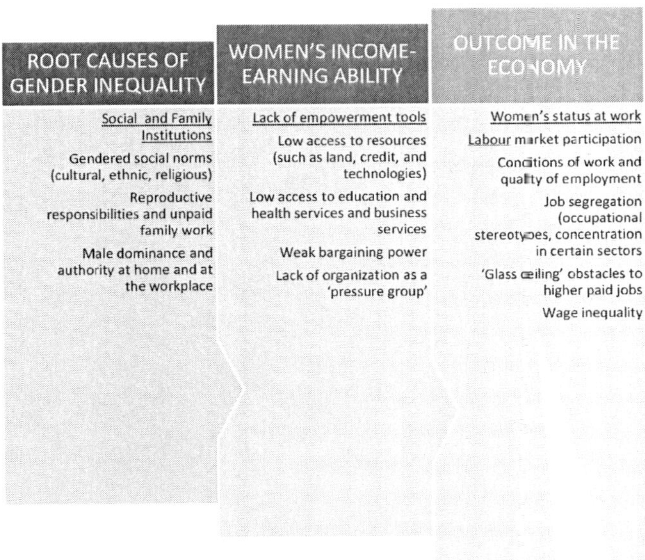

Figure 16.1. Schematic representation of gender inequality in the economy - Adapted from UNCTAD (2004)

Brief Review of Literature

The intrinsic value of gender equality cannot be contested. Extant research has proven that gender inequality acts as a brake on economic development and growth of a nation. There is evidence that there are significant gains in economic growth (Loko and Diouf, 2009; Lagarde, 2016). In developing countries, working women tend to invest more in the schooling of the children (Aguirre et al, 2012; Miller, 2008). Bridging of gender inequality in education has positive effects on employment. Chen (2004) ascertains this by the understanding the effect of average years of schooling on gender equality in education. Also literacy heavily contributes to the variability of female labour force participation within a country (Ogawa and Akter, 2007; World Bank, 2010; Gallaway and Bernasek, 2004). Women in many developing countries have a strong role to play in the creation and preservation of traditional and community knowledge and folklore (UNCTAD, 2004). Changes in education and literacy contribute to the explanation of variation in female labor force participation within a country.

This study attempts to shed light on changes (both positive and negative) that have occurred to few important gender inequality variables that are directly linked to women wellbeing, that occurred on account of globalisation of the economy. The study first looks into the Gender Development Index and Gender Inequality Index. Educational changes are measured by average years of schooling, literacy rates in India, gender-distribution of students across both general and technical/professional courses, percentage of students who dropped

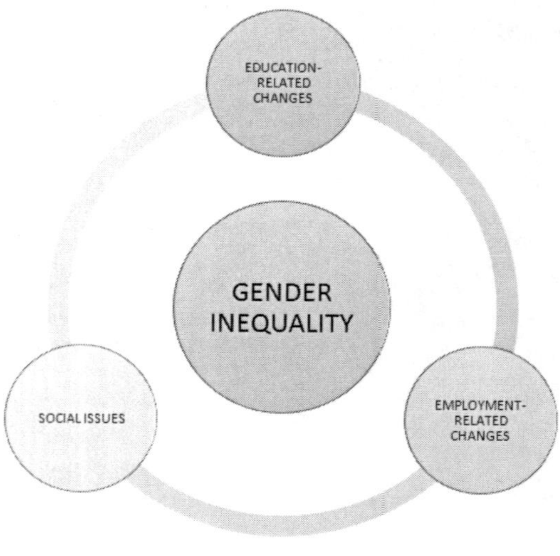

Figure 16.2. Gender Inequality in India

outs/discontinued education, reasons for dropping out/discontinuance, reasons for never-enrolment and levels of computer literacy. Employment-related changes are measured in terms of labour force participation rate, percentage of seats held by women in the parliament. Incidences of violence against women in the Indian society are investigated to provide a social perspective on the status of Indian women in the society. The focus of this research is presented in Figure 16.2.

Measures of Gender Inequality

The Gender Development Index (GDI) is an important measure of gender inequality It is a direct measure of gender gap showing the female HDI as a percentage of the male HDI. The GDI shows how much women are lagging behind their male counterparts on the three dimensions of health, knowledge and living standards and by how much women need to catch up within each dimension of human development. The GDI is useful for understanding the real gender gap in human development achievements. The GDI stands at .819 in 2015 as against the .746 in the year 2000.

The Gender Inequality Index (GII) is another index for measurement of gender disparity. According to United Nations Development Programme (UNDP), this GII is a composite measure to quantify the loss of achievement within a country due to gender inequality. It uses three dimensions to measure opportunity cost: reproductive health, empowerment, and labor market participation. The GII is interpreted as a percentage and indicates the percentage of potential human development lost due to gender inequality. The GII stood at .53 for 2015 indicating a 53% loss in potential human development due to gender inequality. This shows some marginal but steady improvement in the Gender Inequality from .59 in 2010 to .53 in 2015.

Education-related changes

Gender inequality, which is a direct consequence of underinvestment in female education not only inhibits their ability to control their fertility, but also excludes women from participation in the job market thereby reducing the bargaining power of women within households and at work. While on the other hand, better gender equality brings about better children's well-being, making the future labour force more productive, thereby improving economic well-being of the nation in the long run.

Mean years of schooling (both men and women)

Data from 1990 shows that years of schooling for both men and women has improved. However, women outdo the men in number of years of schooling (UNDP, 2016). Till 2011, the average years of schooling of males was higher than the females. And this trend saw a reversal in 2012. Presently the average number of years a female spends in school is more than that of a male person.

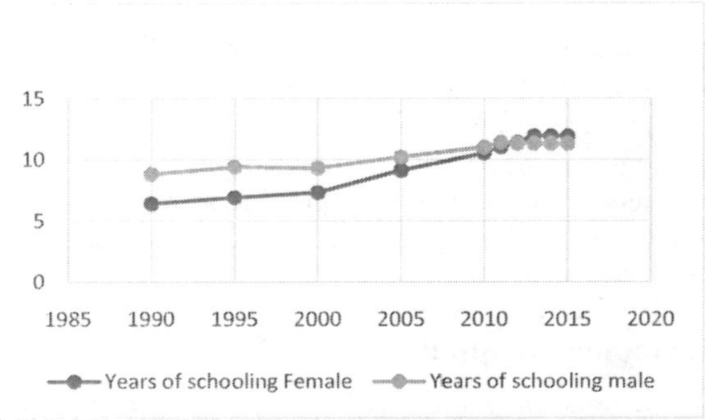

Source: HDR, United Nations Development Programme (UNDP), 2016.

Figure 16.3: Years of schooling (male and female).

Literacy rate

It can be seen from Figure 16.4 that in addition to overall literacy (both male and female) rates going up, female literacy rate has gone up from 39.29% in 1991 to 65.46% in 2011 (Census of India, 2011, a). While the numbers look encouraging at the outset, reports suggest that India's neighbours have outdone her in female literacy. While the first decade after globalisation witnessed a sudden jump in literacy levels, the next decade did not show any major advancement, while the momentum is just sustained. The proportion of women who completed five years of primary schooling in India and were literate was 48%, much less than 92% in Nepal, 74% in Pakistan and 54% in Bangladesh. Also, ranking countries by the earliest grade at which at least half of the women

Source: Census of India, (2011, a)

Figure 16.4: *Literacy Rates of Men and Women in India.*

are literate, ranks India in the 38th place among 51 developing countries (www.educationcommission.org). This means that there is more to do in the realm of female education in India.

Gender distribution of students in both general and technical/ professional courses

Gender distribution of students in both general and technical/professional courses is an important issue because it is a direct determinant of employability and earning potential. It can be seen that except in humanities, where the

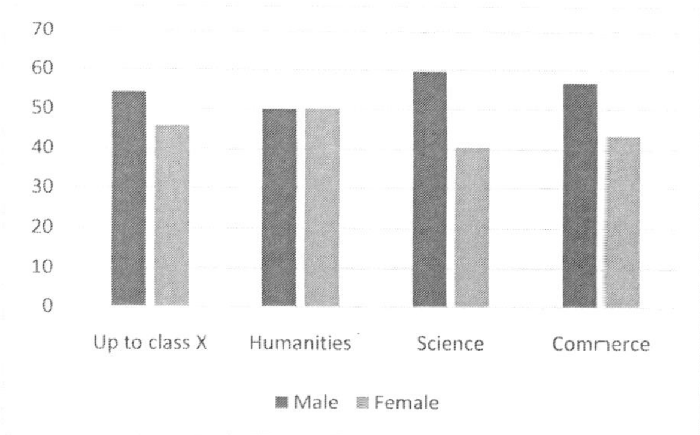

Source: NSSO, 71st round

Figure 16.5: Gender distribution of students (percentages) - general courses.

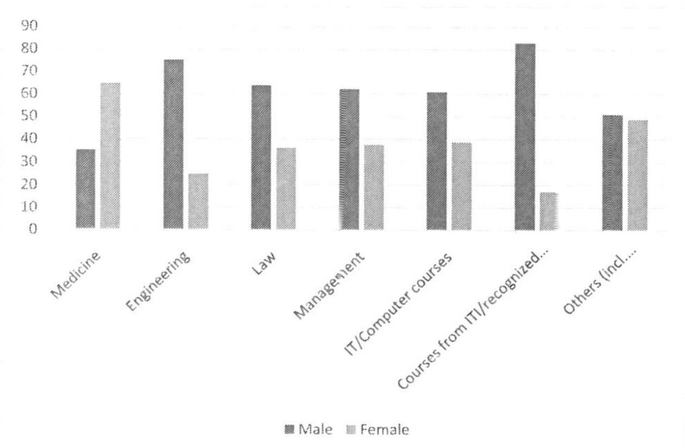

Source: NSSO, 71st round

Figure 16.6: Gender distribution of students (percentages)- technical/professional courses

distribution of women students is very marginally more and medicine, where women students are significantly in greater numbers, every other course, particularly IT, Engineering, Law, Management, etc has a greater concentration of male students (NSSO, 71st round). This directly affects the opportunities that may be available to women upon completion of the courses.

Percentage of dropout/discontinuance of education

In rural areas (Figures 16.7 and 16.8), percentage dropout/discontinuance of education is highest in the 5 to 15 age category followed by the 16-24 category.

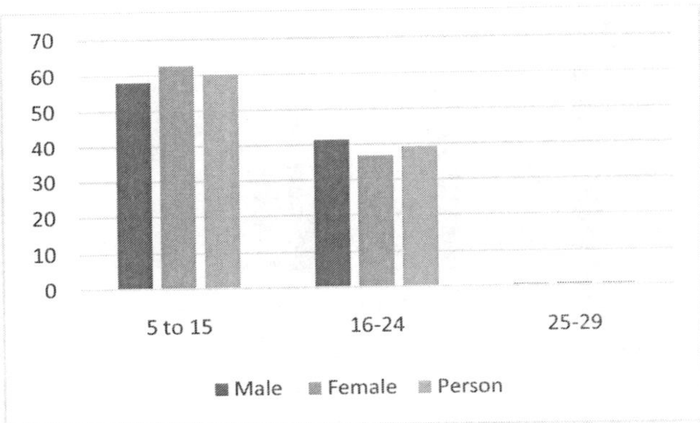

Source: NSSO, 71st round.

Figure 16.7: Percentage of persons (aged 5-29) who dropped out/discontinued in rural areas.

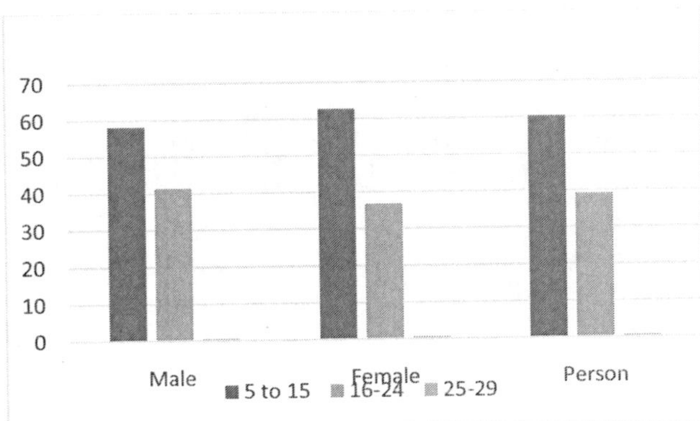

Source: NSSO, 71st round.

Figure 16.8: Percentage of persons (aged 5 - 29) who dropped out/discontinued in rural areas.

Dropout/discontinuance is present, but at very negligible levels in the 25-29 year category. The same trend is prevalent across female students too.

But, in the 5 to 15 age category, the drop-out seemed to be higher in females than males and in the 16-24 year category, more men discontinued/ dropped off than women. This could partially be due to financial pressures of contributing economically to their homes.

In sharp contrast to the rural statistics, urban dropout/discontinuance (Figures 16.9 and 16.10) is higher in the 16-24 age category as opposed to the 5-15 age category. Also, in the 5-15 age group, males are more likely to drop out while in the 16-24 age category, females are more likely to drop out.

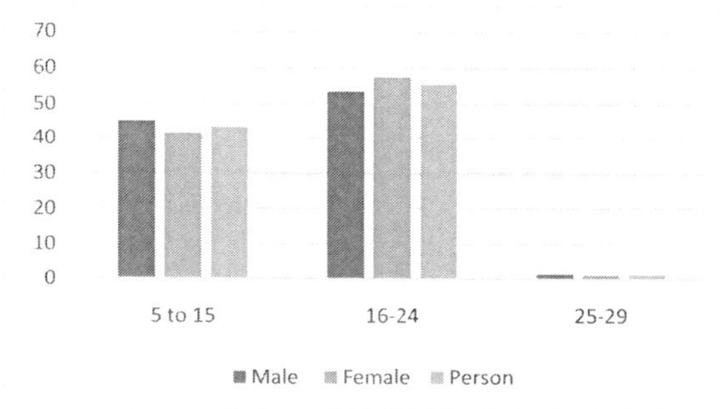

Source: NSSO, 71st round.

Figure 16.9: Percentage of persons (aged 5-29) who dropped out/discontinued in urban areas.

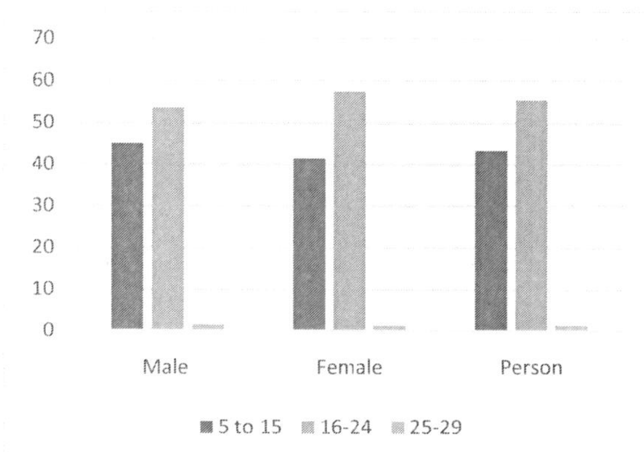

Source: NSSO, 71st round.

Figure 16.10: Percentage of persons (aged 5-29) who dropped out/discontinued in urban areas.

Reasons for dropping out/discontinuance (for persons aged 5 - 29 years) by reasons for dropping out/discontinuance (Per 1000)

The most important reason for discontinuance/dropping out of education is having to engage in economic activities (rural) and financial constraints (urban). In the case of female students, having to engage in domestic activities is the single most reason for having to drop out or discontinue. On the whole, the top reasons (summing rural and urban together) for discontinuance/dropping out are having to engage in economic activities in the case of boys and having to engage in domestic work, in the case of women. Not interested in education and financial constraints also emerge as fairly important reasons for both sexes.

Table 16.1

Major reasons for discontinuance/dropping out of education	*Rural*		*Urban*		*Rural + Urban*	
	Male	*Female*	*Male*	*Female*	*Male*	*Female*
Not interested in education	251	162	208	143	238	156
Financial constraints	236	154	237	149	236	152
Engaged in domestic activities	59	329	24	231	48	297
Engaged in economic activities	299	39	336	69	310	49
School is far-off	6	42	2	18	5	34
Unable to cope up with studies	55	51	53	36	54	46
Completed desired level/class	45	43	83	113	57	65
Marriage		124		171		139
Other reasons	48	57	58	70	51	62
All	1000	1000	1000	1000	1000	1000

Source: NSSO, 71st round.

Never enrolment

The most important reason for never-enrolment for both males and females in rural areas is not being interested in education. Among urban males and females, financial constraints is the primary determinant of never-enrolment followed closely by non-interest in education. Overall, other reasons such as timing of the educational institution not suitable, language/medium of instruction used unfamiliar, inadequate number of teachers, quality of teachers not satisfactory are also important reasons for never-enrolment. For girl students only, additionally, non-availability of female teacher, non-availability of girls's toilet were added to the list of other reasons.

Computer Literacy

Computer literacy is an essential ingredient for employability. The table shows that computer literacy is significantly lower in females as compared to males. Only in the youngest age group (14-29 years) in urban areas, the computer literacy levels are closer to that of males. Overall, urban levels of female computer literacy are better than that of rural levels.

Table 16.3

	Rural				*Urban*			
	Age group (years)							
Gender	*14-29*	*30-45*	*46-60*	*60 and above*	*14-29*	*30-45*	*46-60*	*60 and above*
Male	227	64	22	6	536	309	209	106
Female	135	19	5	1	438	173	87	28
Persons	183	41	14	3	489	243	148	68

Source: NSSO, 71st round.

Therefore, lack of education is an important reason why girl children as forced into marriage. The older the girl gets, the greater is the dowry that is demanded. So, it made economic sense to have the girls married off at a young age. A serious consequence of early marriages of girls was a prolonged child-bearing years leading to many children, again leading to population explosion, lack of employability, lack of financial independence and poverty.

Employment-related
Domestic duties

Females who attend to domestic duties as a percentage of all females in India is shown in the table (ILO, 2014). As we already saw in Table 16.1 that the most important reason for girls to discontinue or drop out of education is having to participate in domestic work. Work done at home is often unaccounted, yields women no income and prevents them from joining the organised workforce. This also coincides perfectly with the drop in participation in the labour force as shown in Figure 16.11.

Table 16.4

Year	*Rural females*	*Urban females*
1993-94	29.1	41.7
1999-2000	29.2	43.3
2004-05	27.2	42.8
2009-10	34.7	46.5
2011-12	35.3	46.1

Source: ILO, 2014.

Proportion of the working-age population (ages 15 and older)

India has one of the lowest Female Labor Force Participation (FLFP) rate, measured as the share of women that are employed or seeking work as a share of the working-age female population among emerging markets and developing countries. The proportion of the working age population (ages 15 and older) has been on a declining trend. It has gone down from 34.8 in 1990 to 26.8 in 2015. This is contrary to the popular assumption that globalisation provides greater employment opportunities to the workforce, including women. Probably it has generated opportunities, but the Indian women have probably failed to capitalize on this opportunity.

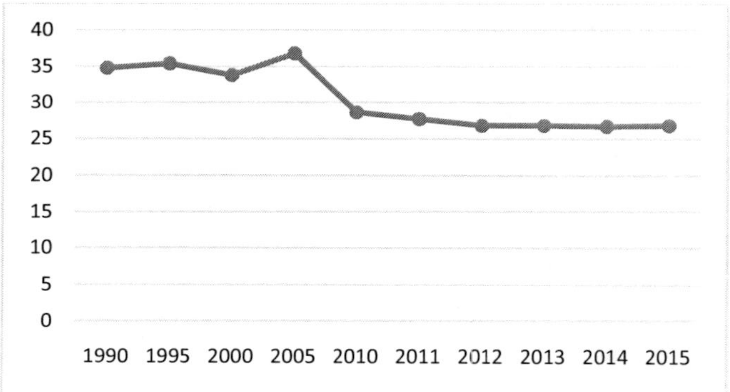

Source: UNDP, 2016.

Figure 16.11: Proportion of the Working-age Population (ages 15 and older)

Women in parliament

In addition to women participation in the workforce, it is also interesting to observe women participation in national political decision-making. This can be ascertained by the percentage of seats held by women in the parliament. The national average stands at around 12.2% which is just about 8% of the overall parliamentary seats. This is an area where women representation has to definitely improve.

Social issues

Crimes against women

According to the National Crime Records Bureau, Ministry of Home Affairs, the total number of crimes against women under Indian Penal Code is 347394 in the year 2015. The number comes to total of 7326099 cognizable crimes under the Indian Penal Code (IPL) and Special and Local Laws (SLL). Of all crimes against women, the cruelty by husband and relatives tops the

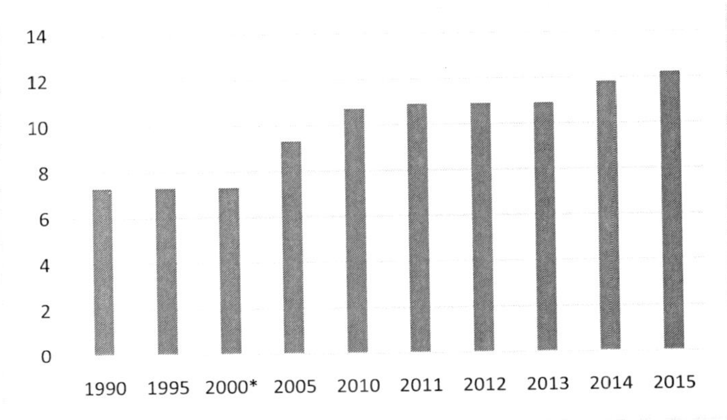

Source: UNDP, 2016.

Figure 16.12: % Seats held by Women in the Parliament.

list. This speaks of very skewed power relations against women in the domestic front. In general, this trend is very deleterious for gender inequality in the country.

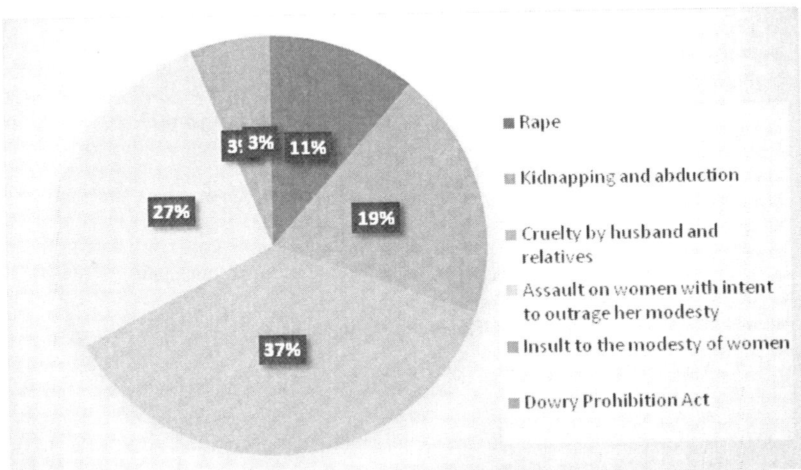

Source: National Crime Records Bureau, Ministry of Home Affairs, 2016.

Figure 16.13: Number of crimes against women in 2015.

While the education scenario seems to be positive for Indian women, the researcher would like to very briefly discuss few demographical changes in the lives of Indian women. The life expectancy of Indian women has gone up from 58.3 years in 1990 to 69.9 years in 2015. The fact that women in 2015 are likely to live almost upto age 70 is indicative of the fact that the general access to and quality of healthcare has definitely picked up. The maternal mortality rate has also dropped significantly from 556 deaths per 100, 000 live births to 174 deaths in 2015. However, it is a very unhealthy trend that the child sex ratio has dipped from 945 in the year 1991 to 914 in 2011. While the education levels have increased, it has not in any way diminished the traditional preference for the male child in our country. Female foeticide and infanticide are practices that are still rampant across the country despite strict bans on determination of sex of a child during pregnancy, leading to roughly 63 million 'missing women' (Economic Survey 2017-18).

To conclude, globalisation has had a mixed set of payoffs for Indian women, who seemed to have gained in a few areas and lost in a few areas. Gender inequality is a serious issue and can have serious deleterious long-run macro economic consequences if not corrected. It has been proven empirically that gender inequality disadvantaging women has negative effects on an economy's long run productivity. It is a systemic social problem and has to be worked from the grass-root level. Research, advocacy, sensitisation of the masses and governmental support in the form of right policies and incentives have to go hand-in-hand if gender equality has to be achieved. If India has to emerge as a super power, it has to certainly focus more on her daughters are treated. In the words of former Secretary General of the United Nations, Kofi Annan, *"Gender equality is more than a goal in itself. It is a precondition for meeting the challenges of reducing poverty, promoting sustainable development and building good governance"*

References

Census of India, 2011a. Provisional Population Totals, Paper 1 of 2011 India, Series-1, Office of the Registrar General & Census Commissioner, New Delhi. www.educationcommission.org

Human Development Reports HDR, United Nations Development Programme (UNDP), 2016.

Key Indicators of Social Consumption in India – Education.National Sample Survey Office.(NSSO, 71st round), 2015.

ILO (2014).International Labour Organisation.Asia-Pacific Working Paper Series.Female Labour Force Participation in India and Beyond. 2014.

National Crime Records Bureau, Ministry of Home Affairs.Social obstacles in Women's Empowerment.Women and Men in India. 2016.

Chapter - 17

Revisiting the Demographic Transition: A Unified Growth Approach

Sk. Md. Azharuddin, Meeta Keswani Mehra

Abstract

The paper utilizes a unified growth theory model to describe the long-run economic growth and demographic evolution of an economy. Using a two period overlapping generations model with two sectors: agriculture and manufacturing, the paper characterizes the transition of the economy from a subsistence pre-industrial Malthusian epoch to a period of sustained modern economic growth. As the representative individual has a life span of two periods: in the first period, she/ he is in childhood and lives off the provision by her/his parents, and in the second period of adulthood, an individual works and makes decision about consumption of the two goods (agricultural and manufactured), number of children to bear and the quality of their children (in terms of education). In the production side, both the goods are produced using learning-by-doing production technologies. The agricultural good is produced with human capital and fixed amount of land with no rent, while the manufacturing good is produced solely with human capital. A pure child quality-quantity trade-off is found in this model. The trade-off suggests that as parents concentrate more on the quality of their children they bear a lesser number of children. Moreover, along the balanced growth path with no population growth, the economy moves with zero productivity, implying that the economy is caught in a Malthusian trap. If manufacturing sector has higher human capital intensity and learning-by-doing elasticity as compared to agriculture, then even if the economy starts with a positive population growth, over time it will converge to a balanced growth equilibrium with zero population and productivity growth. In the opposite situation, if the human capital intensity and learning-by-doing elasticity in manufacturing are smaller than those in the agriculture, then with a positive population growth, the economy moves in an explosive growth path and diverges away

from steady state. Further, the presence of negative population growth implies growth implosion that is incompatible with the basic assumptions of the model. Further, the theoretical outcome of the child quality-quantity trade-off is empirically tested for the pre- and post-independence India, by using an auto-regressive distributed lag (ARDL) estimation method. Using the average years of schooling as a measure of child quality and total fertility rate as an indicator of the number of children borne, the empirical analysis finds a long-run negative and a significant relationship between total fertility and average years of schooling for the post-independence India, implying a child quality-quantity trade-off. However, in pre-independence India, the long-run relationship between total fertility and average years of schooling is found to be positive, indicating toward an absence of long-run child quality-quantity trade-off in that period.
Keywords: *Child Quality-Quantity tradeoff, Unified Growth Theory, Demographic Transition. JEL Classification Codes: J10, J13, J19, J24.*

1. Introduction

Demographic transition plays a significant role in determining the long run economic growth pattern of economies. The interaction between economic and demographic variables is crucial in explaining economic growth and development process from a long-run perspective. Demographic transition has helped economies to reap larger gains from factor accumulation, structural change and technological progress, thus contributing to a sustained rise in per-capita incomes and economic growth (Galor 2011: a). Moreover, economic development is also believed to get enhanced by demographic transition in at least three significant ways. First, reduced population growth leads to an increase in the availability of resources per capita that help generate better resource allocation. Second, reduction in fertility rates help parents to concentrate on child quality rather than the number of children borne, which results in higher human capital accumulation, giving rise to higher per capita income growth. Lastly, demographic transition tends to a change in the age distribution of the population in a manner that the fraction of labor force in the total population rises, thus raising productivity per capita. Thus, demographic transition leads to sustained economic growth and development through its supportive influences on the economy through these channels (Galor 2011: a).

To be on this path of sustained economic growth, empirical regularities point to the fact that market economies must go through three distinct regimes, with differing characteristics of demographic variables to reach sustained economic growth. These three periods are: the Malthusian Epoch, the Post-Malthusian Era and the period of Modern Sustained Economic Growth (Galor 2005). The Malthusian Epoch is the period characterised with very low and stagnant per-capita income. Any resource generation by technological progress or land expansion in this phase is directed towards increase in population size, with little contribution to income per capita. In the Post-Malthusian Regime, while the positive relationship between higher income and population growth continues to operate, with the onset of industrialisation, the diluting effect of higher population growth on per-capita resources is countered by capital accumulation and accelerated technological progress. Thus, a significant increase in per capita income is found to occur in this period. Finally, rapid technological progress and industrialisation in the Post-Malthusian period and its interaction with accumulated human capital and demographic transition paves the way for the period of sustained economic growth, called the Modern Sustained Growth Regime (Galor, 2011: a).

According to the existing literature, there exist several channels through which demographic transition can occur, amongst which the three most important channels are studied under the rubric of (i) child quality-quantity trade-off, (ii) life expectancy, fertility and education acquisition, and (iii) technological progress and education acquisition (see, for instance Cervellati and Sunde (2007), Galor (2011: a), Mason et al.(2016)).

Intuitively, the channel relating to the child quality-quantity trade off describes that, in the Malthusian period, resources generated by technological progress and expansion of land were primarily directed toward an increase in the size of population, with meagre long-run effect on income per capita. But, with industrialisation and technological progress, as parents begin to recognize the importance of human capital, they concentrated more on the quality of the children, the number of children per parent decreased, which led to demographic transition, and finally sustained economic growth (Becker 1960, Becker and Lewis 1973, Croix and Doepke 2003, Galor 2010, Strulik*et al.* 2013). As against this, the second channel states that an increase in life expectancy induced individuals to spend more time on schooling to increase their lifetime income and shift the decision to have children to a later period (Blackburn and Cipriani 2002, Zhang and Zhang 2005, Croix and Licandro 2013). As individuals are less fertile in the later period of life, they will have a fewer number of children overall, which led to demographic transition. Finally, the third channel, which is related to technological progress and education, suggests that with technological progress people needed new knowledge to learn the use of newly emerging technology. This created the need to acquire more education to make use of technologically improved processes and methods. Thus, more time was required to acquire education, leaving less time with the individual to produce children, causing demographic transition (Becker *et al.* 1990, Khan 2008).

To understand the phenomenon of demographic transition and its interaction with the economic variables (such as per capita income growth and development indicators) a need was felt for a suitable economic theory to explain the transition of the economy from subsistence Malthusian economy to the modern economy with sustainable growth. But, most of the conventional growth theories, that have focused on the role factor accumulation and technological progress on growth, did not describe this transition well, while the Malthusian theory was only a depiction of the situation of pre-industrial era of a subsistence economy. Thus, neither the modern growth theories nor the Malthusian theory adequately represented the historical evolution of economies in the Malthusian Epoch, take-off from the Malthusian Epoch to the Post-Malthusian Regime and finally, the transition to a modern economy with sustained per-capita income growth. To address this, Unified Growth Theory (UGT) emerged as a complex framework to motivate the profound shift in human fertility behavior associated with demographic transition (Strulik and Weisdorf 2008). Derived from micro-economic foundations, UGT constructs a dynamical system which allows the analysis of economies as they take-off slowly but steadily from a stable subsistent Malthusian regime to sustained economic growth by endogenizing demographic transition and technological progress.

There exists substantial literature that analyzes this transition from a Malthusian subsistence economy to the phase of modern economic growth. After the seminal paper titled *"An Essay on the Principle of Population"* by Malthus (1798), different authors have tried to explain the process of demographic transition. Becker (1960) tried to explain the demographic transition theoretically via the child quality-quantity trade-off, Becker and Lewis (1973) used a one-period simple utility maximisation problem to analyze this trade-off. Galor and Weil (2000) in their seminal work describe the underlying process of demographic transition and the shift of the economy from the Malthusian regime to one of modern growth transiting through the post-Malthusian era using over lapping generations (OLG) model. After that, several attempts have been made to use OLG model in describing the demographic transition. Croix and Doepke (2003), Moav (2005), Kalemli-Ozcan (2003), Strulik (2004), Yilmazer (2008), Strulik*et al.* (2013), Hanushek (1992), Qian (2009), Li *et al.* (2008), Becker *et al.* (2010) and others have used this framework along with a unified growth setup to demonstrate the process of demographic transition through the channel of child quality-quantity trade-off. In comparison with the above, Murtin (2013), Ehrlich and Lui (1991), Zhang, Zhang and Lee (2001), Croix and Licandro (1999, 2013), Boucekkine, Croix and Licandro (2002), Blackburn and Cipriani (2002), Galor (2011: a) and others have explained the importance of increased life-expectancy in shaping the procedure of demographic transition. Similarly, several others like Becker *et al.* (1990), Galorand Weil (1999, 2000), Galor (2005, 2011:b), Khan (2008) and Greenwood and Seshadri (2002) have showed demographic transition working through the channel of technological progress and education acquisition.

Specifically, Strulik and Weisdorf (2008) have utilised a simple UGT model to describe the phenomenon of demographic transition via the feedback effect of productivity growth on population growth. Using a two-sector closed economy with agricultural and industrial sectors, they describe how fertility responds differently to productivity and income growth, depending upon whether it comes from the agriculture sector or the industrial sector. In equilibrium, the optimal number of off-springs in their model is found to be inversely related to the price of the agricultural commodity, which is consistent with the Malthusian *preventive check hypothesis*.

Our research is motivated by the work of Strulik and Weisdorf (2008), Strulik et al.(2013), Becker and Lewis (1973), Galor and Weil (2000), Croix and Doepke (2003), Moav (2005), Kalemli-Ozcan (2003), Strulik (2004), Yilmazer (2008) and others. The UGT model that we postulate is the closest to the one used in Strulik and Weisdorf (2008) in that we consider a closed economy comprising two production sectors — agriculture and manufacturing. Both the production sectors follow a learning-by-doing production process, where agricultural commodity is produced using land (fixed in supply) and human capital as inputs and manufacturing uses only human capital. In the consumption side, we postulate a two-period OLG model, where individual lives for two time periods — childhood and adulthood. In childhood, individual is dependent on her/ his parents for consumption and human capital formation. But, in adulthood, the individual derives utility from consumption of both agricultural and manufactured goods, number of offspring she/ he bears and the human capital accumulation of the children. It is this last feature in respect of which our model differs from that of Strulik and Weisdorf (2008). Interestingly, in our model as well, the optimal number of children is found to be inversely related to food prices, or the *preventive check hypothesis* plays out. The analysis derives that, in equilibrium, there exists child quality-quantity trade-off, thus leading to demographic transition. In this manner, our work complements the literature on the child quality-quantity trade-off channel of demographic transition and growth.

Our analysis also derives the possibility of a Malthusian trap and the possibility of transitioning from the trap to post-Malthusian period like Strulik and Weisdorf (2008). It is demonstrated that, along the balanced growth path with no population growth, the economy moves with zero productivity, implying that the economy is caught in a Malthusian trap. If the manufacturing sector has higher human capital intensity and learning-by-doing elasticity as compared to agriculture, then even if the economy starts with a positive population growth, over time it will converge to a balanced growth equilibrium with zero population and productivity growth. In the opposite situation, if the human capital intensity and the learning-by-doing elasticity in manufacturing are small enough than those in agriculture, then even with a positive population growth the economy moves along an explosive growth path and diverges away from the steady state and enters into post-Malthusian period. Further, the presence of negative population growth implies imploding growth that is incompatible with the basic assumptions of the model.

In addition, the theoretical outcome of child quality-quantity trade-off is empirically tested for the pre- and post-independence India, by using cointegration with an Auto-Regressive Distributed Lag (ARDL) estimation method. Using average years of schooling as a measure of child quality and total fertility rate as an indicator of number of children, the empirical analysis finds a long-run negative and significant relationship between total fertility and average years of schooling for post-independence India, implying in that period, parents faced a child quality-quantity trade-off. However, in the pre-independence India, the long-run relationship between total fertility and average years of schooling is found to be positive implying that there was absence of a long-run child quality-quantity trade-off in pre-independence India.

The rest of the paper is organised as follows. In Section 2 we setup the basic UGT model for the stylised economy, and derive the presence of a child-quality quantity trade-off. This section also characterizes the balanced and unbalanced growth paths of the economy. In Section 4 we empirically substantiate the evidence of child quality-quantity trade-off for the pre-independence and post-independence India. Finally, Section 5 concludes by summarizing the key results.

2. Theoretical Analysis

The analysis utilizes two-sector closed economy UGT model with endogenous human capital and technical change. Using an OLG structure, it is assumed that while the activities of the aggregate economy extend over an infinite time period, with time denoted by t, where t is discrete. Each individual in such stylised economy is assumed to live for two time periods; an individual is a child in the first time period and an adult in the second time period of her/ his life. In childhood, individual lives on the provision of the agricultural commodity provided by the parents. Moreover, parents also provide for child's training/ education toward human capital formation. Hence, formation of human capital is an endogenous decision of the parents. In adulthood, the individual joins the production process to earn income by supplying human capital either to produce the agricultural good or the manufactured good, while they also devote time toward child rearing. As, in adulthood, the individual takes the decision to bear or not to bear children. Thus, the growth of population is endogenously determined. It is assumed that reproduction is asexual, which means children are born to a single parent[1]. Furthermore, individuals are identical in every respect and each adult has an endowment of h_{t-1} units of homogeneous human capital, which has been acquired in period $(t-1)$ and one unit of labor. She/ he supplies this h_{t-1} unit of human capital to produce any one of the two goods – agricultural or manufacturing — as well as on the rearing of children and formation of children's human capital in period t.

Between any two time periods, t and $t+1$, the change in the size of the labor force is given by:

$$L_{t+1} = n_t L_t, \tag{2.1}$$

where, n_t is the gross rate of growth of population and L_{t+1} and L_t are the sizes of the labor force in periods $t+1$ and t, respectively. As mortality is not considered in our model, n_t measures fertility in period t.

As discussed above, each adult individual is endowed with h_{t-1} amount of human capital in period t and all the adults fully participate in the labor force. Thus, the total human capital in the economy at any period t is defined as

$$H_t = h_{t-1}L_t = h_{t-1}(L_t^A + L_t^M + k) = H_t^A + H_t^M + z, \tag{2.2}$$

where, H_t is the total human capital in the economy, and L_t^A, L_t^M and H_t^A, H_t^M are the aggregate amounts of labor force and human capital that constitute inputs to the agriculture and manufacture sectors, respectively. Thus, $H_t^A = L_t^A h_{t-1}$ and $H_t^M = L_t^M h_{t-1}$. Also, k and z $(=kh_{t-1})$ are the amounts of the labor force and human capital, respectively, that are used in the formation of human capital of the children.

In what follows immediately, the preference structure of this stylised economy is described.

2.1. Preferences

This section discusses the preferences of the individuals in the stylised economy. In this economy each individual lives for two time periods. In the first period, she/ he is in the childhood stage of her/ his life and lives off the parent's income for the consumption of agricultural good and acquisition of human capital. In the second period, when the individual is an adult, she/ he maximizes her/ his utility. The utility of an adult at any period t depends on the consumption of the manufactured good (m_t), consumption of the agricultural good (c_t), the number of children born (n_t) and the acquired human capital of the child (h_t)[2]. Hence, the utility function of the representative adult can be written as;

$$U = \alpha log(m_t) + \beta log(c_t) + \gamma log(n_t) + \delta log(h_t). \tag{2.3}$$

Next, the budget constraint of the adult individual can be expressed as:

$$Y_t = m_t + p_t(c_t + n_t\,\hat{c}) + \tau Y_t n_t h_t\,, \quad \tau<1, \tag{2.4}$$

where, Y_t is the income of the agent, p_t is the price of agricultural good in terms of manufactured good, τ is the fraction of the income spent on human capital formation of the children and $\hat{c}$ is the fixed provision of agricultural good to the children by the parents. In eq. (2.3), the last term pertaining to utility from human capital is additional in our analysis in comparison with Strulik and Weisdorf (2008).

An individual maximizes the utility function in (2.3) subject to the budget constraint in (2.4), which yields the following optimal solutions for m_t, c_t, n_t and h_t:

$$m_t = \frac{\alpha}{\alpha+\beta+\gamma} Y_t. \tag{2.5}$$

$$c_t = \frac{\beta}{\alpha+\beta+\gamma} \frac{Y_t}{P_t}. \tag{2.6}$$

$$n_t = \frac{(\gamma-\delta)Y_t}{(\alpha+\beta+\gamma)P_t\hat{c}}. \tag{2.7}$$

$$h_t = \frac{\delta}{(\alpha+\beta+\gamma)\tau n_t}. \tag{2.8}$$

As can be observed from eq. (2.7), $n_t > 0$, if $\gamma > \delta$. Else, $n_t = 0$, for $\gamma \leq \delta$. Thus, we get that,

Proposition 1: *A positive number of children, n_t, will be borne by an adult individual if she/ he assigns a higher weight on the number of children, γ, than the quality of children in terms of their endowment of human capital, δ.*

Proposition 2: *The optimal demand for children is inversely related to the agricultural good's price, P_t, while it is positively related to the individual's income, Y_t.*

Both of these follow from the solution for n_t in eq. (2.7). Intuitively, to have a strictly positive number of children, an adult must assign a strictly higher weight on the number of children (γ) in her/ his utility function than the weight on the acquired human capital of the children (δ). Further, it can be seen that the demand for children is consistent with the Malthusian *preventive check hypothesis*, as the agricultural good's price effect on the demand for children is negative, that is, $\frac{\partial n_t}{\partial P_t} < 0$. The proposition 2 is consistent with the assumption of Malthus (1798) and complements the result of Srulik and Weisdorf (2008). However, the income effect on the demand for children is found to be positive in such economy.

Next, while deriving the optimal solution of human capital, what emerges is a child quality-quantity trade-off, which is can be easily seen from eq. (2.8).The eq. (2.8) can be rewritten as,

$$n_t h_t = \frac{\delta}{(\alpha+\beta+\gamma)\tau}. \tag{2.8.1}$$

Thus,

Proposition 3: *In equilibrium, there exists a strict inverse relation between the number of children (n_t) and the quality of children (h_t), implying that there exists a trade-off between them.*

Proposition 3 of our study is similar to the result found in the existing literature, such as Galor (2010), Strulik *et al.* (2013) etc, this way our study complements the result of the existing literature on child quality-quantity trade-off.

This can be easily observed in eq. (2.8.1), as the product of n_t and h_t is a constant, given by the right-hand side (r.h.s.) of the same equation. That is, a greater demand for higher quality children (those endowed with higher human capital) implies that individuals choose to have a lower number of children.

In the next section, we discuss the production side of the economy, comprising both the agricultural and manufacturing sectors.

2.2 Production Sectors

This section describes the production side of the economy as well as the process of technological progress exhibited by the two sectors. In line with the existing UGT analytical structure, agricultural production function is assumed to exhibit constant returns to human capital (H^A) and land (V). As land is assumed to be in fixed supply, its total supply is taken to be unitary in value, such that $V=1$. Following Matsuyama(1992), Strulik(1997) and Strulik and Weisdorf (2008), we consider a "learning-by-doing" type of production function for both of the production sectors. Specifically, the production functions have the following form:

$$Y_t^A = \theta\, (A_t)^{\varphi}\, (H_t^A)^x = A_{t+1} - A_t,\ 0< \varphi,\ x<1; \tag{2.9}$$

$$Y_t^M = \mu\, (M_t)^{\sigma}\, (H_t^M)^r = M_{t+1} - M_t,\ 0<\sigma<1, \tag{2.10}$$

where, A_t and M_t are total factor productivity levels in agriculture and manufacturing, respectively. The restriction $0<\varphi,\ ó<1$ represents diminishing returns to learning-by-doing.

Now, denoting the net growth of a variable F between any two periods by, $g_t^F = \frac{F_{t+1}-F_t}{F_t}$, the net growth in productivity in agriculture and manufacture can be expressed as $g_t^A = \theta(A_t)^{\varphi-1}(H_t^A)^x$ and $g_t^M = \mu(M_t)^{\sigma-1}(H_t^M)^r$, respectively.

The following section characterizes the equilibrium for this stylised economy, where the consumption and production sides are combined to solve for the general equilibrium.

2.3. Equilibrium

We characterize the equilibrium for the labor market and as well as for the agricultural and manufacturing sectors.

To begin with, from eq. (2.2), the total labor force in the economy is now given by

$$L_t = L_t^A + L_t^M + k.$$

Further, the fraction of the labor force (as well as human capita) devoted to agriculture and manufacturing are denoted by θ_1 and θ_2, and the specific expressions are given by:

$$\theta_1 = \frac{L_t^A}{L_t} = \frac{H_t^A}{H_t}\ ;\ \theta_2 = \frac{L_t^M}{L_t} = \frac{H_t^M}{H_t}.$$

Since there are no defined property rights on land, the rent from it is driven down to zero. Therefore, human capital in both the production sectors receives the sector's average product. Thus, the relative price of agriculture needs to adjust in such a way that it satisfies the following labor market clearing condition, i.e.

$$w_t = p_t \frac{Y_t^A}{H_t^A} = \frac{Y_t^M}{H_t^M} \tag{2.11}$$

From (2.11), the relative price of food can be written as

$$p_t = \frac{\mu\ (\theta_2)^{r-1} M_t^{\sigma}}{\theta\ (\theta_1)^{x-1} A_t^{\varphi}} (H_t)^{r-x} \tag{2.11.1}$$

Thus, using eq. (2.7), the optimal demand for the number of children by an adult individual can be written as follows:

$$n_t = \frac{(\gamma-\delta) Y_t\ \theta\ (\theta_1)^{x-1} A_t^{\varphi}}{\hat{c}(\alpha+\beta+\gamma)\mu\ (\theta_2)^{r-1} M_t^{\sigma}} \frac{1}{(H_t)^{r-x}} \tag{2.11.2}$$

Furthermore, the share of the labor force devoted to agriculture is determined by the agricultural sector's equilibrium condition. That is,

$$L_t c_t + L_t n_t \hat{c} = Y_t^A \tag{2.12}$$

where the left-hand side of eq. (2.12) represents the economy's demand for, whereas the right-hand side captures the supply of the agricultural good for the entire economy.

Similarly, for the manufacturing sector, the share of the labor force is determined by the manufacturing sector's equilibrium condition, which is,

$$L_t m_t = Y_t^M. \tag{2.13}$$

Substituting the values from eq. (2.11) into eqs. (2.12) and (2.13), we find that

$$\theta_1 = \frac{\beta+\gamma-\delta}{\alpha+\beta+\gamma}, \tag{2.14}$$

$$\theta_2 = \frac{\alpha}{\alpha+\beta+\gamma}. \tag{2.15}$$

Therefore, in equilibrium, the shares of labor force in both agricultural and manufacturing sectors are found to be constant over time. Notably, from $\theta_1 + \theta_2 = 1 - \frac{\delta}{\alpha+\beta+\gamma}$, the remaining share of the labor force, $\frac{\delta}{\alpha+\beta+\gamma}$ (in the form of income), is devoted to the formation of children's human capital through parent's spending on it. This result helps us in deriving the following lemma.

Lemma: *The aggregate labor force in the economy is allocated toward three different uses: in the production of the agricultural good equal to,* $\theta_1 = \frac{\beta+\gamma-\delta}{\alpha+\beta+\gamma}$, *in the manufacturing sector,* $\theta_2 = \frac{\alpha}{\alpha+\beta+\gamma}$, *and the residual share, k, toward the formation of human capital for the next generation's labor force.*[3]

2.4 Growth Paths

In this section, the transition of the economy toward the balanced or unbalanced growth paths is described. Further, we also analyze the economy's break away from the subsistence Malthusian trap.

As we know, along the balanced growth path, all the key variables either do not grow or else grow at a constant rate. Accordingly, the net rate of agricultural productivity growth is defined as

$$g_t^A = \frac{A_{t+1} - A_t}{A_t}.$$

Using eq. (2.9) in the above, we get that,

$$g_t^A = \frac{\theta\left(H_t^A\right)^x}{A_t^{1-\varphi}}. \tag{2.16}$$

Further, utilizing eq. (2.14) into eq. (2.16) yields

$$g_t^A = \frac{\theta(\theta 1 H_t)^x}{A_t^{1-\varphi}}. \tag{2.16.1}$$

The left-hand side of the above is constant along the balanced growth path; therefore, the right-hand side must also be constant. This, in turn, implies that

$$1 + g^A = (1 + g^H)^{\frac{x}{1-\varphi}}. \tag{2.17}$$

Similarly, for the manufacturing sector, the steady state growth path will be characterised by

$$1 + g^M = (1 + g^H)^{\frac{r}{1-\sigma}}. \tag{2.18}$$

Thus,

Proposition 4: *Along the balanced growth path, the productivity growth rates in both the sectors – agriculture and manufacturing — can be solely defined in terms of the growth of total human capital stock of the economy.*

Next, following eq. (2.11.2), the ratio of rates of population growth between the two periods, *(t+1)* and *t* can be expressed as

$$\frac{n_{t+1}}{n_t} = \frac{(1+g^Y)(1+g^A)^{\varphi}}{(1+g^M)^{\sigma}(1+g^H)^{r-x}}, \tag{2.19}$$

whereg^Y is the net growth of income, Y_t. As discussed earlier, each individual in period t is endowed with one unit of labor and human capital of h_{t-1} level, and thus, the income of an individual with h_{t-1} units of human capital can be expressed as,

$$Y_t = w_t h_{t-1}. \tag{2.20}$$

This means that,

$$1+ g^Y = (1+g^w)(1+g_{t-1}^h). \tag{2.20.1}$$

Moreover, from the labor market equilibrium condition in (2.11), we have,

$$w_t = \frac{Y_t^M}{H_t^M} = \frac{\mu \ M_t^{\sigma}}{(H_t^M)^{1-r}}. \tag{2.21}$$

By using eq. (2.15) in eq. (2.21), we find that

$$(1+ g^w) = (1+ g^M)^{\sigma} (1+g^H)^{r-1}. \tag{2.22}$$

Moreover, the use of eq. (2.18) in eq. (2.22) yields that

$$1+ g^w = (1 + g^H)^{\frac{r}{1-\sigma}-1} \tag{2.22.1}$$

and of eq. (2.22.1) in (2.20) yields,

$$1+ g^Y = (1+g_{t-1}^h)(1 + g^H)^{\frac{r}{1-\sigma}-1} \tag{2.23}$$

These derive that,

$$\frac{n_{t+1}}{n_t} = (1+g_{t-1}^h)(1 + g^H)^{\frac{x}{1-\varphi}-1} \tag{2.24}$$

Next, we know, $H_t = L_t h_{t-1,}$ which implies that

$$1+ g^H = (1+g_{t-1}^h)(1+g^L), \tag{2.25}$$

As $L_{t+1} = n_t L_t$, we get,

$$1+ g^L = n_t. \tag{2.26}$$

Using eq. (2.25) and (2.26) in (2.24), we find that

$$n_{t+1} = (1 + g_{t-1}{}^{h})^{\frac{x}{1-\varphi}} n_t{}^{\frac{x}{1-\varphi}}. \tag{2.27}$$

Furthermore, as there exists a child quality-quantity trade-off in equilibrium, from eq. (2.8), we get that

$$n_t h_t = \frac{\alpha}{\tau(\alpha+\beta+\gamma)}$$

$$\Rightarrow 1 + g_t{}^{h} = \frac{n_t}{n_{t+1}} \tag{2.28}$$

Again, use of eq. (3.28) in (3.27) yields,

$$n_{t+1} = (n_{t-1})^{\frac{x}{1-\varphi}} \qquad (2.29)$$

So,

$$(1+g_{t+1}{}^{L}) = (1+g_{t-1}{}^{L})\,\text{a},$$

Where $a = \frac{x}{1-\varphi}$.

We know that, along the balanced growth path, population will grow at a constant rate, that is, $g_{t+1}{}^{L} = g_t{}^{L} = g_{t-1}{}^{L} = g^L$. So, theoretically, there exist two possibilities in this regard: (1) there is no population growth, which implies a constant level of population, or (2) population growth is either positive or negative. We now discuss these two balanced growth path possibilities for the economy.

According to the first possibility, characterised by a balanced growth with no population growth, we have $g^L=0$. This economy experiences a constant level of population over time, or, $L_{t+1} = L_t$. Thus, following eq. (2.1), we get that $n_t = 1$. Further, use of $n_t=1$ in the child quality-quantity trade-off eq. (2.8) yields that

$$\text{h}_\text{t} = \frac{\delta}{(\alpha+\beta+\gamma)\tau}.$$

Therefore, human capital that an individual acquires will also be constant over time along the balanced growth path with zero population growth. This further implies that, with $g^L=0$, $g_t{}^{h} = g_{t-1}{}^{h} = 0$.

Following Proposition 4 and eqs. (2.17), (2.18) and (2.25), we get that

$$1 + g^A = (1 + g^h)^{\frac{x}{1-\varphi}} (1 + g^L)^{\frac{x}{1-\varphi}} \tag{2.30}$$

$$1 + g^M = (1 + g^h)^{\frac{r}{1-\sigma}}(1 + g^L)^{\frac{r}{1-\sigma}}. \qquad (2.31)$$

Since, the case considered is one of balanced growth with no population growth, we will have $g_t^h = g_{t-1}^h = 0$. Thus, eqs. (2.30) and (2.31) will yield

$$g^A = g^M = 0. \qquad (2.32)$$

From eq. (3.32) it follows that both A_t and M_t will be constant over time along the balanced growth path, with $g^h = g^L = 0$.

We next consider the behavior of price, given in eq. (2.11.1). We have

$$p_t = \frac{\mu\ (\theta_2)^{r-1} M_t^{\ \sigma}}{\theta\ (\theta_1)^{x-1} A_t^{\ \varphi}}(H_t)^{r-..x}.$$

Since A_t and M_t are constant over time, the price eq. can be rewritten as

$$p_t = K_p(H_t)^{r-x}, \qquad (2.33)$$

where K_p is a constant.

Thus, the growth of agricultural price can be expressed as

$$1 + g^p = (1 + g^h)^{r-x}(1 + g^L)^{r-x}. \qquad (2.34)$$

From eq. (3.34) it follows that g^p is equal to zero along the balanced growth path with $g^h = g^L = 0$.

Proposition 5: *Along the balanced growth path with zero population growth, all the variables in the economy grow at a zero rate, or they do not grow. Thus, the economy is caught in a Malthusian trap.*

Thus, in the case of a balanced growth path with zero population growth, all the variables — per capita human capital, price of the agricultural product and productivity of agricultural as well as manufacturing sectors — do not grow at all. This concludes that such an economy with no population growth is stuck in a Malthusian trap.

The result in proposition 5 is very similar to the result found in Srulik and Weisdorf (2008), where the economy is also caught at the Malthusian trap with zero population growth.

We now check for the second possibility, of non-zero population growth along the balanced growth path. Let us assume the population grows at some constant rate, s.

Thus, we have $g^L = s = \frac{L_{t+1} - L_t}{L_t} = n_t - 1$, which implies that $n_t = 1 + s$, which is a constant over time. Next, using $n_t = 1+s$ in the child quality-quantity trade off eq. yields,

$$h_t = \frac{\delta}{(\alpha+\beta+\gamma)\tau(1+s)}. \qquad (2.35)$$

From eq. (2.35), it can be inferred that h_t will be constant over time, or $g^h = 0$.

Following eqs. (2.30) and (2.31), the productivity growth in the agricultural and manufacturing sectors along the balanced growth path can be written as

$$1 + g^A = (1 + g^h)^{\frac{x}{1-\varphi}}(1 + g^L)^{\frac{x}{1-\varphi}};$$
$$1 + g^M = (1 + g^h)^{\frac{r}{1-\sigma}}(1 + g^L)^{\frac{r}{1-\sigma}}.$$

Using $g^h = 0$, for the agricultural sector we have,

$$1+g^A = (1 + g^L)^{\frac{x}{1-\varphi}} = (1 + s)^{\frac{x}{1-\varphi}}. \quad (2.36)$$

Since, $\frac{x}{1-\varphi} > 0$, with positive population growth, agricultural productivity will grow over time.

Next, we check for the productivity growth in the manufacturing sector when there is positive population growth. With a constant positive population growth and associated zero growth in per capita human capital, eq. (2.31) can be expressed as

$$1 + g^M = (1 + g^L)^{\frac{r}{1-\sigma}} = (1 + s)^{\frac{r}{1-\sigma}} \quad (2.37)$$

Eq. (2.37) says that if population grows constantly over time, and since $\frac{r}{1-\sigma} > 0$, the productivity growth in manufacturing sector will also grow over time.

We now discuss the change in the agricultural price with non-zero positive population growth. The equilibrium price eq. given in eq. (2.11.1) is,

$$p_t = \frac{\mu\,(\theta_2)^{r-1} M_t^{\sigma}}{\theta\,(\theta_1)^{x-1} A_t^{\varphi}} (H_t)^{r-x}.$$

So, the proportionate price change eq. can be written as,

$$\frac{p_{t+1}}{p_t} = \frac{M_{t+1}^{\sigma}}{M_t^{\sigma}} \frac{A_t^{\varphi}}{A_{t+1}^{\varphi}} \frac{H_{t+1}^{r-x}}{H_t^{r-x}} \quad (2.38)$$

Using $g^h = 0$ and substituting eqs. (2.36) and (2.37) into (2.38) yields,

$$1+g^p = (1 + s)^{\frac{r\sigma}{1-\sigma} - \frac{x\varphi}{1-\varphi} + r - x} \quad (2.39)$$

$$\Rightarrow 1+g^p = (1 + s)^{\frac{r}{1-\sigma} - \frac{x}{1-\varphi}} \quad (2.40)$$

In eq. (2.40), as $s > 0$, we get that

$$\frac{r}{1-\sigma} - \frac{x}{1-\varphi} > 0 \Rightarrow g^p > 0 \quad (2.41)$$

$$\text{Else, } \frac{r}{1-\sigma} - \frac{x}{1-\varphi} \leq 0 \Rightarrow g^{p} \leq 0 \,. \tag{2.42}$$

Now we discuss the situation the first situation when, , $\frac{r}{1-\sigma} - \frac{x}{1-\varphi} > 0$.

We know that with $s>0$, or with constant population growth over time, there is a constant rate of increase exhibited by the productivities in the agricultural as well as manufacturing sectors, as seen in eqs. (2.36) and (2.37). But, with the condition in (2.41) being satisfied, which amounts to a relatively higher intensity of human capital in the manufacturing sector, *r*, coupled with a larger learning elasticity in this sector, captured by φ, than the human capital intensity and learning elasticity in the agricultural sector, denoted respectively by *x* and *ö*, the price of agricultural commodity will increase over time. This price increase will act as the *preventive check* and cause a decline in the number of children borne by the parents, since the increase in agricultural commodity price implies an increase in child-rearing cost. Thus, even if the economy starts with a positive growth of population, through the mechanism of preventive check the economy will eventually reach the balanced growth path with zero population growth. Associated with this, all the variables in the economy will grow at zero rate, including the growth of agriculture and manufacturing as well as the productivity in these two production sectors. Thus, a path starting with $g^{L} = s > 0$ and $\frac{r}{1-\sigma} - \frac{x}{1-\varphi} > 0$ will converge to the balanced growth path. Hence, we derive that,

Proposition 6: *If the human capital intensity (r) and learning elasticity (σ) in the manufacturing sector are high enough as compared to those in agriculture, namely, x and θ, such that the condition in (2.41) is satisfied, then if the economy starts with a positive population growth, s>0, through the preventive check mechanism, over time it will reach a balanced growth path with zero population growth as well as zero output and productivity growth in the both the production sectors.*

We next analyze the situation characterised by eq. (2.42), that is, $\frac{r}{1-\sigma} - \frac{x}{1-\varphi} \leq 0$. If the manufacturing sector is characterised by low enough human capital intensity and learning elasticity as compared to agriculture, such that the condition in (2.42) holds, then, as indicated in (2.42), agricultural prices will decrease over time. This will induce parents to bear a larger number of children, as the child-rearing cost decrease over time. In this situation, however, the output and productivity in both the production sectors will rise over time (through eqs. (2.36) and (2.37)), thus causing an explosive growth path for the economy. Thus, a path characterised by the condition in (2.42) and $s>0$ cannot be the saddle path, and we get that,

Proposition 7: *If the manufacturing sector is characterised by a low enough human capital intensity as well a learning elasticity in comparison to the agricultural sector, such that the* $\frac{r}{1-\sigma}-\frac{x}{1-\varphi}\leq 0$ *holds then, even having started with a positive rate of population growth,* $s>0$*, agricultural commodity prices will fall and the economy will diverge on an explosive growth path, with spiraling population growth as well as productivity growth in both the sectors over time.*

In what follows, we analyze what happens in the case of an economy that starts with a negative population growth, or $g^L = s < 0$.

With a negative population growth rate, the economy will experience negative productivity growth in both agriculture and manufacturing over time, as can be inferred from eqs. (2.36) and (2.37). That is, if in eqs. (2.36) and (2.37), $s<0$, both g^A and g^M are also negative as $\frac{x}{1-\varphi}> 0$ and >0. Since 'forgetting-by-doing' is not an option in our model, a situation with negative population growth that will lead to an imploding growth for the economy is not a possibility.[4]

Proposition 8: *The case of negative population growth, implied by* $n_t<1$*, such that both* g^A *and* g^M *are negative (from* $\frac{x}{1-\varphi}> 0$ *ana* $\frac{r}{1-\sigma}>0$ *and there is imploding growth) is not a possibility as since 'forgetting-by-doing' is not consistent with the assumptions of the model.*

In sum, focusing on a two-sector closed OLG economy, this analysis finds a quality-quantity trade-off faced by the parents. As parents focus more on the quality of the children, they bear a lower number of children. Further, it is derived that, along the balanced growth path with zero population growth, both the sectors of the economy – agriculture and manufacturing - tend to stagnate with zero productivity growth. Thus, the economy is caught in a Malthusian trap. Alternatively, when population grows at a constant rate, and the manufacturing sector is more human capital intensive and has high enough elasticity of learning-by-doing than the agricultural sector, then even if the economy starts with a positive population growth, over time it will converge to a balanced growth path with zero population growth and productivity growth in the two production sectors on account of the population stabilisation effect of the *preventive check* caused by rising agricultural commodity prices. Alternatively, the case of low enough productivity and learning elasticity in manufacturing as compared to agriculture leads to explosive growth path in population and productivity, and hence such paths diverge away from the steady growth path. Moreover, our analysis also suggests the impossibility of imploding unbalanced growth paths for this stylised economy, mainly characterised by negative population growth. These entail forgetting-by-doing, which is inconsistent with the basic assumptions of the analytical model.

The next section of this paper provides an empirical testing of the presence of the child quality-quantity trade-off for the Indian economy, in two separate time periods – pre-independent India and post-independent India. Augmented Dicky Fuller (ADF) and Kwiatkowski–Phillips–Schmidt–Shin (KPSS) unit root tests are used to check the non-stationarity of the variables. Further, an auto regressive distributed lag (ARDL) cointegration approach is used to check for the presence of a long-run stable relationship between total fertility rate and average years of schooling for both pre-independent and post-independent India.

3. Empirical Evidence on Child Quality-Quantity Trade-off

The theoretical possibility of a child quality-quantity trade-off is now tested separately for the pre- and post-independence India. For our analysis, we take total fertility rate as the measure of number of children, while the quality of children is measured by the average years of schooling. We utilize an ARDL co-integration approach to test for a long-run equilibrium relationship between total fertility rate and average years of schooling, along with the other variables (namely, prices of commodities and per capita GDP) that may have some effect on total fertility rate. These estimations are done individually for the pre- and post-independence India. The time period spanned by our study covers 1884 to 1946 for pre-independence and 1960 to 2015 for post-independence India.

In general, in the pre-independence period, the data suggests that all the variables in their natural logarithmic form are I(1) in levels, and hence, they become stationary after taking their first differences. In comparison, in the post-independent period, the natural logarithmic form of total fertility rate and commodity prices are I(0) in levels and the remaining two variables, that is, per capita GDP and average years of schooling are I(1) in levels. The ARDL estimation approach is applicable when all the variables are I(0) or I(1) or a combination of both I(0) and I(1), so this methodology is applied to estimate the long-run equilibrium relationship between total fertility rate and other variables. The ARDL estimation results of our analysis reveal that for the pre-independence India, even if parents face a child quality-quantity trade-off in the short-run, it is insignificant. In the long-run, however, the relationship between total fertility rate and average years of schooling gets reversed, that is, it is positive and significant. In the post-independence time-period, however, a negative and significant relationship between total fertility rate and average years of schooling is found both in the short-run as well as the long-run. Thus, this corroborates our Proposition 3 in Section 2. We now proceed with some details on this empirical estimation.

We first describe the data sources.

3.1. Data Description and Sources

The data set used for our analysis consists of the following variables: total Fertility Rate (TF), average years of schooling (SCH), per-capita gross domestic product (PGDP) and index of commodity prices (PRICE) separately for the pre- and post-independence India. The data under consideration is yearly and covers the time period from the year 1884-1946 for the pre-independence and 1960-2015 for the post-independence India. The data on PRICE for pre-independence India refers to the weighted index of agricultural prices, which are collected from Raychaudhuri, Kumar, Habib and Desai (1983). Further, the net national product data from Raychaudhuri, Kumar, Habib and Desai (1983) combined with population statistics from Maddison(2007) are used for calculating PGDP for the pre-independent period. Finally, the data for TF are collected from ourworldindata.org. For the post-independence period, the data on TF, PRICE and PGDP are collected from the World Bank database. For this period, the PRICE data refers to the Consumer Price Index (CPI). Further, the data on SCH are collected from the Barro-Lee Educational Attainment Dataset(v. 1.0, 07/15) both for the pre- and post-independence period. The dataset provided by the Barro-Lee Educational Attainment Dataset (http://www.barrolee.com/) is spaced at five-year intervals, and interpolation is done to generate the data for the intermediate years.

The description and specification of the data are as follows:

- TF: Total fertility rate;
- SCH: Average years of total schooling;
- PRICE: Weighted index of agricultural prices (Base: 1946-47(for pre-independence period) and 2010-11 (for post-independence period));
- PGDP: Per capita GDP (Base: 1946-47(for pre-independence period) and 2010-11 (for post-independence period));

All the above series are subjected to logarithmic transformation. The natural logarithm of the respective time-series is represented by a prefix '*L*', while a prefix '*D*' represents the first difference of the respective time-series.

3.2. Methodology

This section lays out in detail the different test methods used in our analysis. We have used two different unit root tests, namely, the ADF and KPSS unit root tests for checking the presence of a non-stationarity in the variables. Next, to check for the long-run and short-run relationship amongst the variables (TF, SCH, PRICE and PGDP) the ARDL cointegration methodology is used.

3.2.1 Tests of Unit Root

3.2.1.1. Dickey-Fuller (DF) and Augmented Dickey-Fuller (ADF) Unit Root Test

It is important to check whether the time-series variables under consideration contain a unit root or not. If a variable has a unit root in levels, then it is inferred that it is non-stationary in levels. The pioneering work for unit root test in time-series was proposed by Dickey and Fuller (Fuller 1976; Dickey and Fuller 1979). The idea behind the checking of a unit root for a variable y_t is to check the null hypothesis that ñ = 1 in the following,

$$y_t = \rho y_{t-1} + u_t. \tag{3.1}$$

Taking the first difference and including lags, the Augmented Dickey-Fuller (ADF) test proposes the following form

$$\Delta y_t = \alpha + \delta y_{t-1} + \beta t + \gamma_1 \Delta y_{t-1} + \gamma_2 \Delta y_{t-2} + \cdots\cdots + \gamma_k \Delta y_{t-k} + u_t \tag{3.2}$$

Here again the test of $\rho = 1$ is equivalent to the test of $\delta = 0$ (since $\rho = \delta = 0$) and "k" is the number of lags included in the regression equation and this number is specified by some information criterion (such as, Akaike Information Criteria (AIC) or Criteria (SIC)).

3.2.1.2. Kwaitkowski, Phillips, Schmidt, and Shin (KPSS) Unit Root Test

The standard Dickey-Fuller tests with the null of unit root face some criticism in interpreting the unit root of a variable. Dickey-Fuller tests have lower power against stable autoregressive alternatives with roots near unity (DeJong *et al.* 1992) and these tests have low power against fractionally integrated alternatives (Diebold and Rudebusch, 1991). To get rid of such problems an alternative unit root test with the null of stationarity is proposed by Kwaitkowski, Phillips, Schmidt, and Shin (1992), and in shorter form the test is known as KPSS unit root test. In this test, the time-series variable (y_t) under consideration is written as a sum of a deterministic time trend (β_t), a random walk term (r_t) and a stationary error term (u_t). The null hypothesis of trend stationarity is corresponding to the hypothesis that the variance of the random walk equals zero. That is,

H_0: $\sigma_\varepsilon^2 = 0$, and H_1:$\sigma_\varepsilon^2 \neq 0$, where, σ_ε^2 is the variance of the random walk.

$$y_t = \beta t + r_t + u_t, \tag{3.3}$$

wherer_t is a random walk, that is,

$$r_t = r_{t-1} + \varepsilon_t \tag{3.4}$$

and ε_t follows an iid (0, σ_ε^2).

The initial value r_0 is treated as constant and it works as an intercept. The stationarity hypothesis corresponds to $\sigma_\varepsilon^2 = 0$. Since u_t is assumed to be stationary, under the null hypothesis, y_t is trend-stationary. A special case of the model in eq. (3.3) can also be considered, in which we set $\beta = 0$, and under the null hypothesis, y_t is stationary around a level r_0 rather than around a time trend.

3.2.2. ARDL Estimation

To determine the long-run and short-run relationships among variables, the prescribed traditional approach is the standard Johansen co-integration and vector error-correction model (VECM). But this methodology suffers from several serious flaws, as shown by Pesaran*et al.*(2001). Instead, we use the ARDL method popularised by Pesaran and Shin (1995), Pesaran*et al.* (1996), and Pesaran (1997) to establish the long-run and short-run relationship between the variables being considered. Further, ARDL method yields consistent and robust results, both for the long-run and short-run relationship between variables. Finally, ARDL approach can be applied to find the long-run and short-run relationship between variables irrespective of whether the underlying variables are purely I(0), purely I(1), or a mix of both. This superiority of ARDL estimation over Johansen co-integration motivated us to use ARDL methodology for our analysis.

The ARDL model in our study is used to find the long-run and short-run relationships between total fertility rate and average years of schooling along with GDP per capita and price level for India for the two different time periods – pre- independence and post-independence. For our purpose, the following model is estimated to find these relationships:

$$DLTF_t = \alpha + \beta_1 LSCH_{t-1} + \beta_2 LPGDP_{t-1} + \beta_3 LPRICE_{t-1} + \sum_{i=1}^{P} \delta_1 DLSCH_{t-i} + \sum_{i=1}^{P} \delta_2 DLPGDP_{t-i} + \sum_{i=1}^{P} \delta_3 DLPRICE_{t-1} + \sum_{i=1}^{P} \delta_4 DLTF_{t-i} + \varepsilon_t \quad (3.4)$$

where, α represents the constant term, β_1, β_2 and β_3 denote the long-run coefficients, δ_1, δ_2, δ_3 and δ_4 illustrate the short-run dynamics of the model and $\mathring{a}_t$ is white-noise error term. Further, P indicates the maximum lag length. The maximum lag length is determined in our model by using the AIC.

3.3. Empirical Results

This section summarizes the empirical results of our analysis. We start our analysis by checking for the presence of unit root in the variables with the help of two separate unit root tests — ADF and KPSS both for pre- and post-independence India. First, these two unit root tests are performed on the variables in terms of the levels. If any variable is found non-stationary, or has a unit root at level, then the first difference of the variable is taken and the unit root test is performed again to check whether these first differences are still non-stationary or not. After alluding to the unit root test results, the section outlines the long-run and short-run relationship between total fertility rate and other variables using ARDL estimation. It further reports the error correction term to find the long-run adjustment in the total fertility after any short-run disturbances.

3.3.1. Unit Root Test Results

The ADF unit root test for all the variable is performed allowing for an intercept as well as with a deterministic time trend. The optimal lag included in ADF test is selected by AIC. Similarly, the KPSS test is also performed taking time trend under consideration to detect unit root of the variables.

Table 17.1: Results of the Unit Root Test for Different Variables in Pre-independence India.

Series	*Test Type*	*Test Statistics*	*1% Critical Value*	*5% Critical Value*	*10% Critical Value*
LTF	ADF	-1.381	-4.12	-3.48	-3.17
	KPSS	0.236	0.216	0.146	0.119
LSCH	ADF	-0.099	-4.12	-3.48	-3.17
	KPSS	0.256	0.216	0.146	0.119
LPGDP	ADF	-0.848	-4.12	-3.48	-3.17
	KPSS	0.234	0.216	0.146	0.119
LPRICE	ADF	-2.12	-4.12	-3.48	-3.17
	KPSS	0.117	0.216	0.146	0.119
DLTF	ADF	-3.66	-4.12	-3.48	-3.17
	KPSS	0.173	0.216	0.146	0.119
DLSCH	ADF	-3.36	-4.12	-3.48	-3.17
	KPSS	0.105	0.216	0.146	0.119
DLPGDP	ADF	-7.42	-4.12	-3.48	-3.17
	KPSS	0.213	0.216	0.146	0.119
DLPRICE	ADF	-7.11	-4.12	-3.48	-3.17
	KPSS	0.078	0.216	0.146	0.119

ADF: Null Hypothesis H_0: Series contains unit root.
KPSS: Null Hypothesis H_0: Series is trend stationary.

As can be seen from the results in Table 17.1, the ADF unit root test shows that all the variables — LTF, LSCH, LPRICE and LPGDP — are non-stationary in levels for the pre-independence India. The same conclusion can also be drawn from the results of the KPSS unit root test for all the variables, except LPRICE. But, separately, the use of Phillips-Perron unit root test suggests the non-stationarity of LPRICE at levels[5]. Thus, for pre-independence India, all the variables considered in our analysis contain a unit root in terms of levels. Next, when the first differences of all the variables are taken, then both ADF and KPSS tests confirm the stationarity of all the variables in first difference. Thus, it can be said that, all the variables in our study are integrated of order one, I(1), in terms of levels.

We next run similar tests for the post-independent scenario to detect the non-stationarity of the variables in levels.

Table 17.2: Results of the Unit Root Test for Different Variables in Post- independence India

Series	*Test Type*	*Test Statistics*	*1% Critical Value*	*5% Critical Value*	*10% Critical Value*
LTF	ADF	-5.573	-4.165	-3.508	-3.184
	KPSS	0.258	0.216	0.146	0.119
LSCH	ADF	-0.128	-4.137	-3.495	-3.176
	KPSS	0.227	0.216	0.146	0.119
LPGDP	ADF	0.574	-4.148	-3.50	-3.179
	KPSS	0.234	0.216	0.146	0.119
LPRICE	ADF	-3.420	-4.137	-3.495	-3.176
	KPSS	0.106	0.216	0.146	0.119
DLSCH	ADF	-3.413	-4.148	-3.50	-3.179
	KPSS	0.152	0.216	0.146	0.119
DLPGDP	ADF	-6.646	-4.12	-3.48	-3.17
	KPSS	0.102	0.216	0.146	0.119

ADF: Null Hypothesis H_0: Series contains unit root.
KPSS: Null Hypothesis H_0: Series is trend stationary.

As can be seen from Table 17.2, in the post-independence period, the non-stationarity of LSCH and LPGDP at levels is confirmed by both ADF and KPSS unit root tests. However, for LTF and LPRICE, ADF unit root test suggests stationarity in levels. But according to KPSS unit root test, LPRICE is stationary in level, while LTF is non-stationary. Further, the use of Phillips-Perron unit root test confirms the stationarity of LTF in level[6]. Thus, LTF and LPRICE are variables of order zero, I(0), in levels and LSCH and LPGDP are I(1) as their first difference becomes stationary.

Thus all the variables - LTF, LSCH, LPRICE and LPGDP - are of I(1) in the pre-independence period. However, in the post-independence period, LTF and LPRICE are I(0) and LSCH and LPGDP are I(1). As ARDL estimation methodology is suitable for variables which are I(0), I(1), or a combination of I(0) and I(1), this estimation approach has been used for both pre-independence and post-independence data set to check whether there is any long-run stable equilibrium relationship among the variables or not. In other words, the co-integrating relationship among the variables is checked for, for which the results are presented in the ensuing section.

3.3.2. Results of ARDL Estimation

Table 17.3: Estimated Long-run Coefficients using the ARDL Approach for Pre-independence Period

Variables	*Coefficients*	*t-Values*	*p-Values*
LSCH	0.021035	2.7869	0.007
LPGDP	0.022762	0.46590	0.643
LPRICE	-0.0097610	-1.3076	0.196
Constant	1.7177	6.8388	0.000

After selecting the lag length by AIC and normalizing the result for LTF, the long-run relationship between LTF, LSCH, LPGDP and LPRICE in pre-independence India is estimated; this is compiled in Table 17.3. The results suggest that, before independence, there was a positive significant relationship between total fertility rate and average years of schooling. Specifically, a one per cent increase in the average years of schooling leads to an increase in total fertility by about 0.02 percent, and this relation is found to be stable over time, as the F-statistics of the test is significant at 5% level of significance[7]. Thus, there was absence of a child-quality quantity trade-off in the pre-independence India. However, a preventive check effect was at work through prices, as can be inferred from a negative relationship between commodity price and total fertility, albeit not highly significant. The effect of income per capita remains positive, though highly insignificant.

Next, the results of error correction mechanism for the chosen ARDL model are presented in Table 17.4.

Table 17.4: Error Correction Representation for the Selected ARDL-Model for the Pre- Independence India

ARDL(1,1,0,0) selected based on Akaike Information CriterionDependent variable: DLTF			
Variables	*Coefficients*	*t-Values*	*p-Values*
DLSCH	-0.019494	-1.4160[.162]	0.162
DLPGDP	0.0015761	.48540[.629]	0.629
DLPRICE	-0.6759E-3	-1.1797[.243]	0.243
ECM(-1)	-0.069244	-3.8102[.000]	0.000

These results suggest that there is a negative relationship between total fertility rate and average years of schooling in the short-run, but this relationship is insignificant in pre-independence India. Thus, in the short-run, parents face a child quality-quantity trade-off, but it is not significant enough to display a similar relationship in the long-run. Further, a negative significant error correction term [ECM(-1)] indicates that, if there is any deviation from the equilibrium path in the short-run for total fertility rate, it will retain its equilibrium growth path over long-run. Again, as in case of the long-run relationship, the positive income effect and the negative price effect on total fertility are found to be insignificant.

We next check for the short-run and long-run relationship among the variables for the post-independence period.

Table 3.5: Estimated Long-run Coefficients using the ARDL Approach for the Post-independence India

ARDL(1,0,0,1) selected based on Akaike Information CriterionDependent variable: LTF			
Variables	*Coefficients*	*t-Values*	*p-Values*
LSCH	-0.7642	-3.7179	0.001
LPGDP	-0.2676	-7.3245	0.000
LPRICE	0.1731	2.0320	0.048
Constant	4.3383	12.7939	0.000

The results in Table 17.5 point towards a negative relationship between total fertility and average years of schooling in the long-run in post-independence India. That is, a one per cent increase in the average years of schooling leads to a decrease in total fertility of about 0 77 percent, and it is significant[8]. Thus, there exists a strong evidence of a child quality-quantity trade-off in post-independence India. Further, a negative and significant relationship is found between per-capita GDP and total fertility rate, which means that as per-capita income increases, parents start bearing lesser number of children in the post-independence era. This is a reversal from the effects in the pre-independence period.

We now discuss the error correction for total fertility rate in the post-independence India.

Table 17.6: Error Correction Representation for the Selected ARDL-Model in Post-Independence India

ARDL (1,0,0,1) selected based on Akaike Information Criterion Dependent variable: DLTF			
Variables	*Coefficients*	*t-Values*	*p-Values*
DLSCH	-0.055360	-7.0931	0.000
DLPGDP	-0.019385	-2.9600	0.005
DLPRICE	-0.0015087	-0.24957	0.804
ECM(-1)	-0.072437	-3.7415	0.000

The error correction results for total fertility rate are shown in the Table 17.6 for the post-independence time period. The result point toward a child quality-quantity trade-off in the short-run for the post-independence India as well, as confirmed by a negative and significant relationship between total fertility rate and average years of schooling. There is also a negative and significant relationship between per capita GDP and total fertility rate in the short-run, as can be found from the results in Table 17.6. Further, a negative significant error correction term [ECM(-1)] implies that if there is any deviation in the short-run from the equilibrium path of total fertility rate, then over the long-run, the equilibrium path will be retained.

Thus, to sum up, the ARDL estimation methodology suggests that there is a stable positive long-run relationship between total fertility rate and average years of schooling in the pre-independence period while, in the post-independence period, the sign of this relationship gets reversed. As the total fertility rate is negatively related to average years of schooling, the child quality-quantity trade-off for the post-independence India is confirmed by our analysis, which corroborates Proposition 3 of Section 2. Further, there is a negative income effect on fertility in the post-independence period, which may be attributed to a higher preference for child quality as income rises sufficiently.

Even though, in this section, we find a short run negative relationship between total fertility rate and average years of schooling in the pre-independence India, the relationship is not significant enough to exhibit a long-run stable relationship between these variables. Thus, the long-run positive relationship between total fertility rate and average years of schooling in the pre-independence period may be on account of a lower rate of industrialisation in the Indian economy during that period, when the share of agriculture was high enough. Consequently, the preventive check effect was small enough, so that the trade-off between child quantity and quality is weakened. Thus, in the pre-independence period, in the long run, parents do not seem to face a quality-quantity trade-off.

4. Conclusion

Demographic transition is an important channel through which an economy evolves, achieves better resource allocation, transforms the parents' focus toward quality of the children rather than the number of children, finally modifying the age distribution of the population to support sustained economic growth and development.

The paper lays out a UTG approach as an analytical tool for describing the economy's transition from a subsistence Malthusian economy to a modern economy with sustained economic growth. We utilize a basic UGT model in discrete time with two sectors - agriculture and manufacturing, which is an extension of Strulik and Weisdorf (2008). Considering an OLG framework, each individual/ consumer in this economy is assumed to live for two periods –childhood and adulthood. Further, the economy is assumed to be a closed one. In the consumption side, a child consumes the agricultural good and acquires education, both provided by her/ his parents, and the adult maximizes her/ his utility from the consumption of manufacturing and agricultural goods, number of children she/ he bears and child's education attainment. In the production side, the agricultural sector uses human capital along with a fixed level of land to produce the agricultural commodity, while in the manufacturing sector the human capital is solely used to produce its output. Further, both sectors exhibit learning-by-doing technology.

The key result of our analysis is that if parents assign a higher weight on the number of children than on the quality of children in their (parents') utility function, only then they bear a positive number of children. Further, the demand for the optimal number of the children by parents is inversely related to the price of the agricultural product, implying the presence of a *preventive check effect*. Moreover, as parents care more for the quality of children, they start bearing a lower number of children; thus, a quality-quantity trade-off arises in our stylised economy. We also find that, along the balanced growth path with no population growth, both agricultural and manufacturing sectors of the economy get stagnated with zero productivity growth. Therefore, the economy gets stuck in a Malthusian trap. On the other hand, when population grows over time, then if the manufacturing sector is more intensive in human capital and has a sufficiently large elasticity of learning-by-doing than the agricultural sector, even if in the initial situation there is positive population growth, over time the economy will converge to a balanced growth path with zero population growth and productivity growth in the two production sectors. This will happen via the population stabilisation effect of the preventive check associated with rising agricultural commodity prices. Alternatively, when the manufacturing sector's human capital intensity and learning elasticity are small enough in comparison with those in the agricultural sector, there will be explosive growth in population and productivity, and hence such paths will diverge away from the balanced growth path. Our analysis also discusses the non-feasibility of imploding unbalanced growth paths for this stylised economy, characterised by a negative population growth. These require forgetting-by-doing as an option of growth, which is inconsistent with the basic assumptions of the analytical model.

Further, we empirically test for the possibility of a child quality-quantity trade-off. We run an ARDL model to find the long run equilibrium relationship between the total fertility and the average years of schooling along with some other variables (per capita GDP and commodity prices) both for the pre- and post-independence India. In our study, the average years of schooling is taken as measure of quality of the children. The ADF and KPSS unit root tests suggest the non-stationarity of all the variables (LTF, LSCH, LPGDP and LPRICE) for the pre-independence India. For the post-independence India, LTF and LPRICE are found stationary in levels, while LSCH and LPGDP are non-stationary in levels. Since, in the pre-independence period, all the variables are I(1) and after independence the variables are a mixture of I(1) and I(0), the most suitable framework that is relied upon is the ARDL model to find the long-run relationship among the variables. For the pre-independence India, ARDL estimation finds a long-run positive relation between total fertility and average years of schooling. Moreover, even though parents face a child quality-quantity trade-off in the short-run, as shown by a negative relationship between total fertility and average years of schooling, this relationship is not significant enough to bring a negative relation between these variables in the long-run. In comparison, in the post-independence India, a negative and significant relationship between total-fertility and average years of schooling is found both for the short-runs and long-runs. Further, the error correction terms are significant, both for pre-independence and post-independence India, which suggests that if there is any deviation from the equilibrium growth path of total fertility in the short-run, it will retain its equilibrium growth path over the long-run. One potential reason for the reversal of the relationship between total fertility and average years of schooling could be that, in the pre-independence era, the share of agriculture in the economy was rather high, which coupled with relatively low rate of industrialisation, resulted in a weak preventive check effect and a lower demand for knowledge and skill acquisition. Thus, parents did not face a child-quality quantity trade-off. But, in the post-independence period, a rising share of manufacturing sector and associated technological change deemed it necessary for parents to invest in the education, knowledge and skill acquisition for their children to enable the children to cope with new technologies. Thus, a child quality-quantity trade-off has been faced by the parents. This corroborates our analytical findings in the previous section.

References

Becker, G. S. (1960). "An Economic Analysis of Fertility", *NBER Chapters*, 209-240.

Becker, G. S., and Lewis, H. Gregg (1973)."On the interaction between the quantity and quality of children", *The Journal of Political Economy*, 81(2) Part 2, 279-288.

Becker, G., Kevin, M., & Robert, T. (1990), "Human Capital, Fertility, and Economic Growth", *Journal of Political Economy*, 98: 12-37.

Becker, O. S., Cinnirella, F., &Woessmann, L. (2010), "The Trade-off Between Fertility and Education: Evidence from Before the Demographic Transition", *Journal of Economic Growth*, 15: 177-204.

Blackburn, K., & Cipriani, G. P. (2002), "A Model of Longevity, Fertility and Growth", Journal *of Economic Dynamics and Control*, 26(2): 187-204.

Boucekkine, R., Croix, D. D. L, &Licandro, O. (2002), "Vintage Human Capital, Demographic Trends, and Endogenous Growth", *Journal of Economic Theory*, 104: 340-375.

Cervellati, M., & Sunde, U. (2007), "Human capital, mortality and fertility: A unified theory of the economic and demographic transition" Discussion Paper Series, Forschungsinstitut zur Zukunft der Arbeit Institute for the Study of Labor.

Croix, D. D. L, &Licandro, O. (1999), "Life Expectancy and Endogenous Growth", *Economics Letters*, 65: 255-263.

Croix, D. D. L, &Doepke, M. (2003), "Inequality and Growth: Why Differential Fertility Matters", *The American Economic Review*, 93(4): 1091-1113.

Croix, D. D. L., &Licandro, O. (2013), "The Child is Father of the Man: Implications for the Demographic Transition", *The Economic Journal*, 123(567): 236-261.

DeJong, D. N., Nankervis, J. C., Savin, N. E., & Whiteman, C. H. (1992), "Integration Versus Trend Stationary in Time Series", *Econometrica: Journal of the Econometric Society*, 423-433.

Dickey, D. A., & Fuller, W. A. (1979), "Distribution of the Estimators for Autoregressive Time Series With a Unit root", *Journal of the American statistical association*, 74(366a): 427-431.

Diebold, F. X., & Rudebusch, G. D. (1991), "On the Power of Dickey-Fuller Tests Against Fractional Alternatives", *Economics letters*, 35(2): 155-160.

Ehrlich, I., &Lui, F. T. (1991), "Intergenerational Trade, Longevity, Intrafamily Transfers and Economic Growth", *Journal of Political Economy*, 99 (1991): 1029–1059.

Fernihough, A. (2011), "Human Capital and the Quantity-Quality Trade-off During the Demographic Transition: New Evidence from Ireland", *Working Paper Series, UCD Centre for Economic Research, No.* 11/13.

Frini, O., & Muller, C. (2012), "Demographic Transition, Education and Economic Growth in Tunisia", *Economic Systems*, 36(3): 351-371.

Fuller, W. A. (1976), *Introduction to Statistical Time Series*, New York: John Wiley & Sons.

Galor, O., & Weil, D. N. (1999), "From Malthusian Stagnation to Modern Growth", *The American Economic Review*, 89(2): 150-154.

Galor, O., & Weil, D. N. (2000), "Population, Technology and Growth: From Malthusian Stagnation to the Demographic Transition and Beyond", *TheAmerican Economic Review*, 806-828.

Galor, O. (2005), "From Stagnation to Growth: Unified Growth Theory", *Handbook of Economic Growth*, 1: 171-293.

Galor, O. (2011: a), *Unified growth theory*, Princeton University Press.

Galor, O. (2011: b), *The Demographic Transition: Causes and Consequences* (No. w17057), National Bureau of Economic Research.

Greenwood, J., & Seshadri, A. (2002), "The US demographic transition", *The American Economic Review*, 92(2): 153-159.

Hanushek, Eric. (1992), "The Trade-off Between Child Quantity and Quality", *The Journal of Political Economy,* 100(1): 84-117.

Hondroyiannis, G., &Papapetrou, E. (2002), "Demographic Transition and Economic Growth: Empirical Evidence from Greece", *Journal of Population Economics*, 15(2): 221-242.

Kalemli-Ozcan, S. (2002), "Does the Mortality Decline Promote Economic Growth?", *Journal of Economic Growth*, 7: 411-439.

Kalemli-Ozcan, S. (2003), "A Stochastic Model of Mortality, Fertility, and Human Capital Investment", *Journal of Development Economics*, 70(1): 103-118.

Khan, A. (2008), "The Industrial Revolution and the Demographic Transition", *Business Review, First Quarter*, 9-15.

Kremer, M. (1993), "Population Growth and Technological Change: One Million BC to 1990", *The Quarterly Journal of Economics*, 681-716.

Kumar, S., &Kuglar, A. (2011), "Testing the Children Quantity-Quality Trade-off in India", *Munich Personal RePEc Archive.*

Kwiatkowski, D., Phillips, P. C. B., Schmidt, P., & Shin, Y. (1992), "Testing the Null Hypothesis of Stationarity Against the Alternative of a Unit Root: How Sure Are We that Economic Time Series Have a Unit Root?", Journal *of Econometrics*, 54: 159-178.

Li, H., Zhang, J., & Zhu, Y. (2008), "The Quantity-Quality Trade-off of Children in a Developing Country: Identification Using Chinese Twins", *Demography*, 45(1): 223-243.

Maddison, A. (2007), *The world economy volume 1: A millennial perspective volume 2: Historical statistics*. Academic Foundation.

Malthus, T. R. (1798), 1958. "An Essay on the Principle of Population", in Dent Vol. 2.

Mason, A., Lee, R., & Jiang, J. X. (2016), "Demographic dividends, human capital, and saving", *The Journal of the Economics of Ageing*, *7*, 106-122.

Matsuyama, K. (1992), "Agricultural Productivity, Comparative Advantage, and Economic Growth", *Journal of Economic Theory*, 58(2): 317-334.

Moav, O. (2005), "Cheap Children and the Persistence of Poverty", *The Economic Journal*, 115(500): 88-110.

Murtin, F. (2013), "Long-Term Determinants of the Demographic Transition 1870-2000", *Review of Economics and Statistics*, 95(2): 617-631.

Nicolini, E. A. (2007), "Was Malthus Right? A VAR Analysis of Economic and Demographic Interactions in Pre-Industrial England", *European Review of Economic History*, 11(01): 99-121.

Pesaran, M. H., & Shin, Y. (1995), "Long-Run Structural Modelling" *Cambridge, Department of Applied Economics, University of Cambridge (No. 9419) DAE Working Paper.*

Pesaran, M. H., & Shin, Y. (1996), "Cointegration and Speed of Convergence to Equilibrium", *Journal of Econometrics*, 71(1): 117-143.

Pesaran, M. H., Shin, Y., & Smith, R. J. (1996), *Testing for the 'Existence of a Long-run Relationship'* (No. 9622), Faculty of Economics, University of Cambridge.

Pesaran, M. H. (1997), "The Role of Economic Theory in Modelling the Long Run", *The Economic Journal*, 107(440): 178-191.

Pesaran, M. H., Shin, Y., & Smith, R. J. (2001), "Bounds Testing Approaches to the Analysis of Level Relationships", *Journal of Applied Econometrics*, 16(3): 289-326.

Qian, N. (2009), "Quantity-Quality and the One Child Policy: The Only Child Disadvantage in School Enrolment in China", *NBER Working Paper.*

Raychaudhuri, T., Kumar, D., Habib, I., & Desai, M. (1983), *The Cambridge Economic History of India: Volume 2, C. 1751-c. 1970* (No. 2). CUP Archive.

Sharp, P., Strulik, H., &Weisdorf, J. (2012), "The Determinants of Income in a Malthusian Equilibrium", *Journal of Development Economics*, 97(1): 112-117.

Soares, R., (2005), "Mortality Reductions, Educational Attainment, and Fertility Choice, " *American Economic Review*, 95: 580–601.

Strulik, H. (2004), "Child Mortality, Child Labour and Economic Development", *The Economic Journal*, 114(497): 547-568.

Strulik, H. (1997), "Learning-by-doing, Population Pressure, and the Theory of Demographic Transition", *Journal of Population Economics*, 10(3): 285-298.

Strulik, H., &Weisdorf, J. (2008), "Population, Food, and Knowledge: A Simple Unified Growth Theory", *Journal of Economic Growth*, 13(3): 195-216.

Strulik, H., Prettner, K., &Prskawetz, A. (2013), "The Past and Future of Knowledge-Based Growth", *Journal of Economic Growth*, 18(4): 411-437.

Yilmazer, T. (2008), "Saving for Children's College Education: An Empirical Analysis of the Trade-off Between the Quality and Quantity of Children", *Journal of Family and Economic Issues*, 29(2): 307-324.

Zhang, J., Zhang, J., & Lee, R. (2001), "Mortality Decline and Long-run Economic Growth", *Journal of Public Economics*, 80: 485-507.

Zhang, J., & Zhang, J. (2005), "The Effect of Life Expectancy on Fertility, Saving, Schooling and Economic Growth: Theory and Evidence", *The Scandinavian Journal of Economics*, 107(1): 45-66.

Notes

1. This is only to offer modeling simplicity.
2. Note that the human capital endowment of the adult will be denoted as *ht-1* as this is acquired when she/ he was a child.
3. Proof of the Lemma is available on request.
4. Proof of imploding growth are available on request.
5. The test statistic -2.12 with Mackinnon one sided p-value =0.52.
6. The test statistic is -5.11 with Mackinnon one sided p-value = 0.00.
7. F-statistic value for the test is 9.31 and it is more than 95% lower bound as well as upper bound.
8. In post independent India, in the long-run relationship test F-statistics is also greater than the 95% lower and 95% upper bound.

Bibliography

ACEMOGLU, D. (1998): "Why Do New Technologies Complement Skills? Directed Technical Change and Wage Inequality," Quarterly Journal of Economics, CXIII, 1055–1090.

——— (1999): "Changes in Unemployment and Wage Inequality: An Alternative Theory and Some Evidence," American Economic Review.

——— (2002): "Directed Technical Change," Review of Economic Studies, 69, 781–809.

——— (2003a): "Labour and Capital-Augmenting Technical Change," Journal of the European Economic Association.

——— (2003b): "Patterns of Skill Premia," Review of Economic Studies.

ACEMOGLU, D. AND M. DELL (2009): "Beyound Neoclassical Growth: Technology, Human Capital, Institutions and Within–Country Differences," American Economic Journal: Macroeconomics 2.

ACEMOGLU, D. AND F. ZILIBOTTI (2001): "Productivity Differences," Quarterly Journal of Economics, 116, 563–606.

ACEMOGLU, D., P. A. L. B. AND D. HEMOUS (2012): "The Environment and Directed Technical Change," American Economic Review, 102, 131–166.

AGHION, P., A. D. D. H. R. M. AND J. V. REENAN (2012): "Carbon Taxes, Path Dependency and Directed Technical Change: Evidence from the Auto-Industry," NBER Working Paper No., 18596.

AGHION, P., P. H. AND G. VIOLANTE (2000): "Technology, Knowledge, and Inequality," Mimeo, Harvard.

AUTOR, D. H., A. B. K. AND L. F. KATZ (1998): "Computing Inequality: Have Computers Changed the Labour Market?" Quarterly Journal of Economics, CXIII, 1169–1214.

BECK, N. AND J. N. KATZ (1995): "What to do (and not to do) with Time–Series Cross-Section Data," The American Political Science Review, 89, 634–647.

BONDAREV, A., C. C. AND A. GREINER (2013): "Climate Change and Technical Progress: Impact of Informational Constraints," Economics and Management Working Paper No., 1.

BOSELLO, F., R. R. AND R. S. J. TOL (2006): "Economy-wide Estimates of the Implications of Climate Change: Human Health," Ecological Economics, 58, 579–591.

BROCK, W. AND M. S. TAYLOR (2005): "Economic Growth and the Environment: A Review of Theory and Empirics," Handbook of Economic Growth, 1.

CRIFO, P. (2008): "Skill Supply and Biased Technical Change," Labour Economics, 15, 812–830.

DELL, M., B. F. J. AND B. A. OLKEN (2008): "Climate Change and Economic Growth: Evidence from the Last Half-Century," NBER Working Paper No., 14132.

DELL, M., B. F. J. B. A. O. (2009): "Temperature and Income: Reconciling New Cross-Sectional and Panel Estimates," American Economic Review, 99, 198–204.

EICHER, T. (1996): "Interaction Between Endogenous Human Capital and Technological Change," Review of Economic Studies, 63, 127–144.

FRIEDMAN, M. (1937): "The Use of Ranks to Avoid the Assumption of Normality Implicit in the Analysis of Variance," Journal of the American Statistical Association, 32, 675–701.

GALOR, O. AND O. MOAV (2000): "Ability-Biased Technological Transition, Wage Inequality, and Economic Growth," Quarterly Journal of Economics, 115, 469–497.

GALOR, O. AND D. TSIDDON (1997): "Technological Progress, Mobility, and Economic Growth," American Economic Review, 363–382.

GOLDIN, C. AND L. F. KATZ (1998): "The Origins of Technology-Skill Complementarity," Quarterly Journal of Economics, CXIII, 693–732.

GOULD, E. (2005): "Inequality and Ability," Labour Economics, 12, 169–189.

GOULD, E., O. M. AND B. WEINBERG (2001): "Precautionary Demand for Education, Inequality and Technological Progress," Journal of Economic Growth, 6, 285–315.

GRADUS, R. AND S. SMULDERS (1993): "The Trade-off Between Environmental Care and Long-term Growth – Polluting in Three Prototype Growth Models," Journal of Economics, 58, 25–51.

GREAKER, M. AND T. R. HEGGEDAHL (2012): "A Comment on the Environment and Directed Technical Change," CREE Working Paper No., 13.

GRIMAUD, A. AND L. ROUGE (2008): "Environment, Directed Technical Change and Economic Policy," Environmental and Resource Economics, 41, 439–463.

GROSSMAN, G. AND A. KRUEGER (1991): "Environmental Impact of a North American Free Trade Agreement," NBER Working Paper No., 3914.

——— (1995): "Economic Growth and the Environment," Quarterly Journal of Economics, 110, 353– 377.

HAINES, A., R. S. K. D. C.-L. AND C. CORVALAN (2006): "Climate Change and Human Health:

Impacts, Vulnerability and Public Health," Public Health, 120, 585–596.

HARRIS, R. D. F. AND E. TZAVALIS (1999): "Inference for Unit Roots in Dynamic Panels Where the Time Dimension Is Fixed," Journal of Econometrics, 91, 201–226.

HAUSMAN, J. A. (1978): "Specification Tests in Econometrics," Econometrica, 46, 1251–1271.

LEVIN, A., C. L. AND C. J. CHU (2002): "Unit Root Tests in Panel Data: Asymptotic and Finite– Sample Properties," Journal of Econometrics, 108, 1–24.

MARIA, C. AND S. VALENTE (2008): "Hicks Meet Hotelling: The Direction of Technical Change in Capital–Resource Economics," Environment and Development Economics, 13, 691–717.

MCMICHAEL, A. J., R. E. W. AND S. HALES (2006): "Climate Change and Human Health: Present and Future Risks," Lancet, 367, 859–869.

MILLER, S. J. AND M. A. VELA (2013): "The Effects of Air Pollution on Educational Outcomes.

Evidence from Chile," IDB Working Paper Series No., 468.

RICCI, F. (2007): "Channels of Transmission of Environmental Policy to Economic Growth: A Survey of the Theory," Ecological Economics, 60, 688–699.

SMULDERS, S. AND DE M. NOOIJ (2003): "The Impact of Energy Conservation on Technology and Economic Growth," Resource and Energy Economics, 25, 59–79.

VIOLANTE, G. (2002): "Technological Acceleration, Skill Transferability and the Rise in Residual In-equality," Quarterly Journal of Economics, 117, 297–338.XEPAPADEAS, A. (2005): "Economic Growth and the Environment," Handbook of Environmental Economics, 3, 1219–1271.

Index

J

K

L

M

N

Y

Z